PROSPECTUS LONDINENSIS
CITY of LONDON.
36. The Monument.
37. St. George Botolph lane.
38. St. Mary Hill.
39. St. Margt. Pattons.
41. St. Dunstans in the East.
42. Allhallows Barkin.
43. The Temple.
44. White Frier Stairs.
46. Dr. Salmons.
47. Blackfrier Stairs.
48. Pauls Wharf.
49. Trig Stairs.

CRAFTED IN STONE

A HISTORY OF
THE WORSHIPFUL COMPANY OF

MASONS

OF THE CITY OF LONDON

'The Stonemason'
Gifted by the 2021-22 Master & Mistress Mason, Martin and Susan
Low, in celebration of the 550th anniversary of the Company's grant
of arms in 1472. The sculpture features Yeoman Mason Tom Nicholls
at work.

CRAFTED IN STONE

A HISTORY OF
THE WORSHIPFUL COMPANY OF
MASONS
OF THE CITY OF LONDON

GOD·IS·OUR·GUIDE

IAN W. STONE

EDITOR: MICHAEL ST JOHN PARKER
MANAGING EDITOR: RICHARD WOODMAN-BAILEY

PHILLIMORE BOOK PUBLISHING

2023

Published by

PHILLIMORE BOOK PUBLISHING

www.phillimorebookpublishing.co.uk

© The Worshipful Company of Masons, 2023

This book has been funded entirely
by the generosity of members of the Masons' Company,
and is not being sold for profit

ISBN 978-1-8384510-4-2

CONTENTS

LIST OF ILLUSTRATIONS

Back endpaper: London night panorama, 2016 by Angelo Hornak
Back cover: The Company's arms despicted in the Library Staircase at Guildhall

Author and Editors

IAN STONE, Author, read for his doctorate at King's College London. He completed a Junior Research Fellowship at the Institute of Historical Research, and he has now returned to King's College as a Visiting Research Fellow. He has published extensively on the history of London, and he teaches related courses for Dartmouth College and Skidmore College.

MICHAEL ST JOHN PARKER, Editor, is the Company's Hon. Archivist, and his work among their records helped to lay foundations for the present History. He is an F.S.A., with degrees from both Cambridge and Oxford. Before becoming a research historian, he was head of the history department at Winchester College, and subsequently Headmaster of Abingdon School.

RICHARD WOODMAN-BAILEY, Managing Editor, was Master Mason in 2010. Having initially trained as a stonemason, he qualified as a Chartered Surveyor and Chartered Construction Manager, and has had a variety of technical and leadership roles in a successful career. His wide spectrum of interests led him to produce his firm's centenary history book, a valuable experience … now put to good use!

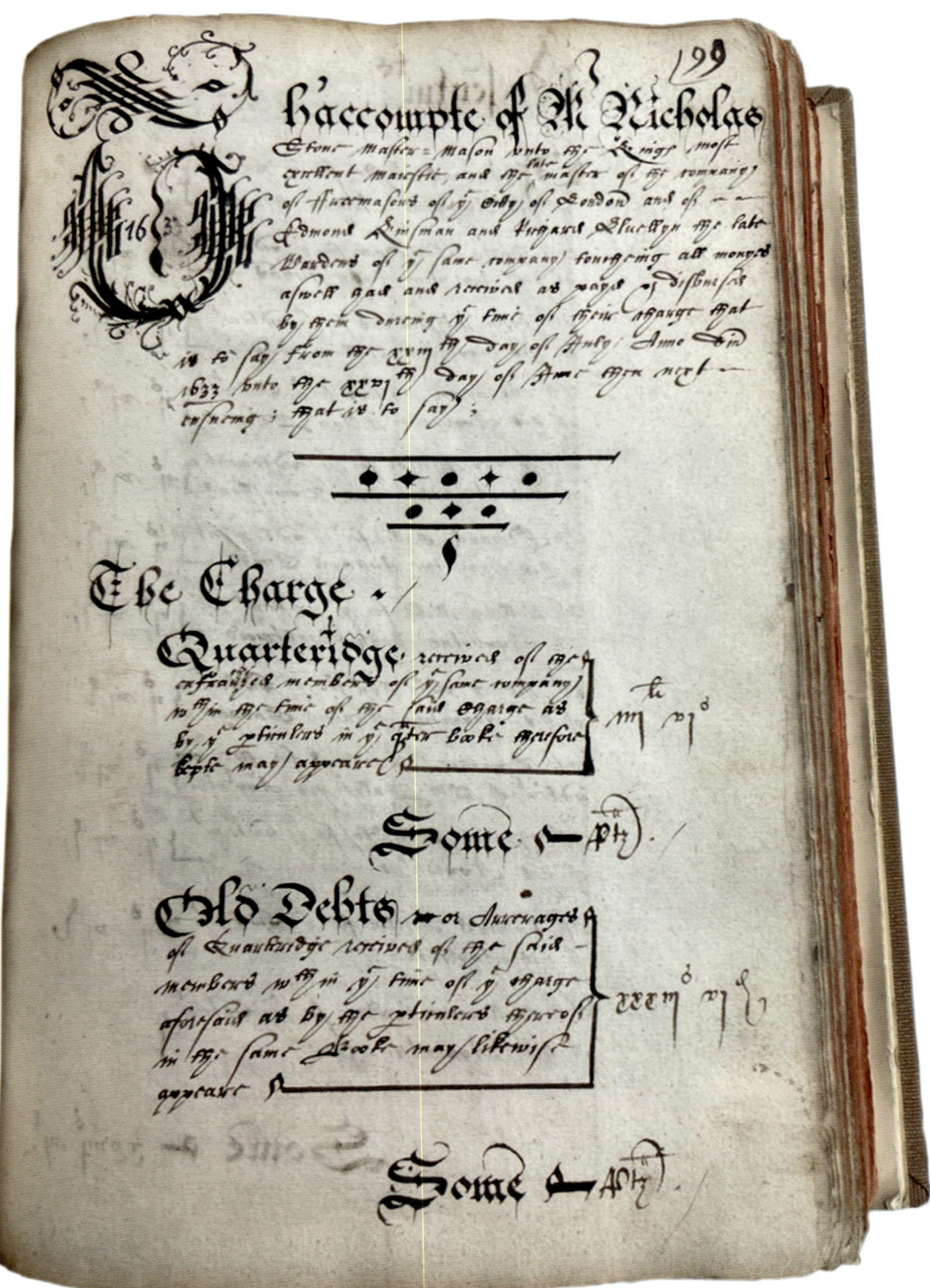

Th'accompte of Mr Nicholas

Stone Master Mason vnto the kings most
excellent Maiestie and the late master of the company
of ffreemasons of the Cytty of London and of
Edmond Kinsman and Richard Gurkyn the late
Wardens of the same company touching all moneyes
aswell had and received as payd or disbursed
by them dureing the tyme of their charge that
is to say from the xx5th day of July Anno dm
1633 vnto the xx5th day of June then next
ensueing: that is to say:

The Charge

Quarteridge receiued of the
enfranchised members of the same company
wthin the tyme of the said charge as
by the pticulers in the after booke therefore
kepte may appeare

ℓℓ vjⁱˢ

Some — ℓvⁱᵗ

Old Debts or Arrerages
of Quarteridge receiued of the said
members wthin the tyme of the charge
aforesaid as by the pticulers therof
in the same Booke may likewise
appeare

xxxⁱ vjˢ ⁱ

Some — xlⁱˢ

1632-3 Accounts Book, when Nicholas Stone was Master.

Principal Supporters

Richard Rowlandson OBE, son of Sir Graham Rowlandson (Master 1964-5), was elected liveryman in 1965 and to Court in 1981. A Chartered Accountant, he became Finance Committee Chairman, having been a founding member of its antecedent in 1982. He was Master 1989-90. In 2002 he chaired the small committee that encouraged the Company's modernisation. A successful businessman, he succeeded his father as Chairman of the family firm, which was a significant benefactor of the Company.

Michael Hall, a liveryman since 1966 and elected to Court in 1983, had a career as a Master Builder. Chairman of Ashby & Horner in the City, he was a familiar figure on construction sites and in stone yards as well as the boardroom, and was deeply involved with the livery – encouraging the use of natural stone. He was a craftsman and diplomat, an artist and sportsman, eloquent, always good humoured, thoughtful, and kind. *In memoriam.*

Past Master Barry Woodman was sworn in to the livery in 1972, the 500th anniversary year of the granting of arms to the Masons' Company. He became a Court Assistant in 1988 and was elected Master in 1996. During his professional career he worked in private practice as a Chartered Quantity Surveyor, being involved in a wide variety of prestigious construction and engineering projects. He retired in 2003 as senior partner in the London office.

Master in 2010-11, Richard Woodman-Bailey commenced work as a stonemason in 1969, although his career evolved and he became a managing director in a major construction company. In 1979 he followed his father, Honorary Court Member Thomas Aubrey Bailey MBE, into the livery, and then to Court in 1998. Inter alia he chaired the Craft Fund charity, 2013 Strategic Review, Finance Committee and Guardian Group, and has been central in this book's creation and production.

Robert Morrow, the Master in 2014-15, was admitted to the livery of the Company in 1990 and elected to the Court in 2003. After a career in international banking, he became Chief Executive of a major membership society, and completed his professional career as a specialist consultant. His year as Master focused on social activity, including leading a visit by a dozen intrepid adventurers to Bulgaria. He is also a liveryman of the Musicians' Company.

Gerry Everett, the Master in 2007-8, was invited to join the Company in 1994 as a consequence of his role as client when the Bank of England received a Stone Award for their successful restoration project. On Court, and as Chairman of the Finance Committee, he was an agent for change in strategic matters and in reforming the financing of general expenditure. He has also been a significant supporter of the Craft Awards for Stonemasonry.

Derek Richard John Smith was elected to the Masons' livery in 1998, having already become a Freeman of the City. When he first started work at Barclays Bank's head office he made daily visits to the Bank of England, which raised awareness of other fine City buildings such as the Tower of London and St Paul's Cathedral. Seeing stonemasons carrying out restoration work, he learnt the importance of the use of stone in our heritage.

Past Master Chris Radmore joined the livery in 2003 and was Master in 2019-20, his year being curtailed by the Covid-19 pandemic. His working life as a stockbroker was the basis of his interest in the livery. Other interests are Lord Nelson, a hero since childhood, researching his family history and freemasonry. Together with his wife he is an active watcher of rugby union and cricket and has an abiding love of music, especially opera.

Past Master Martin Low joined the livery in 2007, became a Court Assistant in 2014 and was Master in 2021. A Chartered Civil Engineer of 37 years who worked in both private and public sectors, after his retirement from Westminster City Council in 2016 he set up his personal consulting firm that helped property owners implement developments with local, regional and national government, and which became a significant and generous corporate benefactor of the Company.

Past Master Dr Christine Rigden became a liveryman of the Masons' Company in 2008, Court Assistant in 2015, and served as the Company's first female Master in 2020-21 during the Covid-19 pandemic. A former London University lecturer specialising in the use of geological materials in the construction industry, Christine has also enjoyed considerable involvement in the wider livery movement and the City Civic, most notably serving as Sheriff of the City of London in 2015-16.

Court Assistant Matthew Hampson has been Chairman of the Communications Committee since 2018, and wishes to record the privilege it has been to work with the talented team who have made this book a reality. He is a keen supporter of the City Mayoralty and is active in Dowgate Ward. Outside the livery, he runs an electronic trading business in the City and has worked in The Square Mile for more than 30 years.

Alderman and Sheriff Alastair King is Alderman for the ward of Queenhithe, where the office of the Worshipful Company of Masons is situated. He has represented the ward (as Common Council Member, Deputy and Alderman) continuously since 1999, and is a long-term resident. His Sheriff's year spans 2022-23. He joined the livery in 2017 and became a Warden in 2019. He applauds the fellowship and commitment to excellence in stonemasonry espoused by the Worshipful Company.

Liveryman Molly Lowell Borthwick joined the Company in 2019. Driven by her passion for stone, particularly the seemingly timeless ancient stone craftsmanship, she has been impressed by the forward-thinking policies of Past Master Martin Low. She hopes to inspire future generations to learn from great works, paying tribute to sculptor Elizabeth Leyh and Ian Jenkins of the British Museum, who have each played a role in creating and understanding the best of stonework through millennia.

Claire Jane Wallbridge joined the livery in 2021 and was elected to the Craft and Training Committee in the same year. The first liveryman in her stonemasonry family, for 20 years Claire's career was retail banking, latterly being involved in training. This enabled a move to the Construction Industry Training Board, which in due course culminated in her position as the Training Officer for the Natural Stone Industry Training Group. Her grandfather would be pleased!

HRH The Duke of Gloucester, KG, GCVO

FOREWORD
HRH THE DUKE OF GLOUCESTER KG, GCVO

From:
HRH The Duke of Gloucester KG GCVO

KENSINGTON PALACE
LONDON W8 4PU

I am delighted to write the foreword to this history of the Worshipful Company of Masons – "Crafted in Stone".

With a keen interest in the built environment, I qualified as an architect, and was very pleased to be elected a Liveryman of the Company in 1975 and Honorary Court Member in 1995. For centuries, and indeed with Stonehenge in mind, millennia, the use of stone has been a key feature in creating our structures, our shelter, our places of worship and our communities. It is therefore self-evident that we all owe much to those who learned the stonemasonry craft.

In London, we can trace stonemasons working, training and even worshipping together in groups as early as the 14th century, at which time 'misteries' and 'fraternities' were part of the life of craftspeople in many trades. During the 15th century, these associations evolved into guilds that are more recognisable to us today, and one of those was the Company of Masons.

For some thirty years from 1455, the complexities of the Wars of the Roses were playing out, dominating the reign of King Edward IV, and his victory at the Battle of Tewkesbury in 1471 secured him the throne until his death twelve years later; it was a victory assisted by finance from the City of London guilds, which may have been a factor in the Grant of Arms to the Masons in 1472.

So, in 2022, the Masons' Company celebrates the 550th anniversary of that Grant, and this book provides a fascinating insight into an ancient guild that is now a thriving livery company. Stonemasonry training is a core focus of its charitable giving, although educational and heritage organisations also benefit; furthermore, in addition to its support for the City of London Mayoralty, it has links with units of His Majesty's Forces.

I am particularly pleased to be associated with The Duke of Gloucester Craft Awards for Excellence in Stonemasonry and The Duke of Gloucester Gold Medal for Lifetime Achievement, and I wish the Company continued success.

PREFACE

As managing editor of *Crafted in Stone*, the writing of this Preface gives me a welcome opportunity to inform readers about the work that has gone into the creation of the book, and to acknowledge the contributions of those involved.

The project has had a long gestation period, but no account of the process by which an ancient craft guild has evolved into a dynamic modern livery company can be dashed off in haste. And if our measured pace needs any further excuse, we can plead that it has brought the publication date into the ambit of the 550th anniversary of the Company's grant of arms, an episode of celebration to which the Duke of Gloucester has referred in his Foreword.

Some minor exceptions apart, this account of the Company's history concludes in 2013. That year was chosen because it was then that the Court adopted the recommendations of the Strategic Review group which I had chaired over the preceding 12 months; it was felt that this was a significant milestone for the Company and so a suitable point at which to pause. Perhaps optimistically, it was also hoped that the lapse of a decade would assist the objectivity of the collective memory. Any who may wish to carry on our story in years to come will at least have a clear starting point!

However, readers in the future can be assured that since 2013 the Company has continued in good spirit, despite disruption from the coronavirus pandemic that commenced early in 2020. Evidence of this vigour may be seen in the level of giving for the 550th anniversary commemoration, which totalled over £80,000 – much of which has been used to fund the research, writing, production and printing of this volume.

So my first message is one of deep gratitude to all those 81 liverymen and freemen who contributed to that total. The Principal Supporters have been exceptionally generous, but the other Supporters have also collectively provided a significant sum, and their names are recorded in this book.

The genesis of *Crafted in Stone* is to be found among the Court Papers of 2009, which show a wish to progress with a comprehensive account of the Company's origins and development. Various research initiatives were undertaken over the subsequent period, and eventually in December 2017 Renter Warden Chris Radmore signed an agreement on behalf of the Company with an external researcher and author, Dr Ian Stone. Delayed by the closure of archives due to the pandemic, his work subsequently took over four years to complete. The Company wishes to acknowledge the magnitude of this task, and we thank him warmly for his diligence and skill. The result of Dr Stone's labours was then edited by Dr Michael St John Parker, our Honorary Archivist, to whom we must pay tribute. Editing is a special skill, and Michael has done a superb job.

In addition to my own role as managing editor, our small working group has been very ably guided by Court Assistant Matt Hampson in his position as chairman of the Communications Committee. Other members of that committee have assisted, and particularly Anne Paranjoti, who has recently joined our team and has made a very useful contribution. Many Past Masters have also contributed their recollections directly to Ian Stone, especially regarding the later chapters, and have commented helpfully upon the drafts. Their names would be akin to the roll of Masters listed later in the book, so, with that on record, we thank them all collectively for sharing their knowledge.

I am also grateful for the guidance of Dr David Bartle, Archivist at the Haberdashers' Company, and Richard Kottler, a Past Master of the Pattenmakers' Company, each of whom has published a history of their own livery in the relatively recent past. Sarah Wearne, an archivist and former colleague of Michael St John Parker, is another person who has kindly given up valuable time, in her case to research suitable images for use as illustrations.

As we approached the penultimate drafts of the text, liverymen Roger Adcock and Richard Nichols thoroughly read and commented upon all the chapters, undoubtedly helping thereby to eliminate errors and enhance clarity. Additionally, Michael St John Parker arranged for the procurement of a leather binding specialist for a small number of the books, and Richard Nichols has used his personal expertise in binding a very special presentation-quality volume, the front of which has been crafted by stone carver and freeman Catherine Martin to make a unique copy that we hope will be admired for centuries to come. Our sincere thanks go to these members.

Whilst it has fallen to me to structure and pull together the assorted sections of the book, and to choose and collate the illustrations, we would never have achieved the result without the talent and experience of Andrew Illes and Noel Osborne of Phillimore Book Publishing. I have had many meetings and conversations with Andrew in particular, and we are extremely grateful to them for their expertise and guidance.

As you will read, there has been an association between the Masons' and the Mercers' Companies for over 400 years, so our gratitude to the Mercers will come as no surprise. As well as their Officers, Court and Clerk, we wish to thank their Hall Manager, Stephen McNally, and all the staff who look after us when we use the Hall and care for our chattels that are kept there.

We are indebted to one of our freemen, Angelo Hornak, for the many days of his time spent using his expertise and specialist equipment to photograph our silverware and then edit the images ready for inclusion. Additionally, he has given us permission to make free use of several of his previously published photographs, including the stunning view across the City of London skyline at night which is displayed on the inside back cover.

Staff have provided helpful support at the London Metropolitan Archives and Guildhall Library where our records are kept, as have the Library and Museum of Freemasonry, and the Institute of Historical Research in particular. We hope that the research work which has underpinned this book will encourage the Company to follow the example of other livery companies in arranging for the digitising of its records in order that they can be made more accessible to the public without risking damage to the irreplaceable originals.

We are grateful to many people who have kindly assisted Ian Stone in his endeavours accurately to portray the factual events that are contained in the text. These include:

Mark Goldman, Richard Martin, Adrian Paye, Michael Poultney and Helen Rogers for providing information and knowledge about stone and stonemasonry.

John Belton, Andrew Prescott, Cécile Revauger and David Taillades for providing advice on aspects of freemasonry.

Richard Shepley for providing a speculative plan of Masons' Hall in the late 18th century, and to Christian Steer for providing help with the wills that are mentioned.

Judy Stephenson, Patrick Wallis and Ian Doolittle for making their research available, the latter also for reading draft chapters, as did Caroline Barron, Adam Chambers, Olivia Clear and Mark Samuel.

The Grant of Arms 550th Anniversary Reception at the Mansion House held on 28 September 2022
(left to right)
Sheriff Andrew Marsden
Major Giles Clapp (Clerk)
The Rt. Hon. The Lord Mayor of London, Alderman Vincent Keaveny
Alistair Wood LVO MBE (Master)
HRH The Duke of Gloucester KG GCVO
Martin Low (Deputy Master)
Peter Blincow (Renter Warden)
Alderman and Sheriff Alastair King DL (Upper Warden)

I wish to thank the Officers, the Court and our Clerk, Major Giles Clapp, for the trust they have had in the team to create and produce this publication to the highest standards; and Giles Clapp, assisted by our Administrator, Jolanta Glas, for supporting Ian Stone and overseeing the distribution of the finished volumes.

Finally, Ian Stone would like to thank his wife, Pippa, and children Sam and Mabel; Michael St John Parker thanks his wife, Annette; and similarly, I thank my wife, Jenny – each in recognition of their forbearance whilst this book was being written, edited and produced.

It has been a very great privilege for us to have been able to take leading roles in bringing this enterprise to fruition. We hope you will enjoy reading the history of our proud Company.

Richard Woodman-Bailey

Edward Conder junior, Master of the Masons' Company 1894-5, wearing the original 1873 Master's badge.

Introduction

The history of the Worshipful Company of Masons has never been given the consideration it deserves. John Stow had evidently read nothing about the Company when he wrote his ground-breaking history of London in 1598, and he thus had very little to say about it. In the three centuries which followed, no surveyor or historian of London had much more to add. That changed in 1893 when Edward Conder junior, then Renter Warden, was given permission to borrow the Company's 'records, books and documents' for the purpose of 'investigating the Past history of the Company'. Over the course of the next 18 months, Conder and his friend William Rylands busied themselves among these records and, in 1894, when Conder was Master of the Company, he produced his *Records of the Hole Crafte and Fellowship of Masons*.[1]

Conder had been initiated as a Freemason just six weeks before he began his research project and there can be little doubt that his interest in freemasonry shaped his history of the Company. During the course of his researches he joined the Quatuor Coronati Lodge, the leading Masonic research lodge, and he freely admitted that his investigations into the connection between the Company and freemasonry had expanded the scope of his work and delayed its publication. But this was not his sole motivation. Conder, like his friend Rylands, was a keen antiquarian. He was admitted as a Fellow of the Society of Antiquaries in 1895 and he read papers there, as well as to the Cumberland and Westmorland Archæological Society. Conder delighted in the social and fraternal aspects of both Company and lodge life, and lauded London for 'its ancient traditions of good-fellowship, good-will, and good-cheer'; so with a pencil he placed crosses next to entries in the Company's records that most interested him: the dinners, feasts, processions and ornaments of Company life.[2]

Conder's stress on the commensality of Company life had a purpose that went beyond mere celebration, however. He produced his work at the end of a difficult period for the livery companies generally, and for the Masons' Company in particular. In the 1880s, reformers had launched a searching inquiry into the livery companies' position in London; the very existence of the companies seemed to be under threat, and the Masons' Company's Assistants had lost a suit in the High Court brought by disgruntled liverymen against their mismanagement of Company affairs. Therefore Conder wrote, not just to explore the history of the Company and of freemasonry, but to justify the contemporary Company's place in the world and to reconcile its members after a bruising and divisive lawsuit.

Conder died in 1934 and the Court paid warm tribute to his efforts. For all the weaknesses of his work, he had undertaken a 'task of great magnitude', and he did produce a book of historical importance. Other works followed in due course. In the same year, Prof. Douglas Knoop, head of the Department of Economics at Sheffield University, was given permission to inspect the Company's records. Knoop and his colleague, Gwilym Jones, were both Freemasons, too, and they were especially interested in the pre-industrial history of the craft of stonemasonry. If Conder was an enthusiastic amateur, these men were dedicated professionals, and throughout the 1930s and 1940s they published extensively, if a little repetitively, on these topics. Their *The London mason in the seventeenth century* and *The London Masons' Company*, in particular, have weighty footnotes and uninspiring prose, but they are solid investigations into the history of the Company and its members. In 1959, the Company's Assistants commissioned Raymond Smith, former Librarian to the Corporation of London, to write a short history of the Company, which became known as the 'black book'; it was a cost-effective update to Conder's history. In the 21st century, David Blake, David Beattie and Richard Woodman-Bailey privately funded Dr Jessica Lutkin to research the history of medieval masons in London. Her work was ready by the end of 2013 and the Company sold copies to members to raise money for the Company's Charitable Trust. Research into the Company's archives, conducted over recent years, has also produced a variety of occasional papers.[3]

None of these works, however, offers a comprehensive history of the Company from its earliest appearance in medieval London to its modern form today. It is hoped that this book will make good that deficiency.

A Note on Names and Gender

Names are given in modern form throughout, so Thomas Daniel not Thomas Danyell, and Richard Banks not Richard Bankes. Where surnames refer to identifiable English placenames, I have used 'of' followed by the place in its modern English form; where I have not been able to identify the place, I have retained the contemporary form preceded by 'de'. However, I have not applied these conventions in cases where modern usage dictates otherwise, or if someone's entry in the *Oxford Dictionary of National Biography* conflicts with this practice, so Henry Yevele not Henry of Yeaveley.

I have used the singular pronoun 'he' to describe the mason, encompassing both male and female.

Dr Ian W. Stone

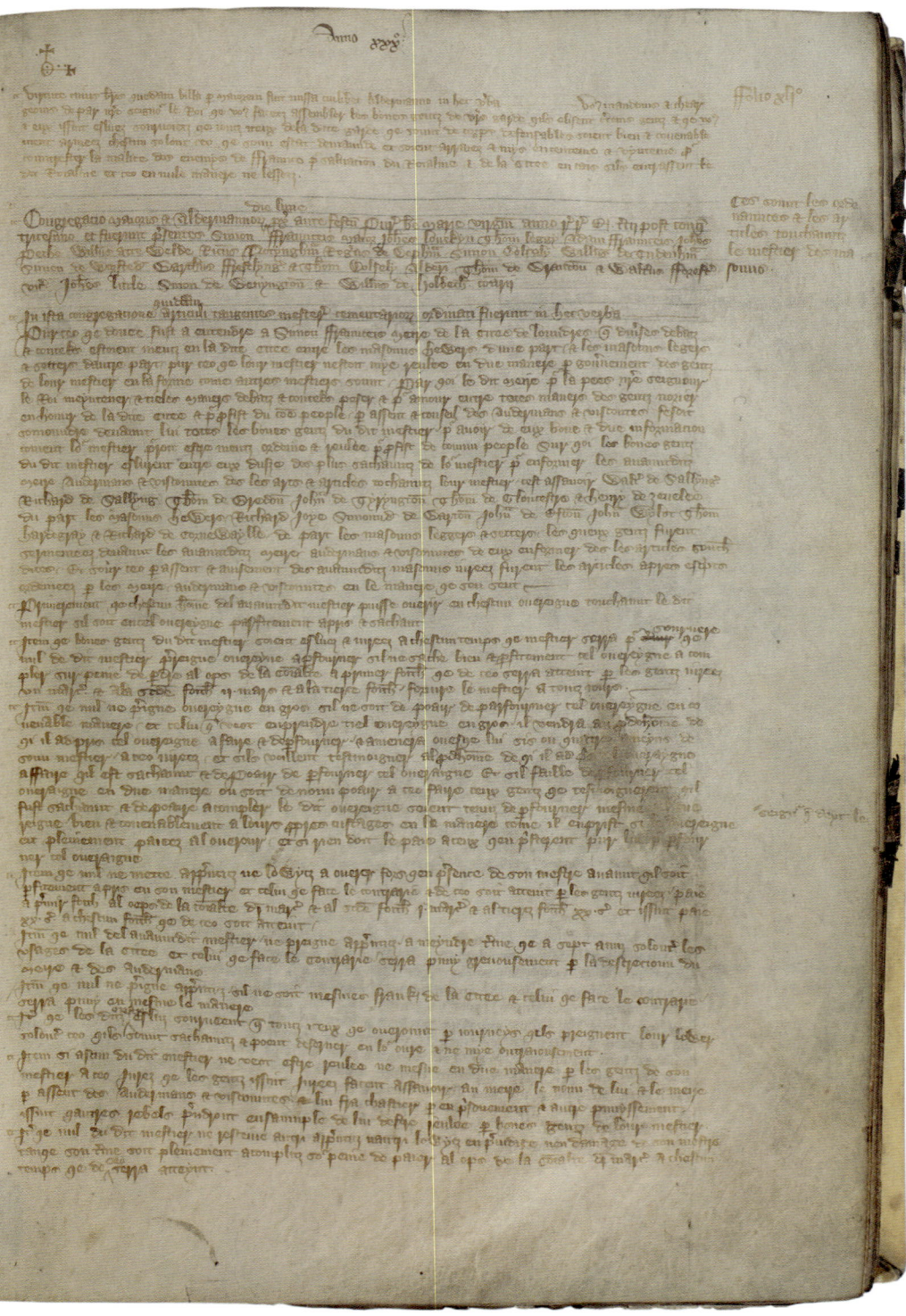

1 *Regulations for the craft of masonry, 1356.*

1

BEGINNINGS

On Monday 1 February 1356, representatives of the craft or trade (*mestier*) of stonemasonry appeared before the Mayor, Simon Fr...ceys, and the Sheriffs and Aldermen of London, to account for quarrels and disputes which had broken out in the City between a number of mason hewers on the one hand, and mason layers and setters on the other. These clashes, it was alleged, had arisen because the craft had 'not been regulated in due manner, by the government of folks of their trade, in such form as other trades are'. The distinctions between the different categories of mason were not always clear-cut at this time; in essence, hewers were those who cut, shaped and worked the stone, and the layers and the setters were those who put the prepared stones into place – and it is easy to see how demarcation disputes might arise on a busy building site. The distinctions were seen clearly enough on that day in the Mayor's court, however, as six masons were chosen to represent the hewers and six to speak for the layers and setters. The outcome was predictable, but in this instance, significant: mindful of the need to maintain the king's peace, preserve the honour of the City of London, profit the common people, and allay dissensions and disputes, the Mayor ordered the masons there present to provide 'good and due information [as to] how their trade might be best ordered and ruled'. As a result, the 12 representatives of the masons agreed a series of written 'acts and articles touching their said trade' arranged under eight headings.*

This was not the first time that attempts had been made to regulate aspects of the craft of masonry in London. A text which can be shown to date from before 1216 had specified that any stone

* Texts of all the regulations, ordinances and by-laws referred to in this book are available on the Company's website. See also Regulations, Ordinances and Charters.

walls between neighbours had to be 3 ft. thick and 16 ft. high, with each party contributing half of the land and the cost. This provision subsequently made its way into London's Assize of Buildings, which regulated construction in the medieval city in a detailed way and governed complaints of nuisance. From 1301 onwards, under the auspices of the Assize of Nuisance, master masons and carpenters are to be found in the City's records acting as sworn, professional viewers, equivalents of the modern 'expert witness', providing technical advice to the Mayor and Aldermen and helping contending parties to settle disputes between neighbours. Following a catastrophic fire in London and Southwark in 1212, other building regulations were issued by 'the advice of wise men' to 'assuage anger, pacify the city and prevent fires'.[1]

The events of 1 February 1356 were therefore not absolutely unprecedented, nor do they necessarily mark the inauguration or foundation of a guild of masons in London. The rulings that were issued on that occasion, however, are the oldest surviving evidence of an attempt to regulate the craft of masonry in London in a comprehensive way. They are, therefore, a good place at which to begin our study of the history of the Worshipful Company of Masons.

In drawing up and submitting regulations for the Mayor and Aldermen to approve in this way, the delegates of the masons were actually doing nothing that would have been considered unusual in 14th-century London. Between 1322, when the Armourers brought a petition, and 1396, when the Coopers appeared similarly, at least 37 London crafts presented ordinances for ratification and enrolment. Thus the first appearance of the masons of London acting in a corporate fashion, in 1356, is typical 14th-century craft behaviour. Similarly, the preamble to the agreement, where the Mayor descants on the importance of the royal peace, civic honour, 'love among all manner of folks', and the primacy of the common weal, employing normative language that can be found extensively among the records of medieval London. In this sense the document probably tells us as much about the self-perception of the civic authorities of the period as it does about the craft of masonry in 1356.[2]

The regulations seem to have been agreed that day without any conflict among the 12 representatives of the craft. However, we know that they had been drawn up in response to 'divers dissensions and disputes' within the craft itself. Explicit admissions of disharmony are rarely to be found in the official records of medieval civic

authorities, and indeed there is nothing quite like the masons'
admission of dispute in any of the other 36 sets of craft ordinances
ratified between 1322 and 1396. The trouble, then, must have been
sufficiently serious to have warranted mention, and it is worth
examining what had caused it, and why, of all the crafts of London,
the masons seem to have been prone to disagreement.[3]

Unsurprisingly, wages were at the root of the problem. In the
period 1280-1350 a journeyman mason, if a wage-earner, could
expect to receive, on average, 4d. or 5d. a day; an apprentice perhaps
half that. Richard of Selling was one of those who represented the
mason hewers in 1356. In 1350-1 he was working at Windsor Castle,

2 An 18th-century representation of mid-14th-century works at Windsor Castle.

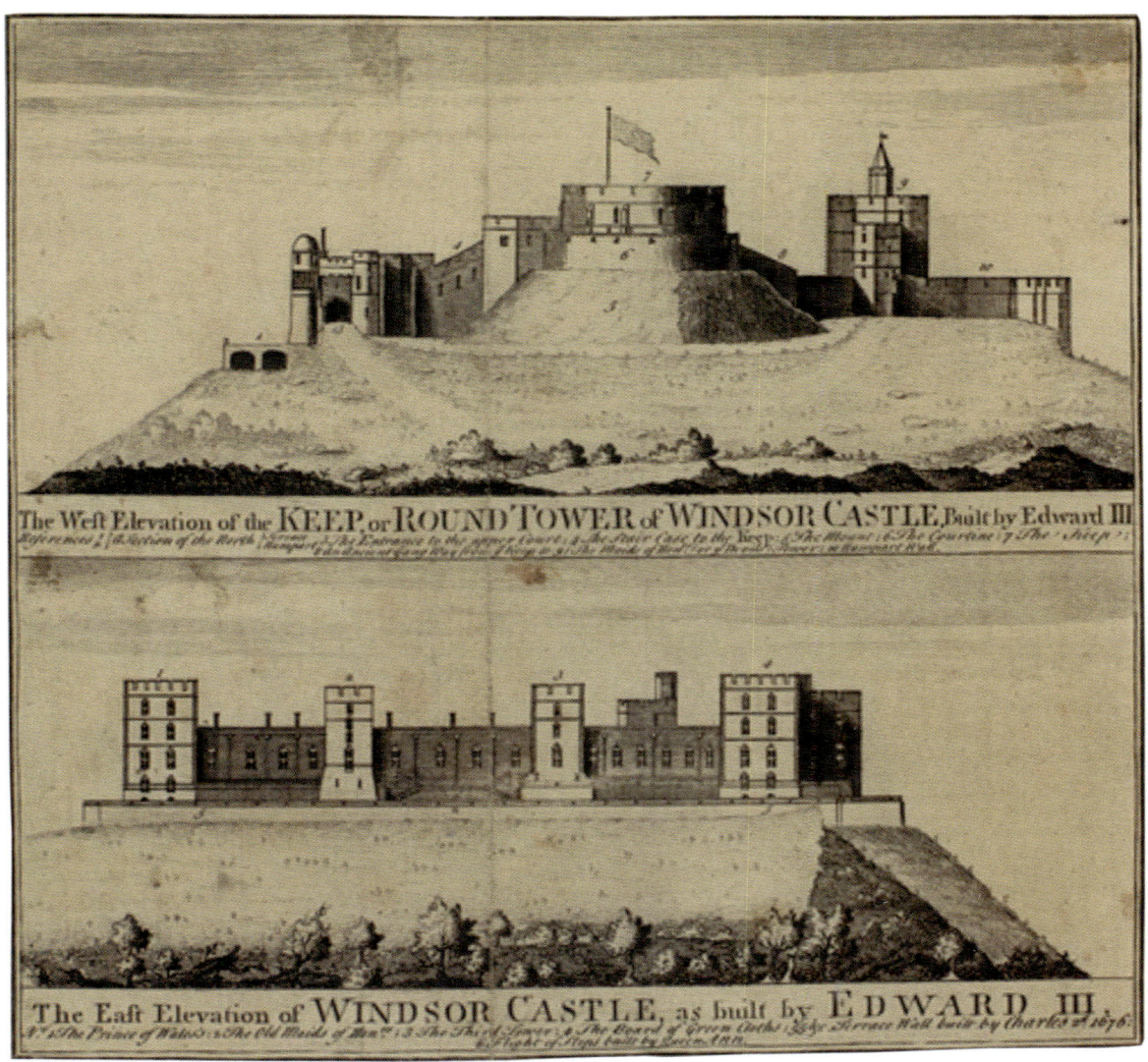

scappling (rough-hewing) stones and taking 5½d. a day. Mason layers working at Windsor at that time were getting 4½d. a day. These sums accord reasonably well with the provisions of two contemporary ordinances, issued in the immediate aftermath of the Black Death, to fix wages at their pre-plague levels. The first of these ordinances, issued by the authorities in London in 1350, after complaining that masons, carpenters, plasterers, tilers, and 'all manner of labourers' were taking 'immeasurably more than they have been wont to take', fixed the wages of masons at 6d. a day in the summer without food or drink, and 5d. a day in the winter on the same terms. This came with a provision that 'if any workman or labourer will not work or labour as is above ordained, let him be taken and kept in prison'. The second, and more famous of the two wage-control attempts, was the 1351 Statute of Labourers, issued by the king and his council, which capped the pay of mason hewers at 4d. a day and of other masons at 3d.[4]

Wage rates in London were evidently higher than those paid outside the City, and it must be likely that the actual going rates were above those set by statute. We know that there had been attempts before the Black Death to establish maximum wage rates paid to masons and other craftsmen, but there is scant evidence that the terms of these early ordinances and statutes were ever breached. By contrast, between 1357 and 1359, 18 masons were among 75 people fined for breaching the Statute of Labourers. In a royal letter of 16 April 1361, the king angrily complained that masons in the royal service were working elsewhere at higher rates. Masons and carpenters were even suspected of coming together to fix their wages at higher levels; this prompted a reissuance of the Statute of Labourers in 1360, banning such associations and forbidding oaths of solidarity. However, surviving building accounts make it plain that wages above the rate specified in the 1351 statute were paid at Ely (1359), Rochester (1368) and York (1371); we can only surmise about the possibility that masons and employers colluded to ignore the law in these instances. The king himself conceded in August 1360 that masons and carpenters working at the Tower of London and Westminster should be paid 6d. a day, well above the 3d. and 4d. set out in his second Statute of Labourers, issued in the same year. In London, it is perhaps not unrealistic to suppose that 8d. or 9d. a day to a mason in the 1350s would have been an achievable daily wage. That is, perhaps twice the amount he could have earned in the

1340s. Certainly that is the amount that masons working at London Bridge commonly took in the 15th century.[5]

It has long been known that in the aftermath of the Black Death there was a shortage of labour which led to higher wages across the country. The shortage was especially acute in the building industry, and presented special problems for the king, who had embarked upon a colossal building programme. Such was the pressure that we see the issuing of record numbers of commissions requiring masons to work under compulsion for the king (impressment), complaints that no masons could be found to work 'except in secret', orders to imprison 'contrariant' craftsmen, threats to fine sheriffs who failed to compel sufficient masons for services required, provision to take security from masons to prevent them running away once impressed, warnings on pain of imprisonment to patrons not to employ runaway masons, proscription of 'Alliances and Covines' of masons, and even outright bans on private people employing stonemasons. It can be fairly said, then, that the 1350s was a period of significant turbulence in the craft of masonry. What we also see in this decade, for the first time, is the appearance of the masons of London before the mayor to request a settlement of their disputes.

All those involved in drawing up the regulations in 1356 had their own interests. For example, with fewer masons across the country, it was in the interests of employers and the lower-ranking masons that any mason capable of working on a project should be free to do so. Thus, we read in the first clause of the regulations 'that every man of the trade may work at any work touching the trade'. Faced with a skills shortage, it was of less importance to an employer whether a mason was classified as a hewer or a layer. What was needed now was labour. With the opportunity for more and better-paid work, it also mattered less to the layers what their designation was. Yet this clause also stipulated that all masons employed must be 'perfectly skilled and knowing' in the craft. Moreover, the second clause provided for the election of overseers from among the craft of masonry to ensure that only those who 'well and perfectly know how to perform such work' do so, on pain of amercement and even a lifetime ban from the craft. It was, of course, in everyone's interests that quality control was maintained. But it was clearly the better-qualified masons in particular who stood to benefit from these means of self-regulation within the craft. In this compromise, then, we can

see the involvement of different groups with competing interests in the drafting of the regulations.

    Not all masons were wage-earners. Many masons would contract with employers, as did Henry Yevele with the Black Prince between 1357 and 1359, to complete work 'at task' or 'in gross'. To protect employers from contracting with incapable workmen, that is those who are not 'skilful and of ability to perform such work', the third clause of the 1356 regulations set out that contractors must provide either four or six men of established reputation within the craft

3 *A vaulting boss at Canterbury Cathedral, believed to show the image of Henry Yevele.*

to act both as referees of their ability and as guarantors that they would complete the agreed works – a form of protection against medieval cowboy builders! But incompetence was not the only reason why a contractor might 'fail to complete such work in due manner'. With masons in short supply, it is likely that contractors were not completing jobs if they received a better offer elsewhere. One imagines, too, that contractors themselves were under pressure, caught between the Scylla of being unable to find masons to work for them on projects unless they paid higher wages, and the Charybdis of recently issued wage regulations. If 18 masons were fined in London for breaching the Statute of Labourers in two years, it must be very likely that many came to view fines against the statute as something of an occupational hazard. In fact, two of the prominent representatives of the craft sworn in 1356 were among those subsequently fined for breaching the statute: Richard of Selling, one of the hewers, was fined 2s., and Simon of Barton, one of the layers, 1s. One likely response of employers and master masons to these pressures would be to employ under-qualified, or even unqualified apprentices and journeymen. But that would not only lead to resentment from properly qualified craftsmen, it would also lead employers to fear poor workmanship. Therefore, the fourth article forbade, again on pain of amercement, a master from setting 'an apprentice or journeyman to work … before he has been properly instructed in his calling'. The fifth clause also made provision for apprenticeships, requiring that they were to last for a minimum of seven years. This stipulation was clearly an attempt to maintain quality, but it does not necessarily imply that indentured apprenticeships were the norm in the craft of masonry at this date. In fact, it may be better interpreted as an attempt by the Mayor and Aldermen to aggrandise their authority.[6]

Further evidence of the fierce competition for labour is to be found in the remaining articles. A prohibition in the eighth article against masters employing apprentices and journeymen who had not completed their terms with other masters tells its own story, as does the emphatic reiteration in the sixth article of the prohibition against taking wages in excess of the regulations. Of course, such prohibitions would be dead letters if there was no mechanism by which they could be enforced. It is in this light, therefore, that we must see the seventh article's provision that those unwilling to be 'ruled or directed in due manner by persons of his trade sworn thereunto' should be punished by imprisonment or other means. It is quite

4 *'The stone which the builders refused has become the headstone of the corner', Psalm 118:22. The Holkham Bible, mid-14th century.*

possible that this article betrays very real tensions within the craft. It is easy to suppose that journeymen and apprentice masons, with a new-found appreciation of the value of their labour, had developed a concomitant understanding of their value as individuals, and were increasingly unlikely to pay heed to figures of authority. Equally, this clause, which provided for the 'good folks' of the trade to choose their own superintendents to work in partnership with the Mayor and Aldermen of London in punishing recalcitrant behaviour, gave substance to the authority wielded by the civic and craft authorities.

In summary, the first known regulations for the craft of masonry were not drawn up in a bubble. The same factors within London, and indeed other towns, which drove crafts to organise in the 14th century affected the masons. However, in the 1350s the craft of masonry came under particular strain as a consequence of the Black Death and an unprecedented royal building programme. In response to these difficulties, and under pressure from the civic authorities in London, the masons of the City are visible to us, for the first time, working in a corporate capacity.

2

THE MASON

The simplest and also most comprehensive definition of a mason is that he is a builder or worker in stone, or someone who is skilled in dressing and laying stone. The reality is a little more complex. The modern mason might think of himself primarily as a quarrier, a banker mason, a fixer mason, a memorial mason, a carver, as a conservator or restorer, or any combination of the above. The modern mason could be a trainee or apprentice, or he could supervise a team of less senior masons. He could be employed, self-employed, or the owner of a business employing a team of other masons. It is more likely than not that he would possess a recognised qualification, for example a City and Guilds certificate or diploma, or a National Vocational Qualification (NVQ) diploma, for which he would either have studied full-time or which would have formed part of an apprenticeship; but a bricklayer could learn to lay stones on a building site and, should he choose, call himself a mason – at least for as long as he could get away with it. In truth, the meaning of the word 'mason' has never been set in stone.

Neither has the gender of a mason. Although female masons are not easy to find in sources, we know that women were present on pre-modern building sites. They collected moss to be used for bedding tiles, they mixed mortar, they acted as porters, and occasionally they dug ditches and quarried stone. It is quite conceivable that they also dressed or laid stone at that time.

Indeed, women could join the Company and play a role in Company life. Widows of Company members, for instance, might be recipients of the Company's charity. A small number of examples from the Company's early modern records also show widows of stonemasons carrying on their husbands' businesses, if not necessarily working as masons themselves.

In fact, lists drawn up in 1696 and 1697 reveal that at least 10 widows had become members of the Company; and in the first four decades of the 18th century alone, at least 18 widows bound apprentices or presented their former apprentices for the freedom. It is clear that not all these widows worked in the masonry trade. Elizabeth Ryland, for example, was the widow of John who was a button maker and spurrier, and she bound three apprentices, each one after the other, in 1725, 1732 and 1739. But others certainly did, like Ann Pickersgill, a mason living in Vauxhall in 1777 and who bound Henry Miller as an apprentice, and Mary Simpson 'who carries on the Trade of a mason and lives at the Old Swan Stairs Thames Street', who bound Robert Stanning as an apprentice in 1807.[1]

5 *Joseph Richards, bound as an apprentice to his mother Elizabeth, a 'Widdow, citizen and Mason of London', 1702.*

Furthermore, apprentices presented by Anne Maslin, Elizabeth Richards, Sarah Yates, Jane Scott and Anne Barrett, all worked as masons in London, which suggests that these women owned workshops or ran masonry operations in some way. Principally, however, most masons have historically been men.[2]

MEDIEVAL MASONS

The beginnings of stonemasonry in Britain are conventionally assigned to the period of the Roman conquest. Many of the earliest stone buildings in the British Isles were military works and their builders were soldiers, but Roman Britain was soon adorned by great works of civic and private architecture, temples and villas which displayed the cosmopolitan sophistication of an imperial power and which, as we now understand, exerted influence on all subsequent generations of builders down to modern times.

Medieval masons were not soldiers, like the legionaries who built Hadrian's Wall, even if they were expected, when working on the English fortress at Calais, to take turns on sentry duty with the troops. In the Latin sources of the period, a mason was usually called a *cementarius* or *lathomus*, while in French records he is usually a *masoun*, and in English a mason. Medieval masons were commonly more itinerant than other contemporary craftsmen, travelling to where they were needed, and they were usually classified according to the type of work they did. As we have seen, the representatives of the masons of 1356 were called hewers (*masouns hewers*), on the one hand, and layers and setters (*masouns leggers et setters*) on the other. The hewers, also called variously cutters (*cissor, taylator, tailleur*) and carvers (*enteiler, intayler*) were those who cut or carved the stones. Because they worked with freestone,* the term 'freemason' (*ffremason, lathomus ffre, liberus cementarius, lathomus vocatus ffree maceon*) was often used interchangeably with 'mason'. They were generally considered to be the highest-skilled masons and they usually took the highest wages. From the 13th century onwards, some of them acquired reputations as specialist carvers of images or sculptures and came to be described as image-makers or imagers (*imaginarius, imaginator, ymaginour*). About the

---

* Historically, the best sandstones and limestones were those which, as a result of their finely-grained texture, could be worked in any direction and cut by the use of a toothed saw. Because they can be undercut and dressed into almost any regular geometrical form, these stones, termed 'freestones', were especially valued for carving tracery and archmoulds in relief, images and figures, window and door frames, and vaulting.

6 *Masons working on the tower of Babel.* The Bedford Hours, *early 15th century.*

same time, some began to specialise in using marble, brass and stone to create sumptuous composite sepulchres or monuments. Often working to standardised patterns, they came to be known as marblers, while others who worked chiefly with alabaster were sometimes called alabasterers.[3]

All these specialist masons would have been able to set stones; indeed, the highest-skilled mason may well have been reluctant to allow anyone but himself to set the finest examples of his carving into place. All the same, because the total amount paid in wages to mason layers (*lathomus vocatus ligier, cubitor, legger*) and/or setters (*positor, setter*), sometimes also called wallers (*murator, impletor muri*) or roughmasons, in medieval building accounts is usually greater than that paid to the hewers or carvers, it would appear that they laid or set the majority of stone. While other distinctions were sometimes drawn between groups of masons – at Eddisbury quarry, for example, the quarriers were classified as master quarriers, cutters and trimmers – throughout the Middle Ages, the differentiation between hewers and layers is the one that is most visible in the sources.[4]

Even so, that does not mean that these distinctions were always tightly drawn. In 1305, 'Adam of Corfe Castle called the marbler of London' (*d*.1331) arrived in London. Corfe is situated close to the Purbeck marble quarries and Adam quickly established himself as a supplier of Purbeck marble. By 1308 he had opened a workshop at Paternoster Row, close to St Paul's Cathedral, and the monumental brasses he produced there became stylistically predominant in London and the South-East. In 1313, Adam contracted to pave four bays with marble in the choir of St Paul's Cathedral and, in 1316, he was one of the masons of London appointed by the Mayor and Aldermen of London to choose six paviors to repair the pavements of the City's streets. So, at different times in his career, Adam was a mason, marbler, pavior, and even a merchant. This was not uncommon.[5]

Today, we might consider some of the most famous and elite master masons of the Middle Ages to have been the architects of their day. After all, medieval buildings were deliberately designed, and master masons were frequently responsible for much – if not all – of the design. When master masons drew up and laid out ground-plans, when they prepared templates for each and every worked stone within the structure, when they liaised with patrons and communicated their vision of the structure to the other craftsmen on site, these masons look very much like the modern architect. These skilled masters also acquired a knowledge of materials passed down through decades and centuries.

In the 16th and 17th centuries, Robert Smythson and Nicholas Stone, two men connected to the Masons' Company, were so

7 *Robert Smythson's memorial, Master Mason and Architect, St Leonard's Church, Wollaton. Note the arms of the Masons' Company above the cornice.*

highly esteemed for their knowledge of building that they may be considered as having been recognised as 'architects'. The concept of 'vision' is of significance here, for vision of a structure's final form is something which both the medieval master mason and the modern architect have, and what the modern structural engineer and contractor do not have.[6]

Contemporaries did not classify medieval masons as architects, however, simply because the term 'architect' was hardly ever used at that time in the way we understand it today. But that did not mean that there was no theory behind the construction of medieval buildings.[7]

Medieval masons used a rudimentary geometrical method, which we now call constructive geometry, in their design and planning work. The main dimensions of a building were set out using polygons and circles, which could easily be drawn using a mason's square, compasses and a straightedge. The lesser dimensions within the building, which could be anything from the width of the aisles to the size of the windows, were then established by rotating or manipulating polygons.[8]

Fig. 2.1: Constructive geometry.

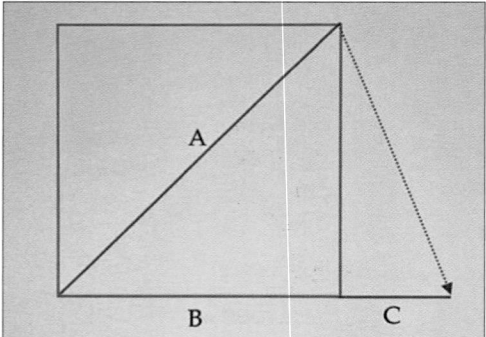

A simple example of how that might be done is shown in fig. 2.1. By drawing a square, a mason might, for instance, establish the plan of the choir of a church. He could then draw its diagonal 'A' and extend baseline 'B' to the same dimension as that diagonal, i.e. A = B + C in length. This section referenced 'C' shown in blue in the diagram could then be used to establish the width of the aisle to the right of the choir. The same technique could be used to establish the width of walkways around a cloister, or chambers adjacent to a hall. The mason would not need to know that the ratio between B and BC was 1:1.414, or to put it another way, 1:√2.* All he needed to know was that this technique 'worked' and that whether he used it to set out a ground plan or to design a window, it both stood up and produced aesthetically pleasing and regular architecture.

Constructive geometry was not the sole preserve of the mason; a majority of medieval structures were the work of carpenters who worked from the same geometric principles. But for masons and carpenters alike, experience, not theory, underpinned the practice: if a building did not fall down, or if it survived for decades with a need for nothing more than minor structural repairs, then it was clearly a success and could serve as a model for other constructions. Of course, the surviving architectural record tells us mostly of the successes of the medieval masons – their failures were cleared away and replaced. However, failures also served to forward the long process which saw rule-of-thumb evolve into genuine understanding, and understanding turn into professional skill.

It was not unknown for master masons to share their empirical knowledge at so-called 'expertises', gatherings at which masons debated the needs and merits of proposed works. 'Expertises' were only summoned for the grandest and most expensive medieval buildings, but they were the germ from which a science of architecture grew in late medieval England, to achieve glorious expression in the works of Henry Yevele and John Wastell and men like them, whose names stand among those of the supreme master masons of all time.

EARLY MODERN AND MODERN MASONS

For reasons which are not entirely clear – perhaps because the distinctions between hewers, layers, image-makers and marblers were always ambiguous – towards the end of the Middle Ages these definitions fell away. Instead, masons came to be most commonly categorised by seniority. The regulations ratified in 1356 make clear that a mason might be a master (*mestre*), a journeyman (*lowytz*) – so called because he was hired (*louer*) by the day (*à la journée*) – or apprentice (*apprentitz*). These terms have remained in use, with more or less the same meanings as they had in the Middle Ages, through

---

* 'Builders did not of course think in terms of square roots. They either worked directly from the geometrical forms that generated the ratios or from arithmetical approximations. Thus the ratio of 12:17 was employed as a convenient equivalent of 1:√2.', Stalley, *Early Medieval Architecture*, 118.

to the modern day. They do not necessarily tell us a great deal about the type of work that masons did. It is unlikely that apprentices in the first years of their indenture would have carved memorial pieces for clients, or that master masons of some seniority would have sharpened their own tools, but it is quite likely that an apprentice in the final years of his term would have done the same work as a journeyman mason, and a journeyman working on the rebuilding of St Paul's Cathedral may well have been responsible for work as fine as that produced by any master in his workshop.[9]

Because national and local government devolved control of economic production to the guilds and companies, and because they were the institutions which produced the most abundant records relating to their trades, there is a natural, but perhaps unprofitable, tendency to view this hierarchy through the prism of company life. However, there were always a great many masons – masters, journeymen, and even apprentices – who worked in London, and indeed elsewhere, who were not free of the Company or in some other way subject to its jurisdiction. Nor should we assume that a majority of masons followed the archetypal path from apprentice to journeyman and then to master all under the Company's auspices. In fact, throughout the early modern period, typically fewer than four in ten apprentice masons took up the freedom of the Company at the end of their term. Moreover, the majority of masons were not small business owners who worked in their own workshops; rather, they were employed on sites and taking wages.

Thus, the distinction between master and journeyman was never that clear in the craft of masonry. Indeed, apart from in its regulations and ordinances, seldom were masons ever classified in these terms in the Company's records. On at least four occasions in the 17th century, when the Company turned to its members for money, it assessed its members either as liverymen and yeomen, or as Assistants, liverymen, householders and other members. Not all liverymen were masters and not all yeomen were journeymen. Finally, from around 1700, when men and women who were not masons began to join the Company in large numbers, the Company's records become next to useless for understanding the status, categorisation or career progression of masons in London.[10]

One development which is clear, however, is the emergence in the 17th century of great mason contractors. Perhaps ironically, these men – arguably the most famous masons of all – are most visible in an era when the high status of the elite mason in Britain was supposedly superseded by the emergence of the professional, learned, and gentle architect. In truth, while most of these men almost certainly could work, dress or lay stone, and therefore be described as masons, that was not their primary role at all. Instead, we should best understand them as businessmen and 'entrepreneurs who managed large teams of skilled men [and] complex supply chains' and men who 'profited richly from financing contracts with Crown and City'. We need not look far to explain their appearance. In the 17th century, the English economy was moving inexorably to what we might understand as a more capitalistic model. Hitherto, masons had been paid, usually weekly, by officers or clerks employed by the patron for each day they had spent working. This simple system was still in use in the 17th century: in 1681, in a frequently-quoted letter sent by Sir Christopher Wren to Dean Fell of Christ Church, Oxford, Wren called this the 'By Day' method of organising construction. It gave patrons and employers flexibility to manage their workforce, but it required them to have enough cash to pay the craftsmen each week and there was very little incentive for the craftsmen to finish work quickly – Wren believed it was preferred by 'lazy' contractors.[11]

But Wren also set out two other possible methods. One which was actually little used was 'By Great' (by task), whereby a contractor undertook to complete a specified job for an agreed price. This put the greatest burden of risk on the contractor, and thus encouraged him to rush the job or to use unsatisfactory materials. Wren's preferred method, and indeed increasingly the most popular one in the 17th century, was 'By Measure', by which method a contractor agreed to complete a specified measure of work, for example a certain number of yards of stone laid, at an agreed price. Once the work was completed, a measurer would assess the work and either authorise payment to the contractor, perhaps discounted if the work was wanting in some way, or ask the contractor to make the work good before reassessing it for payment. 'By Measure' involved more administrative effort, but it had the advantage of incentivising the contractor to work quickly while ensuring that no money would be paid without checks. It also required the contractor to finance each section of the work until he was paid by the patron – which might take months, if not years. In the real world, contracts might employ two methods or specify different requirements for labour and materials, but Wren's analysis is good enough for our purposes, and it is evident that contracting 'By Measure' was 'increasingly capitalistic'.[12]

At the same time, after the Great Fire of London – but not simply *because* of the Great Fire – there was unleashed a building boom, the like of which London had never seen before. At least £290,000, and probably much more than that, was spent rebuilding 51 parish churches in London. By the time that allowance is made for covering the cost of loans which were taken out, over £1.1m was spent rebuilding St Paul's Cathedral. Annual expenditure on new royal buildings, which had averaged some £20,000 during the reign of King Charles II, had more than doubled to £45,000 by the end of the century; much of this money was spent in and around London, at sites such as Chelsea and Greenwich. The contracts for the masonry work at Westminster Bridge between 1738 and 1750 were worth £155,000. There is no way of knowing how much money was spent on the great private developments in London's new West End, but surely we must suppose the total also to have been in the tens of thousands of pounds.[13]

Mason contractors rose to prominence in this age because they were successful, experienced and well-capitalised businessmen. They were able essentially to finance a great deal of this work for extended periods of time while they waited for payment, and the work was profitable enough to make the wait worthwhile. Many of them owned, or had well-established connections with, quarries all over the country, too. It becomes much easier to wait months for payment when one does not have to pay one's own suppliers. The Strong family had owned quarries in the Cotswolds for at least three generations before Thomas and Edward Strong senior came to London. Thomas Strong was already sending 'great Quantitys' of stone from these quarries to London before he came to the City, bringing several masons with him, almost immediately after the Great Fire. The Kempsters owned a quarry in the same area of the country, from which Christopher Kempster was supplying stone to London in 1668. The Wise family, Thomas Gilbert and Stephen Switzer were all connected with the quarries at Portland. All these men established large enterprises in the City.[14]

In 1678, Thomas Strong employed 35 men at St Paul's Cathedral where, by the time of his death in 1681, he had been paid over £8,500 to provide labour and over £700 to supply stone. Thomas's contracts to rebuild three parish churches in London, between 1672

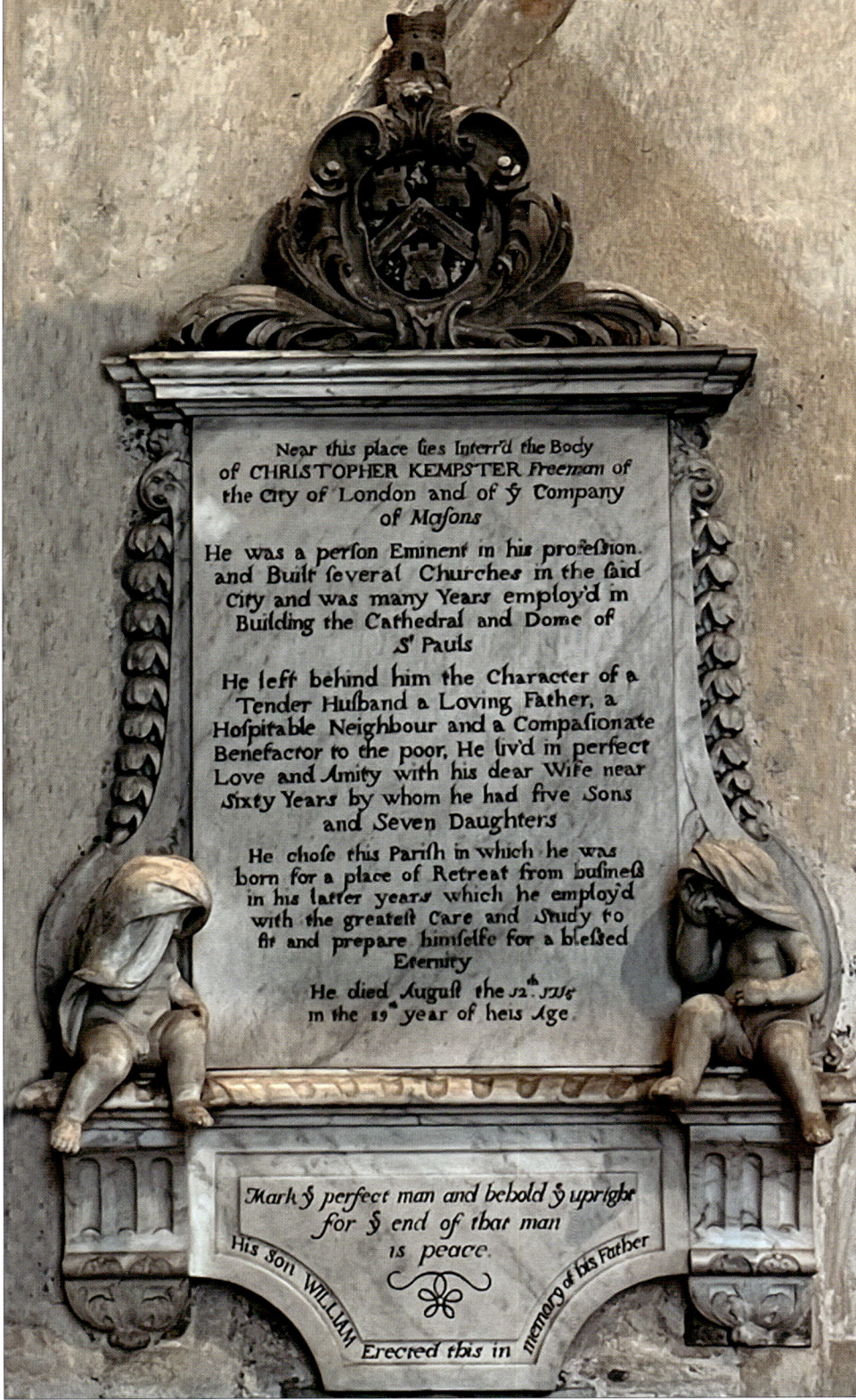

8 *Memorial to Christopher Kempster, twice Master of the Masons' Company, at the Church of St John the Baptist in Burford, Oxfordshire.*

Near this place lies Interr'd the Body of CHRISTOPHER KEMPSTER Freeman of the City of London and of ỹ Company of Masons

He was a person Eminent in his profession. and Built several Churches in the said City and was many Years employ'd in Building the Cathedral and Dome of S⸍ Pauls

He left behind him the Character of a Tender Husband a Loving Father, a Hospitable Neighbour and a Compasionate Benefactor to the poor, He liv'd in perfect Love and Amity with his dear Wife near Sixty Years by whom he had five Sons and Seven Daughters

He chose this Parish in which he was born for a place of Retreat from business in his latter years which he employ'd with the greatest Care and Study to fit and prepare himselfe for a blessed Eternity

He died August the 12⸍ 1715 in the 89⸍ year of heis Age.

Mark ỹ perfect man and behold ỹ upright for ỹ end of that man is peace.

His Son WILLIAM Erected this in memory of his Father

and 1681, were worth over £5,500 and, during the 14 years he was in London, he turned over not less than £1,000, in addition to the above sums, in private work and in selling stone to others. After Thomas's death, his brother, Edward and then his son, Edward, took on and expanded the family business. Edward senior, for example, was paid over £66,000 for supplying labour and materials at St Paul's Cathedral. On 26 October 1708 (three years before the work at St Paul's would officially be declared complete), he laid the last stone on the lantern on the Cathedral's dome, meaning that he was engaged from beginning to end in the Cathedral's reconstruction. Together with Ephraim Beauchamp, another contractor from the Cotswolds, Christopher and William Kempster contracted for some £25,000 worth of work at St Paul's Cathedral alone, while Thomas Wise and his son Thomas, together with Thomas Hill, had contracts there worth £30,000.[15]

But ownership of, or an association with, a quarry was not a prerequisite for success. Edward Pearce, Jasper Latham, Samuel Fulkes and Nathaniel Rawlins all contracted for sums in excess of £10,000 at St Paul's Cathedral. Thomas Cartwright, John Thompson, Edward Tufnell and his son Samuel, Christopher Cass, Andrews Jelfe and many others all profited handsomely as well from the new market conditions.[16]

As the great mason contractors benefited from their ability to finance and organise masonry work on a huge, national scale, so the emergence of organisations – building contractors – which could do this across different crafts and trades was a logical next step. There was no moment in time when 'mason contractors' disappeared from view, but they are much less visible from the 1730s onwards as London's building boom ran out of steam somewhat. At or around the same time, men who described themselves as 'builders' or 'master builders' begin to appear more frequently in the sources of the period. At first, they were probably master craftsmen who undertook the responsibility for all aspects of a construction project, employing workers in their own trade, but sub-contracting with other master craftsmen for the work with which they were less familiar. By the start of the 19th century, however, as Britain industrialised and as credit and financial markets became more sophisticated, building contractors, firms which employed craftsmen from all trades and which had their own workshops, depots and factories, as well as transport and other equipment, become visible.[17]

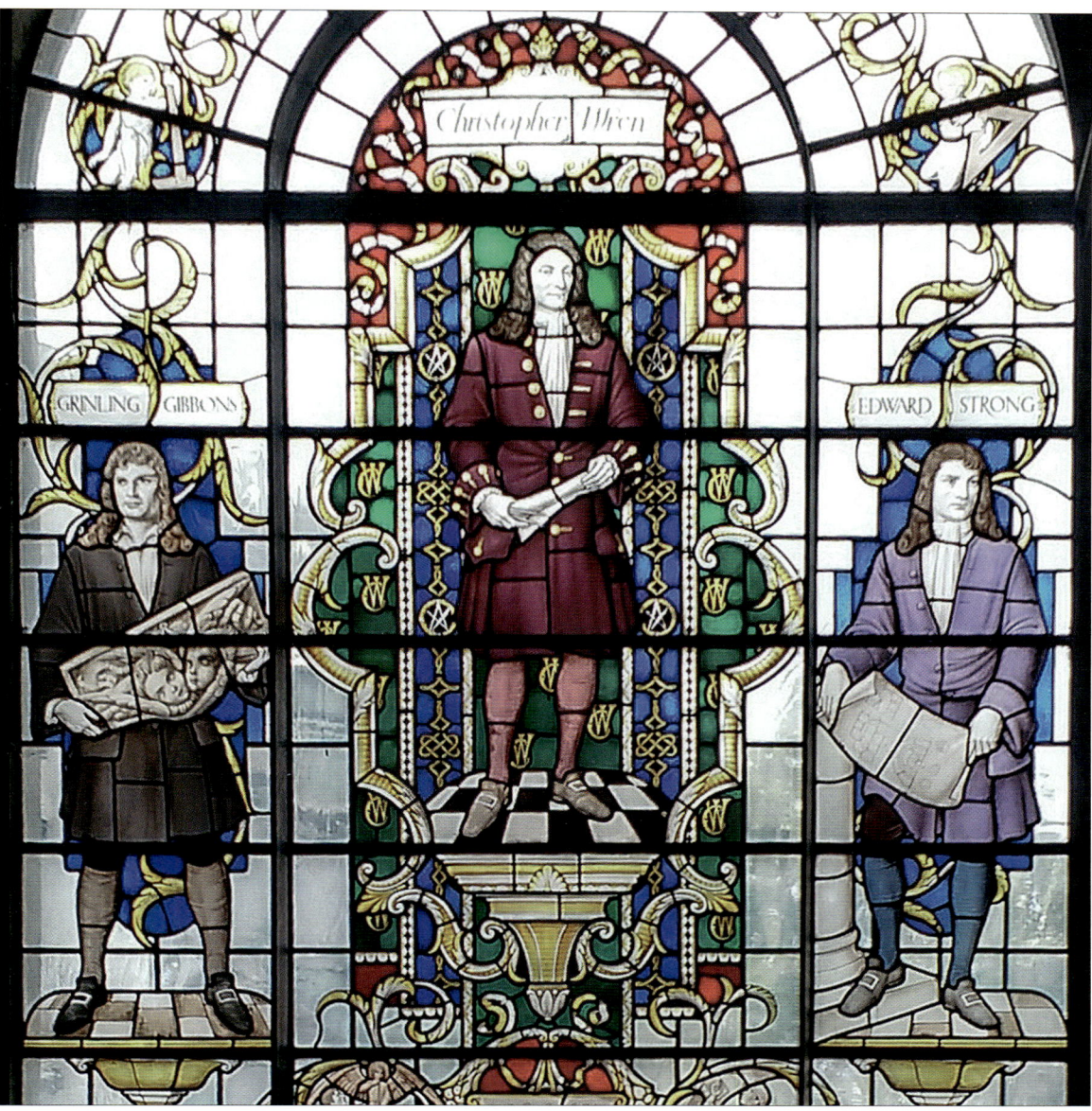

9 *Edward Strong senior, depicted in the Christopher Wren window at St Lawrence Jewry Church, alongside master woodcarver Grinling Gibbons with whom he worked at St Paul's Cathedral.*

The most famous enterprise of this kind in early 19th-century London was that created by Thomas Cubitt (1788-1855). At first through winning contracts with his brothers William and Lewis, and then on his own with speculative developments in Belgravia and Pimlico, Cubitt provided his enormous workforce of masons, carpenters, bricklayers, plumbers, architects, surveyors, lawyers and lettings specialists with continuous, and in many cases permanent, employment. There were plenty of other big contractors, too. In December 1846, Messrs Grissell and Peto, a civil engineering firm and one of the main contractors working on Barry and Pugin's Palace of Westminster, had 1,470 men employed on that one project alone, while the census taken in 1851 recorded 57 building firms in London which employed 50 or more men; nine had workforces in excess of 200 men. In 1875, James Holloway set up his building and contracting business that eventually became Holloway Brothers. Of course, not every mason in 19th-century London worked for one of these great enterprises, but many did, and, as wage-earners dependent on these great employers for their subsistence, they were, to all intents and purposes, more a constituent part of Britain's 19th-century proletariat than the artisan mason of earlier times.[18]

Modern building companies, with their large teams of continuously employed workers – structural engineers, quantity surveyors, managers, foremen, and legal and human resources departments – are descendants of these Victorian master builder companies. However, very few of them will employ many masons on permanent contracts. There are probably a few thousand masons – and perhaps not even that many – working in the United Kingdom today. In an age when brick, glass and concrete are the materials most commonly used in construction, there simply is not the same demand for masons' labour as there is for other building workers.

Masons' Marks

We know more about the wage rates paid in the building industry over the centuries than we do for any other industry. In fact, building workers comprised the only sizeable social group in pre-modern Britain who were paid, usually weekly, wages which were calculated by the day, and evidence for their rates of pay is not hard to come by. This material has been analysed extensively in numerous places. However, the Masons' Company was hardly ever involved in setting or administering wages or pay and we need not detain ourselves with that material here.*

One way that masons ensured they received the correct pay was through the use of insignia now known as 'masons' marks'. These marks were usually quite simple, formed from combinations of lines, shapes or letters which were cut or scratched into the stone. In

---

* An exception came in 1521, when the Company ratified ordinances which restricted the wages that could be paid to apprentices and which gave the Wardens of the Company the right to set the wages of apprentices who had not completed at least four years of their term.

a society with limited literacy, they served as a simple and effective way for the employer or patron to calculate how many stones the mason had carved or set and how much he should then be paid. Over time, masons' marks came to be used much more widely than just on stone for the purpose of calculating wages. It is possible that they would have functioned as a rudimentary form of quality control. Members of other contemporary crafts in London, for example the heaumers (makers of helmets), the blacksmiths, the bladesmiths, and brasiers, were all expected to set their 'own mark upon his work' so 'that people may know who made them, in case default shall be found'. In some instances, the name of a mason appears next to his mark and we can safely assign the mark to the man. In most cases, however, marks cannot be attributed to any known mason, or are

10 *Lease dated 18 June 1573 showing the marks of several leading members of the Masons' Company, including John Tanner (upper right).*

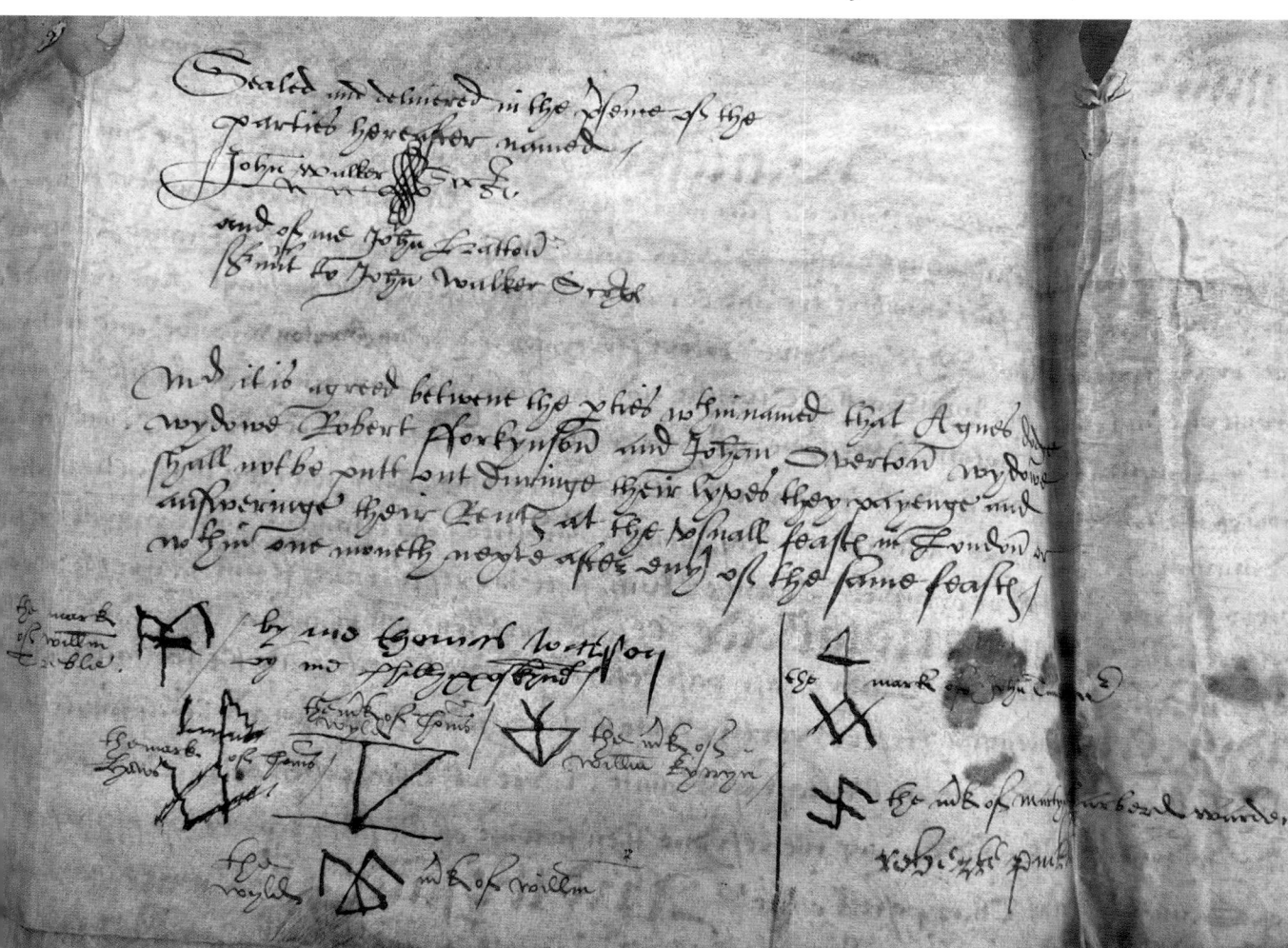

so indistinct or generic that they cannot nowadays be used with any certainty to identify the work of an individual mason.[19]

We know that masons' guilds in Torgau and Strasbourg actively concerned themselves with the marks used by their members, but in London the Masons' Company never sought to assign, regulate or police the use of marks – presumably because quality control on building sites was the responsibility of an officer of the works or a surveyor, rather than the Wardens of the craft. However, marks did come to represent individual masons in the way that a signature does for us today, and they appear frequently enough in the Company's records. In the 16th century, John Tanner and Philip Paskin both engraved their marks on to mazers which they presented to the Company, while up to the beginning of the 18th century, masons would use their mark to sign or witness records or texts now found in the Company's archive. In 2012-13, the Company began a project to build a comprehensive catalogue of marks used by modern masons so that future generations can match masons to the stones they carved. The marks are displayed on the Company's website and the first mark on the register was that of Chris Berridge, a freeman *honoris causa* in recognition of his winning the Gold Medal for architectural stonemasonry at the World Skills competition in London in 2011. This is, in its own way, a good example of how the Company in recent years has reimagined its connections with its craft and those who work in it.[20]

3

THE MEDIEVAL COMPANY

Walter Walton, 'citizen and mason of London', died at some point between 16 August and 6 October 1418. Walton first appears in the historical record in a royal letter dated 26 September 1383, which granted Walton and Simon at Hook, a fellow mason, protections from royal impressment as they were rebuilding the church of St Thomas [Becket] of Acre in London 'from devotion to the saint, who is said to have been born and educated in that hospital'. Thereafter, Walton appears frequently enough in the sources of the period: at Westminster Hall as a carver of tabernacles and images, and as Henry Yevele's warden; at Portchester Castle and Sheen Palace, impressing masons and supplying materials; at Little Hallingbury in Essex as a surveyor; in London as a sworn viewer; and as 'chief surveyor of all stone-cutters and masons for the king's works in England', that is, right-hand man to an ageing Yevele. He was also trusted and respected enough to be called upon by other masons to perform important duties. With Stephen Lote, he witnessed the will of Richard Style (d.1412), before he executed Lote's own will in 1418. He also acted as a surety, very much in the spirit of the third article of the 1356 regulations, for the work of Thomas Wolvey in Henley on Thames, Oxfordshire.[1]

Walton was, then, a citizen and mason of some standing, with a wide network of contacts in the craft of masonry, as was evidenced further by his own will. In this document, among his many donations of property and money, were four, perhaps five, bequests to men who can be identified as masons. His apprentice, John Oldland, was to receive a hewing axe and six irons for masonry at the end of his term; Ralph Oldland, mason, presumably a relative of John, was granted a compass; Richard Brent, who received another compass, may well

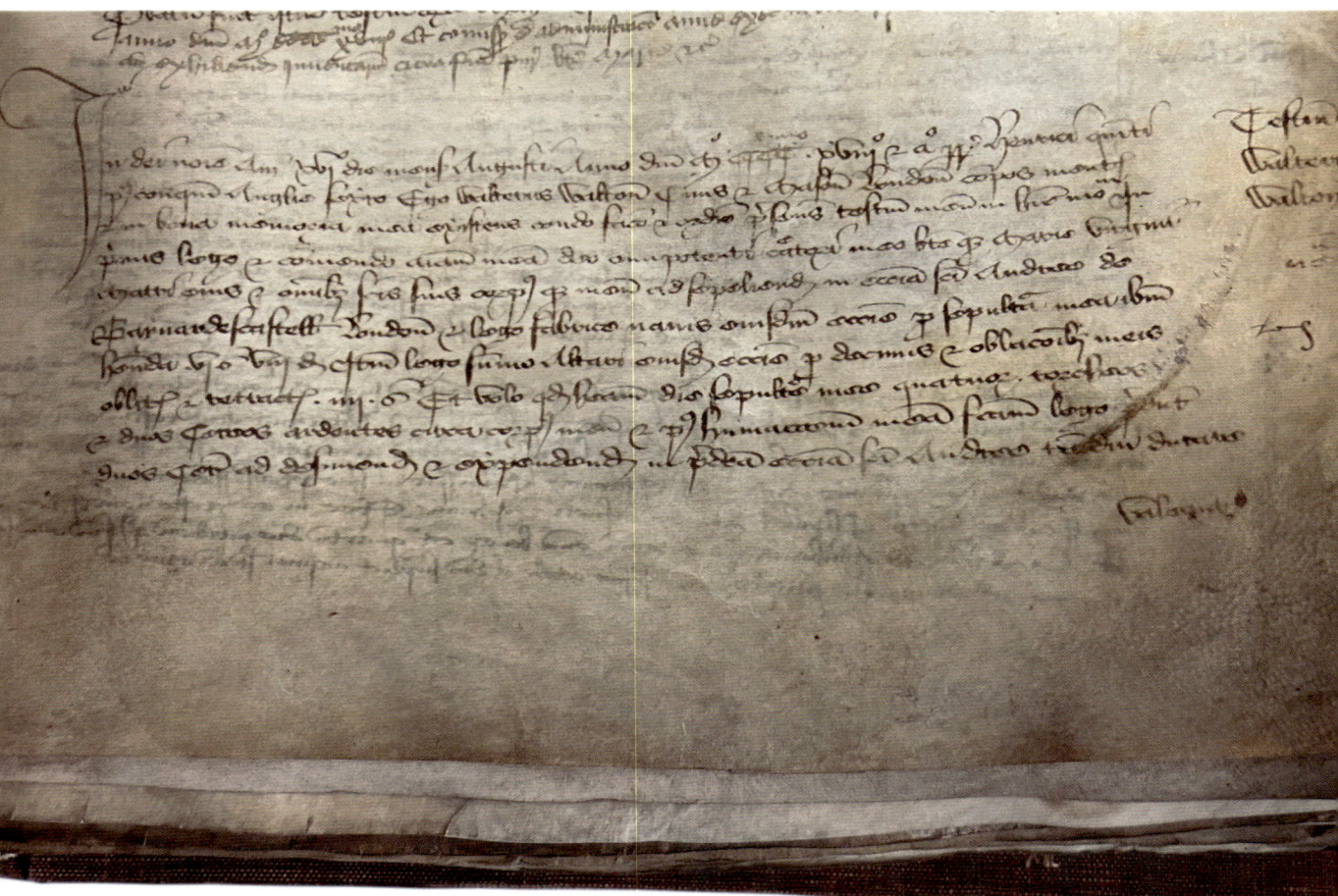

11 *The will of Walter Walton, citizen and mason, who died in 1418.*

have been a mason. John Croxton, the recipient of Walton's best compass (*optimum compas*), certainly was a mason; in 1416 and 1419 he was sworn as master of the mistery of masons, and he was the man most responsible for the design and construction of the London Guildhall. More significant for our purposes, however, are two further bequests. The first to Thomas Pierpoints, mason, of Walter's 'livery cloak of my old and free mistery' (*meum capucium de vetere liberata mistere mee*). The second, one of a series of Walton's pious bequests, of half a mark, that is 6s. 8d., to the 'fraternity of my craft' (*fraternitas artis mee*). Walton's will does not provide us with our earliest evidence either of a mistery or of a fraternity of masons in London. What it does offer, however, is the earliest instance of these two associations together in one document and of one man who belonged to both.

The Mistery of Masons

The term 'mistery' derives ultimately from the Latin, *ministerium*, a simile of *officium*, meaning craft or trade. Ministerium became *mestier*, *mestera* or *misteria* in the French of the period, whence *métier*/metier in modern French and English. The representatives of the craft of masons, in 1356, agreed to a series of 'acts and articles concerning the craft (*mestier*) of masons'. But *mestier* and its variants also had another sense, that of an institutionalised or formalised body. This body was what we now sometimes call a 'mistery': an association formed of and by a group of freemen who exercised a given craft. The term, in its modern form of 'mystery' survives to this day – it is, for example, to the 'Master and Wardens of the Art or Mystery of Masons of London' that the Company's Beadle swears to 'give and use his faithful advice and counsel'.[2]

The 'mistery' of masons in due course appear as a 'guild'. The word 'guild' (*gilda*) was freely used in the Middle Ages to describe almost any social, religious, economic or political association. In 1388, the Crown demanded that all guilds answer questions about their status and organisation. Forty-two returns from London guilds survive – clearly just a fraction of the true number. Among these we find evidence of a wide variety of different types of guild, ranging from religious fraternities of an entirely devotional nature, through religious fraternities with charitable objectives, to fraternities partially associated with a particular craft, and straightforward craft or mercantile misteries.

No return survives from the masons of London. But that need not be of any significance. As part of this enquiry, each guild was asked whether its members wore a common livery; evidently by 1388 it was a commonplace that many did – a gown or a hood, or both. In the aftermath of this investigation many guilds began to seek royal charters, and it was a feature of these charters that they commonly granted the exclusive right to wear a common livery. Thus, by 1418, when Walton died, many if not most misteries in London were probably in possession of their own livery. This would have been distinct from the royal livery worn by masons in the employ of the king, or the cloaks and robes often given to masons by their patrons. So Walton's bequest to Thomas Pierpoints of a livery cloak of his 'old and free mistery', clearly refers to an item of what might be called civic uniform, peculiar to the masons of the City of London.[3]

The emergence of these craft associations, or misteries, was a phenomenon of urban life across 14th- and 15th-century England,

and following their growth it quickly became common practice for municipal authorities across the country to delegate to the relevant mistery the responsibility for supervising a particular craft in their town. In effect, this meant that what was often a self-appointed group was given considerable power over the practitioners of their craft. It is easy to understand why this happened. Misteries provided the urban authorities with a cheap means of regulating labour and production for the common good, and they could also become sources through which fines and amercements might be levied. In most cases, there would be interests in common between the leading members of the misteries and the men who ran the town; the two groups might in some cases even become interlocked. The institutional development of misteries across the country was given momentum by a statute of 1363-4 which set out that all artisans and craftsmen were to belong to just one mistery; the statute also provided for the election of two men in each craft 'to [ensure by] survey, that none use other Craft than the same which he hath chosen'. In London in particular, where, from the early 14th century onwards, the freedom of the City carried with it important rights and privileges, the men of the craft misteries had every incentive to organise and control access to that freedom.[4]

A mistery of masons must have existed in some form in 1376, because in that year Thomas Wrek, John Lesnes, John Artelburgh and Robert Henwick were elected by the mistery of masons to London's Common Council. Masons were subsequently chosen for the common councils elected in 1377, twice, and again in 1381. The masons were, then, one of about 50 crafts which were sufficiently well organised to elect representatives to the contemporary councils.[5]

Whether a mistery of masons existed before then is a matter of debate. The preamble to the 1356 regulations did set out that the craft of masonry had 'not been regulated in due manner, by the government of folks of their trade, in such a form as other trades are'. That does not mean, however, that no mistery existed at that point. Perhaps there was a craft association which, in the opinion of London's Mayor and Aldermen, regulated the craft in an 'undue manner', or which operated in a way other than 'by the government of folks of their trade', which had a form unlike those of other contemporary misteries, or which had simply not felt the need to come before the Mayor and Aldermen and agree to a normative set of ordinances.

It is equally possible that a mistery was established or ordained for the first time in 1356. After all, some form of administrative machinery was necessary to elect and swear the overseers of work and discipline. Knoop and Jones accepted that three of the articles agreed in 1356 were 'typical gild ordinances of the period, which might have been borrowed from almost any set of ordinances', yet they still concluded that whatever was established at that time was not a regular guild. But what was a regular guild in 14th-century London? Certainly, we have no record of men being sworn as masters of the mistery before 1386, but that does not mean that no masters existed. After all, the next recorded occurrence of masters being sworn is not found until 1416, and they appear only irregularly thereafter, a fact suggesting incomplete record-keeping rather than anything else. It is also true that the regulations did not provide for the regular election of officers, but then nor did at least 14 other sets of ordinances which were ratified in 14th-century London. Indeed, it was only in 1364 that the civic authorities can first be seen ordering the crafts of London to elect 'good men' from each mistery who might lawfully rule and govern the mistery 'in its kind'. Nor is it of any consequence that the regulations did not provide for the division of fines – this was by no means a *sine qua non* of contemporary guild life either. In point of fact, there was no one-size-fits-all pattern of development which can be applied to each mistery and to each craft. As Elspeth Veale has argued, 'different groups' of workers within London 'set up and used different forms [of organisation] for different reasons at different times'.[6]

Perhaps it would be best not to imagine a mistery being founded on one precise date anyway. It is unlikely that a quorum of medieval masons met in a lodge or in one of London's taverns or churches and constituted a mistery in the way that we might expect a football or cricket team to be founded today. Instead, we should look for the earliest evidence of an association of masons performing the typical duties of a mistery – maintaining quality control within the craft, resolving disputes between craftsmen, policing admissions to the freedom of the City and controlling apprenticeships. If we do that, we might conclude that the regulations of 1356 provided for those things. Admittedly, there is nothing in these regulations about search, an important means by which quality control could be enforced, nor is there any clause which sought to prevent non-freemen from working as masons in London. But research suggests that 27 sets of ordinances brought before the Mayor and Aldermen by 14th-century crafts of London say nothing about powers of search, and the itinerant nature of medieval masons' employment may have militated against attempts to prevent non-freemen carrying out the trade. Indeed, it was not unknown for some craft regulations specifically to regulate or to allow the employment of foreign workers – that is anyone not free of the City of London – and, in 1481, a further set of regulations agreed by the masons made provision for the fair employment of foreign workers.

THE FRATERNITY OF MASONS

While misteries were, quite specifically, associations of craftsmen, the fraternity was a much less narrowly defined form of guild organisation.* Gervase Rosser has recently suggested that there may have been at least 30,000 guilds or fraternities which 'operated in England at some point between 1350 and 1500'. The importance of the fraternity in medieval London has long been understood. Caroline Barron found evidence of between 150 and 200 parish fraternities existing in London in the years 1350 to 1500. Normally, but not always, a religious element was at the heart of the fraternity; a typical fraternity might be centred on the parish church, on the cult of a saint, or on a particular feast day or a religious festival such as Corpus Christi. Fraternities offered the laity a chance to express their piety in their own idiom, through a model of communal, participatory worship and devotion. They were open to almost all ranks of society, high and low – membership fees were typically modest – and most fraternities were willing to admit women. Usually the members would come together on their patron saint's day to worship collectively, feast communally and, perhaps, elect their officers.[7]

Fraternities were of critical significance to their members also in preserving that continuity between the community of the living and the greater community of the dead, which was such an essential feature of later medieval social and religious belief. Members of a fraternity were expected to attend the funerals of their colleagues and to ensure that masses and obits were celebrated for the souls of deceased colleagues; indeed, the medieval fraternity had a major role as a 'communal chantry'. It is no surprise, then, that so many appear to have been founded in the decades after the trauma of the Black Death. Barron found evidence of the existence of 74 fraternities in London between 1350-1400, compared with only 10 in the preceding half century.

* Called variously *fraternitas, compaigne, congregatio, confrarie*, Veale, *The Great Twelve*, 238.

As evidenced in Walton's will, a significant minority of fraternities drew their members exclusively or predominantly from one or other particular craft. Sometimes, these craft fraternities even developed from parish fraternities, particularly as in medieval towns it was common for those engaged in a certain craft to live close by others of their craft. The first evidence for a fraternity of masons in London is to be found in the will of a mason called William Hancock, which was proved in the Commissary Court of London on 4 April 1389. Among his several bequests, Hancock left 12d. to the 'fraternity of masons of London founded at St Thomas of Acre'. Outside London, a fraternity of stonemasons is visible at an even earlier date: in 1313 the masons of Lincoln established the Fraternity of the Blessed Virgin Mary. There is no hard and fast rule as to what came first, craft fraternity or craft mistery; in Lincoln the fraternity of masons appears long before any mistery, and fraternities of the great mercantile crafts of London are usually visible at an earlier date than their misteries. In the case of the masons of London, however, the mistery is evident before the fraternity.[8]

It is possible that fraternities were especially popular among masons. Masons were likely to be itinerant, and some may have found the immobile parish church an unsatisfactory or inadequate location for their piety. The fraternity, on the other hand, offered much more flexibility. For example, masons who were impressed for the king's works at Windsor Castle could both take their fraternal connections with them, and also expect to encounter kindred spirits on site. Many masons joined fraternities unrelated to their craft, too. Henry Yevele, for example, was a member of the Salve Regina Fraternity based at St Magnus the Martyr church close to London Bridge; John Mappleton (d.1407) was a member of at least two fraternities: one in his parish of St Dunstan and another, providing an example of the diversity of loyalties which was typical of the time, the Fraternity of St John the Baptist of the Tailors of London.[9]

Whether the 'fraternity of masons of London founded at St Thomas of Acre', and mentioned in Hancock's will of 1389, was indeed the same fraternity as that to which Walter Walton belonged in 1418 is uncertain. Certainly, in 1383, Walton was working on the church of St Thomas from 'devotion' to the saint. Like so many contemporary Londoners, he appears to have been conventionally devoted to Becket's cult. It was, however, the Mercers who developed the closest relationship with the Order of St Thomas of Acre, even acquiring the site of its London home for Mercers' Hall after the Order was suppressed in 1536. Indeed, there may well have been more than one fraternity of masons in late-medieval London – perhaps even one centred on Holy Trinity Priory (also known as the church of Christchurch), Aldgate, or devoted to the Four Crowned Martyrs, which site and cult appear in the ordinances the Company ratified in 1481.[10]

What is undeniable is that a trend towards the unification of craft mistery and craft fraternity was widespread in 14th-century London. This happened so commonly that by 1400 very few misteries did not have an attached fraternity. There was no single way in which the two fused – different dynamics played out at different times. As Veale noted, the institutions which emerged from the fusion of mistery and fraternity derived strength and authority from the 'common economic interests' of the mistery and the 'social cohesion' of the fraternity. Walton's will, in 1418, offers us our earliest evidence of this coalescence of mistery and fraternity in the craft of masonry, and it is a process of the first importance in the development of the Masons' Company.[11]

THE COMPANY OF MASONS

There was, then, by 1376, if not before, an established mistery of masons in London. By 1386 this mistery can be seen electing and swearing-in masters and by 1418 it had its own livery cloak. In 1422, the craft of masonry was one of the 111 crafts 'exercised of old in London' named on a list drawn up by the Clerk of the Brewers' Company. By 1389, there was at least one fraternity of masons in London and early in the 15th century, perhaps even before, at least one prominent mason was a member of both associations. Thereafter, the mistery and fraternity of masons appear to have fused and the new body appears frequently and regularly enough in the records of the 15th and early 16th centuries. In 1439, 'the wardens and society' of the 'craft and Felishep' of masons went to law in a dispute with John Brown, one of the masons sworn as a Viewer in London. In 1449 and 1456 the masons were one of about 50 misteries who made a financial contribution towards the cost of soldiers. In 1453, 1461 and 1518 they were again one of about 50 misteries who played a part in keeping of the peace or of the watch in London. By 1463, the mistery of masons had a hall. In 1472-3 the 'hole crafte and felawship of masons' acquired a coat of arms. In 1481, the 'goode folke of the craft, mistere or science of masons' came before the Mayor and Aldermen of London to seek ratification of a series of ordinances for the better rule and guiding of the craft. In 1510 'the hoole felliship of the craft, mistere or science of fremasons' had a number of articles registered at the Guildhall which clarified the Wardens' power of search. In 1521, 'the wardeyns and company of the mistere of masons fremen' of London had another set of ordinances approved and enrolled by the Mayor and Aldermen.[12]

On each of the occasions mentioned above, a different group of masons would have come together or acted together, for different reasons, and each of their associations would have been of a distinct character. Nevertheless, it would also be safe to assume that whether described as a mistery, craft, fellowship, science or company, singularly or in combination, it was, from 1439 to 1521, essentially the same institutional body which appears in the examples given above. Therefore, for ease of reference, the term 'Company' may be used to describe the association of masons visible from this time onwards.

Strictly speaking, the guilds of London only became companies proper once they were incorporated by royal charter. The first examples of these charters were issued in the 1390s, usually to the wealthier property-owning guilds, in the aftermath of the 1388 inquiry into the guilds. A royal charter granted the companies a perpetual legal personality and it is from this model of incorporation that modern livery companies descend. Possession of a royal charter also enabled a company to administer bequests as charitable and religious trusts, with significant consequences for the future. Royal charters did not, however, come cheap, and their real value was to those companies with significant property holdings. Primarily because it was not a major holder of property, the Masons' Company of London would not obtain its charter until 1677.[13]

The 15th and 16th centuries were an 'age of iron' for the London companies. As a network of institutions playing a significant role in the lives of medieval Londoners, the companies were second only to the parishes in importance and size. It is, therefore, not surprising that the Masons' Company should appear as growing in confidence and authority during this period. Certainly, by the end of the 15th century, the Company was a strong presence in the City's political and physical environment. The masons were a distinctive, rather than a typical group, not least in that they were specialised among themselves (as between hewers, layers, wallers) to a greater extent

than those working in other crafts; they were itinerant, liable to be impressed, and reliant on a handful of prominent patrons for work; moreover, they were ordinarily based in their masons' lodges rather than in the workshop.

However, the idea that the lodge should be seen as the equivalent of the guild in the craft of masonry, or that the differences between the masons and their craftsmen contemporaries were so great that masons could not form a 'normal' guild or that they were 'outside the normal medieval craft structure' cannot be sustained. Guilds appeared in various forms; not all were urban, nor did all members of craft associations share the same skills; it is not the case that misteries and guilds could only exist if they were in possession of ratified ordinances – or even that all guilds were first and foremost economic institutions. Thinking in those narrow terms has sometimes led historians, when they have found evidence of guilds of masons, to attempt to explain them away as aberrations. It is certain, however, that the masons of London were fully and effectively able to participate in the guild system which was fundamental to late medieval urban life.[14]

12 *Edward IV, king at the time of the Company's grant of arms in 1472 and ratification of its ordinances in 1481.*

THE 1481 ORDINANCES

On 15 October 1481, the 'goode Folke of the craft, mistere or science of masons' came before the Mayor and Aldermen of London humbly to seek ratification of a further set of ordinances. As in 1356, this certainly was not an action which occurred in isolation.[15]

In the 15th century, more and more of London's guilds began to by-pass the civic authorities and obtain recognition of their institutional status from the Crown by way of royal charter. Between 1462 and 1515 at least 16 crafts and trades in London – by no means all great mercantile ones – bought a royal charter. This threatened the authority of the Mayor and Aldermen who, in response, ordered in both 1437 and 1487 that the 'Wardens of divers Misteries' should bring their books of ordinances before them to have any unauthorised ones cancelled. Granted that the masons appeared before the Mayor and Aldermen six years before the 1487 civic ordinance, it is also quite possible that the Mayor and Aldermen were bringing pressure, which we cannot discern, to bear on the masons and other crafts in London to ratify ordinances prior to the formal order of 1487.[16]

On the other hand, it is equally possible that the Masons came before the civic authorities because they thought they could drive a hard bargain. One consequence of this competition between City and Crown was that the crafts and trades within London could negotiate good terms from the civic authorities. They could, for example, seek increased powers for company officers, or for the right to keep a share – or a greater share – of fines levied by these officers. Both of these provisions were granted to the Masons in 1481.

The Masons may also have been motivated by the actions of the Paviors in 1479. In that year, on 26 October, the 'goode folke of the craft and occupacion' of paviors had come before the Mayor and Aldermen of London to ratify their first set of ordinances. These ordinances are of a similar nature to those the Masons had drawn up two years subsequently. Perhaps the Paviors were prompted to act by the appointment of Edward Stone, a carpenter, as 'master of the city works' in 1478, with responsibility for the repair of the City's walls, cleaning the ditches and maintaining the streets. Were the civic authorities dissatisfied with the activities of the Paviors and did they in turn seek better regulation of their craft? We cannot know, but that the Paviors set off something of a chain reaction is suggested by the appearance of the Marblers before the Mayor and Aldermen, on 31 August 1486, similarly seeking approval of a first set of ordinances for the better government of *their* craft.[17]

Of course, all manner of companies were ratifying ordinances at this time – some 16 crafts had their ordinances enrolled in London's *Letter Book L* between 1460 and 1500. All the same, within the space of seven years, the representatives of what we might think of as three different branches of the craft of masonry sought not only formal recognition of their own specific aspect of the craft, but also their right to govern and police the craft broadly defined. We have already noted that the distinctions between the work undertaken by paviors, masons and marblers were never drawn that tightly; indeed, in 1585, the Masons' Company and the Marblers' Company were even 'united, incorporated and conjoined' to each other. The Mayor and Aldermen of London were no doubt happy to have three different companies regulating the working of stone within the City: all three were sources of revenue from fines, which were split equally between the Chamberlain and the common box. More generally, a proliferation of companies expanded the bases of civic activity – more pageantry at the City's festivals, more business coming before Lord Mayor and Aldermen, more substance and complexity underpinning the City's claims to liberties and freedoms.

The first two clauses of the Masons' ordinances reveal that there were also specific problems within the Company. The incumbent Wardens, Thomas Hill and Richard Rede, had long been in office and had consequently 'born grete charges'. Therefore, the ordinances provided for two new 'honest and discrete' Wardens to be elected biennially at a peaceable assembly of the members of the Company held within 10 days of the Feast of Holy Trinity, and to be sworn at the Guildhall within 12 days of their election.

The Company's accounts and inventories appear to have been in some disorder, too, so the newly elected Wardens were to take charge of the Company's property, and within a fortnight of their presentation at the Guildhall they were to receive the accounts of the old Wardens in the presence of six or more honest persons of the craft. Any Warden not presenting his accounts within this period was liable to an initial fine of 20s., rising to 40s. if the delay stretched a further fortnight. The fine was to be split, with a half going to the City Chamberlain and half to the Company's common box. This equal division of fines stands in contrast to the 1356 regulations, in which the proceeds of all fines levied were to be paid only to the 'commonalty' of London. Hill and Rede were given a year to present their accounts. It is not hard to find evidence for why Hill and Rede had held office for so long; a fine of 40s. for members who refused to take up office, once elected, must suggest that many had avoided service.

A more or less contemporary note entered into John Carpenter's *Liber Albus* gives an indication of what the oath taken by the Wardens of the Company would have comprised. They would have sworn, invoking the help of God and the company of saints, to supervise the art or mistery of which they had been elected as Masters or Wardens; to keep the ordinances of the mistery which, it was stressed, had been approved by the Court of Aldermen; to present all defaults without fear or favour to the chamberlain; not to use the dignity of their office to extort money from, or do wrong to, anyone; to do nothing against the dignity or peace of the king and City; and to behave well during their time in office, according to the good laws and freedoms of the City. The oaths taken by the Company's Master and Wardens today are not that different.[18]

Five subsequent clauses in the 1481 ordinances set out a raft of obligations for all members of the Company, many of which were enforceable by not inconsiderable fines, the proceeds of which were to be split in the same manner as above. Members were to be clad in the livery 'convenient to their powers and degree' at least once every three years; to attend Holy Trinity Priory annually on the feast of the Four Crowned Martyrs, and biennially on election day, clad in their livery and prepared to offer 1d. at each Mass to charity; to come to a biennial fellowship dinner; to pay quarterage of 3d.; and to appear whenever summoned by the Beadle or other officer 'for any besinesses of our soveraign Lord the kyng or for any causes of this citee or for any other matiers concernyng the wele of the said feolashippe'.

The financial burden of membership was not that heavy. Over the course of two years, membership of the Company and attendance at the church services and dinners, assuming no extra payments for 'recreation', would have cost the enfranchised mason a minimum of 3s. 3d. (39d.) with an extra 8d. were his wife to attend the biennial dinner. On top of that, once every three years he would be expected to pay an unspecified sum for his livery clothing. By way of comparison, a mason who worked at London Bridge in the 15th century would reasonably have expected to earn 8d. a day, meaning that in five days he would have earned enough to cover the minimum cost of his membership of the Company, excepting the cost of the livery cloak and hood, for two years. Working an extra day would have covered the cost of his wife's dinner; doubtless many contemporary masons reckoned the expense in this way. Membership of the Company was, then, quite clearly within the means of all but the humblest of late medieval masons.

The remaining six clauses were concerned, more or less, with regulation of the craft of masonry. Again, breaches of the ordinances were punishable by amercement. No one was to be admitted to the freedom of the Company by redemption until he had been 'duely examyned' and judged to be properly qualified by the Wardens of the craft and a body of four or six honest members. Masters were barred from employing any 'foreyn or allowes' (an allow – French alloué – was a hired journeyman)* or 'any mans servaunte' contracted to work for another master who was a member of the Company. No one was to 'hire any other persone enfraunchesed or brothere oute of his hous, shop, logge or dwelling place', that is to say that no employer was to 'hire out' their workers to other employers and profit at the expense of the employee. Members of the Company were forbidden to disobey the

---

* Cf. 'lowyt' in the 1356 regulations.

Wardens, use contumelious words towards the Wardens or each other, or slander anyone else of the craft. Finally, the Wardens were granted, for the first time, the formidable power of search and correction. That is, they had the authority to check that all those practising the craft were entitled to do so, and to inspect tools, measures, materials and premises. There was no provision in these ordinances for the regulation of apprenticeship, presumably because it was felt that this was covered under the 1356 regulations.

Together, these clauses represent an attempt to reconcile competing interests from within the ranks of masons. Employers and contractors gained protection from their workers being enticed away by others, and their right to employ foreigners was explicitly noted. Humbler masons were protected from being exploited by their masters. All members of the Company could take comfort from the guarantee that only competent workers would be admitted to the Company. This provision upheld the value of the freedom – both corporate and civic – that they had all so diligently acquired. Likewise, all members of the Company who played by the rules had good reason to accept and support the search. Why should they, for example, pay to enrol their apprentices if those who did not escaped punishment? All masons benefited, too, from the prohibition of slander and 'unhonest words of liying'. To contemporaries, reputation mattered a great deal. It was a form of social capital upon which livelihoods depended.[19]

If the 1356 regulations show us the mistery in embryo, the 1481 ordinances demonstrate a company reaching its maturity. What we see in 1481 is an institution with a coherent structure and organisation. There are procedures for electing Wardens, and their duties – or at least some of them – have been codified. This text also provides us with our first evidence of a body within the Company resembling a Court of Assistants. Time and again there is reference to a grouping of four or six 'honest men of the craft'; they are to present the newly elected Wardens at the Guildhall, they are to be there when the accounts of the old Wardens are rendered, they are to oversee the new Wardens' custody of the Company's property, they are to advise the Wardens on the giving of the livery and the hosting of the dinner, they are to judge the knowledge of those seeking admittance to the Company by redemption. Admittedly, there is no procedure set out for choosing these men, there is no indication as to who qualified as an 'honest person'; there is not even an expectation that the same body of 'honest persones' should

13 The 1481 ordinances.

appear on each occasion. Nevertheless, for all the ambiguities, this body of 'honest persones' looks very like the consultative bodies which appear in the ordinances of other 15th-century companies. Moreover, in addition to its Hall and coat of arms, the Company of 1481 had property, jewels, money and a common box – into which half the proceeds of the fines were to be paid. Even without a charter of incorporation, this was an established company with a very visible presence and personality.[20]

There is also, in 1481, a very different hue to the character of the Company. Fraternity was now at its heart in a way that it never was in 1356. Throughout, the Company is called not just an art, craft and science, but also a fellowship. The members were enjoined to speak well of each other, not using 'unmanerly language nor unfittyng or unhonest wordes'; they were expected also to come together for elections, church services and for dinner. It also seems that there were, in 1481, what we might think of as two grades of membership: those enfranchised of the craft, and the 'brothers of the said craft'. Many of the provisions applied equally to both types of member. 'Every persone of the said feolashippe' was to pay quarterage, all members were required to attend when summoned and to show respect towards each other, and all members had to obey the rules on the enticement of another's workers. However, only those enfranchised could vote for the Wardens, be elected as Wardens, attend the Company's dinner and services of Mass, and, perhaps, wear the livery.*

We should probably understand 'brothers of the craft' as the equivalent of the yeomen commonly found among other crafts. The term 'yeoman' meant different things to different people at different times in medieval London. In the second half of the 14th century, yeomen were the 'dissident' groups which emerged in some crafts to press for higher wages and, perhaps, recognition. In the 15th century, we see the emergence of yeomen craft fraternities. At all times, however, the yeomen generally comprised the junior members of the craft. Relations between the yeomen of the craft and the masters could be antagonistic, but they could also be cordial. For many young artisans and craftsmen, membership of these yeomen fraternities marked nothing more than a normal stage in their life cycle prior to entering the livery of the company. Over the course of the 15th century, the tendency was for the yeomanry to form a subordinate or junior body within the livery company, sometimes – but not always – maintaining a separate fraternity and/or electing their own officers. Unwin has suggested that by the end of the century, there would have been very few companies which were not 'supplemented by a yeomanry organization' in this way.[21]

The distinction between the yeomen and the more senior members of the company was sharpened by wearing of the livery. A clear pattern emerged in many companies at this time, whereby only the more senior – and usually more prosperous – members of the company were expected to wear its livery. These men naturally came to dominate the administration and governance of the company.

---

* The language of the third clause is ambiguous on this point.

It even became common for those in the livery to dine separately, usually in the parlour of their hall, away from the yeomen who would dine in the main hall. The exalted position of the liverymen was given external consolidation in ordinances issued by the Mayor and Aldermen of London and, in 1467, Common Council ordained that only its members, the 'Masters and Wardens of each Mistery of the City, coming in their livery, and by other good men specially summoned for the purpose' could elect the Mayor and Sheriffs. In 1475, it was made clear that the 'good men' were those in the livery.[22]

There is no evidence that the 'brothers of the craft' of masonry belonged to a different fraternity in these ordinances. Nor is the term 'brothers of the craft' commonly used as a synonym for 'yeomen'. Instead, they are often called 'bachelors', 'journeymen', 'young men', or 'servants'. On the other hand, it is quite clear that in 1481 these 'brothers of the craft' played a lesser role in the Masons' Company. In this way, too, with its hierarchical structure and differentiated membership, the Masons' Company appears to have been similar to its contemporary companies.

The 1481 ordinances provide us with an excellent snapshot of the Company. As with any snapshot, however, we should ask ourselves 'who or what is not in the picture?'. Frustratingly, the names of only two masons, Rede and Hill – men of quite modest standing – are given. To what extent, if at all, were more famous masons such as Thomas Jordan, Chief Bridge Mason at London Bridge and Master Mason of the king's works, and his successor Thomas Daniel, involved in Company life at this time? What role was there for the lesser-skilled and unskilled workers, the mortarmen and hod-carriers, in the contemporary Masons' Company? Where are the women? We know that when John Mappleton died in 1407, his widow Agnes took on his apprentice, Walter Show. This was a common enough arrangement at the time; indeed, many apprentices went on to marry their late master's widow. Were women like Agnes, who took on their husbands' apprentices, considered to be members of the Company?[23]

We might well ask many more questions of these ordinances. Why Holy Trinity Priory? The importance of the feast of the Four Crowned Martyrs in these ordinances seems easy enough to understand. The Martyrs were a group of Persian sculptors who had refused to carve a pagan statue for the emperor Diocletian (284-305), and suffered for their faith. Their craft was sufficient to recommend them to the

14 The Legend of the Four Crowned Martyrs by Rueland Frueauf the Younger in 1515.

devotion of medieval stonemasons. The connection with the Priory, however, is more difficult to explain. Had a fraternity of masons ever gathered there? John Stow had sight of manuscripts which were in the possession of the Priory before it was dissolved in 1532, yet he knew nothing of any connection with the masons of London. It is more likely that the relationship developed when the Masons' Company obtained a 99-year lease of land for a hall, in Haslewood Alley, Bassishaw Ward, from the prior. The benefits to the Priory from such an arrangement were obvious: they would receive any offerings made by the masons at the church. If this were indeed the case, then a transactional explanation may best account for the Priory's emergence as the foremost devotional site of the association of 15th-century London masons.[24]

How well-attended were the dinners and church services provided for in the ordinances? A list drawn up in 1501-2 suggests that there were just 11 liveried masons. Andrew Eliot was a friend of Hill and a prominent mason who died just before these ordinances were ratified. From his will, we learn that he had a great deal of affection for the Company – but as a fraternity rather than a mistery. Yet it is the mistery, not the fraternity, which dominates these ordinances.[25]

How many members of the Company paid fines – if indeed they were ever levied? The ordinances granted the Wardens authority to search and correct all manner of works and things 'which apperteigne to thoccupacion and science of masons within the Citee of London and the Suburbes of the same'. What exactly appertained to the occupation and science of masons, what counted as the suburbs of London, and what penalties could the Wardens inflict upon transgressors? To what extent did the medieval Wardens ever enforce the search in the manner set down in these ordinances? There can be little doubt that much remained uncertain, and, on 19 February 1510, the 'good men' of the Masons' Company appeared before the Mayor and Aldermen to ratify a new set of ordinances which aimed to clear up the evident ambiguities with regard to their power of search. They also sought to define, and perhaps expand, their jurisdiction vis-à-vis the Marblers and Paviors, claiming the right to inspect 'alle marblestones' and 'any paving stone', and to have oversight of any craftsman in London who used the plumb rule, compass, level and square.[26]

The best way to understand these ordinances is as a text which represents the wishes of those who drafted and agreed the ordinances. In this way, the ordinances tell us how the Mayor and Aldermen of London and the Wardens and 'honest persones' of the Company thought the Masons' Company should be instituted and the craft of masonry governed in the City. Theirs was a mutual interest. The presence of an officer of the Mayor at the search reinforced the authority of the Company's Wardens; the Company's promise to present all defaults to the City Chamberlain underpinned the power of the Corporation.

The price of civic sanction was that the Company should attempt to control and regulate the craft of masonry, to raise money for the Chamberlain, to provide men when called upon, and to take part in civic ritual and pageantry. In return, its members received certain privileges and its officers were co-opted into the civic ideal. There is no evidence to suggest that all, or even a majority, of those who worked as masons in London were members of the Company, nor that these ordinances entirely exemplified their concerns. In this way, the ordinances provide us with a window through which to perceive the medieval Company. It is however, a view taken through rather opaque glass.

4

THE COMPANY'S ARMS

The earliest known petition for a grant of arms in England by a trading corporation was that of the Worshipful Company of Drapers. They received letters patent dated 10 March 1439, granting them arms to bear on their common seal or elsewhere. This grant is, in fact, also the oldest known surviving patent of arms given in England. Within the space of the next 60 years, 25 more London companies had been granted arms; their grants represent just under a quarter of the 115 or so known grants made during this period.[1]

The Masons' Company were the 16th London company to be given a grant of arms. They were issued in the 12th year (1472-3) of the reign of King Edward IV by William Hawkeslowe, Clarenceux King of Arms (1461-76).* The original patent survives and, after several adventures, it is now kept in the British Library. It is one of only 13 such patents issued in the 15th century known to be extant. A note on the document, which is hard to decipher but which seems to say £5 2s., may indicate the fee which was paid to Clarenceux for the grant. On the patent the arms are described as 'a feld of Sablys a Cheveroun silver grailed thre Castellis of the same garnysshed with dores and wyndows of the feld in the Cheveroun a Cumpas of Blak'. This translates in modern heraldic language as follows: Sable, on a chevron engrailed between three castles argent, garnished with doors and windows sable, a pair of compasses extended also sable.[2]

In layman's terms this signifies a black (sable) background, upon which is an inverted V-shaped band (chevron). The chevron is engrailed, meaning that its edges are composed of a series of concave

---

* There are three Kings of Arms, or senior heralds, who interpret the laws and conventions of arms and who can grant arms in the sovereign's name: Garter, the senior King of Arms; Clarenceux, the senior provincial king who controls England south of the Trent; and Norroy and Ulster, who controls England north of the Trent and Northern Ireland.

indentations. Within the chevron is a pair of extended compasses which are also black. Around the chevron are to be found three silver (argent) castles, which are depicted with black doors and windows.* On the original patent there is a chiaroscuro drawing of the arms.

We have already seen the frequently close connections between the medieval crafts of London and the various contemporary religious fraternities. It is, therefore, not unusual to find religious symbols

---

* Because of the difficulty in printing silver as a colour, any silver devices in arms are commonly depicted in white, Bromley and Child, *Armorial Bearings*, 269.

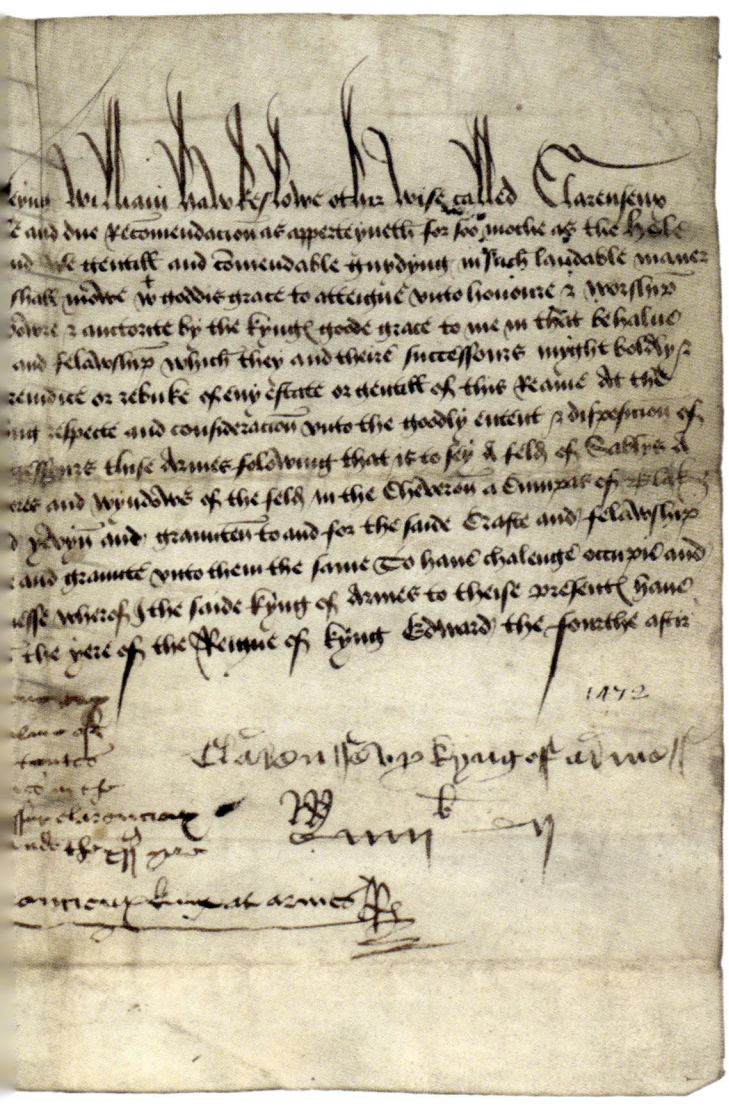

prominently displayed on the companies' earliest grants of arms. Indeed, after the Reformation many coats of arms had to be changed in order to remove what were then perceived to be superstitious elements. However, from the start, the Masons' Company chose imagery associated with the craft of masonry, rather than religious metaphors, to represent its corporate identity. The Company did not choose to portray St Thomas of Acre or a device associated with the Four Crowned Martyrs on its armorial bearings; it did not show the Tower of Babel or King Solomon's Temple. Instead, castles and compasses symbolised the Company's place in the world.

From 1530 onwards, it became customary for the Crown to send out heralds on 'visitations' across the country, usually every 20 or 30 years, to check that all those bearing arms were doing so correctly and legitimately. The Masons' arms were inspected on at least three occasions in the next 150 years by visiting heralds. The first was Thomas Benolt, Clarenceux, who made a note on the original patent confirming that he had ratified the grant in 1520–1; he subsequently had a version of the arms entered into his own manuscript copy of a visitation of London made in 1530. The arms were next inspected and confirmed at a London visitation held in 1590 by Robert Cooke, Clarenceux. The third inspection took place in 1634 by Sir Henry St George, Richmond Herald. On 28 October 1634, Richmond summoned the Master and Wardens of the 'Company

16 *Masons' Company arms depicted in the visitation book of Thomas Benolt, Clarenceux King of Arms, in 1530.*

of Masons and Marblers' to appear before him at the Guildhall, by 9 o'clock on 10 November, bringing with them evidence of their right to bear arms. The Master and Wardens must have taken the original patent with them because Richmond, too, made a note on the document confirming that the arms had been inspected. He also had a fine drawing of 'the armes of the company of free Masons of the Cytty of London' added to his record of the visitation, in which he set out that the arms had been 'entred and approved' by the Master, Edmund Kinsman, the two Wardens, Hugh Jones and

17 *Masons'*
Company arms
depicted in the
visitation book
of Sir Henry St
George, Richmond
Herald, in 1634.

Thomas Moore, and the Clerk, Edmund Roberts. There were no visitations after 1686.[3]

Despite all the emphasis on regulation, discrepancies between authorised blazons and their appearance in actual use were not uncommon. Furthermore, there is some scope for artistic licence in any depiction of armorial bearings. In the case of the Masons' arms, irregularity seems to have occurred from the very beginning: the very first illustration of the Company's arms, found on the original patent, shows a crest above the shield. The crest is formed of a castle mounted on a torse (a wreath formed of two pieces of cloth twisted together), atop a left-facing helm, attached to which is a mantle or cloak, sable on the one side, argent on the other. Yet there is nothing whatsoever said about the crest in the grant. At some unknown point this crest acquired a standardised format: 'on a wreath of the colours a castle argent'. By the rules of armory, the colours must be argent and sable, that is, silver and black. However, the oldest surviving illustration of the arms with a clearly painted wreath is that made by Thomas Benolt, Clarenceux, in 1530; he showed the wreath as or (gold) and azure (blue). Benolt may have misread the original patent, but it is his, strictly irregular, interpretation which is used in modern practice. In his manuscript, Benolt also depicted the castle on the crest above a mount vert (a green hill), something else unspecified in the original patent which has now become common practice.

In the 16th and early 17th centuries, the importance attached to displays of heraldry reached new heights. In the face of rapid social change, families claiming gentle or noble status, often for the first time, began to make prominent use of heraldry to celebrate their eminence. Non-armigerous individuals often took pride in the arms of institutions with which they were connected. William Kerwin (d.1594), a very prominent mason in late 16th-century London, had the Masons' Company's coat of arms engraved on his tomb in St Helen's Bishopsgate. The Company's arms were also displayed on memorial tablets or tombs raised to Robert Smythson (d.1614) in the church of St Leonard at Wollaton, Nottinghamshire; William Smith in St Olave Hart Street, London; and to Christopher Kempster (d.1715) in the church of St John the Baptist in Burford, Oxfordshire.[4]

The arms of the Masons' Company are frequently to be found, hand-drawn or hand-blazoned, in many 16th- and 17th-century manuscripts. In the 16th century, catalogues of corporate heraldry in London began to be printed from engravings, suggesting that there was a market for these collections beyond antiquarian interest. Early modern compilers and copyists of the Old Charges, texts connected with freemasonry, also took great interest in the Masons' Company's coat of arms, and it was probably through the world of freemasonry that the Company's arms came to be engraved on a rummer (a large drinking glass) which the Company acquired towards the end of the 1960s. The care given in these reproductions to accuracy and detail varied a great deal. Towers appear in place of castles, and plain instead of engrailed chevrons. The first printed catalogue, Benjamin Wright's *The armes of all the cheife corporatons of England Wt the Companies of London*, published in 1596, represented the Company's arms with towers, not castles. Such mistakes were replicated in numerous popular works, right through into the 19th century. Indeed, mistakes can still easily be made. Even in the early years of the 21st century, the Company developed the unfortunate habit – now corrected – of depicting the castles in gold rather than silver. The anomalous colours of the crest wreath have survived all revisions.[5]

At some point subsequent to 1722, the original patent of arms disappeared from the Company's archive, and its whereabouts was unknown until around 1870, when a solicitor discovered the document and sold it to a certain Ebenezer West, an antiquarian dealer living in Clerkenwell. West offered it for sale to the British Museum, but they refused to pay what he had demanded. They did, however, bring it to the attention of Frederick Gwatkin, the Company Clerk. By November 1870, the Company had bought the patent for seven guineas from West and donated it to the British Museum. In return, the Assistants asked that the 'Company be supplied with some photographic facsimiles of the Grant and that the Company have access to the original whenever they may desire to refer to it'. On 24 January 1871, John Winter Jones, Principal Librarian at the British Museum, wrote to the Company acknowledging receipt of the grant and thanking them for their 'addition to the National Collections'. Subsequently, nine photographic copies of the grant were distributed to the members of the Court of Assistants, and one to the Clerk for his own use, and a vote of thanks was recorded for Master Henry Burnell's 'valuable assistance in recovering the grant' and his liaison with the Museum.[6]

The Company's arms can be seen in various places – not the least on several signs outside pubs known as the *Masons' Arms*. In the 1840s, the Company paid 10 guineas to Thomas Willement, a celebrated writer on heraldry and stained-glass artist, for a representation of the arms which was installed in the great hall of Christ's Hospital School, now at Horsham. Another window of stained glass, dating from 1874, on the staircase of the Guildhall has provided inspiration for the design of the Company tie. In the 1970s, Brian Thomas depicted the Company's arms for the crypt of the Guildhall.[7]

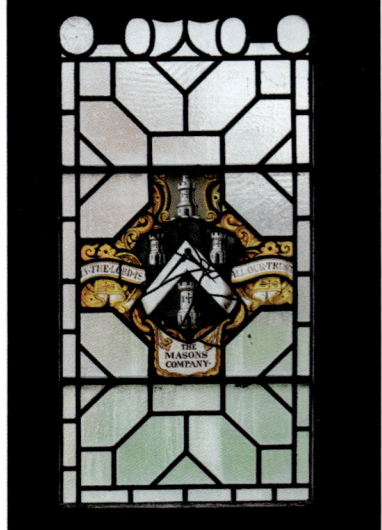  

18 *The Company's arms, depicted in three windows (left to right).*
Hall at Christ's Hospital School; Library staircase in Guildhall; Crypt in Guildhall.

Because the grant of arms is securely dateable to 1472, many members of the Company have come to imagine that year as the one in which the Company was founded. That is, of course, not the case. However, to celebrate the 500th anniversary of the grant in 1972, a new exemplification was prepared by Somerset Herald, Robert Dennys, and a lavish celebration took place at Mansion House.[8]

THE MOTTO

A similar tale of confusion is attached to the Company's motto, the oldest surviving example of which is found on Kerwin's tomb in St Helen's church. Here, 'God is our guide' is quite clearly engraved underneath a fine depiction of the Company's arms. However, a manuscript which can be dated to 1599 gives 'In the Lord is all our trust' as an alternative form of motto. It is possible that the compiler of this manuscript had sight of Wright's *The armes of all the cheife corporatons of England*, published in 1596, which may have given the variant version.[9]

A motto is actually not an integral part of a coat of arms, and it can be changed at the will of the armiger. Nor is it clear that one version of the Company's motto is much older than the other: the first witnesses of the two variants can be dated to within five years – perhaps even two years – of each other. We might think that Kerwin's tomb is the better authority. After all, he was a member of the Company, while the early modern antiquarians and cataloguers were not. However, until the end of the 19ᵗʰ century, 'God is our guide' is found or displayed nowhere else other than on his tomb, whereas the longer form is quite commonly seen.

19 *Tomb of William Kerwin, 1594, St Helen's, Bishopsgate, depicting the motto 'God is our guide'.*

20 *Somerset Herald's new exemplification of the Masons' arms, prepared in 1972.*

We need not think in terms of a 'right' and a 'wrong' Company motto. Variant mottoes have been used by, or attributed to, several of the London livery companies. It was probably Conder who first became aware of the existence of 'God is our guide' as an alternative motto, as a result of his undertaking to write the Company's history. In January 1894, a committee formed of the Master and Wardens (Conder was the Upper Warden at that time) 'was appointed for the purpose of conferring and reporting as to the Arms of the Company'. On 29 March 1894, when the committee came to report its findings to the Court of Assistants, it advised that 'the Kirwin [*sic*] tomb 1594 appears to be the earliest extant authority', and that as the Company was 'reverting to the original form of the arms', it would be 'desirable to resume at the same time the earliest recorded Motto'. Although this version of the report was unanimously accepted, in October 1894 the Court agreed, rather strangely, to accept an estimate 'not exceeding £6' to alter the badges of office 'without altering the mottos'. Until the 1960s, Past Master badges continued to be made each year with 'In the Lord is All Our Trust'.[10]

All of the most modern depictions of the Company's arms display the 'Kerwin' version, 'God is our Guide'.

5

THE REFORMATION

In February 1532, in what may have been something of a test run for the subsequent general dissolution of religious houses, the Priory of Holy Trinity, Aldgate was surrendered to King Henry VIII (1509-47). This action affected the Masons' Company in various ways. From at least 1463, the Company had held a lease on its Hall from, and paid its rent to, the Priory; now the Priory's properties were possessions of the king. The Company's calendar had been centred on the cult of the Trinity since at least 1481, when the ordinances had specified that 'the persones enfraunchesed' of the Company should meet on or within 10 days of the feast of the Holy Trinity to choose Wardens, and demanded that members attend Masses at the Priory. This second provision was now overthrown. Henceforth the Company was entirely and consciously secular.[1]

The effects of the Dissolution were also felt by London's masons in other ways. At the start of the 16th century, 23 important religious houses stood in or near London. By 1547, the Priory of Holy Trinity was one of five houses that had become great mansions in the hands of nobles. Masons had built and maintained them; now they were set to work demolishing or converting them. There may have been mixed emotions about the process; John Stow lamented how the workmen – presumably masons – engaged by Sir Thomas Audley on converting the Priory into a residence, 'with great labour beginning at the toppe, loosed stone from stone, and threw them downe, whereby the most part of them were broken, and few remained whole, and those were sold verie cheape, for all the buildings then made about the Citie were of Bricke and Timber'.[2]

There can be no doubt that the livery companies, indeed all institutions in London, had to adapt as they charted a course through

21 *Ruins of part of the Priory of the Holy Trinity, called Christ Church, near Aldgate.*

the Reformation. The Masons' coat of arms survived unscathed, but the Bakers, Brewers, Innholders, Drapers, Parish Clerks and Scriveners all had to change their arms to remove 'superstitious imagery'. Inquisitions of 1546 and 1548 revealed much about the religious and charitable endowments of the parishes, colleges, hospitals and fraternities of London; but as a relatively poor Company, and one without a charter, the Masons appear to have managed no endowments which could be described as dedicated to superstitious purposes, so they do not appear in the London and Middlesex Chantry Certificate Report, which was issued as a result of the investigations. There is, however, another class of evidence which we can use to good effect to examine the extent to which the Reformation affected the lives of masons and how it changed the nature of their Company, and which has survived in relative plenty: the wills of masons in 15th- and 16th-century London.[3]

WILLS

Most medieval wills were drawn up along common lines, such as those followed by Andrew Eliot, a citizen and mason of London, who wrote his 'present testament' on 13 January 1478. By 23 July he was dead. Eliot was a mason of senior standing in London. In 1439, he had been one of the four men chosen as arbitrators in the dispute between John Brown and the craft and fellowship of masons. In 1444, he appears as one of the Wardens of the Masons' Company. At the time of his death, he was wealthy enough to have his will proved in the Prerogative Court of the Archbishop of Canterbury. Only a minority of masons in London possessed goods to the value of £5, the minimum wealth required to prove their wills in this court; the majority of wills were proved in the Commissary Court of the Bishop of London and the Archdeaconry Court of London.[4]

Despite Eliot's important roles in Company life, it is only through his will that we hear his voice, and then only distantly – the picture that wills provide is never complete. Eliot may or may not have owned property, within or without London; if he did, he made no mention of it in his will. He may have transmitted some of his goods and property before his death – then as now there was the financial incentive of avoiding death duties; he may equally have failed to mention the devise of property, as real estate would automatically pass to his heir-at-law. In Eliot's case it is uncertain who his heir-at-law would have been. He makes no mention of a wife, alive or dead, or children in his will. The only individuals named as beneficiaries in his will were Maud, possibly his sister, the wife of Walter Grant, who received 10 marks, and her daughter Isabelle, possibly his niece, who was given the same amount. In sum, therefore, Eliot's will is disappointingly uninformative about his economic situation.

However, the wills of the period do usually allow us to see the religious belief of an individual. Admittedly, a deathbed declaration of devotion might speak more to the unfortunate circumstances in which the testator found himself or herself, than to any deeply held religious conviction in life. Equally, wills tended either to be drawn up by professional scribes, often priests, or in the presence of clergy administering the last rites, and as such they may tell us more about what the attendant clergy thought the testator should believe than what their belief actually was. That said, the scribe was expected to read the will back to the testator and it is unlikely that in that age of belief, and at the very end of life, a testator would willingly subscribe to a false credal statement.

Such limitations notwithstanding, a will such as Eliot's is still a valuable historical resource, particularly when set in the context of other wills drawn up by masons, marblers and stonecutters connected with London between 1500 and 1580. The wills of 18 masons were proved and enrolled between 1500 and 1539, the year of the Act of the Six Articles, and they may be taken as defining a cohort who drew up their testaments largely according to the tenets of the traditional religion.[5] They are examined fully in the following section. A second group comprises 18 wills which were proved between 1540 and 1579, that is an equal period of 39 years after religious belief had been more or less reshaped.[6] They are analysed more fully in a subsequent section of this chapter.

PRE-REFORMATION PIETY AND CHARITY

After the customary opening 'In the name of God, Amen', Andrew Eliot began his will by giving the date on which it had been prepared, his name, and his status and place of residence, namely that he was a citizen and mason of London. He then avowed that he was 'in gode and hole mynde, thankes be almighty God', and therefore mentally capable of drawing up a legal testament. Eliot's next concern was with the fate of his soul, which he bequeathed 'to almighty God, my savioure, and to his moder saint Mary, and to all the hoolly saints of heven'. Up to the very eve of the Reformation, three-quarters of wills which were proved in London's Commissary and Consistory Courts professed belief in the doctrine of mediation in this way. Only very rarely did wills drawn up by masons and marblers before 1539 not contain a similar preamble. The masons of London appear in this respect as even more than typically pious.[7]

Eliot did not ask that he be laid to rest in his parish church nor that any outstanding tithes be discharged. Instead, he sought only interment in the church of the parish in which 'it shall happen my soule to pass out of this worlde'. We might be tempted to take this seeming absence of attachment to a particular place as more evidence of the itinerancy of the lives of contemporary masons. That would probably, however, be wrong. Eliot had put down roots in London. His will opened with his declaration that he was a citizen of the City, and we know that he was an important member of the Masons' Company. Two of his three executors were citizens of London: John Fouler, a skinner and William Rolls, a mason. The presence of Rolls enables us to place Eliot at the heart of a network of masons and their families which was absolutely centred in late medieval London. Rolls, like Eliot, was a mason of some standing among his contemporaries. He served as executor to Robert Young in 1453, and in his own will, drawn up in 1480, he left many of his tools, including his great compass, to his godson William Kingsfield. William Kingsfield is one of at least

22 *Arms of five masons depicted in a glass window in the pre-Fire Hall; Kingsfield is top left. Early 17th-century manuscript.*

five men bearing that surname who can be shown to have connections with the craft of masonry in the 15th and 16th centuries; by the middle of the 17th century the arms of the family were displayed in glass at Masons' Hall. They were men of a certain status, even something of a dynasty. Rolls also appointed Thomas Hill, a mason and one of those named as Warden of the Company in the 1481 ordinances, as an executor of his own will. In the year following Eliot's death, Hill joined the religious fraternity of St Nicholas, the fraternity of which Eliot had been a member. Hill's wife, Elizabeth, had been a member of the same fraternity. At the very least, Eliot, Rolls and Hill knew and trusted each other, and Eliot was devoted to the same fraternity as Thomas and Elizabeth Hill.[8]

Such men, clearly, were not itinerants; on the contrary, the parish church, unmistakably fixed and local, was evidently very important in their lives: 16 of the 18 masons who drew up their wills between 1500 and 1539 asked to be buried in a named church, 15 directed that any tithes they owed in their parish be paid 'in discharging of my soul', and 13 even specified, more or less exactly, where in the precincts of their named church they wished to be buried. At times, these requests provide us with quite an intimate picture of the testator in question. Thomas Pope (d.1533), for example, rather touchingly asked to be buried in the churchyard near the spot where Elizabeth, his wife, and his children were buried. Thomas Hill (d.1484), Walter Martyn (d.1513), John Molton (d.1547) and John Paskin (d.1557) all made similar requests, as indeed did Elizabeth Burpham, who, in 1555, asked to be buried next to her husband Gilbert, a mason. Equally evocative was the wish of Nicholas Merche, a citizen and freemason of London who died in 1517, to be buried in the south aisle of the church of St Bartholomew-the-Less, 'where I am wont to walke'. This burial place cost him 6s. 8d., which appears to have been the going rate for burial in the choir or other prominent place within a church.[9]

Eliot may have been a little unusual in requesting that his body be buried in whichever parish he might die, but his religious orthodoxy emerged strongly in the request that his executors 'fynde within the convent chirch of the Trynyte of London a chanon of the convent' to sing, for the next four years, a weekly mass for his soul, taking 7d. a week for his trouble – and should any canon be disposed to sing for his soul on a daily basis, he, too, should receive 7d. for a week's effort.

There are, in fact, three key themes in Eliot's will, themes which recur time and again in the wills of masons in pre-Reformation London. The first is a desire to shorten the time spent by the testator in purgatory. There were several ways in which this might be achieved. Most masons asked that their outstanding tithes be paid, and besought Marian and saintly mediation on their behalf. Many also left money to pay for masses, prayers of intercession, trentals (30 masses sung a month after the funeral), obits and anniversaries. Any mason might leave a few pence for a single mass, but to provide, as Eliot did, for weekly masses over a term of years was clearly a matter of much more consequence, and such bequests were the preserve of better-off craftsmen. When Thomas Wells, a freemason of London, died in 1526, he bequeathed £6 13s. 4d. (or 10 marks) for one honest priest 'to sing masse and to pray for my soule and all Christen souls' in his parish church of St Martin Orgar for a year, 20s. for two trentals of masses in the conventual church of the Austin Friars, and 5s. to Thomas Marshal, a priest, to pray on his behalf. This was a sum of almost £8, an amount that was the equivalent of a respectable annual wage for masons at the time.

Susan Brigden has shown that fully one-half of richer testators in the Prerogative Court of Canterbury between 1520 and 1522 made bequests for chantry priests to sing masses for their souls, compared with 9 per cent in London's Commissary Court between 1522 and 1530. This unequal pattern is replicated in our study of the masons. In the first group of 18 masons, seven had their wills enrolled in the Prerogative Court; of these seven, six made clear bequests for prayers, masses, obits or trentals. By contrast, only three of the 11 masons whose wills were enrolled in the Commissary Court made similar bequests.[10]

The fraternities offered the masons of London an alternative means of providing intercession for their souls, which appears to have been as popular with masons as it was generally with Londoners. Four of the 18 masons in our first cohort remembered at least one fraternity in their wills, almost an exact match with the proportion of Londoners, generally, who did the same. The fraternity of St Nicholas received 6s. 8d. from Eliot and from Hill 3s. 4d. Hill was a member also of two other fraternities, St Giles without Cripplegate and Our Lady St Mary in the church of St Stephen, to both of which he left money. He asked the brothers and sisters of all three fraternities to pray for his soul. For good measure, he also bequeathed 6s. 8d. for the repair of buildings and tenements belonging to the same church of St Stephen, hoping that its parishioners would also pray for his soul.[11]

In what ways might Eliot, Hill and other masons typically have expected the fraternity to intercede for their souls? The fraternity of the Holy Trinity at St Botolph without Aldersgate paid a priest 10½ marks annually. In return, he said a weekly requiem for the souls of departed members and kept the personal obits of benefactors. All living brethren were expected to attend an annual service on the weekend after All Souls (2 November), at which a dirige and requiem would be performed, whereupon the priest would read the names of all the brothers and sisters, quick and dead, and recite the *De Profundis*. At least five masons in late medieval London were members of this fraternity. William Flint and William Emery were two. John Lesnes, one of the masons who represented the craft on the Common Council elected in 1376, was listed as a member along with his wife Margery. Another who joined the fraternity with his wife was John Canning, a citizen and stonecutter, who paid 12d. to enter the fraternity with his wife Alice, in 1377. Canning's son and daughter-in-law, William and Cecilia, paid the same sum to enter in 1393-4.[12]

John Canning must have been an important member of the fraternity as in the 1390s he witnessed several of the fraternity's charters, alongside aldermen, sheriffs and mayors of London, including the famous mercer, Richard Whittington. The fraternity was dissolved in 1548, but as late as 1536 George Simpson senior, a citizen and freemason of the parish of St Botolph, bequeathed £5 to the 'bretherhode of the holly Trinitie founded in the same church whereof I am a brother'. All these masons, and their wives and families, hoped to benefit in death from the efforts of the fraternity's priest and living members.

Fraternities provided Londoners with more than just intercession for their souls. They also offered the prospect of the best possible funeral – and preoccupation with funerary rites is the second of our key themes. What late medieval Londoners feared especially, in Caroline Barron's words, was not death itself so much as 'the prospect of an indecent burial'. Members of a fraternity, or clerks in its employ, would attend funerals, usually clothed in the livery of the guild or fraternity; they would sing psalms, diriges and masses; and they would provide or hold candles, lights and tapers to burn at the funeral, usually around the corpse.[13]

The Masons' Company's ordinances of 1481 made no special provision for the funerals of its members, but this was not unusual, because by the late 15th century the functions of the fraternities had assumed a scope which made separate provision for funerals less necessary. But the importance attached to the funerary rituals is clear in the wills of contemporary masons. In addition to the 6s. 8d. which he bequeathed to 'the fraternitie of saint Nicholas founded by the clerks of London', Eliot left the same sum to be distributed among the clerks of the fraternity that came to his funeral, a further 6s. 8d. to the clerks of the fraternity attending his month's mind, 4d. each to four clerks of the fraternity who carried his body at the funeral service, and 5s. to the four orders of friars in London (the Black, Grey,

Austin and Carmelite Friars) 'so that they come to my bueryng'. A special value was attached to the services of the friars in connection with obsequies in late medieval London. William Rolls, for example, the mason who executed Eliot's will, left 5s. to the Grey Friars and 3s. 4d. to the Black Friars so that they might say masses for his soul.

The fraternity of St Nicholas was also popular – Londoners requested the attendance of members of this guild more often at their funeral obsequies than that of any other fraternity. As Eliot's will suggests, it had been founded by the parish clerks of London (the modern-day Parish Clerks' Company grew out of this fraternity after the Reformation) and it offered its members 'a more elaborate funeral than could be provided through membership of the average parish fraternity'. At least three prominent masons in late 15th-century London – Eliot, Hill and Thomas Daniel – all of whom were probably known to each other, were members of this fraternity.[14]

Another way in which Londoners provided for a decent burial was to ask that money be distributed to the poor, whether on the day of their decease, funeral, month's mind or other anniversary. Eliot, for example, left 3s. 4d. to be distributed among the poor of the parish in which he died. Remembering the poor in this way was an elementary act of charity, but it was also an act of piety, and contemporary Londoners were expected to display both virtues openly. Many Londoners believed that giving money to the poor repaid itself in the treasure which the donors consequently accumulated in heaven. 'He that hath pity upon the poor lendeth unto the Lord; and that which he hath given will He pay him again.' There was even a widely held sense that the poor were specially blessed, and that their prayers were particularly valuable in hastening one's deliverance from purgatory. 'Item, I bequeath to be gyvyn and dalt the day of my buryall among poor folks to pray [for] me and all Christen souls .xx.s', ordained Thomas Wells in 1526. Wells was one of four masons who, between 1500 and 1539, made explicit provision for the poor in their wills.[15]

Undoubtedly, there was also an element of status affirmation in the custom of funeral doles; as Ian Archer has noted, bequests to the poor to attend funerals and anniversaries emphasised the 'bonds of patronage and deference'. But we should not be too cynical: the giving of doles to the poor was understood as virtuous in itself, and their prayerful attendance at the funeral served to make it a more effective occasion. For those like Eliot, who did not have families to speed them on their way at their burials, this would have been of even greater value.[16]

One last provision in Eliot's will can also be taken as evidence of his desire for the finest possible obsequies. Eliot asked that his executors provide four torches and four tapers 'for to burne the daies of my decesse and monethes mynde'. Lights, torches and candles were prominent elements in the ceremonies of late medieval funerals, and were often elaborately deployed. When John Painter, citizen and freemason of London, died in 1536 he specified that his executors 'shall provide for my burial .xij. half pounde tapers and .xij. childern to bere them and they to have for their labours .xij. rochetts [surplices] of newe clothe'. He also requested that his executors 'shortly after my deceas shall provide and ordeyn foure great tapers of .iiij. lb a pece to stonde aboute my herse and also twoo braunches of virgin wax of .iij. lb a pece.'

The third and final theme of special importance in Eliot's will was the significance of his membership of the Masons' Company. The only parish mentioned in his will was that of St Michael Bassishaw,

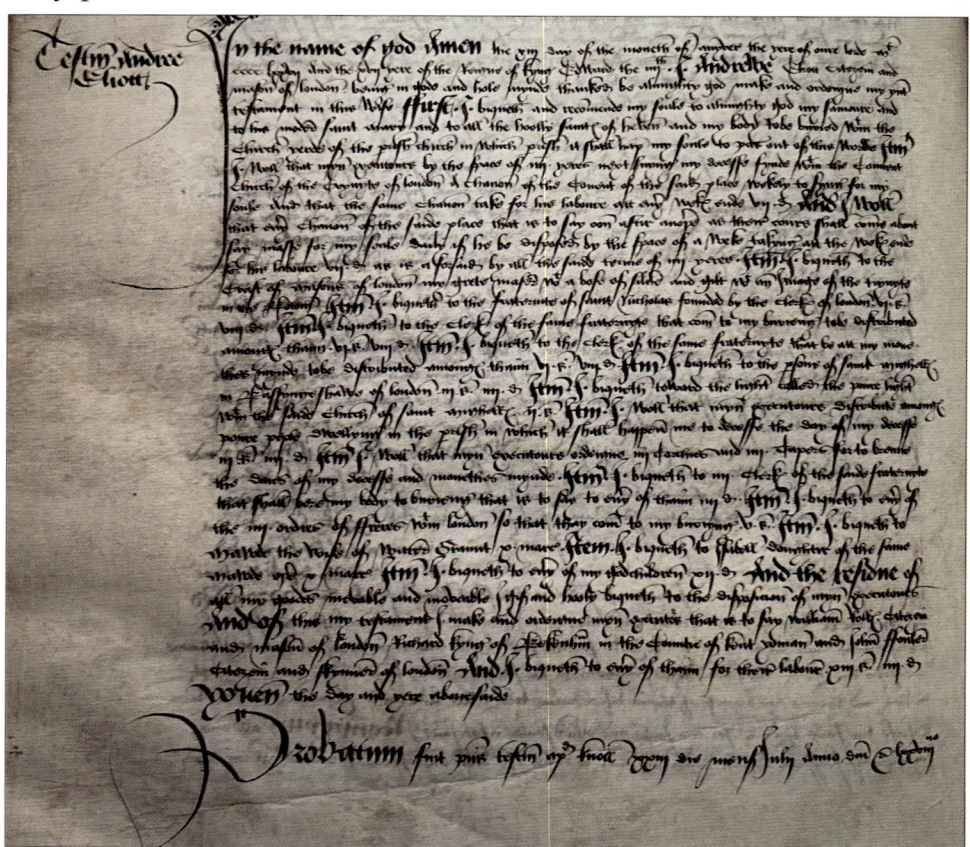

23 *The will of Andrew Eliot, citizen and mason, who died in 1478.*

to the parson of which Eliot bequeathed 3s. 4d. along with 2s 'toward the light called the poure light within the saide chirch'; Masons' Hall, where presumably Eliot spent a fair amount of time, stood in St Michael's parish. Further, Eliot's request that a canon of Holy Trinity Priory should sing masses for his soul is a clear indication of the connection between the Priory and the Company. Finally, Eliot's bequest to 'the craft of masons of London' of his 'grete maser [or drinking bowl] with a boss of silver and gilt with an image of the Trynyte' strongly suggests that in his mind, at least, the Masons' Company and the cult of the Holy Trinity were intimately associated. Perhaps the fraternal and religious aspects of Company life at Masons' Hall and Holy Trinity came to assume a special meaning for Eliot, in some way at least, because he was unmarried and childless.

By remembering the Company in his will, Eliot was following an established, if somewhat occasional, tradition. He was one of at least three masons in the second half of the 15th century who gave something to the Company at their deaths.[17] In the period 1500-1539 three other masons, Richard Aylmer, Walter Martyn and John Painter, all left bequests to the Company in their wills. Eliot's loyalty to Holy Trinity Priory, the religious institution most obviously connected to the Company, does not appear to have been shared by his fellow masons – at least on the evidence of their wills. None of the 18 masons who prepared a will between 1500 and 1539 made mention of the Priory; various other religious houses, in London, Canterbury and elsewhere, were remembered by the testators in this group, but there is no evidence of links between them and the Company. No single house seems to have been held in particular collective reverence by them.

On the whole, the masons of late medieval London appear to have been an orthodox bunch; at least, their wills afford no evidence of reformed or Protestant religious sympathies before 1539. Rather, in a very traditional idiom, they sought intercession for their souls, joined and remembered religious fraternities, left money for the poor and a few even made provision for the Company. Masons were not the wealthiest men in contemporary London, so we do not see them bequeathing enough property or money, either to the Company or to religious houses, to support perpetual endowments. Instead, we find the better-off masons making bequests of cash which might provide for a few years' worth of intercession, while their less well-off fellows usually discharged their tithes and bequeathed more modest sums for the benefit of their soul and their poor neighbours.

Post-Reformation Piety and Charity

John Paskin, a citizen and mason of London, died late in 1557. His will epitomises many of the difficulties we face when we use wills as evidence in the decades after 1540. Few wills drawn up by masons in this second cohort contained a preamble more obviously evangelical than Paskin's. 'I commend my sowll into the hands of almightie God, my Saviour and Redemer, by the merits of whose most bitter and paynfiled passion I stedfastly trust and beleave through his most mercyfull mercy to be partaker of his most glorious kingdome of heaven.' Yet Paskin also went on to ask that his executors, 'in the day of my buriall and at the masse of Requiem to be donne for my sowll and all Christen sowlles shall dystribute and gyve unto the poure as unto theym shall be thought conveniente.' Should we see Paskin as a mason with evangelical sympathies who, at the end, hedged his bets somewhat with a provision for a Mass for his soul and those of other Christians? Alternatively, might this instead be evidence of a superficial submission to orthodoxy? It is perhaps significant that Paskin did not ask for a requiem Mass; rather he referred to the one which would 'be donne for my sowll'. Paskin died in 1557, when Mary I (1553-8) was on the throne and Roman Catholic rites had been restored to the Church. There is certainly a sense here that this was a requiem Mass more obligatory than it was optional.

There was, in mid-16th-century London, a great deal of pressure on people to conform outwardly to the religious orthodoxy. Sentiments expressed in a will were even sometimes used to condemn people as heretics, which could lead to the exhumation of their corpse and the burning of their remains. Under Mary the requirement of orthodoxy was intensified; more than 75 people were burned to death for heresy in London and its suburbs between 1554 and 1558. Was Paskin toeing the line with a minimal level of enthusiasm? Possibly. At some point during the reign of Edward VI (1547-53), he bought a child's cope of blue velvet from the churchwardens of St Benet Fink, his parish church, for 2s. 2d. We know that some such purchases were opportunistic acquisitions of luxury material which could be bought at a knockdown price, but others were, quite certainly, born of a reverent desire to preserve a sacred object. Perhaps it is significant that Robert Smythe, curate of St Benet Fink, was a witness to the will.[18]

While we do not know when Paskin was born, at the time of his death he must have been an old man. In his will, he bequeathed his 'sylver potte and .iij. spones of silver' to his grandson, Richard Paskin. Grandchildren are mentioned in only a minority of 16th-century wills; John Paskin would have been at least 50 at his death, and probably older than that. In 1538, the citizens of London were ordered to arm themselves according to their status. As the companies were to administer this provision, they submitted to the Lord Mayor, Richard Gresham, a list of their members ranked as Wardens and Assistants, liverymen, and householders and freemen. Paskin was one of 12 masons in our second cohort who appear in this list. In that year, he was a householder and freeman so he must have been in his mid-20s then at least. Nine masons from our cohort, who appear as Assistants and liverymen on the list, would have been older than that. John Aylmer must have reached a good age when he departed his life in 1548: he had served as a Viewer in London from at least 1509 until the year of his death. John Molton, who was not named in 1538, but who was 'master masonne unto the kinges maiestie', when he died in 1547, must also have been a senior mason. Paskin's generation were men who had lived the majority of their lives professing traditional beliefs, but who faced death at a time when those beliefs had been thrown into disarray. Therefore, we can expect that, on the whole, they might have been more conservative in disposition, in matters of religion at least.[19]

It is possible, therefore, that the wills of the masons in this second cohort understate the extent to which reformed ideas had spread among the masons of London in the decades after 1540. This was partly, at least, because the structural template for wills remained largely unchanged. But variations crept in; many wills of the period feature a preamble which mixes tenets of the old and new faiths. 'I do recomend my soule into thandes of almightie God my maker, redemer and onely saviour' began George Simpson junior, a citizen and freemason of London and cousin of George Simpson senior, in 1556, before adding 'and to our blissid ladie seynt Mary the virgyn, his glorious mother, and to all the holie companye of seynts in heaven'. As Paskin's will also demonstrates, even when a preamble was clearly evangelical in tone, it could still quite easily be followed by traditional provisions, or vice versa.

Paskin and Simpson junior were the only two masons to have had their wills proved during the reign of Mary, when Roman Catholic orthodoxy was restored and reformers were severely persecuted. It would be hard to draw any general conclusions from a sample this

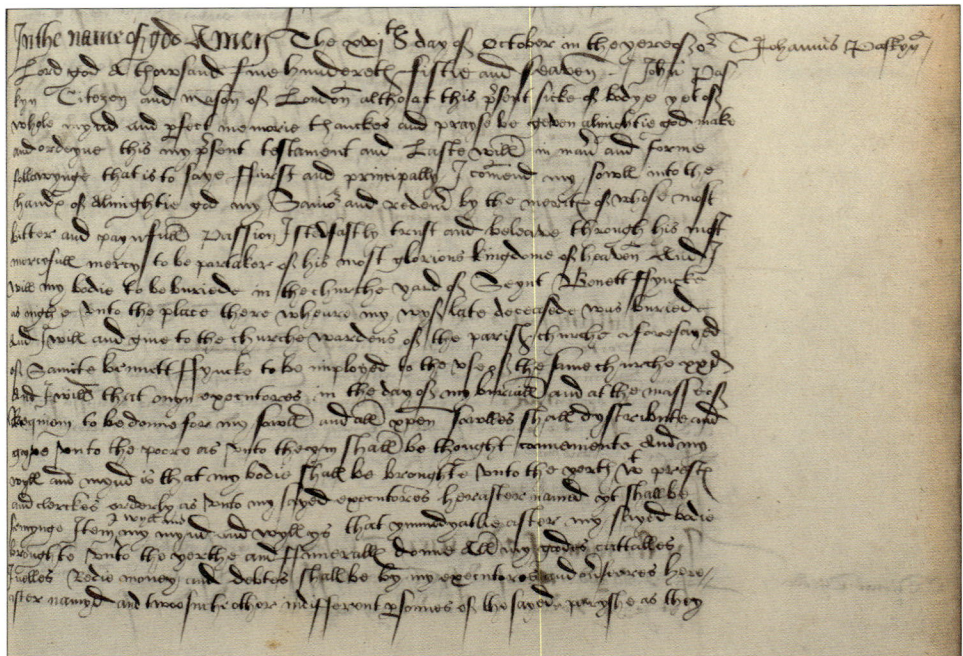

24 *The will of John Paskin, citizen and mason, who died in 1557.*

small in any circumstances, but there can be no dispute about the fact that the will of every mason who died in the period 1540 to 1579 shows to a greater or lesser extent the influence of the new religious teaching.

England was not suddenly converted to Protestantism. The process of reform, for it was indeed a process, took decades. Comparison of the five wills drawn up by masons in the final years of Henry VIII's reign (1540-7), with the five wills we have from the reign of his son Edward VI (1547-53), is particularly instructive for showing how masons adapted to the doctrinal changes which were imposed from above. Under Henry, Londoners could and did still ask that candles be borne at their funerals and placed around their corpses. Thus, John Molton left 24s. to buy torches 'for to burne at my buriall and moneth mynde'. Likewise, while purgatory had been denied and the houses which existed to pray for the souls of the dead had been dissolved, private masses for the dead were allowed to continue and Londoners carried on making provisions for masses, trentals, obits and chantries. John Orgar, in 1546, asked that his executors spend 6s. 8d. a year, over a term of seven years after his decease, maintaining an 'obit or anniversary for my soule, my wiffes soule and all Christen soules'. We have no way of knowing whether his obit was ever established and observed. It is almost certain that it would have ceased to be observed, as indeed would all those of his fellow masons, when the chantries and fraternities were suppressed and obits declared superstitious in 1548.

Three masons during the last years of Henry VIII, namely William Holmes, John Orgar and John Molton, invoked the Virgin and the saints when committing their souls, while two, Robert Hawte and Francesco Benall', used the neutral formulation of simply leaving their souls to Almighty God. None of the five masons whose wills were proved during the reign of Edward VI requested masses, trentals or obits for their souls, and only one, John Aylmer, who died in 1548, asked for intercession from the living. 'I will and bequeathe to .xij. poor men of my nighbours to praye for me at the daye of my buryeng and at my monythes mynde, to every of them .xij.d.' Under Edward, just two masons, Aylmer and Geoffrey Orgar (d.1551), invoked the company of heaven, two, Gilbert Burpham and Thomas Fant (both d.1550), left their souls to God alone, while one, William Chamberlain (d.1550), chose the perhaps slightly more evangelical commendation of giving his 'soull unto almightie God, putting me holely in his mercy'.

In all of this, the masons of London were quite typical. Between 1539 and 1547, two-thirds of Londoners committed their souls to the Virgin and/or the saints, and one in five to God or Christ alone. In the same period, the attacks on purgatory weakened the case for the fraternities' existence – even before they were abolished in 1548, fewer than one Londoner in ten provided for a fraternity in his or her will. The last mason to remember a fraternity in his will was George Simpson senior, who died in 1536.[20]

As the religious houses and fraternities of London disappeared, so the companies, many of which had derived from or absorbed a fraternity, assumed some of their functions and responsibilities. Comparison of the two groups of wills makes this quite plain. Whereas just three of the 18 masons in the first cohort made provision for the Masons' Company in their wills, five of the 18 in the second cohort did. All five of these masons appear either as Assistants or liverymen in 1538 – they were evidently men with sincere attachment to the Company. Four of the five, Thomas Harris, Thomas West, Aylmer and Simpson junior, left money on tightly defined terms to pay for a celebration in the Company's hall at the time of their burial – an innovative change of practice. Only Gabriel Caldham left money to the Company without clear direction as to how it should be spent. Prior to 1540, it was usually friars and members of the parish fraternity who came to the burial of the citizens, and it was in the churches of the religious houses and the convivial environment of the fraternal feast that deceased Londoners were remembered. Now, Harris and Simpson requested the presence of members of the Company at their funerals, and Aylmer and West left money to the Company for a 'recreation' in their memory. The desire to be sent onwards in the best way possible had clearly not changed and in the second half of the 16th century it appears that masons increasingly turned to their Company to provide some of the religious and social functions which the fraternities and religious houses no longer could.

The value of such bequests as these is not easily computed in modern terms, nor is the significance of other charitable provisions to be found in masons' wills, such as those relating to donations to the poor, not least because we know nothing about the efficiency or integrity of the testators' executors. In his *The Charities of London, 1480-1660*, published in 1960, Wilbur K. Jordan put forward a convincing argument that Londoners actually increased the amount of money which they gave to charity after the Reformation, and that it was provided in more sophisticated and established ways. Since then, historians have broadly accepted that once Roman Catholicism had been displaced, charitable giving did increase, and that bequests to the poor were increasingly channelled through the institutions of London – the hospitals, companies and parish vestries. However, few now believe that giving grew by as much as Jordan suggested, and it is still far from clear how the Reformation really affected charitable behaviour. Londoners may have increased the amount they gave to charity in response to the hard economic conditions of the 1540s and 1550s, rather than to any doctrinal changes. There are hints of a shift towards a more institutional framework of charitable giving in the wills of the post-Reformation masons. William Chamberlain, Thomas Fant, Paskin, West and Peter Maye all left money either to their parish poor boxes, from which the churchwardens would provide for the poor, or to the churchwardens of the parish to distribute as they saw fit. This form of giving is more systematised and vicarious than the direct distribution of alms by the executors of wills to the poor, such as we usually find before 1540. Aylmer's undoubted humanity also took another form: in 1548, he asked that 'the poor presoners of the Marshalsee and of the Kings Benche', the unfortunate residents of two altogether unwholesome institutions, be given 'breade, drinke and meate to the valor of vj s.viij.d'.[21]

CONCLUSIONS

No detailed account of the impact of the Reformation on the masons of London has so far been written. Such evidence as there is suggests that, as a group, they were neither more markedly radical nor more staunchly conservative than the majority of Londoners. As the structures of traditional belief were swept away, so the masons of London stopped leaving money to the fraternities, they stopped requesting masses and obits for the benefit of their souls, they stopped discharging their tithes, and they stopped committing their souls to the Virgin and the heavenly company of saints. The last mason in our study either to settle his tithes or to invoke the Virgin and the saints in his will was Simpson in 1556. The next will proved in this cohort was that of Thomas Harris, a freemason of St Olave in Southwark, who died in 1563. He commended his soul to almighty God, 'my only maker and redeemer', by the shedding of whose blood he did 'truste and faithfullie beleve only to be saved'. Belief in intercession for the soul had been replaced by justification by faith alone. In fact, rather than request intercession, in a clear demonstration of his Protestant faith, Harris left 3s. 4d. 'to some godlie preacher to make a sermon at my buryall'.

Burial customs, at least in their ceremonial aspects, changed under Protestant influence. On the whole, though, for the masons of London who lived before, through and then after the Reformation, the desire for a decent burial and to provide charity for their fellow Londoners remained as important as ever. To achieve this in late medieval London, they had turned to their fraternities and religious houses; as the teachings of the reformed faith replaced those of the traditional kind, the masons of London continued to request the presence of the poor at their funerals, but they also much more obviously turned to their Company to replace the institutions which could no longer provide them with a seemly despatch, or offer charity in the way that they wanted. In this way, we learn something of the evolution of the Masons' Company in the 16th century through the wills of its members.

These developments permanently changed the character of the Company. When, in 1603 and 1643-4, John Kempton and John Shuttleworth left money to the Company for funeral suppers in their memory, they followed in the footsteps of Aylmer and West. When in 1635 Thomas Jordan bequeathed £3 'unto such of the livery of the Company of Ffreemasons [of] London as shalbe present in their liveryes at my funeerall', when in 1681 Edward Strong paid £5 to the Company for having attended the corpse of his brother Thomas, and when in 1700 John Thompson provided mourning rings for the Assistants and asked that they all came to his burial, these men acted in the same tradition as did Simpson and Harris. In fact, sometimes masons in later centuries went beyond precedents which we see at the time of the Reformation. In January 1634, for example, Henry Wilson paid £2 for the livery of the Company to attend his wife's funeral. Today's custom, whenever a liveryman dies, of sending a representative of the Company to attend his or her funeral maintains a tradition now centuries old.[22]

There is one final detail concerning wills to be noted here. In 1478, Andrew Eliot bequeathed his 'grete maser' to the Masons' Company. A century later, two leading masons, John Tanner (d.1600) and Philip Paskin (d.1580), son of that John who is mentioned above, both gave mazers to the Company. Eliot's mazer bore religious imagery, while Tanner's and Paskin's were engraved with their marks, but the choice that these masons made to give the same type of gift, on either side of all the changes that we have witnessed here, indicates that they all had the same understanding of what the Company actually was, and placed the same value on the fraternal aspects of Company life.

25 *The mark of Philip Paskin, centre, from a deed sealed in 1563.*

6

THE EARLY MODERN COMPANY

From 1619, we have an almost complete series of the Company's accounts.* From 1663, we have the first surviving book containing a record of quarterage payments, along with the names of all those bound as apprentices and those admitted as freemen. From 27 March 1677, the Company's Court of Assistants began to keep a record of its minutes; the Court's minute books survive in an unbroken sequence from then until the present day. None of the original sets of ordinances and regulations for the craft of masonry drawn up before this time are to be found among the Company's own records; the by-laws ratified shortly after the granting of the charter were copied out by a contemporary into a book which does remain in the Company's archive. Thanks to the improvement in record-keeping, from the 17th century onwards we can get an increasingly detailed insight into the life of the Company.

COMPANY CONTROL BEFORE THE GREAT FIRE OF LONDON
It has been argued that in the 16th and 17th centuries the character of the Masons' Company 'underwent relatively little modification, apart from the absorption of the Marblers in 1585, such modification as there was being in the direction of more pronounced oligarchy.'[1] This may be true in a narrow constitutional sense, but it focuses only on certain economic and institutional aspects of the Company's character, paying too little heed to the fraternal, charitable and social elements, and above all it fails to integrate the Masons' Company into the dynamic history of both nation and City within these years.

*An older ledger has probably been lost. Among the disbursements in 1619-20 was 5s. for the purchase of a 'new ledger'.

73

There can be no doubt that, towards the end of the 16th century, London's livery companies began to face significant challenges. Between 1550 and 1666 London's population rose nine-fold, placing the City's system of economic and political control under intolerable strain. In 1632, the Corporation complained to the Crown that 'the freedom of London which was heretofore of very great esteeme, is grown to be little worth, by reason of the extraordinary enlargement of the suburbs, where greate numbers of traders and handicraftsmen doe enjoy without charge, equall benefit with the freemen and citizens of London.' It is this context that explains the provision in the royal charter which was granted to the Masons' Company in 1677, which granted them authority over all masons within the 'citties of London or Westminster, in the suburbs of the same citties or seaven miles compasse of the same on every side'.[2]

The surging growth of London was not the only development which challenged the companies' dominance as economic supervisors and

26 *Likeness of Nicholas Stone: engraving made in 1798, believed to be from the memorial plaque in St Martin-in-the-Fields church.*

regulators. The traditional economic structure of the medieval town, based on the independent artisan operating as master of his own workshop, was increasingly superseded by the emergence of a new economic model, one in which larger manufacturers subcontracted their labour – a system ill-suited to regulation by companies of the medieval type. The career of Nicholas Stone (1586/7-1647) illustrates the contradictions which resulted.

He was perhaps the most successful mason of his generation; he was responsible for the building of Inigo Jones's Banqueting House at Whitehall (1619-22), and served as the king's Master Mason for at least eight years from 1632, in which capacity he regularly employed sub-contractors. Between 1613 and 1642 from his bustling workshop in Long Acre, which was conspicuously outside the City boundaries, he produced dozens of sculptural monuments to order for patrons. But this prosperous exponent of modern industrial organisation was also an eminent member of the Masons' Company; he served as Renter Warden (1626-7) and Upper Warden (1629-30), before, very unusually, serving a two-year term as Master between 1632 and 1634.[3]

27 *Painting by Thomas Hosmer Shepherd of Banqueting House, Whitehall, which was designed by Inigo Jones and built by Nicholas Stone.*

In theory, at least, the companies' legal rights within London remained intact for much of this period. The Masons' Company and the Corporation certainly worked hand-in-hand – as they had done in 1356, 1481 and 1510. In 1521, the Mayor and Aldermen of London ratified ordinances which increased the Masons' Company's control of apprenticeships and which limited the opportunities available for apprentices and foreigners to work as masons in London. In 1580, in response to the increased employment of Purbeck stone in the City, the Mayor and Aldermen gave two Wardens of the Masons' Company, together with 'two persones skilful or more of the cloathinge [i.e. livery] of the same companye and one offycer of the lord maior of this cytie', the power of view, search and oversight of all Purbeck stone coming into the City. These men had the right to seize any stones which were defective, ill-wrought or falsely measured, or to force the owner to amend them at his own cost. The Company also had the authority to fine anyone in London who bought stone which had not been examined and to charge buyers of Purbeck stone 1d. for each hundred feet of stone which they assessed.[4]

However, legal developments, usually on a national rather than local level, were imperilling the City companies' authority. In 1599, the companies' power to confiscate goods seized during search was declared illegal. In other cases judged in the same year, the companies were told that their ordinances had to be 'consonant to law and reason', and that blanket prohibitions on contracting work out to foreign labour had 'no binding force'. The Tolley case of 1614 was another significant blow to the right of companies to compel freemen practising their trade to join their company.[5]

According to the old custom of London, confirmed in the 1563 Statute of Artificers and again in 1614, anyone seeking to practise a trade or craft in the City of London had to obtain the freedom, but he did not necessarily have to do so through the Company connected to his trade. Many Londoners were attracted to the wealthier and bigger companies, and so the lesser companies lost revenue, authority and prestige. Problems of protocol arose and multiplied; who, for example, had the power to regulate a mason who was a member of another company? What would happen if men unconnected with a company's craft became masters and wardens? How could they enforce the power of search if they were ignorant of the craft or trade?

These developments affected the Masons' Company in different ways. The Company continued to search Purbeck stone until the end of the 17th century. Indeed, it raised significant sums of money through its power to do so. In the 1620s and 1630s, the search for Purbeck stone brought in more money than admissions to the freedom or quarterage payments. As late as the 1650s the Purbeck search was still yielding an average of £6 5s. 11d. a year. Some of this money came in from fines from those who broke the rules, but most appears to have been raised by charging the buyers for assessments made by the Company – in this way, something like a customs duty on the import of this stone into London. In 1654-5, when the fee charged by the Company had increased to 4d. for the examination of each hundred feet of stone, the Company received £10 1s. 4d. from the search of 60,000 feet. More controversially, the Masons' Company did, at least occasionally in the 17th century, continue seizing illicit Purbeck stone, some of which it sold off.[6]

The Masons' Company had never forbidden the employment of foreigners: its ordinances of 1481 and 1521 had actually sanctioned foreign labour in clearly defined circumstances – probably because it suited large employers to employ foreigners. It was not, however, in the interests of journeymen masons who were free of the Masons' Company that unfree workers could be easily employed. At times, perhaps under pressure from its yeomanry, the Company's Assistants did act in the interests of the journeymen. In 1521 the Assistants restricted the employment of foreign and apprentice labour at a time when the Crown was limiting the opportunities for aliens to work in London and when wages in the construction industry were very low. Indeed, in 1514, London's building workers had even drawn up a petition in which they complained that their wages did not cover their cost of living. In 1548, in response to demands from artisans for higher wages, a law was enacted which sought to make it easier for unfree workers to find work in towns. This Act prompted 'fifteen companies of handy occupations', of whom the Masons' were one, to meet at St Peter's Westcheap, on an unknown date to formulate a response. The meeting appears to have had some effect, for a year later the Act was repealed.[7]

Between 1620 and 1641, the Company was involved in a protracted dispute with the Plaisterers over whether plasterers were using plaster to cover up defective stone, which ought to have been

replaced by masons. In 1621-2, the Company spent 30s. on petitions addressed to the Solicitor-General, the Bishop of London, the Lord Mayor and the commissioners for the works at St Paul's Cathedral, which requested that only freemen of London be employed on the works at the cathedral. Subsequently, the Company worked with the Bricklayers and the Carpenters to regulate the construction industry in London, and especially to suppress the use of unfree workers. While it would not, and after 1599 could not, prohibit foreign labour, on these occasions, at least, the Company was a vigorous and effective actor and lobbyist on behalf of its humbler members.[8]

Well into the 18th century, the Company would also persist in seeking the translation of masons to its ranks. Sometimes, these battles would be quite lengthy. In 1637, for example, John Young, a mason who was a member of the Weavers' Company, finally translated to the Masons' Company after a six-year legal battle and after the Aldermen of London had specified that all craftsmen (although not merchants and retailers) had to join the Company connected with their trade.[9]

28 The King's Commissioners for Building uphold a complaint brought by the Company of Masons in its dispute with the Plaisterers in 1637, signed by Inigo Jones and others.

ENFORCING THE RULES

There were various ways in which the early modern Company could impose discipline on its members. Throughout the period, the officers and Assistants might invoke the help of the Lord Mayor and Aldermen. Recourse to the civic authorities, however, was expensive and slow, and so something of a last resort. The Company's Court of Assistants also had the power to administer and enforce regulation. It was in this Court, for example, that apprentices were enrolled and freemen admitted. The Assistants also heard cases of debt, and they might be called upon to resolve a dispute within the trade, perhaps over poor-quality workmanship or for breach of contract, or to adjudicate in presentments of slander or assault. They levied fines on liverymen who did not attend or who came late to quarter days, or on those who came to Company events without their livery cloaks. Members of the Company were also fined for using bad language towards the Company's officers, for abusing each other, and for missing the funerals of fellow liverymen or other church services. Men and women, rich and poor, came before the Masons' Company's Court of Assistants and to transact this amount of business courts would commonly meet some seven or eight times a year.[10]

In the 17th century, the general search appears to have taken place once a year, usually in February or March. On the search day the Master, Wardens and Beadle of the Company, perhaps accompanied by some of the Assistants and even officers of the Lord Mayor, would have passed through a certain area of London. They would have inspected premises, tools, goods and materials to make sure that all masons were working in line with the Company's regulations. They would, too, have ensured that all master masons were members of the Company and verified the employment status of those employed, especially as apprentices, by master masons. Usually, those involved in executing the search dined together in the evening.

However, the Company does not appear to have generated much, if any, net income from the general search. In 1624-5, the general search raised 9s. 10d. but 57s. 8d. was spent on the day of the search itself. In February 1630, it yielded 12s. 4d., a sum dwarfed by the 43s. 2d. spent in expenses enforcing the search and dinner at the *Queen's Head* tavern. In fact, by the 1620s, the search was only really of symbolic value. When the Company's officers carried out the search, they reassured masons who were members of the Company that the Company was active in protecting their conditions and rights. In this way, it helped to reinforce members' obedience to the Company's authority. As an economic and quality-control tool, however, the search was rather less effective. In 1630, the search officers could not hope to visit more than, say, two dozen premises on the search day, in a city of 300,000 people. Moreover, the writ of the officers would not easily have run outside the bounds of the City. By the 1650s, the search seems to have been little used. Between 1650 and 1666 the Company's account book records just two instances of the general search; 7s. 9d. was raised from that in 1650-1 and 9s. from the search in 1654-5. It is, of course, possible that the search was carried out on more occasions than were recorded, and that it simply failed to raise any money. This would, however, seem to be unlikely.[11]

Typical punishments in the court of a livery company might involve a fine or amercement, the seizure and destruction of goods – often in a very public and ceremonial fashion, the closure of a workshop, even corporal punishments and, in the very last resort, expulsion from the company. We only have the Court's records from 1677 onwards, by which time the Company's authority to punish recalcitrant members had been greatly weakened. The most common punishments visible in these sources are fines for refusing to take up the livery or to serve as stewards when asked. With only the accounts ledger to guide us before 1677, we see a very partial picture of the Court's activity: fines paid but not those unpaid, for example, and we have no idea of the extent to which the Masons' Company applied stricter punishments than those early in the 17th century.

The Company's Wealth

Meeting the financial demands of the Crown and the Corporation was a further challenge for all London's companies. In the 16th century, the companies had become a favoured medium for the taxation demands of royal government. On 71 out of 75 occasions during the Tudor years, when the City had to raise men or money for defence, to provide the watch, to purchase grain or to collect money for poor relief, the quotas were assessed through the companies of London. The companies did gain, in return, reiteration of their authority, royal charters and an audience for their petitions, but they were institutions too rich and too well-organised for the Crown and Corporation not to exploit.[12]

In 1540 the Masons' Company supplied four men for the midsummer watch. In 1579, 1580, 1585, 1586 and 1591 the Company paid towards the cost of soldiers, weapons, gunpowder and ships. By October 1618, the Masons had contributed £150 towards the Ulster plantations. Throughout the 17th century the Company paid towards poor relief in the parish of St Michael Bassishaw; in the 1630s and 1640s, typically about 26s. each year. In 1635-6, the Company was involved in the impressment of masons for work at Castle Cornet in Guernsey.[13]

At times of stress, these demands could become quite onerous. In 1640-1, as the country slid towards civil war, the Company was forced to pay £100 to the Chamberlain of London which formed part of a greater sum of £50,000 lent, by and through the companies, to the king. In addition to which, in that year the Company also spent totals of £2 8s. 8d. on muskets, gunpowder and ammunition, £1 16s. 2d. on making a store for the weapons and munitions and 2s. 6d. for a man to keep watch on Sundays in the streets and at the church doors at night. In 1643-4, as the companies were asked to provide £50,000 for the defence of London, this time against the king, the Masons' Company paid £4 18s. in subsidies and £7 9s. on supplying a soldier.[14]

Some of these demands might seem rather modest. Certainly, as one of the smaller and poorer companies of London, the Masons were not expected to contribute as much as larger and richer companies. In 1579, for example, when the companies were required by the Crown to purchase gunpowder for the defence of the realm, the Merchant Taylors supplied 40 firkins, the Masons just one. Nevertheless, levies such as these were not always easy to accommodate. In 1627-8, the Company only avoided posting a loss after it raised £17 3s. 6d. from selling some of its silver to pay royal subsidies. To obtain the money for the royal loan in 1640-1, the Company had to borrow £100 at interest from Richard Hide, a prominent member of the Company. To meet Hide's interest payments over the next two years, the Company borrowed £9 from several liverymen and it sold two silver bowls – was Eliot's mazer one of them? – and a little silver drinking dish. On 30 September

THE MARBLERS

From Wallis's *Londons Armory*, 1677; as reproduced in *Coat-Armour of the London Livery Companies*, by Charles Welch, F.S.A., 1914.

1643, the Company mortgaged three tenements at the Company Hall to Robert Buckland, a glover who lived in the parish of St Saviour in Southwark, in order to raise the capital needed to repay Hide. Buckland's money was, however, not used for that purpose. In 1642, Parliament had demanded £100,000 of the companies and the £120 from Buckland was instead paid to the Chamberlain of

London for Parliament's use. By 1658, the Company's accounts record that over the course of 14 years the Chamberlain of London had repaid just £35.[15]

It is clear that, even with the injection of capital via these loans, the Company was struggling to keep up with the demands made of it. Between 1639 and 1646 it posted a financial loss in every year apart from 1644-5, when it accounted for a surplus of just 27s. Throughout the 17th century, the presentation and auditing of the Company's accounts was, to say the least, of variable quality. In at least nine years between 1619 and 1666, despite being signed off by the auditors, the balance carried forward cannot be reconciled with the totals given for income and expenditure. It cannot be a coincidence, however, that five of these occasions came in the 1640s when the Company was under severe financial pressure.[16]

When the Company amalgamated with the Marblers in July 1585, the union was hardly an alliance from strength on either side. We know very little of the Marblers' Company's fortunes in the 16th century; there may have been particular difficulties within the marblers' craft which led to what they described as the 'great decaie and disabilitie of theire said companie'. But it is just as likely that the general challenges faced by all the companies of London had weakened the Marblers to the extent that their very existence was no longer viable, while the Masons needed all the reinforcements they could find.[17]

THE COMPANY YEAR

Each year, the newly elected Master and Wardens had to be installed in office in a way that ensured that authority was transmitted from one set of officers to the next without any loss of continuity. Before 1677, this transfer took place at the Guildhall, in June or July, because it was the Mayor and Aldermen of London who had ratified the Company's ordinances. There, the new officers swore their oaths of office. The Company's charter, however, authorised the Company to administer its own oaths of office, and so, from 1678 onwards, the new officers were usually sworn at Masons' Hall at the court meeting subsequent to their election. Throughout the period, the election of the new officers was always celebrated in some style and it can fairly be said that it inaugurated a new year in Company life.

On 18 July 1629, the Company spent £7 14s. 1d. on an election feast at the *Windmill Tavern* in Old Jewry, to which the Assistants even brought their wives. Over the course of the year, officers and Assistants also dined together following the four quarterly Court meetings: Midsummer, Michaelmas, Epiphany and Lady Day. In 1629-30 the Company dined on these occasions at the *Star Tavern* in Coleman Street (twice), the *Mitre* (presumably one of two hostelries called the *Mitre* on Cheapside), and the *Dog Tavern*.[18]

In addition, there was a series of other occasions throughout the year, for example on the day of the general search, when the Assistants would meet to dine. Early in the 17th century, the foiling of the Gunpowder Treason Plot on 5 November was almost always celebrated with a dinner; in November 1629, the Company spent £4 18s. 1d. dining at the *White Horse* in Lombard Street. London's new mayor would take his oaths of office at the Guildhall and the exchequer on 28 and 29 October each year, and dinner was held on the day of the Lord Mayor's Show to celebrate. In 1620, the Company spent £7 3s. 3d. in total on celebrating the installation of the new Lord Mayor, of which sum £6 was spent on dinner with the members' wives. The remainder of the money was spent on hangings to decorate Masons' Hall, ribbons and streamers, and staves to be carried by attendants (whifflers) who might clear a path through a crowd. A subsequent note reveals that the whifflers wore black and white ribbons, that is to say, ribbons in the Company's colours. This remained an important day in the Company calendar. Just under 100 years later, the Company spent over £35 celebrating Lord Mayor's Day. It was clearly a jolly occasion well into the 18th century, with the Company providing tobacco and pipes, as well as music, alongside meat and drink for members, though in 1735 the Court resolved not to allow dancing to the music![19]

The regular cycle of dinners was supplemented by others held irregularly. In 1626-7, the Company met the Bricklayers on three occasions and dined with them each time. In 1629-30 the Company dined at the *Mermaid* and the *Star* following meetings about building work, and at the *Queen's Head* in Queenhithe, when four men were made free of the Company by patrimony, which was a common cause for celebration in the Company. On 18 October 1626, 'all the livery and divers of the yeomanry' were invited to dinner at the *Three Tuns* in Holborn, 'itt being a special court day'.[20]

It is striking that so many dinners appear to have been held at various inns and taverns in London rather than at Masons' Hall.

Perhaps the dining room at the Hall was too small, or the kitchen inadequate to meet the needs of some of the larger groups which may have assembled, so that it was necessary to resort to taverns. Certainly, the Court meetings themselves were held at Masons' Hall: the accounts frequently record the purchase of bread, beer and fuel, and materials to strew across the floor, on the days when the Court met. To take just one example, on 10 January 1632, at the meeting of the Epiphany Court, 2s. was spent on provisioning Masons' Hall for the meeting in the morning, and then 26s. 10d. on dining at the *Dagger* thereafter. For those who served on the Court of Assistants and who held office as Master and Warden, the dinners would have been, to some extent, a reward for their service to the Company.[21]

BUILDING COMMISSIONERS AND CITY VIEWERS

The Crown had long worried that the growth of London's population would push up food prices, make administration more difficult, create conditions in which the plague could spread more easily and lead to the irrevocable loss of open space within and without the City. Consequently, from 1580 onwards, a stream of royal proclamations and acts sought to curtail the building of houses outside the City walls, and to control construction work inside the historic City. Responsibility for the enforcement and policing of these new regulations was initially delegated to the Mayor and Aldermen of London, and the sheriffs and justices of the peace in the counties adjacent to the City. Almost certainly as a result of frustration with the inability of these local officials properly to administer these directives, the Crown, in 1615, established a special commission for buildings to contain and to manage London's physical growth. Until the outbreak of civil war in 1642, this commission was a powerful body in London.[22]

There is no evidence that the Masons – or indeed the Bricklayers or Carpenters – played any formal role in the administration of the new building regulations. In this way, then, the establishment of the commission could be seen as evidence of the diminished role played by the companies in general, and the Masons' Company in particular, in the government and administration of London. That would, however, fail to take account of other ways in which the Company was an important administrative institution in early modern London. To give just one example, the Masons were one

of only three companies which nominated men to serve as City
Viewers.

The office of Viewer had a long pedigree in London. It can be
traced back to 1301 when Richard of Witham, a mason, took an
oath of office, albeit at that time the office had no official title.
The custom thereafter developed in London wherein two masons
and two carpenters would take an oath as 'sworn masons' and
'sworn carpenters' of the City to advise the Mayor and Aldermen.
The Viewers acted in cases of public nuisance (e.g. the blocking
of ditches and alleys), encroachments into the street or even onto
the river, quarrels over the extent or conditions of boundaries,
clashes between neighbours over access to light and air, and
the partitioning of properties. To fulfil this role, the masons and
carpenters would inspect buildings and pavements; they would
take often quite detailed measurements; they would interview
plaintiffs and defendants, as well as witnesses and neighbours; and
they would examine documentary evidence, for example deeds,
leases and wills. At the end of their investigation, they would
present a report or a certificate to the Mayor and Aldermen. While

30 *Hollar's map of
London before the
Great Fire of 1666.
Note the shields of
the Great Twelve
livery companies.*

the final decision always rested in each case with the Mayor and Aldermen, the masons and carpenters were seldom overruled. There is no evidence that it was a salaried position, but holders may have taken a cut from the fees paid by private parties, and they were often granted gifts or given exemptions from holding other offices.[23]

Masons who served as Viewers were senior members of both craft and Company. We have already met, for example, Richard of Selling, Simon at Hook, Walter Walton, John Croxton, John Aylmer and William Kerwin. On each occasion when a vacancy for a Viewer arose, the Masons and Carpenters would nominate two men for office, from which pair of names the Mayor and Aldermen would choose one man to hold office for life or until he was no longer capable of performing the duties. From 1550 onwards a Viewer was also chosen from among the men of the Tilers' Company, which amalgamated with the Bricklayers' in 1568. Well into the 17th century, the Viewers continued to issue certificates, examples of which survive, and in them we can see them applying their minds to questions of London's laws and customs, as much as they did to matters concerned with building safety and demarcation. The masons of London who held this office, and their Company who presented them for election, thus performed an important role in the City.

The Viewers gave useful service at an intermediate level of the City's administration. None of the masons of early modern London, however, held office as one of the 26 Aldermen or 200-odd Common Councilmen. These functionaries were drawn from the richest strata of London's society, and almost invariably from the ranks of the Great Twelve companies. In the assessment of a subsidy in 1582, just 75 householders in London were assessed in the highest £200 bracket; 24 of London's 26 Aldermen were among this number. By contrast, the wealthiest mason to appear in the assessment was William Kerwin. He was assessed in the £50 bracket to pay 50s. He was exceptional; most of his colleagues who were assessed are to be found in the £3 bracket.[24]

The transformation of the City into a metropolis in the 17th century diminished the Viewers' importance. London was becoming 'too large, too populous for four men, no matter how expert and diligent, to act effectively as building inspectors, arbitrators of private quarrels, surveyors, protectors of the integrity of public streets and ways and the like.' Nevertheless, Viewers continued to be appointed and they still performed the duties of their office. In the end, though, the Fire of 1666 was to prove fatal for the office of Viewer. After the conflagration, it was the surveyors of the City, men such as Robert Hooke, Peter Mills and Edward Jerman, who were not members of the Masons' Company, who ensured that the City was rebuilt in accordance with the terms of the 1667 Rebuilding Acts.[25]

Apprenticeship and Training

If there is a traditional view of apprenticeships in the early modern craft of masonry, it would describe a young man beginning a seven-year apprenticeship at the age of 14 by entering into an indenture which was, in London and its environs at least, administered and regulated by the Masons' Company. At the end of their terms, apprentices became freemen of their companies.

There is, at first sight, certainly some evidence to support that view. From 1563 until 1814, the legal status of apprenticeship in England was defined by the Statute of Artificers. Among other things, the Statute gave householders in towns and cities the right to take apprentices for a minimum term of seven years, it forbade the employment of anyone who had not served an apprenticeship, and it sanctioned the imprisonment of those who refused to serve as apprentices. In London, the legal status of apprenticeship was defined even longer than that. In fact, the Statute took what was already the existing 'Custome and Order of the Citie of London' and applied it nationwide, and in the City the final vestiges of company control of crafts were only removed in 1835 and 1856. Before 1563, the Crown had occasionally interfered in the regulation of apprenticeship in London, but for the most part apprenticeships were controlled by London's companies acting with, and to an extent on behalf of, the City's Mayor, Aldermen and Sheriffs.[26]

There can be little doubt of the importance of apprenticeship in pre-modern London. In the mid-16th century, some 1,400 men started an apprenticeship each year in London, almost all of them born outside the City, and apprentices comprised 10 per cent of the urban population. This meant that two-thirds of all men in contemporary London had served apprenticeships and apprentices who had completed their terms accounted for nine in every ten admissions to the freedom of the City. In 1700, after 150 years of colossal population growth and a supposed weakening of company control, some 3,800 youths continued to start apprenticeships each year in London and together they still accounted for about 10 per cent of the capital's population. The figures for the Masons' Company are no less remarkable. From 1619, when we can count the number of apprentices bound to masters under the auspices of the Masons' Company, over 2,700 youths began a corporate apprenticeship and, until the start of the 19th century, admission by servitude was by far the most common route to membership of the Company.[27]

However, indentured apprenticeship, as defined above, and training are not the same thing. Training is the process by which masons are taught to dress, carve and lay stone. Early modern masons were trained by other masons exclusively at their places of work, whether at the quarry, on the building site, in the lodge (which was probably on a building site), or in a workshop. An indentured apprenticeship was an economic, legal and social institution in the lives of pre-modern Londoners that provided a structure for training, but it does not follow that all training took place through apprenticeships of this sort. In 1359, for example, John of Evesham was appointed by the dean and chapter of Hereford to teach the arts of masonry and carpentry to the craftsmen placed under him, while between 1603 and 1606 Nicholas Stone spent just two years as an apprentice before working as a journeyman with Isaac James in Southwark.[28]

Indeed, because next to nothing from the Company's records before 1619 survives, we actually have very little idea of the use or practice of apprenticeship in the craft of masonry before the 17th century. If anything, based on studies of the evidence which we do have, apprentice masons appear to have been something of a rarity in the Middle Ages. Medieval building accounts and wage ordinances survive in relative abundance, but within them we find very few references to masons' apprentices. A recent study of official records produced at the London Guildhall in the 14th and 15th centuries found just *one* mason among 605 apprentices. Of course, there may be particular reasons why we do not find many apprentice masons in these sources. For example, if a master mason was expected to pay the wages of his apprentice from his own wages, then this would explain the absence of apprentices in building accounts and wage ordinances. Alternatively, apprentices might be hiding in plain sight in the records behind other names: 'masons' servants' or 'masons' mates' for example. Moreover, there is actually no reason why building accounts would record whether someone was an apprentice or not. In 1475, for example, Adam Vertue (d.1485) was taking 3s. 4d. a week for his work at Westminster Abbey, while his son Robert (d.1506) took just 1s. 8d. Robert must have been Adam's trainee or apprentice in some way, but what did that matter to the clerk who paid his wages or who wrote up the accounts? His only concern was to record Robert's payment, not his status.[29]

It is unlikely that masons trained through some other quasi-institutional system. What is more likely is that apprentice masons are so few and far between because the traditional system of indentured apprenticeship was for the most part unsuitable for the craft of masonry. Masonry depended upon the existence of a large workforce of mobile, wage-earning journeymen, who were themselves seldom in a position to train and support apprentices, whereas apprenticeship was designed primarily to train independent masters for industries based in workshops in fixed locations. In sources which pre-date 1619, at least, it would seem that the exceptions prove this rule. When we do find evidence of apprentice masons, they are most visible at London Bridge, an evidently immobile site, or else they are apprenticed either to masters who described themselves as marblers, or to highly-skilled masons of the calibre of Walter Walton, Stephen Lote, Robert Vertue and John Molton – men most likely to own workshops and least likely to be itinerant.[30]

If, however, indentured apprenticeships were unsuitable for the craft of masonry, we must then explain why more than 2,700 youths were bound as corporate apprentices and why apprenticeship features so prominently in the ordinances the Company ratified in 1356 and 1521, in its charter, and in the by-laws of 1678. Indeed, for a period of some 500 years from the middle of the 14th century onwards, the regulation and administration of apprenticeships appears to have been at the heart of Masons' Company life.

First, apprenticeship was much more than just a system through which people learnt a trade in early modern London. It was the most common route by which people obtained the freedom of the City and, in the same way that mass higher education is today, apprenticeship was a social institution in the lives of pre-modern Londoners. When an apprentice mason entered his master's household, he learnt not just the craft of masonry and how to run a business within the craft, but also the mores of City life, how to act as the head of a household, and how to be both a reputable citizen of London and a member

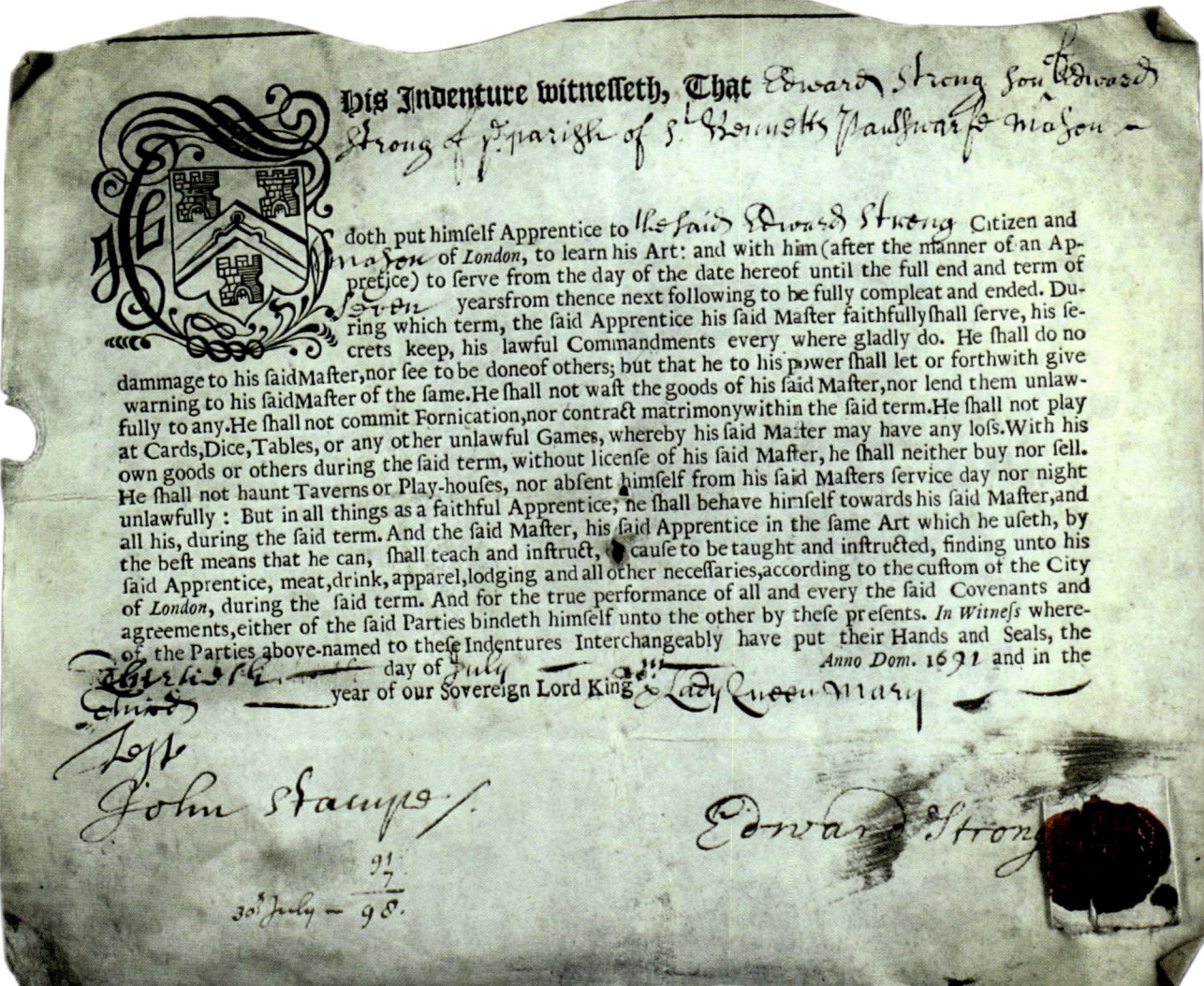

This Indenture witnesseth, That Edward Strong son Edward Strong of ye parish of St Bennetts Paulswharfe mason

doth put himself Apprentice to the said Edward Strong Citizen and mason of *London*, to learn his Art: and with him (after the manner of an Apprentice) to serve from the day of the date hereof until the full end and term of seven yearsfrom thence next following to be fully compleat and ended. During which term, the said Apprentice his said Master faithfully shall serve, his secrets keep, his lawful Commandments every where gladly do. He shall do no dammage to his said Master, nor see to be done of others; but that he to his power shall let or forthwith give warning to his said Master of the same. He shall not waft the goods of his said Master, nor lend them unlawfully to any. He shall not commit Fornication, nor contract matrimony within the said term. He shall not play at Cards, Dice, Tables, or any other unlawful Games, whereby his said Master may have any loss. With his own goods or others during the said term, without licence of his said Master, he shall neither buy nor sell. He shall not haunt Taverns or Play-houses, nor absent himself from his said Masters service day nor night unlawfully : But in all things as a faithful Apprentice; he shall behave himself towards his said Master, and all his, during the said term. And the said Master, his said Apprentice in the same Art which he useth, by the best means that he can, shall teach and instruct, cause to be taught and instructed, finding unto his said Apprentice, meat, drink, apparel, lodging and all other necessaries, according to the custom of the City of *London*, during the said term. And for the true performance of all and every the said Covenants and agreements, either of the said Parties bindeth himself unto the other by these presents. *In Witness* whereof the Parties above-named to these Indentures Interchangeably have put their Hands and Seals, the _____ day of July _____ *Anno Dom.* 1691 and in the _____ year of our Sovereign Lord King & Lady Queen Mary

John Stamp

Edward Strong

91
—
7

30 July — 98

31 *Indenture binding Edward Strong to his father, Edward, 1691.*

of the Masons' Company. When he was bound, the apprentice swore to swerve his master faithfully and to keep his secrets, not to 'commit Fornication, nor contract Matrimony', not to gamble, and not 'to haunt Taverns or Play-houses'. At the same time, his master covenanted to train and look after the youth in his charge. Hundreds and then thousands of these contracts were agreed each year. They were a glue that helped to hold society together.[31]

Second, it is surely no coincidence that the Company only ever drew up provisions to regulate apprenticeship at times of significant stress in its craft. The regulations of 1356 were drawn up in the aftermath of the Black Death, while the Company's next attempt to reinforce its control over apprenticeships, in 1521, came at a time when real-term wages for construction workers were probably lower than in any years since 1490. Similarly, the Company obtained its charter in 1677 and ratified its by-laws in 1678, when the labour market in London's construction industries had been enormously distorted by the influx of large numbers of building workers and the passing of the two Acts for the Rebuilding of London. Of course, at each time the dislocation was of a different nature, but on each occasion the answer was the same: restrict employment opportunities available to apprentices in London to allow masters and journeymen to benefit from higher wages. In this way, we find evidence of the Company acting, in Adam Smith's words, to 'restrain the competition to a much smaller number than might otherwise be disposed to enter the trade'. In short, to engage in a conspiracy against the public to raise the price of labour.[32]

The question then becomes: how effective was the Company's control over apprenticeship in the craft anyway? Before the 17th century, it is impossible to tell. The regulations ratified in 1356 give the impression that there existed a system for indentured apprenticeships in the medieval craft of masonry in London, but tell us nothing about how and by whom it was administered. The ordinances of 1521 provide evidence for structures of enforcement, but we have no idea of how effective or exclusive they were. Thereafter, even when we do have the Company's records, we cannot accept them uncritically. We simply have no way of knowing how many apprentices or trainees ever learnt how to be masons in London at any time outside the authority of the Masons' Company. Even in the 17th and 18th centuries, when thousands of youths were apprenticed at Masons' Hall, there were still plenty of trainee masons who had not been indentured. The Company's records often note the prosecution of those who had not completed apprenticeships – how many escaped prosecution is unknown – and the Court would not have gone to the trouble of appointing a committee of Assistants in 1714 to draw up a case against those 'who follow the Trade of Masonry not having served apprenticeships thereto', to deal only with a trivial issue.[33]

While 2,700 Company apprentices might seem an impressive number, over the course of 250 years it actually equates to fewer than one apprentice binding a month. Moreover, after 1700, when large numbers of men and women who were not operative masons joined the Company and then subsequently bound apprentices, the

32 *Court Minutes, 10 January 1765, showing the admissions of Daniel Durant and William Weedon.*

Company's records tell us less about training in the craft of masonry and more about the changing composition of the Company's membership. On 10 January 1765, for instance, three men, Daniel Durant, William Weedon and Richard Jackson, were made free by servitude, but we cannot draw any conclusions from this about training in the craft of masonry at that time. All three had in fact served apprenticeships to carpenters who happened to be members of the Masons' Company.[34]

The fact is that there was both a theory and reality of apprenticeship, and the reality was much more fluid and flexible than the theory supposes. Masters and apprentices appear to have disregarded the rules when it suited them. William Bussey, for example, was prohibited from taking any more than two or three apprentices by the Company's rules, yet between 1664 and 1676 he bound 11 apprentices and presented nine former apprentices for the freedom of the Company. Perhaps he managed a large operation and he used cheaper apprentice labour in place of journeymen; perhaps some of these young men spent periods away from London, back with their families or working elsewhere in the country. Whatever the case, this is not an example of an artisan master and his trusty apprentice working exclusively together over a period of years in a workshop.

Notwithstanding the solemnity of the oath they took at the time of their binding, young men in their late teens and early twenties did, unfortunately, go to taverns, gamble, fornicate and even marry. Many more did not complete their indentured terms; they simply walked away from unhappy households, or in search of better-paid work once they had enough skill to find work as journeymen, while others who did complete their indentures simply refused to take up the freedom. In fact, the rules were actually never as rigid as they might first appear. The Lord Mayor's Court, for example, provided an institutional forum in which apprenticeship indentures could be cancelled. Between 1725 and 1785, at least 29 apprentices of the Masons' Company were discharged and turned over to new masters in this court. Numerous studies have shown that by the time we account also for those who died – perhaps as many as one in ten apprentices – then only 40 per cent of apprentices, across all crafts and trades in London, ever took up the freedom at the end of their terms.[35]

Table 6.1. Bindings and admissions 1619-63.

Years	No. of apprentices bound	No. of admissions	Conversion %
1619-29	162	70	43
1629-39	150	75	50
1639-49	105	76	72
1649-59	175	68	39
1659-63	91	31	34
Total	683	320	47

Table 6.2. Number of apprentices bound 1663-1872.

Years	No. of apprentices bound
1663-1672	311
1673-1682	182
1683-1692	169
1693-1702	137
1703-1712	147
1713-1722	211
1723-1732	181
1733-1742	142
1743-1752	90
1753-1762	108
1763-1772	79
1773-1782	44
1783-1792	48
1793-1802	23
1803-1812	44
1813-1822	37
1823-1832	38
1833-1842	35
1843-1852	13
1853-1862	2
1863-1872	1
Total	2,042

The figures for the Masons' Company tell a similar tale. From 1619-63 we have the Company's account book which typically records the total number of those bound as apprentices or admitted in each year, but not their names nor always the means by which people became free. From 1663 onwards, we have a (presumably) complete record of the names of all those who were bound as apprentices or made free of the Company. From these records, we learn that from 1619 to 1872, 2,725 youths were bound as apprentices in the Masons' Company: 683 between 1619 and 1663 (table 6.1) and 2,042 from 1663 to 1872 (table 6.2).* For the earlier period, we can try to estimate a conversion ratio by comparing the number of bindings with admissions, which appears to show that 47 per cent of apprentices became free of the Company between 1619 and 1663.[36]

However, this is a very crude measure. First, the admissions for the 1620s are those of men who completed apprenticeships in the decades before 1619, and we have no idea of how many apprentices there were then. Similarly, many of those who were bound in the 1650s and early 1660s would only have taken up the freedom after 1663. Second, approximately 10-15 per cent of the 320 admissions in these years would have been by patrimony and redemption, as opposed to servitude. We cannot know, therefore, how many apprentices completed their terms and took up the freedom in this period, but it seems clear that less than 40 per cent did. For the period after 1663, six five-year samples were taken (table 6.3) and they show that, again, fewer than four in ten apprentices typically ever became free of the Company.

Table 6.3. Apprentices and admissions, 1675-1804.

Years	Apprentices	How many free	Conversion %	How long (years)
1675-79	108	31	29	11
1700-04	69	28	41	13
1725-29	82	36	44	10
1750-54	56	20	36	9
1775-79	22	13	59	10
1800-04	11	4	36	8
Total	354	132	37	10

* Because the account book was structured not around a calendar year but rather a financial year, the beginning and end of which year either changed or at times was not even noted, it is hard to tabulate its data alongside that from after 1663. Therefore, the data has been given in two tables.

If we return to the traditional view of apprenticeship with which we started this study, that is of apprentices learning their craft over a period of seven years before taking up the freedom of the Company, then we can now see that this was only a model ever followed by a small minority of masons. Many thousands of masons must have learned their craft in ways other than through an indentured apprenticeship, and there is little compelling evidence that apprenticeship was either the most suitable or the most popular training method in the craft of masonry.

Even among those who did start a corporate apprenticeship, fewer than half would ever go on to be admitted to the Company and most of those who did waited much longer than seven years. Thomas Trippett, for example, was bound in 1711 and only became free in 1738; Ralph Parker only took up his freedom in 1744, 22 years after he was first bound; while John Pegg waited 26 years to become free, in 1784, and then only so that he could bind an apprentice – a common occurrence. On average, as is shown in table 6.3, freemen were admitted 10 years after they were first bound. In fact, we should dispense with the idea that a seven-year term was the norm in early modern London. In 1625-6, for example, the first year for which we have more detailed information, eight of the 15 young men enrolled as apprentices were bound for terms of eight years and one for nine.[37]

The figures given above also reveal just how ineffective were the Company's attempts to enforce its authority on the practice of apprenticeship. The numbers of Company apprentices fell as a consequence of the civil wars during the 1640s and the Napoleonic Wars of the 1790s, as young men went off to fight and as there was less civilian building work, but rose between 1713 and 1732 as the Company's membership increased thanks to an influx of non-operative masons. These trends had nothing whatsoever to do with the Company's regulations. It is also plain that the numbers of indentured apprentices in the Masons' Company – of whom not all were masons of course – was in slow but terminal decline from the middle of the 18th century, that is long before the Statute of Artificers was repealed and the final vestiges of Company control in London were abrogated between 1814 and 1856.

We must not overstate the importance of the Company's role in training. True, in a given year in the 17th century, a dozen or a score of young men would begin a Company apprenticeship, but outside the City and its suburbs, the Company has never wielded any authority or responsibility. Nicholas Stone honed his skills while living in Amsterdam with Hendrik de Keyser, the city's master mason and sculptor, from 1606 to 1613, while Thomas Strong and his brother Edward learnt their craft working with their father and each other on various projects, and perhaps at their quarries, in the Cotswolds before coming to London. What role did the Company play in training these masons, three of the Company's most famous sons? Within London, people learnt the craft of masonry long before the Company existed and they have continued to learn the craft long after the Company's institutional role came to an official end in the 19th century.

The Company has never actually trained a single mason, in any complete sense, and it is only in the last 100 or so years that the Company has provided any financial support for trainee masons. In pre-modern London, the costs of training were borne by the masters themselves and then, in the 18th century, in some instances and to some extent, via premiums which some apprentices paid to their new masters.

7

HENRY WILSON
A 17TH-CENTURY LIVERYMAN

On 22 January 1627, Henry Wilson became free of the Masons'
Company by servitude having completed an apprenticeship under
William Wilson – probably his uncle or cousin and a man of some
standing in the Masons' Company.* Having paid the Company a total
of 23s. 10d. to admit Henry as a freeman, William and Henry would
have gone to the Chamberlain's office at the Guildhall together.† There,
they would have paid an additional sum of 4s. to have Henry's name
entered on a register of freemen, or citizens, of London. National and
local legislation passed in the middle decades of the 16th century had
set the minimum age for citizenship through apprenticeship at 24,
and, on average, men were 26 when they became free.[1]

In finishing his term and becoming a citizen, Henry Wilson was
in a minority. However, a majority of the adult male population in
early modern London were citizens: approximately three-quarters
of men in the middle of the 16th century and just above half
by the end of the 17th century. When Wilson became a freeman
of London, he secured significant economic and political rights.
Under the auspices of the Masons' Company, he had the right to
set himself up in business, for example, or to bind an apprentice.
In 1636-7, he took Simon Walton as his apprentice. Previously,
in 1628-9, he had paid 2s. 6d. to have William Sommers, who
had been apprenticed to John Williams, turned over to him – a
common request.[2]

---

* William had served as Upper Warden in 1623-4, and Master in 1625-6. The fee for admission
to the freedom of London was lower for those admitted by patrimony than it was for those
admitted by apprenticeship. If William was Henry's father, there would have been a clear
incentive to admit him by patrimony.
† The maximum fee a company could charge for admittance was 3s. 4d. To increase its income,
however, the Company levied an additional 6d. fee, which was payable to the Clerk, and a
'gratuity' of 20s.

As a freeman, Wilson also had the right to take part in the election of the City's Common Councilmen in his ward, and the ward's officers. With these rights, however, came responsibilities. In his ward, for example, Wilson was now expected to participate in keeping the watch under the supervision of the Beadle and Constable, to present offenders to the Alderman of his ward for justice, and to pay taxes and national subsidies. Within the Company he had to follow the Company's rules as set down in its various ordinances, and pay quarterage. He was also expected to hold office in the Company when elected, and attend Company events when summoned.[3]

The most onerous expectation was to serve as Steward. Each year, the Assistants would elect several members to serve as Stewards, which meant that they were obliged to pay the cost of the Company's dinner on Lord Mayor's Day. This was commuted in the 17th century to a fine of a set amount – then £6, perhaps more than two months' wages for a journeyman mason – and it became customary for many freemen to compound their Steward and livery fines, as Wilson did in 1630. The Assistants were understandably keen to ensure that freemen served as Steward when required. After all, the fines brought significant sums of money into the Company's coffers, and they were even happy to agree payment plans which allowed newly elected Stewards to stagger their payments. Equally understandably, many members were keen to avoid this expensive obligation altogether.[4]

The threat of prosecution was frequently enough to bring recalcitrant members into line – even as late as 1809. At other times, however, things turned more acrimonious. In 1654, Thomas Cartwright was committed to Newgate Gaol when he refused either to serve as Steward or to pay a fine in lieu of holding the office. In 1726-7, the Court prosecuted Joseph Stanfield after he had similarly refused to accept his election, which prompted Stanfield to rail against the Assistants 'in a very Rude and Indecent Manner' telling them that 'he did not get his Money by picking of pockets'. In the end, both Cartwright and Stanfield submitted to the Company's authority, but the Company did not always succeed in its prosecutions. In 1708, for instance, the Lord Mayor found in favour of the four masons summoned before him for not paying their Stewards' fines.[5]

In 1630, Henry Wilson became a liveryman and he thereby acquired additional rights and responsibilities. He could now have two apprentices working under him at any one time and he could participate in the election of the Company's Master and Wardens. He could also now take part in elections for the City's MPs, the Lord Mayor, and one of the Sheriffs, as well as the City Chamberlain and other officials. In return, however, the Company expected much more of him.

In the first place, there was his fine of £3 for becoming a liveryman. The fine was not the only extra cost that liverymen bore. As we have seen, a liveryman was expected to attend quarter days in his livery gown, on pain of fine. Any time spent on Company business, such as this, was time not spent working. On these occasions, and indeed others, he would have been expected to attend Company dinners, which would have entailed associated costs. All liverymen, Wilson included, were expected, usually, to pay greater sums in assessments levied upon the Company. In the 1630 assessment for corn, 44 liverymen were asked to pay £1 each, whereas 72 yeomen of the Company were assessed at sums ranging from 2s. to 10s. In the 1631-2 assessment for pageants in the City, 32 liverymen paid 3s. 6d. per head, while 30 yeomen paid sums ranging from 1s. to 3s.

34 *List of Masons' Company members assessed for King Charles I's Ship Money in 1636. Includes,*
(a) James French, Master.
(b) William Smith, Upper Warden.
(c) Thomas Stanley, Renter Warden.
(d) Nicholas Stone
(e) Henry Wilson
(f) Edward Marshall.

Table 7.1. Totals of Assistants, Liverymen and Freemen, 1501-1636.

	Officers and Assistants	Liverymen	Yeomen	Total
1501-2	N/A	11	N/A	N/A
1538	8	14	15	37
1630	25	19	72	116
1631-2	20	17	30	67
1636	43		81	124

per head. In 1636, 43 liverymen paid 9d. each towards Ship Money, but 78 yeomen paid just 6d. each.*[6]

The lists drawn up to administer these assessments provide us with a useful means of understanding the nature and extent of the contemporary Company's membership. To be sure, they usually record only those who were assessed or who, as in 1631-2, actually paid, so many poorer members, or those who managed to evade assessment, may not be represented. Indeed, in 1631-2, only the 'greater parte of the assistents' paid 3s. 6d. each towards the assessment. Nevertheless, what matters is the trend over time and here the pattern does seem clear enough; in the century between 1530 and 1630, membership of the Masons' Company may well have risen by perhaps a multiple of three or four.

Of course, we would expect the number of members to have risen as the population of London rose across that period. The Company's 43 or 44 liverymen in the 1630s, with a yeomanry perhaps three times as large, was very typical for a minor craft company. By contrast, perhaps more than 2,600 men were members of the Merchant Taylors' Company in 1595.[7]

Only a minority of men in early modern London ever became liverymen. Most remained in the yeomanries of their companies. In the mid-16th century, just one man in ten who acquired the freedom would become a liveryman; and at the end of the 16th century just 10 per cent of householders, that is to say perhaps just 2,500 men, wore their company's livery. Men who joined the minor companies, like the Masons, had a greater chance of becoming liverymen than those who joined the Great Twelve with their larger memberships. On average a Londoner would expect to wait 12 years to become a liveryman. However, the period of time between admission and

* Three yeomen who had their names entered on the list but no money entered next to their names have not been counted.

becoming a liveryman varied considerably. Henry Wilson rose to the rank of liveryman within four years of his admission to the freedom – a rapid ascent, and probably a consequence of William Wilson's seniority. Those who had been apprenticed to liverymen and Assistants were much more likely to become liverymen themselves.[8]

Liverymen of the Masons' Company were further required to serve as Court Assistants, if elected. In 1651-2, a unique entry records that five men paid a fine of £2 each when they became Assistants. Whether this was an innovation in that year, or a chance survival pointing towards an established practice is not clear. As previously noted, courts of assistants emerged in the 15th century as governing bodies for the livery companies, and the 1481 ordinances provided for a body of six men which looks very much like a Court of Assistants in the Masons' Company.[9]

The Court of Assistants would meet at least quarterly to transact the regular business of running the Company, and usually more often than that. In 1677, the Company's royal charter specified that the Court should comprise 24 men; prior to that, we cannot tell how many men were meant to serve as Assistants at any one time. In 1538, eight men were listed as Assistants for an assessment while, in 1630, 25 appear on a list. In reality, the size of the Court would naturally have varied as death, retirement and changes of residence removed individuals from its numbers, while the induction of new members would have fluctuated according to how many men could be persuaded to take on its potentially onerous responsibilities.

The 1481 ordinances provided for two Wardens of the Company who were to serve two-year terms in office. In 1607, the Assistants of the Company petitioned the Mayor and Aldermen to change the organisation's structure for the Company's better governance. Thenceforth, the liverymen of the Company were to elect a Master and two Wardens each year within 10 days of the feast of Holy Trinity (the eighth Sunday after Easter), whom they would promptly present to the Mayor and Aldermen of London. The names of all the incumbents are known from 1619-20. In 1677, the Company's royal charter specified that the election must take place 'upon the Foureteenth day of June (if it bee not Sunday), and if it bee Sunday then upon the next day after.'

Office-holding in the Masons' Company was not exactly cheap. The Master and Wardens were traditionally expected to pay sums of money towards the lavish election dinner held in their honour –

early in the 17th century, typically £1 or 10s. each. Over time, this requirement was commuted to an entry fine which to this day is still demanded of the newly elected officers. Anyone who tried to avoid office was liable to pay an even higher fine. The officers' other obligations were not always light either. They had to collect the taxes and assessments demanded by both Crown and Corporation of London and, in 1632, Thomas Priestman and John Shuttleworth, the two Wardens of the Masons' Company, were both committed to Newgate Gaol for failing to collect an assessment levied to pay towards the cost of buying and storing grain for the City.[10]

Since the 1740s, it has been customary for the Master to have served as Upper and Renter Warden in the two years before his elevation to the chair. Before then, men spread out their service in the three offices over a longer period. The Renter Warden is the junior role, but it is the one that bore a much heavier responsibility. It was the job of the Renter Warden, until well into the 20th century, to account for all the money that the Company received and spent, and to present his accounts to the Court of Assistants at the end of his year in office. The Company has often closed its accounts in the red – on at least 16 occasions between 1619 and 1666, for example, the Company ended the year with a debit balance – and in those years it was the Renter Warden who made up the shortfall until the Company could reimburse him.[11]

Henry Wilson was Renter Warden in 1641-2. Unfortunately, at the end of that year the Company owed him £25 3s. 5d. Over the course of the next three years Wilson received £5 3s. 5d. back from the Company; security was given for the £20 balance which seems never to have been paid to him. He was, perhaps, fortunate. The deficit of £52 4s. 10d. in 1659-60 was so great that the Master, Thomas Stanton, had to bear some of the load alongside Stephen Switzer, the Renter Warden.[12]

To ensure that the Renter Warden could cover any potential deficit, and that he would deliver up any credit balance and property, the by-laws of 1678 required him to enter into a bond of £200 with the Company, which would be cancelled once he had made 'a perfect, full, true and plaine Accompt in writing, fairely written, of and for all such Receipts and Payments as hee hath made within the time of his Renter Wardenship', and delivered up all the Company's money and property which he had in hand. It is not clear whether bonds were drawn up every year, but they certainly were in many cases, and several remain in the Company's archive. With all these obligations, it is no wonder that many masons chose rather to pay a fine of £6 to avoid the office altogether. In 1653-4, for example, Thomas Moore and John Parker both paid £6 to be excused.[13]

In 1645-6, Henry Wilson served as Upper Warden. The Upper Warden is the senior warden. Traditionally, his role was ill-defined, but it provided a candidate for Mastership with a year close to the chair. Two years later, Wilson paid the customary fine of £2 13s. 4d. to avoid holding this office again. In 1648, he was installed as Master; he served for a second time in 1654-5. Only a tiny proportion of those men who began apprenticeships in early modern London ever held the most senior office in their companies. Those who did become Master were senior men, who tended to be in their fifties when they were elected. Wilson, who had been born while Elizabeth I still ruled, must have been about fifty, if not older, when he was installed as Master.[14]

His responsibilities as Master were surprisingly ill-defined in the 1607 ordinances which established the office. Much as the Master does today, as the highest-ranking officer of the Company, he would have represented the Masons' Company in the civic life of the City. He would have presided at meetings of the Court and he was, ultimately, responsible for the Company's good governance.

Wilson rose to the top of the Company tree despite a record which included various clashes with the Company's Court. He was fined on more than one occasion for carrying away Purbeck stone which had not been examined and once he was amerced 7s. for faulty workmanship at St Botolph without Aldgate. In 1631-2, he paid 30s. for several unspecified misdemeanours and he was committed to the Compter in mysterious circumstances. Four years later, he paid 12d. after offending contrary to orders the nature of which was not described. In 1638-9, he was one of 15 men fined for not coming to Court in his livery gown. Such a record was not at all unusual, however, among the Company's office holders; in fact many Masters had what might be described as chequered careers behind them – such were the rough edges of a career in the building trade, then as perhaps now. Indeed, notwithstanding his early-career disregard for the regulations concerned with Purbeck stone, from 1649 to 1659 he was responsible, either solely or primarily, for collecting monies received from the Purbeck search.[15]

When Henry Wilson made his will he opened by declaring that he was a parishioner in St Martin Vintry and 'a free mason of London'. He then went on to make detailed provision for his wife and children. The Masons' Company was clearly not the only association or community in London to which Wilson belonged; his household, his neighbourhood, his ward and his parish were all important institutions to him, and to all of these he would have felt, at various times and in different ways, loyalty and affection. As Rappaport has rightly noted, 'Londoners lived in a multitude of worlds within worlds'. This system of overlapping institutions had emerged gradually and sometimes painfully, but it kept society stable in early modern London at a time of great political, social, religious and economic upheaval. Becoming a freeman of the Masons' Company and the City in 1627 was, however, probably the single most important step which Wilson took in his adult life. Certainly, it was the most fundamental.[16]

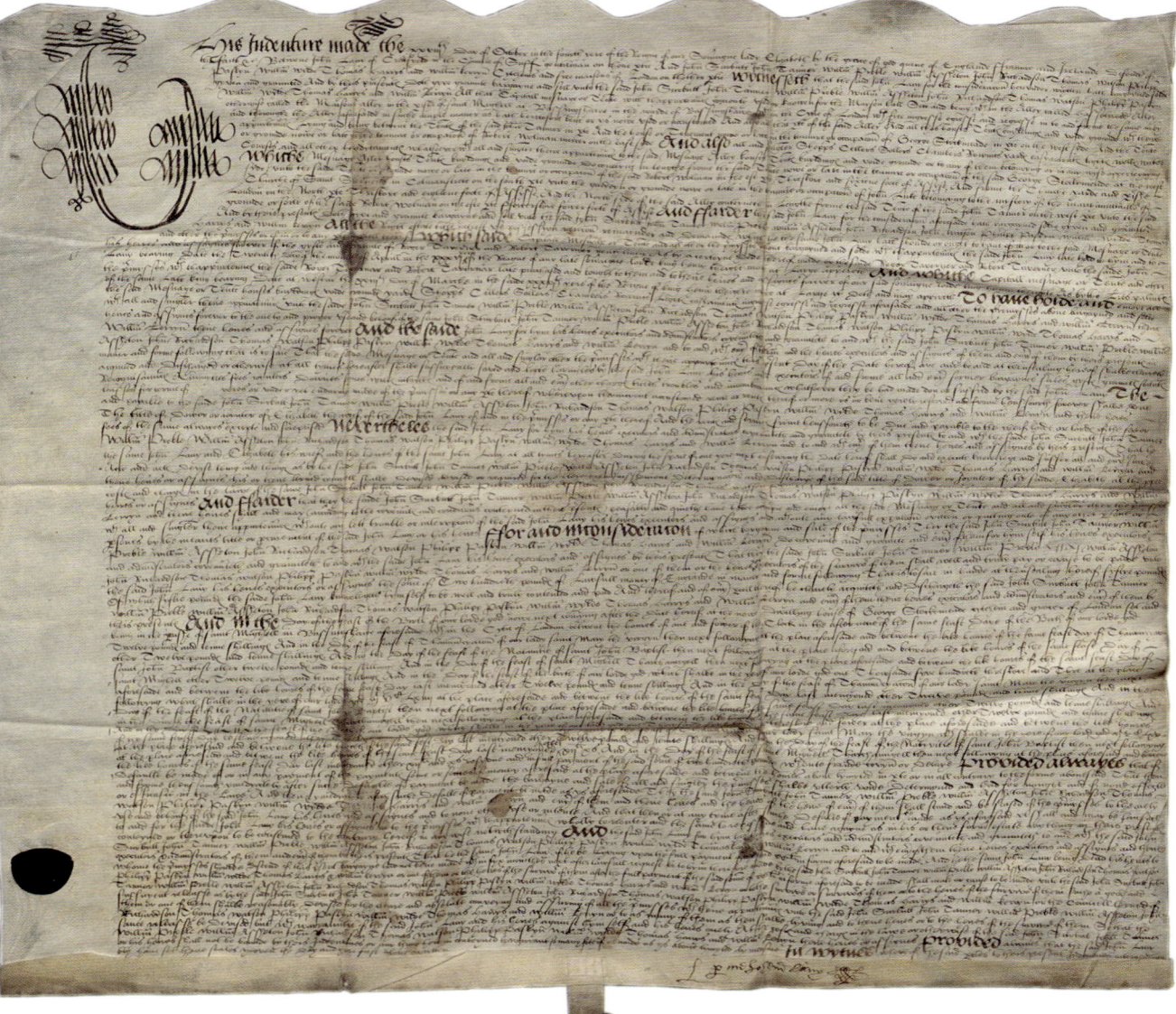

35 Indenture by which representatives
of the Masons' Company purchased the
freehold of Masons' Hall from John Lany,
28 October 1562.

8

MASONS' HALL

Recovering the history of Masons' Hall is a difficult endeavour. There are no known engravings or paintings of the buildings which stood on the site, either before or after the Great Fire of 1666, nor any reliable early plans of the area in which it stood. It seems that Masons' Hall was never of much interest to the early modern surveyors of London. John Stow, for example, recorded nothing of the pre-Fire Hall's appearance, while in the 18th century, John Strype and John Noorthouck noted little more about the second Hall than that it was 'small'. A number of relevant leases, deeds and mortgages do, however, survive; they throw a great deal of light on the Company's financial position over the centuries, but they are less useful as tools with which to recreate the detailed reality of the building.[1]

To take just one example. The Company purchased the freehold of the Hall in 1562. According to that indenture, the premises measured 76ft. by 78ft. These figures are seriously at odds with later ordnance survey maps, which give 66ft. by 42ft. There is no evidence to indicate that the Company ever alienated any of the site area, nor to suggest that the boundaries were altered as part of the rebuilding after the Great Fire, when, famously, most boundaries remained as they had always been. The simplest explanation, although unprovable, is that this single uncorroborated source recorded the measurements incorrectly. It is particularly frustrating that Conder did not supply any plan or image of the post-Fire Hall, which must have been familiar to his older colleagues, if not to Conder himself.[2]

In what follows, the term 'premises' is used to denote all the buildings which stood on the whole site, including any tenements or houses let as private dwellings. The term 'Masons' Hall' or 'the Hall' describes the series of connected rooms and chambers, for example the kitchen, the parlours, the buttery and, of course, the great hall itself, all of which are outlined in brown on illustration 37 (p.120), which were used for Company business and events; adjoining tenements which were not part of the Hall proper are outlined in blue. The term 'great hall' is reserved for the largest and grandest room in the Hall. Unless otherwise indicated, all rental figures are annual amounts.

The pre-Fire Masons' Hall

In 1400 only six companies, all of them merchant rather than craft companies, had halls. Over the course of the next century, the Masons were one of 31 companies to acquire halls. Then and thereafter, Masons' Hall fulfilled many functions. It served as an administrative centre for the Company, providing the Master, Wardens, Assistants and Clerk with a place to create and store records, and to keep the Company's plate, treasures and money. It had an important social purpose, as a place where members could come together to meet, to feast, and to conduct the ceremony and ritual which was central to Company life. It was also a place for charity; members bequeathed money to Masons' Hall, and it was at the Hall that the pensioners were paid, the poor box was kept, and its contents disbursed. That commemoration of the dead which was at the heart of the medieval fraternity was focused especially on the Hall, and there it continued well into the 16th and 17th centuries. It was of course, and not least, a commercial asset which could be rented out and used as security for loans. Finally, it had a symbolic value: it gave the Company a very real and obvious sense of belonging in the heart of the City of London.[3]

The earliest evidence that we have concerning the Hall is the lease which the Company obtained on the site in what was then known as Haslewood Alley, in the ward of Bassishaw and the parish of St Michael Bassishaw, from the prior and convent of Holy Trinity, Aldgate. This lease, post-dated 28 May 1463, but effective from Midsummer (24 June) 1462, was for a term of 99 years. The document was still in the Company's archive in the late 17th century, but it would appear to have been lost by 1722. Similarly, very few of the Priory's records have survived, so we do not know the details of the property which the Company acquired from the Priory. Did the Company acquire a virgin site upon which they built a hall? Alternatively, was there a large private house there already? In a number of cases, companies first acquired halls when a wealthy member donated or devised a suitable property, usually a large courtyard house, to his company for use as a hall. The common arrangement of such medieval domestic buildings was and indeed still is visible in the nomenclature of the halls, almost all of which had and have parlours, kitchens, chambers and pantries.[4]

What is clear is that the premises leased by the Masons were but a tiny part of the Priory's property portfolio in London. In the early 16th century the Company was paying 26s. 8d. in rent to the Priory, at a time when the Priory's property holdings generated a total annual income of between £278 and £432. Following its suppression in 1532, all the Priory's properties passed into the king's hands. On 14 January 1538, the king granted the lease of the premises of Masons' Hall, along with 10 other properties in the parish of St Michael Bassishaw which had previously belonged to the prior and convent, to a certain John Lany, a gentleman from Cratfield in Suffolk, for a term of 41 years. Notwithstanding this grant, on 23 March 1545, Roger and Robert Taverner, two brothers from Norfolk, concluded a separate deal by which they purchased a whole batch of properties, including the Company's premises, from the king. One month later, on 20 April 1545, the Taverners sold the freehold of the premises to John Lany.[5]

It is not easy to make sense of this apparently circular sequence, but the artificial conventions of the law of property at that time, combined with the wild conditions of the land market in the immediate aftermath of the Dissolution, frequently caused what might be described as rigged deals to be recorded as a sort of legal pantomime. One of the Taverner brothers, Roger (d.1572), was a surveyor and writer who was employed in the 1540s in the Court of Augmentations, the court established by Henry VIII in 1536 to administer the properties and revenues of the religious houses which had come into his hands at the Dissolution. Positions of this nature could be lucrative for men willing to make the most of the opportunities which they provided, and there is, in this mysterious conveyance, more than a hint of some financial chicanery.

Be that as it may, it probably affected the Company little. What was more significant in the Company's history was its purchase, on 28 October 1562 (at the end of the 99-year term of the lease), of the freehold premises from Lany for £200. Because the Company had not yet been incorporated by charter, it could not hold title to property, so 10 named masons held it as feoffees or trustees. The masons agreed to pay Lany £50 on the sealing of the agreement, or indenture, followed by 12 quarterly instalments of £12 10s. Upon payment of each instalment, Lany provided the masons with a receipt, 10 of which remain in the Company's archive.[6]

The masons who acted on behalf of the Company were John Surbutt, John Tanner, William Preble, William Ashton, John Richardson, Thomas Watson, Philip Paskin, William Wild, Thomas Harris and William Kerwin. These men were significant figures in the contemporary Company. Twenty-four years before this conveyance, in 1538, Preble had been a member of the Court of Assistants, Harris a liveryman, and Ashton, Richardson, Surbutt, and Watson all yeomen of the Company. Tanner was a successful mason who was assessed to pay 10s. on £10 worth of property in the subsidy of 1582 and who owned property in Masons' Alley immediately adjacent to the premises on their western side. Philip Paskin was City Mason and, after his death in 1580, he was succeeded in this role by William Kerwin. As we have noted elsewhere, Kerwin was also a City Viewer and he is visible as Warden of the Company in 1585. It is quite possible that these 10 masons comprised, either wholly or partially, the Court of Assistants in 1562.[7]

In the indenture of 1562, the premises were described as the 'capitall messuage or tenement with thappurteaunces comonly used or knowen for the Mayson Hall sete and being within the alley called Haslewood Alley otherwise called the Maisons Alley'. By this time, so it would seem, the premises had become enough of a feature of London's topography for one of the surrounding streets to acquire a name connected with the Company – Masons' Alley.

How the Company raised £200 to pay Lany is unknown. On 17 September 1563, the 10 masons who had acquired the property in 1562 transferred it to a group of 34 masons for the sum of £120. Between 1566 and 1572, nine of them (Thomas Harris died in 1563 and passed his title and interest in the premises to his son William) subsequently acknowledged that they had been paid the sum of £12 each by the Company in discharge of the £120.[8]

Perhaps John Richardson contributed a greater sum than £12. In a deed dated 23 November 1565, but possibly evidencing a transfer which took place in 1562, ownership of three chambers or tenements on the first floor of the premises was transferred to Richardson. Subsequently, Richardson leased these chambers to the Company for a term of 99 years in return for an annual payment of 26s. 8d. for the rest of his natural life, and 15s. thereafter to his heirs or assigns. In September 1619, Richardson's grandson, Benjamin, sold his interest in the chambers back to the Company for the sum of £20. What is clear is that London property values were rising: 26s. 8d. was the sum which the Company had paid in rent for all the property on the site between 1463 and 1562, yet between 1562 and 1619 it paid that same sum just to lease the three small tenements.[9]

Analysis of the surviving pre-Fire deeds and leases reveals that from 1562 until 1666, when the premises were entirely destroyed, ownership of the Hall and chambers, often as separate entities, passed regularly from one group of feoffees to another, as did possession of their leases, in an often-bewildering series of transfers. Carefully interpreted, these records tell us a good deal about the location, appearance and layout of the premises.

The Hall was situated roughly midway between Basinghall Street and Coleman Street, two streets which, then as now, ran north to south. On the ground floor the property comprised a great hall with a small parlour or separate dining room, a kitchen, a pantry with two cellars, and a yard with some sort of shed. In 1636-7, two loads of stone seized during the search were carried from the river to the premises; presumably they were stored in the yard. On the first floor, there was a garret (a small attic room) above the parlour, together with three chambers or tenements. Two of the chambers, measuring 22ft. 5in. north to south and 11ft. and 10ft. 4in. east to west, were located above the kitchen. The third chamber, which was smaller, measuring just 12ft. north to south and 13ft. east to west, was above the gate into the Hall. This chamber may also have been in some disrepair at the time when the Company bought the freehold, because shortly thereafter the Master and Wardens committed to rebuilding it within the space of 20 years to the same dimensions as before, but with its joists, floor and eaves equal to those of the other two chambers.[10]

INCOME AND EXPENSE

Many livery companies had tenements and chambers attached to halls, which were used as almshouses for poor or infirm companymen, or their widows, who paid reduced rents or even no rent at all. Whether the Masons' Company let these tenements as almshouses in the 15th century or not is unknown, but they did so subsequently. In 1565 three widows, Overton, Thomson and Spede, rented the chambers from the Company. In 1573, Joan Overton was still living in one of these tenements, and Agnes Dodge, another widow, was in another. In 1619-20, the first year for which we have the Company's accounts, widows lived in all three chambers, paying £1 13s. 4d., £2 and £2 4s. annually. By 1630-1, however, the two larger tenements were let for £3 10s., and the smaller one above the door for £2, bringing in a total of £9 in rental income. Between 1640 and 1657, the tenements regularly generated a yearly income exceeding £10. This was probably a consequence both of the tenements' increased value and of letting them at market rates to tenants who were not pensioners or widows.[11]

Indeed, from as far back as the Company's records allow us to see, through to the time when the premises were sold, the Company was willing to let part or all of the premises. From 1631 to 1642 the Gardeners' Company paid £10 a year, falling to £8 a year from 1640, to the Company for the use of the great hall, parlour, buttery, kitchen and yard. From 1651 to 1659, the Porters' Company paid £8 for a similar arrangement. In the 1620s, rental of the various buildings on the premises brought in an average of £14 9s. 1d., increasing to between £22 12s. 0d. and £23 12s. 0d. between 1630 and 1660, and then to £25 6s. 8d. in the 1660s.[12]

The higher average figures for the 1650s and 1660s are all the more impressive when one considers that from 1659 to 1661, the Company received no rent at all as it undertook a substantial rebuilding programme. The money paid by the Gardeners and Porters must have been only for occasional use of the Hall, because from 1674 onwards the Company let the great hall, parlour, kitchen and buttery on the ground floor of their new Hall, along with the rooms on the first floor above, on a series of long leases for continual occupation for sums much greater than this. Edward Hulse, 'Doctor in Physicke', took the Hall on a lease for £50 a year, and he was followed by Mr Jackson who paid £37 10s. and Caleb Smith who paid £40. Throughout the 18th and 19th centuries, the Company's income from renting property on the premises was significant. In 1778-9, some £70 of the Company's total income of just under £160 came from tenants in the Hall and the two tenements. In 1840-41, by which time the Hall was let for £75, the gross income from renting the premises had almost doubled to £137.[13]

The Company could also raise money by using the premises as security for loans. This was something which the Company did both before and after the Great Fire. In September 1643, the three tenements at Masons' Hall were mortgaged to Robert Buckland in return for a loan of £120. In 1664-5, the Company agreed a 51-year mortgage with Edward Marshall, secured on the premises in return for a loan of £200 at 5 per cent, while in 1676, Anthony Light's loan of £800 to the Company was also secured on the 'lately new built' premises.[14]

There were, of course, running and recurring costs associated with the premises, while the drawing up of deeds, mortgages and indentures incurred legal and professional costs. Insurance also appeared as an expense after the Great Fire, when the Company insured its premises, first at the Hand In Hand Fire Office, and subsequently with the Westminster Insurance Office. Higher property taxes in the 18th century also significantly reduced the Company's income from the premises. By the 1720s Caleb Smith's quarterly payments of £10 gross were often only worth £7 net to the Company, and by the 1740s as little as £6 net.[15]

Not all of the Company's tenants proved reliable and secure. In 1826, Messrs Lloyd and Goodman, who worked in the woollen trade, surrendered their lease owing to financial difficulties and for almost five years the Company could not find a tenant for the Hall. In 1831, they finally found a tenant in John Fryer Smallman, a factor of 74 Basinghall Street, but within a year he was in arrears, he had sublet the Hall, and his creditors were in possession of his goods and running his business. At least some of his arrears were paid in the end, but the void period and trouble collecting the rent had a significant effect on the Company's financial position, pushing the Company into the red in six of the seven years from 1829 to 1835.[16]

Repairs and maintenance were a constant drain on the Company's resources, too. In 1710, the Company paid over £140 to contractors for work on the premises. In 1743, the Company decided not to play its usual part in the celebrations for Lord Mayor's Day as so much money had been spent on repairs that year, while in 1782 the Company entered into a bond with John Scott for £80 at 3 per cent interest for repairs which he had carried out at the site. More often than not, the money for repairs and maintenance had to be found from the Company's ordinary income, although it was not uncommon for members to contribute to these costs through gifts and loans.[17]

Routine repairs were inescapable adjuncts of property ownership, but the Company's finances were more radically affected by expenditure on two major programmes of capital works which followed each other in quick succession in the third quarter of the 17th century. In 1657-8, the Company embarked on what might now be called a redevelopment programme, which involved the construction of two new tenements for rent, at a cost of almost £300. To finance works on this scale, the Company had to borrow from its members: Clement Cole lent the Company £215 and Henry Banks lent £75.[18]

Within the space of just a few years, of course, all the new work lay in ruins. It is hard to know precisely how much was spent on rebuilding after 1666, but Edward Sleamaker, the carpenter, billed the Company for at least £629 16s. 11d. When we factor in what was paid to the bricklayers, masons, painters, glaziers, labourers and others, then we should surely allow for a sum in excess of £1,000. Perhaps it was even much more than that. Between 1668 and 1674 the Company raised a total of £486 12s. 6d. from its members, presumably by way of an assessed subscription, and borrowed £700 from Past Master George Dowswell, to pay for the rebuilding. These costs were a considerable factor in the Company's financial woes of the 1680s and 1690s, and as late as 1702, that is 36 years after the Fire, the Court of Assistants was still lamenting 'the present circumstances of the Company and the greatness of the debts wherewith it is incumbred occasioned cheifly by the hall's being burnt in the late dismall Fire'.[19]

THE POST-FIRE HALL

All the same, the decision was taken to press on and rebuild immediately after the Fire – a decided vote of confidence in the Company's future on the part of its members. Work began almost immediately, when the Company met its tenants to discuss how best to proceed, and money was spent clearing debris. In 1669, the Company leased the plot of land, outlined in yellow dashes on illustration 37 (p.120), from Benjamin Needham in return for an annual payment of £4. Needham may not have been the freeholder of the land; certainly, by the 1720s the freehold was held by Christ's Hospital, and it is quite possible that Needham only ever held a lease from them which he sublet to the Company. Be that as it may, this land gave the Company improved access to the Hall through a small gateway and a plot on which to build a tenement for rental. Once this lease had been sealed, all the foundations were set out, more of the debris was cleared, and a bricklayer began work.[20]

Work was well under way in 1670, when meetings were recorded to discuss the rebuilding, as a result of which over £500 was spent on materials, carriage, clearing away of rubbish, and contractors' bills. One year later, Mr Blunt, a plasterer, was hard at work, so the project must have been approaching completion. By 1672, the work was more or less finished. Among the workmen's bills that year were some for cleaning, and for rushes and other material to strew upon the floor, and the first rental payments were received. The Company continued to pay contractors in arrears, however, for a few years yet.

What did the Company actually build? We do not know who designed the buildings, nor do we know anything of their exterior appearance. We have simply no idea whether the exteriors were plain or decorated, or whether there was any statuary or sculpture. From certain leases, deeds and maps we can surmise that the Hall comprised perhaps four storeys in total: a basement, a ground and first floor, and then an attic storey in the pitched roof. From these same sources, along with some contractors' bills and the Company's accounts and minutes, we know that, in line with the regulations for the rebuilding of London after the Fire, the walls were built almost entirely of brick, while the interiors were panelled in wood. There was some masonry work; in 1669-70, 40 tons of Portland stone were bought and in the same year about £85 was paid to two masons for their work on site. This stone may have been used to make a cornice around the roofline, and possibly also to provide ornamental frames for the windows and doorways.[21]

In the same year 1669-70, some £400 was paid to carpenters and bricklayers, and while the two leading contractors on the rebuilding were both members of the Masons' Company, neither was a mason by trade: Edward Sleamaker was a carpenter and Edward Ellen was a bricklayer. On domestic and semi-domestic sites, such as Masons' Hall, opportunities for specialist stonemasons tended to be confined to decorative work, and paving, as seems to have been the case here. In 1672-3, for example, a mason was paid £6 to pave the yard.

As to the organisation and arrangement of the premises, frustratingly, only three of the many surviving leases provide us with much information, and they do so only in the most general terms. An inventory 'of the Goods, Chattels and things whereof mention is made in the Indenture' granted to Dr Hulse on 11 September 1674

supplies a list of rooms with descriptions of each. It tells us, for example, that there was a 'Cellar behind the Kitchen and Buttery' which was connected to another 'Cellar under the Parlor', and that there was a 'little Roome on the right hand of the hall' which was 'paved with Freestone'. The lease that was sealed with Caleb Smith in 1710 affords a more detailed schedule along the same lines, but it is unfortunately very faded. From these two leases we can compile a list of rooms which comprised the Hall, but there are hardly any measurements in either lease and neither makes a serious attempt to orientate the rooms.[22]

36 *Plan of tenement to be demolished in Masons' Alley, from lease agreed with Christ's Hospital, 1767.*

We know also that there were two tenements on the post-Fire site, which the Company let out to tenants. They were only numbered for the first time in the 19th-century records of the Company, the tenement to the west as 2 Masons' Alley and the tenement to the east as 4 Masons' Alley; the Hall, with its entrance between them, was 3 Masons' Alley. For ease of reference, these numbers will be used for the tenements throughout their history. In October 1767, the Company sealed a new 61-year lease on the site of the passage to the yard and 4 Masons' Alley, covenanting to pull down the house which stood on the site and to build a new and substantial brick house. This lease contains a plan with measurements of the house to be demolished.[23]

At first sight, all this is rather unpromising material, but when it is combined with scattered references in the Company's minute books and other records, we can begin to put the pieces of the puzzle together. For example, although we do not know the measurements either for the tenement at 2 Masons' Alley or for the Hall, we do know their rental and insured values and we can compare these with those of 4 Masons' Alley, the dimensions of which are known.

2 Masons' Alley, first let for £16 in 1674 to William Bashford, a cooper, was consistently let for between £10 and £12 in the 50 or so years thereafter, while 4 Masons' Alley, which was first let in 1672 for £12 to Lewis Langley, also a cooper, was usually let for £10 to £11 in the same 50-year period. In 1723, both houses were insured to the value of £150. From this information, therefore, we can suppose that the two tenements were roughly the same size, with 2 Masons' Alley being somewhat the larger of the two.[24]

Comparing the rent paid by the tenants in the Hall and those in the tenements is more of a comparison between apples and pears, and we have to allow for the fact that exclusions and restrictions in the leases granted on the Hall would have negatively affected their value. For example, the Company always either excluded certain rooms from the leases, or it ensured that it could use the Hall on a number of days throughout the year. More useful, then, is a comparison of the insured values, which were presumably calculated per square foot. In 1723, the Hall was insured for £1,000, suggesting it was between six and seven times the size of each tenement.

A speculative reconstruction of the site-plan is suggested at p.120, with the caveat that the arrangements of the premises were never fixed. The house at 4 Masons' Alley was completely rebuilt in 1767-8; in 1707, a doorway was opened from the yard into 2 Masons' Alley; in 1735, a music gallery was built, presumably above the great hall; and in 1791, a door was opened from the great parlour or court room into the yard.[25]

The premises were entered from Masons' Alley through a gateway and passage measuring 6ft. wide and just under 12ft. long. This

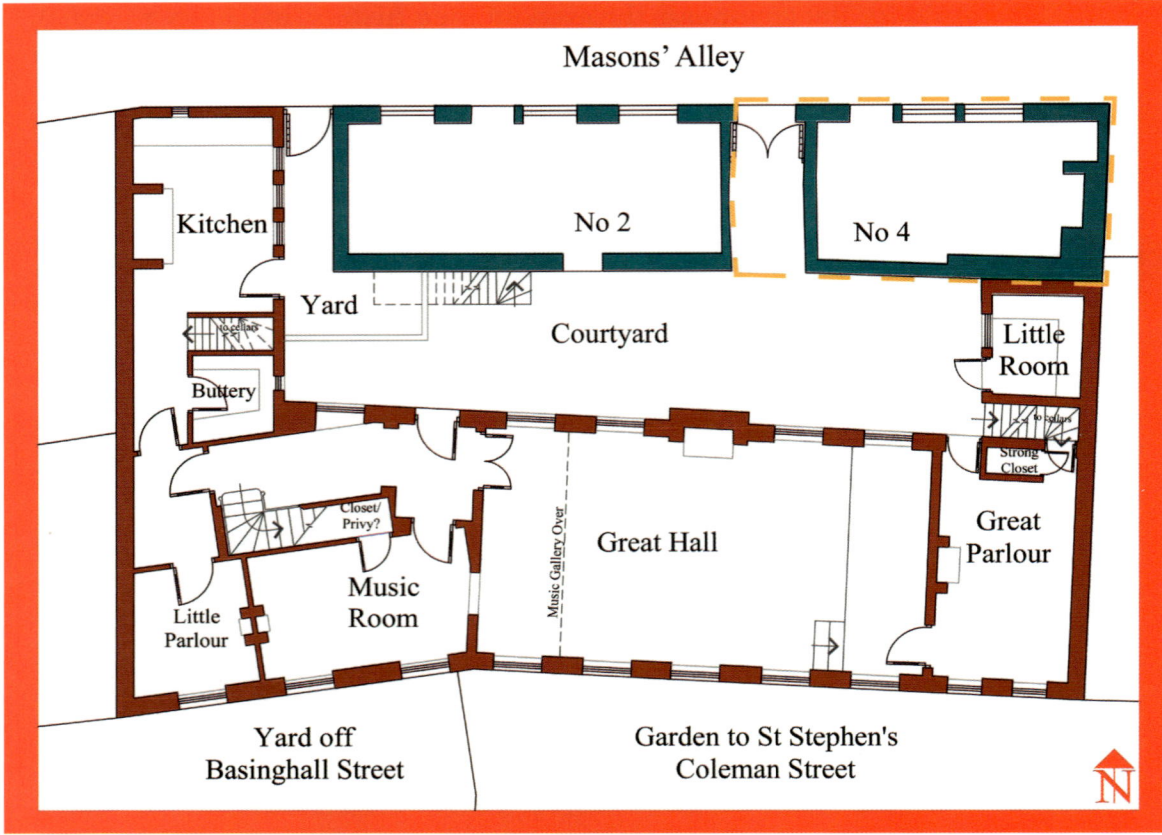

37 Speculative plan of Masons' Hall in the late 18th century.

passage opened into a courtyard. The best comparison today for such an entrance might be that which survives at Apothecaries' Hall in Blackfriars, but similar passages gave access to numerous courtyard properties located off the street lines of the old City. On the west side of this passage was 2 Masons' Alley, a brick tenement with a staircase between it and Masons' Hall. This, the other tenement, and the kitchen of the Hall, would have been two storeys high – the maximum height allowed under the terms of the Act for the Rebuilding of London in 1667 for buildings which fronted 'by-streets and lanes'. Completed by 1674, it was let, as noted above, to a series of tenants; in 1807 the rent was sharply raised to £21 per annum. Between 1811 and 1826, and from 1840-65, it was let to the same tenants as were in the Hall.[26]

Extending over the passage and standing on its eastern side was 4 Masons' Alley. As we have seen, this was let first to Lewis Langley and then to other tenants until 1727, in which year the lease sealed with Needham in 1669 expired. At that point, the Company was able to negotiate a new lease for the passage only, paying one-off premiums of £35 and £25 to hold that small strip of land until 1770. Between 1727 and 1767, ownership of 4 Masons' Alley reverted to Christ's Hospital, the freeholder of the site, and the Company lost the income from renting the house on the plot. However, in 1767 the Company agreed a new 61-year building lease for 4 Masons' Alley from Christ's Hospital in return for an annual ground rent of £5, and

38 Present-day passageway providing entrance to Apothecaries' Hall, likely to be similar to that at Masons' Hall.

Joseph Barlow was engaged to build a house on the site for £210, an agreement that was financed by selling some of the Company's 3 per cent consols. The new house must have been a considerable improvement on what was there before because it was soon let for £19 and by 1834, by which time a new lease on the site had been agreed with Christ's Hospital for £20 ground rent, it was bringing in £36. All in all, even allowing for the upfront costs of rebuilding the house, the usual running costs of owning property, and the ground rent, this was good business for the Company.[27]

To the immediate south of 4 Masons' Alley and opening directly onto the courtyard's eastern side stood the 'little room paved with stone'. Usually excluded from leases sealed with the Hall's tenants, it was used as a counting house, and it was the room in which the pensioners were paid their quarterly pensions. It may also have accommodated the Company's treasury and archive.[28]

At the western end of the premises were the kitchen, buttery and cellars. The little parlour, music room, great hall and great parlour / court room extended along the southern edge of the premises. Above these rooms were several chambers on the first floor, for which the Company may have had little use and which were presumably used as bedrooms or perhaps even sublet as lodgings by the tenants who took leases on the Hall. Above these were garret rooms with dormer windows. This arrangement allowed for the grandest rooms to be the biggest and brightest rooms, and it also explains why the Company took a lease on the passage from Masons' Alley, namely so that those entering the Hall did not have to enter past the kitchen.

At the main entrance to the Hall from the courtyard was a pair of wooden doors and the floor here was paved with black and white stone. The great parlour, little parlour, staircase and great hall were all wainscoted. It is most likely that the music room, which had two glazed external windows and an opening into the great hall, stood at the western end of the great hall, while the great parlour, which also had two external windows, stood at the eastern end. In the great hall itself there were wainscot benches and 8ft.-high wainscot panelling which ran around the walls. Anyone who has been to the halls of the Clothworkers, the Armourers and Braziers, or the Cutlers, or to any one of Wren's many post-Fire churches in London, will have seen an arrangement whereby wainscoting runs around the structure at about half the height of the walls with the windows above. The great hall of the Masons' Company must have been a double-height room of a similar type. We know that there was a 'great window', which would have opened southwards onto the garden and churchyard of St Stephen Coleman Street. The floor of the Hall was paved in black marble, apart from at its upper end, where there was a 'great table' on a dais paved with black and white marble. The arms of the king, the Corporation of London and the Masons' Company were displayed in carved wooden panels against the wainscot on the walls.

In 1910, the Company established a committee to try to find out if any carvings, monuments or relics in any way connected with the Hall could be found. In the end, just 'two carved panels of the Arms of the Company removed from Masons Hall' were discovered in the possession of Frederick Cox. They were almost certainly the 'armorial escutcheons' which were committed to the charge of Alfred Gwilt, the Company's Surveyor, in 1866. According to Conder, the Company 'never afterwards claimed' them and they passed from Gwilt to a 'late member of the Court of Assistants', presumably John Cox, who passed them to his son, Frederick. In due course Frederick Cox handed them back and, in December 1911, an agreement was reached with the Guildhall Library and Museum to keep them there. From there they passed to the Museum of London.* It is probable, but not certain, that the 'armorial escutcheons' of 1866 and 1910 were the same as the carvings of the Company's arms mentioned in the leases of 1674 and 1710.[29]

39 *Carvings of City and Company arms hung in Masons' Hall.*

* Not located in Museum archive, 2022.

We can but speculate on what other ornaments or memorials there might have been at Masons' Hall – in the great hall or elsewhere. We know that in the pre-Fire Hall, Robert Buckland's generous agreement to remit a debt owed to him, on the understanding that the Company would pay pensions worth 10s a year to 10 poor freemen or widows, was commemorated on a wooden board at the Hall 'to bee seene and knowne to all the severall members of the Companie'. The arms of at least five leading masons were depicted in glass in the pre-Fire Hall – an interesting, perhaps slightly surprising, comment on the social status attained by some, at least, of the early modern liverymen. Were benefactors and armigerous members of the Masons' Company remembered in the post-Fire Hall in similar ways? We do know that the table with the names of those who were known for a while as 'accepted masons' was kept in the great parlour of the post-Fire Hall. It is likely that the 18th-century Company would have followed the fashion set by others at the time, and hung portraits of Masters and benefactors on the walls; the records show that in 1738, when Miles Mann resigned his clerkship after his election as Town Clerk at the Guildhall, the Company considered engaging John Vanderbank (1694-1739) or William Verelst (1704-52), both famous portraitists, to paint Mann's picture 'to be fixed up in their Hall'.[30]

The dais at the end of the great hall, the carved panels, and the means by which prominent members of the Company were remembered, all remind us that the authority and hierarchy of the Company were made manifest in the architecture of Masons' Hall. The arms of the king, Corporation and Company were a visible embodiment of the way in which power flowed, or at least was meant to flow, from the Crown to City and then to Company. Only the Assistants, and perhaps even only the most senior of them, would have dined at the great table on the dais. It is also quite possible that certain rooms or chambers, perhaps even the great parlour, were reserved for the sole use of the livery. In the same way that the parlour of the large private house was the withdrawing room for the owner, so it was common for parlours of company halls to become rooms in which only the Assistants or liverymen would dine. Over the course of the 18th century the great parlour seems to have become the Company's Court Room, used for meetings of the Assistants, and it was either excluded from leases granted to tenants, or the Company reserved the right to use it for Court meetings on a given number of days.[31]

Masons' Hall and its two adjoining tenements were neither wholly private nor wholly public structures. The Masons' Company had, and indeed has, both a private and a public role in London – a duality reflected at the Hall. The Hall was a private building, but one of its most essential functions was to stand as a public representation of the Company in London. The Company's meetings were not open to the general public as a rule, but they had a public aspect and members of the public who were not members of the Company would often be in attendance. For example, those suspected of carrying out the mason's trade in London without having completed an apprenticeship or having taken up the freedom would be summoned to courts at the Hall. Conversely, many of the Company's meetings and celebrations took place in public venues: coffee houses, inns and taverns. It is easy to imagine members of the Company processing to these venues from Masons' Hall, as they did when going to their stand on Lord Mayor's Day. Nor were celebrations which took place at Masons' Hall hermetically sealed events: companymen would bring guests to feasts and dinners.

While many of the Company's tenants took leases on the understanding that they were renting private dwellings, the extent to which any building in early modern London afforded its owners or occupants complete privacy is questionable. Both of the tenements bordered a communal passage and a courtyard that was used for Company business, while the tenants in the Hall had to agree to the Company using some or all of the rooms for its meetings and dinners. Doubtless some resented this more than others. Edward Davis, for example, a difficult and querulous man with whom the Company had a trying relationship throughout the period of his tenancy at the Hall (1743 to 1788), was probably more of a private man than Dr Hulse, who presumably welcomed patients to the Hall. Mary Bashford, who lived at 2 Masons' Alley until 1727-8, used the tenement as a schoolhouse – it was her request that a door be opened from the yard into her parlour so that her scholars could enter more easily – while Elizabeth Sharpe, the tenant from 1757 to 1760, ran a lodging-house. Daniel Gossett, a warehouseman who paid £45 annually between 1790 and 1803 to rent the Hall, hosted public sales at which it was not unusual for some of his goods to be 'pilfred'. Gossett filled the Hall with so much of his stock that the Company had to write to him in 1799 with a request that he tidy up and take better care of the property. In 1827 the Court gave serious consideration to letting the Hall to Frederick Geswick, a weaver, who wanted to install looms at which 100 men might work. Just over 10 years after that, the Hall was converted into a tavern.[32]

In 1836, John Baily and his wife Elizabeth took a lease on the Hall for £75 rent. Shortly thereafter, they turned it into a public house called *Masons' Hall Tavern*. In 1840, they also took 2 Masons' Alley for £20, and the 1841 census records John, described as a tavern keeper, and his wife Elizabeth living with four servants at the tavern. Baily and the Company appear to have had a good relationship. The Company became accustomed to dining in one of the rooms at *Masons' Hall Tavern*, and many of Baily's bills and receipts survive. In 1843-4, the Company spent £92 11s. od. on four dinners, more or less equal to the amount which they received from Baily in rent. Essentially, by this arrangement the Company paid nothing for their dinners, and Baily paid nothing by way of rent. In 1843, Baily joined the Company, and at his admission he donated 10 guineas to be distributed among the Company's pensioners. By this time, Baily had already drawn up plans to take down 2 Masons' Alley and the service rooms on the western side of the premises, in order to make 'one spacious and convenient Building', but he appears to have died before work began. His widow, Elizabeth, took the business on, until in 1853 she assigned the lease to Charles Hicks. who became the licensee of the tavern. The Company continued to dine at the tavern, and in 1854-5 they paid over £103 for four dinners, easily in excess of the net rent, which was just under £90. In 1855, Hicks also took 4 Masons' Alley on a lease for £40, and he then drew up plans for substantial changes at the premises. Among other things, he wanted to install a glazed, iron roof over the upper rooms used as a billiard room, to convert the basement, or cellars, into a kitchen, and to knock through between 2 Masons' Alley and the Hall. These plans were all agreed, but they were soon waylaid by another project.[33]

In August 1858, the year which became famous as 'the year of the Great Stink' in London, and following intermittent cholera outbreaks, an enabling act was passed allowing the Metropolitan Board of Works to begin constructing the great sewerage system devised by Joseph Bazalgette. In June of the same year, however, the City of London's Commissioners of Sewers had already contacted Christ's Hospital to purchase compulsorily the freehold of 4 Masons' Alley and the passage to the courtyard in order to carry out improvements in Masons' Alley. Christ's Hospital had little choice but to agree:

they sold the freehold for £640 and the Company surrendered its lease to the Commissioners for £200. The work must have been completed quite quickly, because in October the Company opened negotiations with the Commissioners to buy the freehold of the site, only to discover that Hicks had already agreed a lease on the plot of 4 Masons' Alley. Both Hicks and the Company appear to have accepted that it was an embarrassing mix-up, and the Company settled for a new lease from the Commissioners on the passageway only.[34]

In 1860, however, the Commissioners put both freeholds up for sale and the Company bought them for a total of £1,560. The purchase was financed by selling some of the Company's stock and the taking of a mortgage of £700 at 4 per cent, the capital of which was quickly reduced by sealing a new lease with Hicks with a £300 premium and an annual rent of £150, along with the receipt of almost £175 as a dividend from the Ulster plantations. Thus, from 1860, there was just one freeholder for the entire premises: the Masons' Company. There was, too, just one leaseholder, Charles Hicks. Hicks held a lease on all the buildings on the premises, apart from the court room which was reserved for the use of the Company. *Masons' Hall Tavern* was a substantial tavern, restaurant and hotel. In 1861, 12 of its staff – the manager, his wife and daughter, two waiters, a porter, three barmaids and three maids – all lived on site. It is quite possible that many others worked there as well.[35]

In 1865, Hicks sold the business for £7,500 and asked to assign the lease. At the same time the Company received a letter from a firm of solicitors, acting on behalf of an unnamed client – almost certainly the purchaser of Hicks's lease – asking if the Company would sell the freehold. A six-month process of offer and counter-offer followed until, on 18 December 1865, the Company accepted an offer of £9,000. It would take another year for the sale to complete – the delay was possibly a consequence of litigation between Hicks and the purchaser. But while the sale of the freehold dragged on, the Company made preparations to leave. In January 1866, the Court agreed that the Company's pensioners could collect their pensions at the Clerk's office in Lincoln's Inn so that they need not follow the itinerant Company; that the Clerk should take charge of the books, writing and plate; and that the Company's Surveyor, Alfred Gwilt, should look after the armorial escutcheons and flags. In that year, not one of the Company's meetings was held at the Hall. There

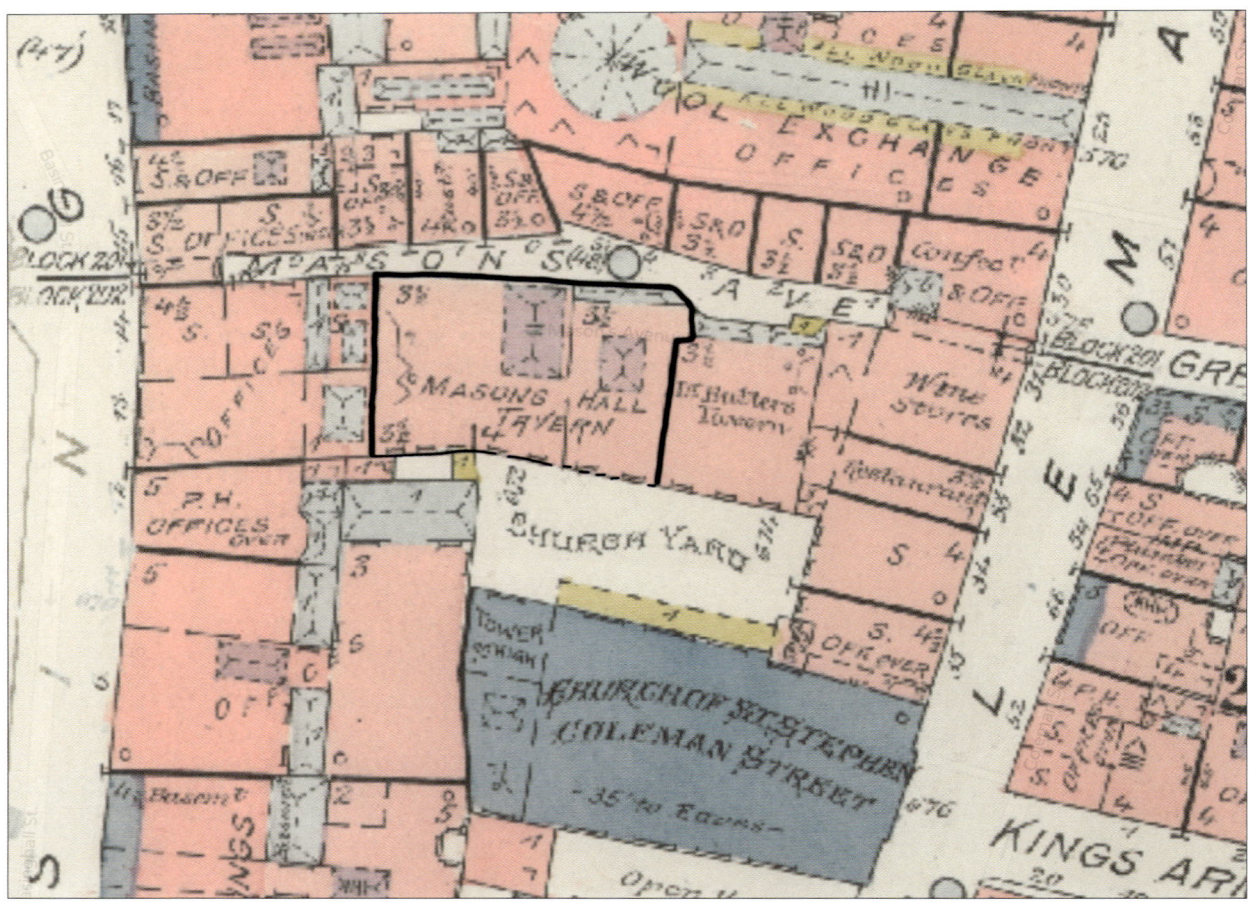

were four parties to the purchase, which was eventually completed in December 1866. The Company were obviously one. The buyers were Walter Federan Nokes, a gentleman of 8 Finch Lane in London; Masons' Hall Tavern Ltd.; and Isaac Moses Marsden, who appears both to have been something of a property investor in London and to have provided most, if not all of the capital. The premises remained in use as a tavern well into the 20th century.[36]

40 Map showing Masons' Hall Tavern in 1887 to help assess fire risk for insurers, produced by Charles E. Goad Ltd.

The Company's minutes never record exactly why the Court decided to surrender the historic premises. No doubt the sale was presented to a Court comprised of hard-headed, if possibly short-sighted, Victorian businessmen as making good commercial sense. £9,000, the sale price, was a lot of money in 1866 – especially when compared with the annual rent of £150 (£9,000 was 60 years' purchase) which the Company had been collecting. Certainly, better returns were achievable and the Company immediately sank £8,500 from the proceeds into Gordon Willoughby James Gyll's development of the manor of Wraysbury in Buckinghamshire, at 4.5 per cent return. This investment brought the Company an annual dividend of £620 – more than four times the amount they used to receive from letting the Hall.[37]

However, not all the increased income was invested. Frederick Gwatkin, the Clerk, saw his salary increase from £25 to £31 10s. and, in 1867 when he was granted the freedom and livery of the Company *ex gratia* as a reward for his long service, the Court noted 'particularly the good judgement and prudent conduct exhibited in carrying through the sale of this Company's property in their Hall'. The Beadle's pay went up by £2 to £12, and the pensions by £4 to £10.

The biggest winners, however, were the Assistants. Alfred Gwilt, who appears to have been on some form of commission for negotiating the sale, picked up a fee of £52 10s. The Court also resolved to set £300 aside each year for entertaining. In 1905, John Hunter even suggested in a letter that 'the chief object [of selling the hall] was to get a better dinner than the old joints and plum pudding'. Furthermore, if the Clerk and Beadle were to get pay rises of 26 and 20 per cent, then surely there was enough money to ensure that the Assistants were better rewarded too? Since 1861, just £5 had been divided among those who attended Court meetings punctually, so in January 1867 the Court resolved to double this to £12, and then in August 1869 to lift the amount to two guineas each. An Assistant who came to each of the seven meetings held in a year could expect to pick up 14 guineas for his trouble, and enjoy a much better repast than he had previously.[38]

The cost of the Court fees was hereafter a significant annual expense in the Company's accounts. In 1869-70, the £135 18s. paid in fees comfortably exceeded the £115 which was paid to the Company's pensioners. In 1887-8, by which time the size of the Court had increased following the legal judgment given against the Company in 1885 by Mr Justice Day, the £212 paid to the Assistants was almost double the £108 paid to the pensioners. In that same year, too, almost £280 was spent on entertaining, in addition to £86 which was paid for 43 gold £2 pieces to celebrate Queen Victoria's Golden Jubilee which were distributed to the Court and livery. In the interwar years, it was not unusual for the Court fees to account for one-third of the Company's total expenditure and sometimes they were the single largest expense recorded.[39]

It could be, and doubtless was, said that the sale of the premises made little fundamental difference to the conduct of the Company's business. Its affairs could be administered from the offices of Hunters in Lincoln's Inn Fields, and its records and plate were kept safely elsewhere. The Company had always used a variety of venues for their meetings and dinners, and they soon settled into a peripatetic routine. The favoured places in London, at least in the first few itinerant years after the sale, were the *City Terminus Hotel* at Cannon Street, the *Albion Tavern* in Aldersgate Street, and the *Ship and Turtle Tavern* in Leadenhall Street. The Court evidently decided that it was pleasanter to go out of town, or at least out of the City, for the summer Courts – these were held at the *Trafalgar Hotel* in Greenwich, *The Star and Garter Hotel* at Richmond, and even the *Rosherville Hotel* in Gravesend.[40]

Despite *Masons' Hall Tavern* remaining in use as a public house, the Court never returned there for its meetings. Why not? Although it was quite small – at 2,700 sq. ft. it was smaller than the investment property the Company owned at Bishopsgate – it is hard to believe it was too little for what was one of London's smaller companies. Perhaps it was simply not the best venue for the Company's meetings and dinners, or perhaps the Court was glad to shake the historic dust of Masons' Alley from off their modern feet.

There is little evidence in the Company's records that the Court looked back on the sale episode with any feelings of loss or regret. In October 1949, even when a sub-committee was formed to look into a proposal to build a hall which all the homeless livery companies (of which there were many more after the Second World War) might use, it recommended that the Masons' Company should decline to take part. Subsequently, it has been suggested that the Company might acquire a hall by taking over an existing building in the City (e.g. St Michael Paternoster Royal) or by sharing a site with another construction company, but none of these proposals has been seriously entertained by the Court. Today, Masons' Alley has become Masons Avenue,* and since 1980 a series of plaques have informed the passer-by that Masons' Hall once stood in that small lane, but otherwise no trace of the Hall survives on the site where once it stood.[41]

The fact is that by the late 18th century the Hall had largely ceased to function as the social heart of the Company; instead, it

41 *(right, inset) Present-day plaque in Masons Avenue on the site of the Hall that was sold after 400 years.*

42 *Present-day view along Masons Avenue with Guildhall at the end. Plaque affixed to modern building on left of picture.*

* According to the Corporation of London, the alley should be known as Mason's Avenue; according to the Royal Mail, it is Masons Avenue; according to The Worshipful Company of Masons, it should be known as Masons' Avenue!

ON THIS
SITE STOOD
THE HALL OF THE
WORSHIPFUL
COMPANY OF
MASONS

1463 - 1865

had become, primarily, a source of revenue. That being so, it could be seen as perfectly rational to sell it off and generate better returns elsewhere. But the question then becomes: is revenue maximisation the point of the Masons' Company? The liverymen of the later 19th and early 20th centuries seem to have been content to answer in the affirmative – with the proviso that the profits of their shrewdness should be deployed in supporting their corporate lifestyle. A later, more philanthropically-minded generation might disagree. In any case, there can be little doubt that when the Company sold the premises – its Hall, its home – then something which cannot be totted up on a balance sheet was lost.

9

THE IRISH VENTURE
AND THE ASSOCIATED COMPANIES

Today, the Masons' Company takes a rather equivocal view of its participation in the Ulster project. On its website and information sheets, it laments the 'failure' and 'poor investment returns of the scheme', but celebrates the relationship 'which had been built up over the centuries' with its associated companies and the 'important shared history that underpins a supportive fellowship'. In what follows, we shall see that there is good reason not to take either of these assumptions at face value.[1]

Over the course of three centuries, the Irish venture was, for the Masons' Company at least, a financial success. An initial contribution of £150, paid in instalments from 1610-16, provided the Company with an investment which realised a sum of £6,422 18s. 2d. once the final proceeds of the sale had been divided in 1909. Moreover, over the course of 200 years from 1710, the Company had received on that original investment of £150 an average annual dividend in excess of £60. By any measure, and even allowing for inflation, a return such as that would usually be counted a success.

As for the 'supportive fellowship', there is no doubt that it is vibrant and meaningful today, but there is rather less evidence that it was built up by centuries of close, fraternal association. Instead, for some 250 years the relationship between the companies was purely transactional, and it was only towards the very end of the companies' collective involvement in Ulster that it developed into something more communal and charitable.

THE EARLY PLANTATION, 1610-35

In September 1607, Hugh O'Neill and Rory O'Donnell, the earls of Tyrone and Tyrconnell, boarded a French ship off Rathmullan in

County Donegal. Both men were magnates in Ulster, a province which had long been the most Gaelic, Roman Catholic and lawless part of the British Isles. Fearful of arrest for rebellion, and accompanied by perhaps 90 followers, they fled into what became a permanent exile in Europe. As a result of this 'Flight of the Earls' an enormous area of land escheated to the Crown, and the way was opened for resettlement, or 'plantation', by English, Scottish, and above all Protestant tenant farmers.[2]

There was nothing particularly novel in this idea – in fact, the Crown had instituted plantations in Ireland before. Nor was it especially surprising that the City of London should have been approached to undertake the plantation project; the livery companies had often been called upon to supply the Crown with money or men, and this scheme, which promised the Londoners favourable trading privileges, found support among wealthy and influential members of the City's mercantile elite. Many liverymen, however, wanted nothing to do with a proposal which seemed to them dangerous, expensive and of little certain benefit to them personally. The Assistants of the Mercers' Company, for example, 'in all humility' returned a firm rebuff to the royal offer. In the end, however, it was clear that the Crown was not going to take no for an answer, and enough Londoners came to the conclusion that the wisest course was to agree the most advantageous terms that they could.[3]

Eventually, on 28 January 1610, the City of London and the Crown settled conditions for a plantation. The City covenanted to spend £20,000 on settling an area of more than 300,000 acres in a newly-formed county of Londonderry, and to build two new towns, at Derry and Coleraine, suitably fortified, which they could colonise. In return, the citizens were granted the woods and fisheries of the county, along with trading and admiralty privileges. To manage the plantation, the City established the Irish Society, effectively 'a Standing Committee of the Court of Common Council to which full authority to manage the affairs of the Plantation had been delegated'. The £20,000 investment was to be raised from a levy on 55 City companies, paid in four instalments of £5,000, with each company's contribution calculated according to the City's corn assessment. The Masons' Company was rated in that assessment at 25 quarters, which meant that it was called upon to pay £50, in four instalments of £12 10s. 0d.[4]

43 *Lord Mayor's precept demanding £50 from the Masons' Company in January 1610 [Note: until 1 January 1752 the calendar year commenced on 25 March; therefore the January 1609 date written on the document is now considered to be January 1610].*

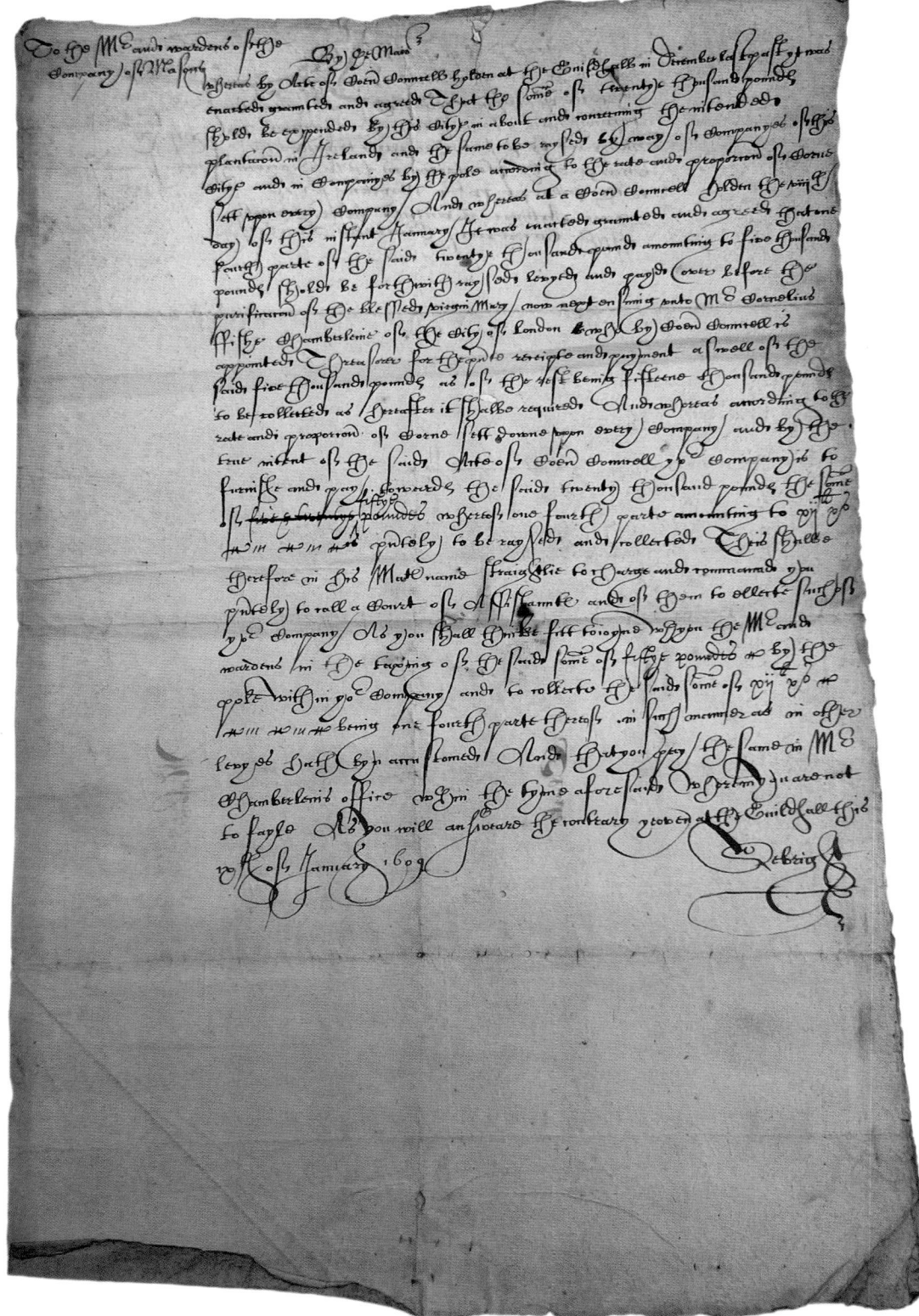

To raise the sums demanded, most companies taxed their members. There was, however, widespread reluctance to pay, and the money came in very slowly indeed. The Mayor and Aldermen issued threatening reminders, some companies were forced to borrow money to meet their obligations, and the Wardens of several companies were committed to prison for non-payment. We have no way of knowing how the Masons' Company collected its contributions, but a series of precepts and receipts kept in the Company's archive show that it made its payments, albeit sometimes late, between 1 March 1610 and 23 April 1611. By the latter date, however, it was clear that more money would be required from the Londoners and in July 1611 a demand for a further £10,000 was issued, to which the Masons had to contribute £25. Over the course of the next five years, an additional £30,000 was levied on the London companies, so that by 1616 they had paid a total of £60,000 to the Crown, of which the Masons' share was £150, or a quarter of 1 per cent of the final amount. This might seem very modest, but a score or so of the companies involved in the project contributed less than the Masons did – an indication of the contemporary Company's wealth relative to its peers.[5]

In March 1613, the Crown established the county and city of Londonderry by royal charter. The charter provided for the government of the city on a model very similar to that of London, and it incorporated the Irish Society. The new county comprised just over 500,000 acres (795 square miles). The Irish Society was granted about 30,000 acres of this total, essentially the two towns of Londonderry and Coleraine and their respective liberties, and it managed and controlled the undertaking on behalf of the City of London. It also collected certain monies, for example from rents in the new towns and from fishing rights on the county's rivers and lakes, which it divided among the companies by way of an annual dividend. There were other landholders in the newly chartered county: the Church of Ireland, Sir Thomas Phillips (a soldier, adventurer and military superintendent), and native Irish freeholders between them held some 188,000 acres. The remaining 290,000 acres, that is over 57 per cent of the county, was to be divided among the companies.

Clearly, it made no sense to carve the land into 55 or so 'proportions' and to grant tiny parcels of land to those companies, like the Masons' Company, which had contributed relatively small amounts to the venture.* Instead, it was decided in 1613 that the lands should be divided into 12 proportions, each of which would be assigned to an 'association' of companies. Each association was to be headed by one of the Great Twelve companies, and was supposed to have contributed 1/12th, more or less, of the total raised towards the venture so far. Some associations were not really associations at all. The Grocers and the Merchant Taylors, for example, had both contributed more than 1/12th of the sums raised, so they formed 'associations' entire of themselves, while other associations, for instance that headed by the Vintners' Company, comprised as many as nine companies. The Masons' Company were associated with the Mercers, the Cooks, the Broderers and the Innholders – although the last of these soon dropped out of the scheme. By 1616, when the companies had made their final payments to the Crown, this association had paid £4,903, or just under 1/12th of the £60,000 levied. The Masons' Company, with its contribution of £150, was easily the junior partner: the Mercers had contributed £3,920, the Innholders and the Cooks £300 each, and the Broderers £233.

On 17 December 1613, lands were allocated by lottery to each association. Each portion (see map) was given a number, and the numbers were drawn by the City's Swordbearer. The Drapers and Skinners were unfortunate enough to draw lands scattered across the south of the county, areas that were populated by hostile native Irish, while the Grocers, Goldsmiths and Fishmongers all did well, getting lands close to Lough Neagh and the river Foyle. The Mercers drew lot eight, one of the larger portions (21,600 acres or 33.5 square miles) which lay in the east of the county, and this portion along with some other small estates was finally conveyed to the Mercers and their associated companies by the Irish Society on 17 October 1618.

The four companies appear never to have constituted a formal body to settle and manage their estates; instead, this was a responsibility assumed solely by the Mercers' Company. Nor is there any evidence to suggest that the four companies ever drew up a written agreement to confirm how the profits of the venture were to be divided; rather, the junior partners trusted the Mercers to distribute proportionate dividends from the revenue of the estates. By a single, self-regarding elision, the scheme became known to the four companies' members as the Associated Companies, and in what follows that term is used to describe their collective participation and relationship.

* So termed; hereafter referred to as 'portions' or 'estates'.

As soon as they received their proportions, the other 11 associations immediately farmed them out to undertakers who agreed to pay them a fixed sum each year and to satisfy the companies' obligations to the Irish Society and to the Crown. The Mercers, however, for reasons which are far from clear, went a different way, and managed the Associated Companies' portion themselves, employing agents to collect rents, oversee building works, and generally to run the estates.[6]

44 *Map of the county of Londonderry depicting land allocated to the Great Twelve.*

The portion was bounded to the east by the river Bann, rich with salmon and eels. Here the land was fertile, there was a great deal of timber in the woods, and, while there were no towns or villages, there was a small settlement on the Bann at Movanagher. In addition, there was basalt and clay in abundance, both of which could be used with the plentiful timber in construction projects on the lands. Less happily, the estates yielded no minerals and very little quality building stone. There was some unproductive land – boggy or mountainous, and hitherto unsurveyed. The estates were divided in two geographically, with an Irish freehold, and some glebe and church properties, lying between the two parts.

It has been estimated that in this first period of the Ulster plantation, some £3,000 was spent on buildings on this portion. The hamlet at Movanagher was fortified and a mill was built there, and some British freeholders and tenants were established on the land. But there is every reason to think that some of the Associated Companies' agents were dishonest men who profited from rack-renting tenants. Strategically, the fort at Movanagher, at the very easternmost boundary of the portion, protected only the fisheries, the woodlands and the ford by and across the river Bann; in no way did it command the estates as a whole. There was no church at Movanagher, and its mill appears to have been inefficient. Some woods were over-exploited for their timber, while others provided shelter for hostile natives.

The biggest problem was that there were never enough British settlers. In the late 1620s, there were perhaps three- or four-score of settlers on the Associated Companies' portion, easily a minority of the population. This was mirrored across County Londonderry. A royal inquiry in 1627-8 found that 1,412 able-bodied British men lived on the plantation, compared to 2,293 Irish – and that figure does not include the Irish who were resident on lands not owned by the Londoners. This was hardly surprising. By English

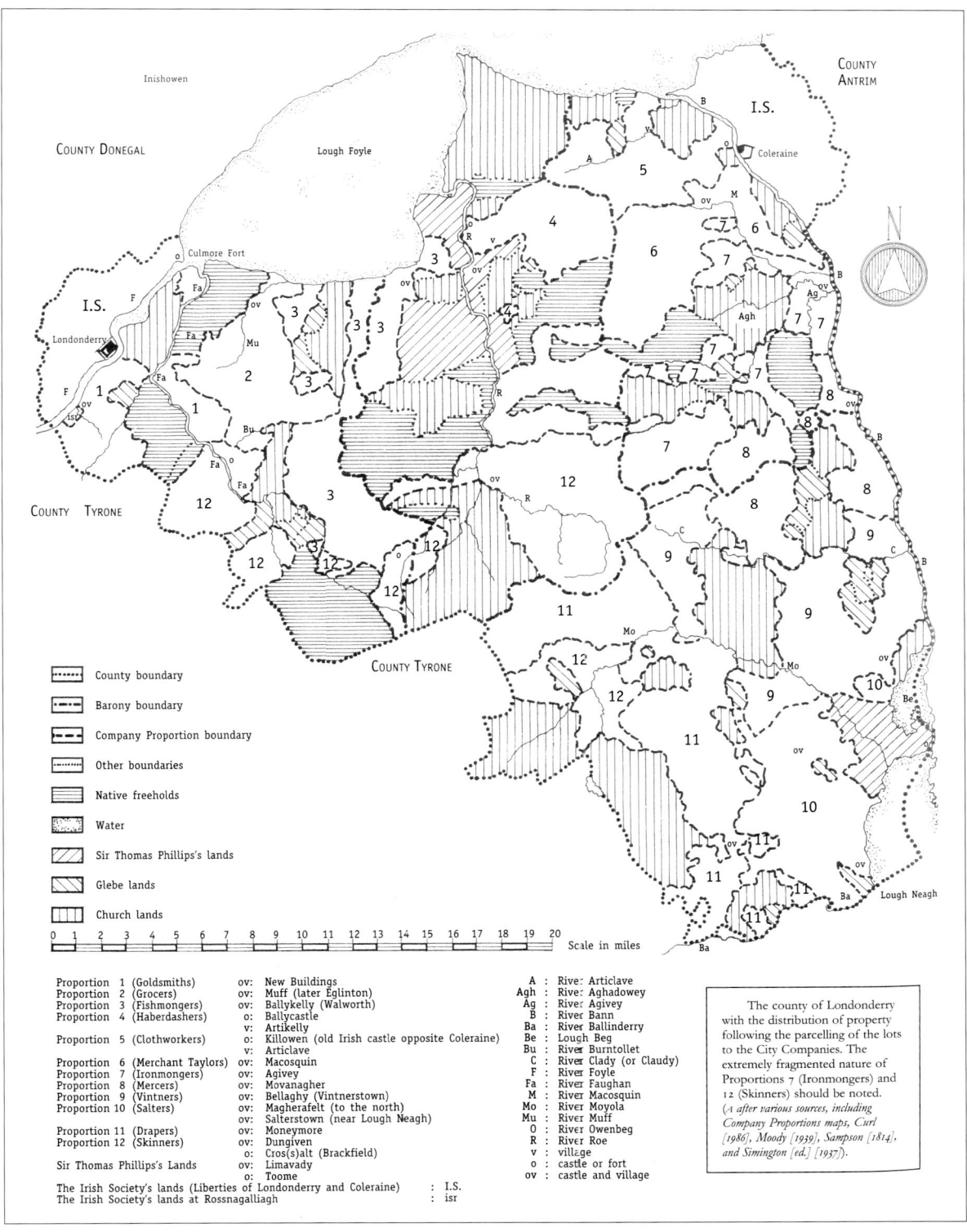

The county of Londonderry with the distribution of property following the parcelling of the lots to the City Companies. The extremely fragmented nature of Proportions 7 (Ironmongers) and 12 (Skinners) should be noted. (*A after various sources, including Company Proportions maps, Curl [1986], Moody [1939], Sampson [1814], and Simington [ed.] [1937]*).

County boundary
Barony boundary
Company Proportion boundary
Other boundaries
Native freeholds
Water
Sir Thomas Phillips's lands
Glebe lands
Church lands

Scale in miles
0 1 2 3 4 5 6 7 8 9 10 11 12 13 14 15 16 17 18 19 20

Proportion 1 (Goldsmiths)	ov: New Buildings	A :	River Articlave
Proportion 2 (Grocers)	ov: Muff (later Eglinton)	Agh :	River Aghadowey
Proportion 3 (Fishmongers)	ov: Ballykelly (Walworth)	Ag :	River Agivey
Proportion 4 (Haberdashers)	o: Ballycastle	B :	River Bann
	v: Artikelly	Ba :	River Ballinderry
Proportion 5 (Clothworkers)	o: Killowen (old Irish castle opposite Coleraine)	Be :	Lough Beg
	v: Articlave	Bu :	River Burntollet
Proportion 6 (Merchant Taylors)	ov: Macosquin	C :	River Clady (or Claudy)
Proportion 7 (Ironmongers)	ov: Agivey	F :	River Foyle
Proportion 8 (Mercers)	ov: Movanagher	Fa :	River Faughan
Proportion 9 (Vintners)	ov: Bellaghy (Vintnerstown)	M :	River Macosquin
Proportion 10 (Salters)	ov: Magherafelt (to the north)	Mo :	River Moyola
	ov: Salterstown (near Lough Neagh)	Mu :	River Muff
Proportion 11 (Drapers)	ov: Moneymore	O :	River Owenbeg
Proportion 12 (Skinners)	ov: Dungiven	R :	River Roe
	o: Cros(s)alt (Brackfield)	v :	village
Sir Thomas Phillips's Lands	ov: Limavady	o :	castle or fort
	o: Toome	ov :	castle and village
The Irish Society's lands (Liberties of Londonderry and Coleraine)		: I.S.	
The Irish Society's lands at Rossnagalliagh		: isr	

© *Professor James Stevens Curl.*

45 *The Buildings of the Company of Mercers at Movanagher, depicted by Raven in his map, c.1622.*

standards, Ulster was a wild province with primitive agriculture and industry – why would an English farmer choose to settle there? Hopes that large numbers of Londoners themselves would leave the overcrowded City to settle in Londonderry and Coleraine had been quickly dashed. Worse, those that did come from England and Scotland to settle often found themselves living, without sufficient arms or means of defence, in isolated farmsteads where they were vulnerable to attack.

All in all, the plantation was not a happy place. In Sister Diamond's words, 'the gulf between the old inhabitants and the newcomers was very wide – in origin, language, laws, religion. Fear and suspicion kept the two groups apart so that there was no real fusion or integration. The Irish were hostile and aggressive towards the settlers, and the latter, through lack of security, armed themselves against the native attack.'[7]

No doubt some unscrupulous agents and undertakers were profiting from the Ulster plantation, but there is little evidence that, at this stage at least, the companies or the Irish Society were. The Irish Society only began to make profits and pay a dividend in 1623, 10 years after it had been incorporated. The Masons' Company may have received some dividends before 1629, but this is far from clear. The Company's account book only records the first receipt of money from the Mercers' Company in 1629 and, between that payment and one in 1635, the Masons' Company received dividends totalling just under £43. It is not clear whether these sums represent the whole, or only a part, of the story between 1618 and 1663.[8]

The Crown repeatedly ordered surveys and inquiries to ascertain what was going wrong in the plantation. In truth, there was blame on all sides. At the very start of the business, the Crown had essentially compelled the Londoners to finance the plantation at a final cost three times higher than that originally agreed. It had been slow to grant title to the companies and the Irish Society, and it had not upheld its obligations to pay and provide for soldiers to defend the settlers. The companies for their parts had been reluctant participants and several had baled out at the earliest opportunity. Having laid out considerable sums of money for a plantation, in which they had little interest and expertise, most entrusted the running of their estates to untrustworthy undertakers and agents. Collectively, the companies and the Irish Society had failed to build enough houses, to undertake the necessary infrastructure projects, to attract anything like the number of settlers which they had agreed, or to displace the native Irish from the land.

For all these difficulties, however, there was, in the first half of the 1630s, a possibility, at least, that the venture could have produced worthwhile results. But the few successes of the plantation so far were about to be undone completely.

COLLAPSE, 1635-58

By 1630, the Crown had lost patience with the Londoners and an inquiry was commenced in the court of the Star Chamber into what was termed the 'utter ruin' of the Ulster plantation. This was the decade of King Charles I's 'personal rule', when he turned to every expedient to raise money without summoning a parliament, and the City knew that the king's primary motivations were pecuniary. It therefore offered increasing sums to bring the inquiry to an end – at first £20,000 and then £30,000. Crown pressure continued to mount, however, and in 1635 legal proceedings began against the City in Star Chamber. The judges, under pressure from the king, were only ever going to find against the City, and when the final judgment came, it was everything the Londoners would have feared. Found guilty of not adhering to the original articles of agreement, their lands in Ulster were to be surrendered to the Crown, their royal charter was to be cancelled, and they were to pay a monstrous fine of £70,000. Further negotiations bargained the fine down to £12,000, but the lands were lost and the Irish Society was dissolved.[9]

It seemed, then, that the Associated Companies' venture was over. Maybe some in the Masons' Company were glad to see the back of it. Certainly, in 1639, representatives of the Masons' Company agreed to deliver up the Associated Companies' title to the estates in Londonderry to the Crown 'if they may be freed by the Mercers' Company from all Taxes that shall come hereafter'. In 1640, however, Charles was forced to summon two parliaments and this provided the Londoners with a chance to seek redress. Accordingly, in January 1641, London's Common Council submitted a petition to the Long Parliament in which it claimed it had been unjustly treated in the Star Chamber. In August, the House of Commons declared that it agreed with the citizens and that they should have their properties in Londonderry restored to them. In late November, the king, now in a greatly weakened position, intimated that he was willing to restore the properties, but he was already in no position to do so. On 22/23 October, Catholic Ireland had risen in rebellion and by the time that Charles tried to woo the Londoners with promises of returning their lands, thousands of Protestants in Ireland had lost their lives and their homes. Most of County Londonderry fell to the rebels very quickly indeed. We have no idea how many settlers on the Associated Companies' estates were killed, but certainly some were, while the rest fled with thousands of other refugees to the towns of Londonderry and Coleraine.[10]

The atrocities perpetrated against their Protestant 'brethren' in Ireland enraged many in London, and in 1642 the companies 'most freely and with great alacrity' voted to supply Parliament with £100,000 for the 'relief and preservation of the kingdom of Ireland'. But the Irish troubles were quickly subsumed into the greater chaos of the civil wars, together known as the Wars of the Three Kingdoms, that engulfed England, Scotland and Ireland from 1639 to 1653. In these wars, Movanagher, the other settlements on what had been the Associated Companies' proportion, and pretty much everything else that had been built there was destroyed.

MIDDLEMEN, 1658-1831

Following Parliament's victory against the Crown, the Londoners sought either the restitution of their estates or compensation for their seizure. In March 1657, Cromwell's government reconstituted the Irish Society by charter, and one year later London's companies were put back in possession of their lands.[11]

Once bitten, however, the Mercers evidently decided that they had not the time nor inclination to deal with the troubled lands of Londonderry and, on 1 November 1658, they let the Associated Companies' portion on a 41-year lease to a certain Gervase Rose, for an entry fine of £500 and an annual rent of £300. After the restoration of Charles II, this lease was renewed in 1663 for a further 41 years on the same terms, and, at some point before 1688 (probably in 1670-1), the lease passed to the Jackson family of Coleraine who held it until its expiration in 1712.

The closing decades at the end of the 17th century were a difficult time for all London's companies. During this period, the Masons' Company had neither the capacity nor the will to pay much attention to their estates in Ireland. Instead, they were happy, perhaps even relieved, simply to collect the rent from their lessee and their dividends from the Irish Society. This established a pattern that would hold for a period of 173 years, during which time the Associated Companies became absentee landlords of the type against which much resentment would be directed in the 19th century.

In 1663-4, the Masons' Company collected £51 10s. 0d from the Mercers' Company – its first dividend since 1635. This was a bumper payment, probably made up of monies paid by Rose since 1658 and a renewed entry fine in 1663, after deductions for costs incurred by the Mercers in regaining title and arranging the leases. Thereafter, for the next 25 years the Company received an annual dividend of between £10 and £14, apart from in 1666-7 when it collected £17 18s. 10d. The Company's record-keeping broke down at the end of the 1680s, but dividends continued to accrue more or less regularly. Indeed, the stability of these payments was to prove something of a godsend to the Company at a time of considerable financial stress. In the 1680s and 1690s the Company was able either to secure loans or mortgages on its revenues from Ireland, or to ringfence its dividends in order to satisfy its creditors. It is hardly an exaggeration to state that the revenues from the estates in Londonderry helped ensure the Company's survival.[12]

In 1712, with two years left of Jackson's lease, the Masons' Company appointed a committee to join with the Mercers' Company in arranging a new lease for the Company's estates. In 1714, John McMullan took a new lease, again for 41 years, for an entry fine of £6,000 and an annual rent of £420. McMullan was a speculator. He had borrowed the money he needed to take on the lease and he hoped to turn a profit by subletting land on the estate. He died two years after taking on the lease, with his accounts in chaos, and the lease passed to his financier, James Wilson, and then to Wilson's son. When this lease expired in 1755, a new lease was taken by Alexander Stewart of Newton, County Down, for a fine of £16,500 and an annual rent of £420. This was a 'lease for lives', that is to say that it was to run for the lives of three specified people, and the third life was that of another Alexander Stewart, his surviving second son, who died in 1831. Jackson, McMullan, Wilson and Stewart were Protestant gentry who saw landholding as a means to further their mercantile and political careers. Stewart was by far the most successful; he was already rich through his marriage to Mary Cowan, the daughter of a Londonderry alderman, and he sat as MP for Londonderry. His son and grandson were the first and second marquesses of Londonderry and holders of high political office. The Associated Companies' estates, however, passed not to Robert, the first marquess, but to his younger brother, Alexander.[13]

From 1714 to 1831 the Masons' Company received a dividend which varied from year to year, but which over the period averaged in excess of £16 a year. There were actually two components to the money that the Company received from the Mercers. The first was the Company's share of the rent from the Associated Companies' estates which, in theory at least, should have been the same each year (in reality, it seldom was); the second was the Company's share of the dividend paid by the Irish Society to all the companies for fishing rights and rents in the cities of Londonderry and Coleraine. But the arrangement was inflexible; the Associated Companies were due the same annual rent payment of £420 in 1815 as they had been in 1715. This meant, of course, that the Masons' Company saw no perceptible increase in their dividends over the course of the 18th century, despite the fact that, towards the end of his term, Stewart was collecting over £10,000 in rents on the estate.[14]

There were some positive developments on the Associated Companies' estates during this period when the lands were leased to middlemen. Whereas the companies had failed to attract enough settlers in the first 50 years of the plantation's existence, in the 50 years following, that is between 1660 and 1710, tens of thousands of Scots, mostly Presbyterians, came to settle on the cheap lands in Ulster. Kilrea, Maghera and Garvagh all matured as bustling market towns, and communications were improved across the estates. Following Acts of Parliament in 1696 and 1704, linen production increased across Ulster, with industrious Huguenots (French Protestant refugees) very much involved in this process, and linen mills were established on the Associated Companies' lands in the middle of the 18th century by Alexander Clark and Sons at Upperlands and John McKinney at Moneygran. The Associated Companies occasionally sponsored charitable efforts on their lands, too.[15]

For the most part, however, conditions on the Associated Companies' estates during this time were far from prosperous. Penal laws which prohibited Roman Catholics from owning land or taking long leases as tenants created a cycle of deepening poverty among the Irish peasantry, who yet clung desperately to what they considered to be their ancestral lands. The recently-arrived Scottish Presbyterians did not have the same attachment to the land, however, and, being subject to many disabilities themselves and resentful of their obligations to pay tithes to the established Church, they began to leave, in droves, for the American colonies during the second decade of the 18th century, thereby draining the province of some of its most energetic inhabitants.

The Associated Companies were not really much interested in the state of Ulster. They drove the hardest bargains they could with Rose, McMullan and Stewart who, in turn, had to exploit the estates harder and harder to recoup their investments. The obvious consequence of agreeing long leases to middlemen with high entry fines was that there was little incentive for anyone to invest in or improve the land on the estates; the Stewarts proved to be the worst landlords of the lot. When they agreed their lease with the Mercers' Company with its enormous entry fine, the Mercers, who were at that time under great pressure following the Annuity Scheme disaster,* had no wish to complicate negotiations by insisting on onerous covenants to improve the Associated Companies' estates. Instead, they confined their involvement to extracting their profits from Ireland and using them to maintain their concerns in London.

* A failed, high-risk life assurance scheme.

As a result, it can fairly be said that, in the early 19th century, some tenants on the Associated Companies' estates lived lives as wretched and miserable as those of serfs in imperial Russia.

ENLIGHTENED LANDLORDISM, 1831-1909

From 1780 onwards, the penal laws were gradually eased and voices began to be raised urging reform of social conditions, if only in the interest of political tranquillity. In the first decades of the 19th century, the Mercers' Company 'listen[ed], with mounting impatience, to the depressing accounts of the condition of its property', and as soon as the last Stewart lessee died, the Mercers took the Associated Companies' estates back under direct control. There was clearly much to do but the Mercers set about the task with an energy and compassion that had been absent for the previous 200 years. They sent deputations to County Londonderry to survey and report on the estates, and they appointed a succession of competent resident agents, with a remit to be neutral in matters of religion and politics in their dealings with the tenants.[16]

In theory, the rents on the estates were worth some £10,000 a year, but there were arrears of twice that amount, which shows just how hard the tenants had been driven. Within the space of a few years the Mercers' Company had reduced rents across the estate by 19 per cent, to some £8,500 a year, and bought the arrears for £12,000, thereby relieving their tenants of £8,000 worth of debt, that is about one year's rent, and protecting them from harassment by Stewart's heirs. A review of the rental value in 1855 saw rents rise to just over £10,000, but this was still less than Stewart had been extracting from the estate a generation before, and in 1876 they increased again to just over £12,000.

On the other side of the ledger, between 1831 and 1873, £215,168 was spent either on improving or on administering the Associated Companies' lands, that is some 55 per cent of the £388,658 revenues in the same period. Schools, dispensaries and churches were built, planting and drainage schemes were implemented, new and improved roads, houses and public buildings were constructed. Benevolent landlordism such as this could not avert the catastrophe of the famine of 1845-52, or counter-balance the deeply-rooted Irish practice of divisible inheritance, but at least there is little evidence of political discontent on the Associated Companies' estates in the later 19th century, which may suggest that landlord and tenant relations were fairly amicable.

The period of direct control was also transformative for the Associated Companies back in London. From 1832 to 1909 the Masons received a little over £10,000 in dividends at an average of £130 a year – a significant sum of money for a small company. By 1880, the Company's annual pension bill was £129, so we might say that this was effectively financed by dividends received from the Londonderry estates. The most significant development in these years, however, was the slow emergence of a good-natured fellowship between the four Associated Companies. In 1872, the Assistants of the Masons' Company invited the Masters of the Mercers, Cooks and Broderers to join them at one of their dinners in the ensuing year, and this appears to have started an arrangement whereby the Masters of those companies would dine with the Masons' Company at the Court's Midsummer Dinner. Over the course of time the nature of this dinner evolved and in the first decade of the 20th century it assumed the form it has today.[17]

As well as dining in fellowship, the association has been celebrated in gift-giving. In 1883, the Cooks' Company sent the Masons a china plaque – now unfortunately lost – marking the 400th anniversary of their incorporation, and in 1911 Christopher Holford sent the Masons a copy of his book *A Chat About the Broderers' Company*, for which he was thanked and sent a copy of Edward Conder's *Hole Crafte* by return. The winding-up of the Associated Companies venture in County Londonderry was marked by the exchange of silver cups between the companies, and in their winding-up statement, the Mercers welcomed their 'esteemed partners in the Irish Estates' to Mercers' Hall, expressing their 'fervent hope' that 'the traditional friendship of nearly three hundred years of the Associated Companies may in no wise be impaired', and they looked forward to remaining associated with the Cooks, the Broderers, and the Masons in 'ties of everlasting friendship'. In 1910, the Masons' Company's Assistants resolved to engrave the cup they had received from the Mercers' Company with the words of the Mercers' Clerk which had accompanied the gift, namely that 'my Court hope that this Cup may be accepted as a small memento of the partnership which lasted in uninterrupted harmony for nearly three centuries, and as an omen of a still more durable friendship in the future'.[18]

THE LEGACIES OF THE VENTURE

For a period of 300 years, the Associated Companies' venture was of only marginal importance in the history of the Masons' Company, and the records of occasional administrative episodes show that the Masons had little interest in, and made little impact on, the processes of collective decision-making. The Mercers' decision in December 1831 to take the estate back under direct management was made without consulting their Associated Companies beforehand. In 1904, after the Mercers' Company had let the Masons know that it was considering a sale of the estates, the Masons' Assistants once more resolved 'that the Company leave itself in the hands of the Mercers Company with regard to a sale'. Two years later, the Court similarly resolved 'to leave the Mercers' Company to carry out the sales and receive the entire purchase moneys'.[19]

There is no evidence to suggest that anyone from the Masons' Company ever visited the Associated Companies' proportion in County Londonderry, in an official capacity at least, before Charles Emmerson travelled to the province in 1952, in which year he

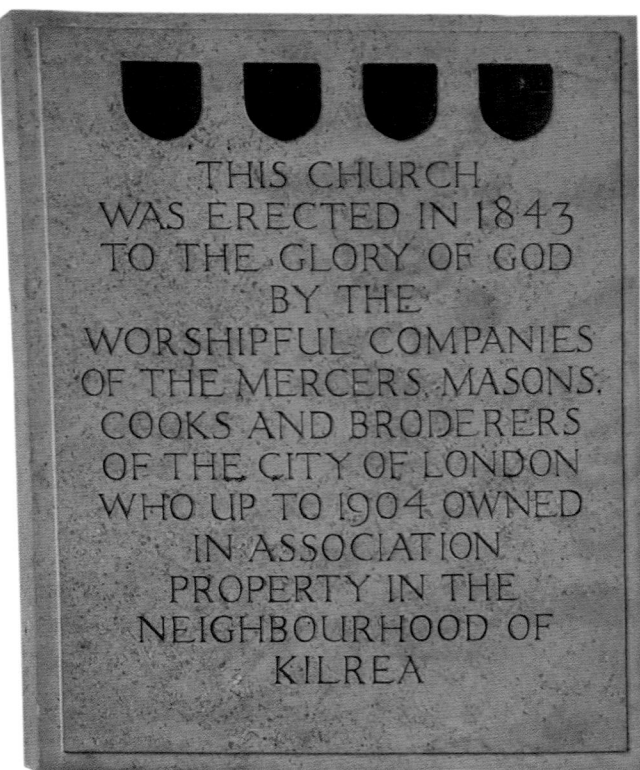

46 *Tablet in St Patrick's Church, Kilrea, acknowledging the construction of the church and incorporating the coats of arms of the four Associated Companies.*

represented the Company at the unveiling of a memorial tablet commemorating the Associated Companies' involvement in the rebuilding of the parish church of St Patrick's in Kilrea some 100 years previously.[20]

Change began to occur at the end of the 19th century, when the Associated Companies began to socialise together and to exchange gifts. These two traditions have been built on ever since. In 1958, the Masons' Company gave the Mercers a wooden Master's chair and a stone font for their rebuilt hall, while in 1994 they presented them with a stone plaque to mark their 600th anniversary. The Livery

47 *The chapel font, commemorative plaque and the Master's chair presented by the Masons to the Mercers.*

Dinner with the Associated Companies is now one of the Company's two annual formal functions.[21]

Over the course of the 20th century, close connections developed in other ways, too. From 1930, the Broderers began to hold their banquets at Mercers' Hall, while 10 years later the Masons' Company began to use Mercers' Hall for its Court meetings. Mercers' Hall was largely destroyed by enemy action on 10/11 May 1941, but the Masons' Assistants were able to meet there again in 1942. The Hall was formally reopened in 1958 after it had been rebuilt and since that time the Masons' Company has used it for its Court meetings, Common Hall, some committee meetings and storage. One reason why the Masons' Company has been so uninterested in acquiring a Hall of its own in recent decades is that the Court is satisfied with the current arrangements at Mercers' Hall and of the Company's 'special relationship' with the Mercers. In 2000, the Masons and Cooks held a joint carol service at Christmas; the Broderers have since joined in the celebration, and now each company takes a turn hosting the event triennially. Members of the Mercers' Company have attended from time to time. In 2002, for example, at the joint carol service held at St Helen's Bishopsgate, the Master Mason, Peter Johnson, laid a wreath on the tomb of William Kerwin, while the Master Mercer laid a wreath on the tomb of Thomas Gresham.[22]

Despite the troubled history of the Ulster plantation, there was even a joint commercial enterprise in the post-war years. In 1948, the Mercers wrote to their Associated Companies inviting them to take shares in a new venture in what was then Southern Rhodesia, now Zimbabwe. At that time, the economy of Southern Rhodesia was experiencing something of a post-war boom, attracting investors and immigrants alike, and the proposal was to farm cattle and tobacco on an area of land measuring some 90,000 acres, that is about four-and-a-half times the size of the former proportion in Londonderry. The Masons' Company's Assistants were very keen to participate, giving their unanimous approval to the immediate suspension of any standing orders which prevented them from committing to the project forthwith, and expressing their hope that the other Associated Companies would be similarly enthusiastic. As it turned out they were, and all four companies duly invested in the Charter Estate Co. Ltd. The Mercers' Company subscribed to £80,000 in debentures and £8,500 in equity shares, while each junior company took £500 worth of equity shares.

By 1962, the Masons' Company had yet to receive a penny in income and the Mercers' Company wrote offering to repay the Masons' Company its original investment of £500. Having discussed the matter, the Court replied to the Mercers in suitably loyal terms that 'notwithstanding the fact that no income had been received from the investment for the last past ten years, the Company wished to remain in association with the Mercers' Company over the Charter Estates investment no matter what difficulties the Company might encounter.' In the end, the venture limped along for a further 20 years, making no money whatsoever for the Associated Companies, until it was sold for £50,000 in 1981, which should have led to the Masons' Company recovering £2,500. However, with Robert Mugabe in power there was little chance of the money ever leaving Zimbabwe and a year or two later the Masons' Company Assistants were discussing first, whether they could sell the cash to Oxfam at a discount to use for charitable purposes in Zimbabwe, or, second, whether the Company should simply donate the money to charity there. In the end, the Associated Companies did agree to use the money for charitable purposes, the money was distributed and the venture brought to a close between 1986 and 1989.[23]

In contrast to this commercial enterprise, the Associated Companies have shown a willingness in recent years to engage in charitable endeavour independent of any property interests, such as the Bishop of London's church appeal in 1946, or appeals from the Lord Mayor in 1950 and 1956.[24]

In 1988, after much discussion between the Companies, it was agreed to go even further and launch a common charitable enterprise which would be known as the Joint Venture Scheme. Each company agreed to contribute an annual sum to the Scheme: the Mercers £5,000, the Cooks £3,000 and the Broderers and Masons £1,000 each, that is a total of £10,000. Every four years, each company would then receive £10,000 which it would be free to use in furtherance of its own charitable endeavours. The Scheme was well supported by the members of the Associated Companies, and in 2001-02 the decision was taken to increase each company's contributions by 50 per cent. For a relatively small organisation like the Masons' Company, the Joint Venture Scheme proved something of a blessing. In 2007, for example, having contributed a total of £4,500 over the course of the three preceding years, the Company received £15,000 which it paid into its craft fund to support students studying stonemasonry.[25]

Mercers

Masons

48 *An enduring association for more than 400 years: Mercers, Masons, Cooks and Broderers.*

Cooks

Broderers

49 *Richard Woodman-Bailey, Master Mason, and Neil Barnes, Chairman of the Charitable Trust, present a cheque for £20,000 to St Ethelburga's Centre.*

In late 2008 and early 2009, within the context of the 400th anniversary of the Associated Companies' inception, the Mercers' Company tabled proposals to develop the Joint Venture Scheme yet further, both by increasing each company's contributions, and also through support for the Gullion Link Project, which sought to promote peace in South Armagh and to widen the horizons of young people in Northern Ireland and East London, primarily through exchange visits. This Project was run by the St Ethelburga's Centre for Reconciliation and Peace, an organisation in London which, in turn, had a good relationship with the East London Mosque. The Project was discussed in detail by the four companies, after which they all committed their share of the Joint Venture funds to the Project. Richard Woodman-Bailey, Master Mason, and Neil Barnes, Chairman of the Company's Charitable Trust, presented a cheque for £20,000 to St Ethelburga's Centre on 2 March 2011. Later that year, five representatives of the Masons' Company (Ralph and Rosie French, Sarah Grundy, Allan Daire and John Crook) travelled to Northern Ireland to join other Associated Companies members in walking the 26-mile Ring of Gullion, a volcanic ring-dyke in South Armagh.[26]

Support for the Gullion Link Project may have been qualified across all four companies, and the Joint Venture Scheme has since returned to its original form, but there can be no doubt that on the 400th anniversary of the formation of the Associated Companies, and on the 100th anniversary of their withdrawal from their Irish estates, in committing to support a multi-year project in Northern Ireland to the tune of £80,000, the four Associated Companies had come a long way indeed.

10

TURBULENCE

On Tuesday 4 September 1666, a fire which had been raging in London since Saturday night reached Masons' Hall. Fortunately George Dowswell, Master of the Company in that year, had the good sense to get to the Hall before the Fire did. He was, thus, able to preserve 'the Companyes writings and goods'. But there was nothing he could have done to protect the Hall itself. Within a short space of time, Masons' Hall, only recently rebuilt at considerable expense, was reduced to a smoking ruin. Two days later, the Great Fire of London burned itself out. The damage wrought was scarcely conceivable. About 80 per cent of the area of the historic City had been destroyed; 44 livery company halls and 87 parish churches across London had been razed to the ground. St Paul's Cathedral and the Guildhall were devastated. Thousands of houses were no more. Dozens of companymen and their families must have been rendered homeless.[1]

For the Company, the loss of its Hall – and the associated rental income – was a catastrophe. But even while dismay was almost universal, there must have been a few sharp-witted, optimistic spirits who could discern opportunity in the disaster: London would have to be rebuilt, and the new City would be one of brick, stone and tile. There would be huge demand for materials, which could only benefit the quarry owners, merchants, and mason-contractors; the labour of both masters and journeymen would be in great demand. Even the dusty apprentices could look forward to enhanced opportunities. All of which promised much for the Company; more masons working in the City should translate to more admissions to the freedom and more apprentice bindings.

Perhaps, indeed, the Masons' Company, which nominated men for the position of City Viewer, from whose ranks the king's Master

50 *A depiction of the Great Fire of London, 1666.*

Mason was often chosen, and which policed the craft of masonry within the city's limits and suburbs, would play an important role in planning, administering and regulating the reconstruction?

REBUILDING THE CITY

On 8 February 1667, the king gave royal assent to two Acts which allowed the reconstruction of London to begin in April of that year. Although administrative complications, initial difficulties with the supply of money, and war with Holland meant that it was not until the spring of 1668 that reconstruction really got going, nevertheless the prevailing mood was one of keen determination – the City must be restored, and made better than before. In April 1670 another Rebuilding Act was passed, which increased the amount of money available for the work by raising the duty on coal arriving in London; it also increased, from 39 to 51, the number of parish churches which were to be rebuilt in the City. This was no mere genuflection to what might today be called 'the heritage of the past'. The churches were symbols of an ardent faith, vital expressions of the Londoners' hopes of salvation; they were also critically important as nodal points in the City's network of social solidarity. When, in June 1675, Thomas Strong laid the foundation stone of St Paul's Cathedral, he was, in a sense, setting the keystone of the whole structure of London's rebuilding, even though at that

time, work had yet to begin on more than half the City's parish churches.[2]

Seen in perspective, the speed and scale of the City's recovery was nothing short of astonishing. By 1672, most companies had a hall complete enough to allow for meetings and dinners, and by 1676, the City's secular public buildings were almost all complete. These were the buildings that demanded the greatest supply of stone. It was also clear, by 1676, that many of the medieval City's worst features had

been corrected. Londoners lived in better houses and moved around improved streets that allowed for safer circulation. Steps had been taken to prevent flooding and improve drainage. The City's markets had been moved to more suitable buildings, and the area around the Royal Exchange had been transformed so that it became a fitting mantle for the mercantile hub within.

51 St Paul's Cathedral, west front, etching, 1747.

The success of the rebuilding owed much to the facts of well-established supply chains and a large, existing pool of building workers. All the same, this was a building boom the like of which London had never seen before. We have already noted the opportunities which arose for the great mason contractors of the time; whether journeymen masons and those who relied on wages benefited as much is less clear. Skilled and unskilled construction workers poured into the City, and the greater supply of labour appears to have limited significant wage growth. That said, it is quite possible that stonemasons in and around London saw their annual incomes rise because of the greater availability of work.

Surprising as it may seem, this exuberant building boom was not matched by an equivalent surge in prosperity on the part of the Masons' Company. The critical fact which advanced the prosperity of individuals, great and small, in the building trade at this time, without affording corresponding benefit to their representative body the Masons' Company, was an officially authorised opening up of the labour market. The decision, born of emergency, to abandon the age-old system of regulation that had given the Masons' Company its origin and *raison d'être*, was given express sanction in chapter 16 of the First Rebuilding Act, which set out that all those working on the rebuilding of London – 'who are not Freemen of the said Citty shall for the space of seaven yeares next ensueing and for soe long time after as untill the said buildings shall be fully finished have and enjoy such and the same liberty of workeing and being sett to worke in the said building as the Freemen of the Citty of the same Trades and Professions have and ought to enjoy.'

Further, the Act declared that at the end of the seven-year term they were to 'have and enjoy the same Liberty to worke as Freemen of the said Citty for and dureing their naturall lives'. Simply put, this allowed any unfree workman, artificer or labourer to come to London and work on the same terms as a freeman of the City for seven years. At the end of that period, they were to receive the same privileges as freemen. For any workman considering a move to London, this was an enormous incentive. For the Company, however, it threatened ruin. What now was the point of joining the Masons' Company, with all the attendant costs and responsibilities, if one could work as a mason in London without taking up the freedom? This provision, which threw the construction labour market in London wide open to all-comers, had the potential to imperil the Company's very existence.

And yet, in the first instance, there was an increase in the numbers of those looking to join the Company. In the three years from March 1663 to March 1666, on average each year, the Company bound 20 young men as apprentices and admitted just over 10 men to the freedom. In the three years from March 1667 to March 1670, each year an average of over 51 young men were bound as apprentices and over 15 men were admitted to the freedom. The monies received from the admission fines and apprenticeship bindings, and thereafter other fines as the new freemen progressed through the Company's ranks, helped the Company to carry forward a credit balance of over £39 in 1668 and almost £84 in 1669. In 1669-70, the Company had a livery 40 strong; one year later, there were 59 liverymen in the Company's ranks; by 1673, there were 69. In 1670, the Company declared a (relatively) colossal credit balance of £358 17s. 0d.[3]

Even so, the growth in the Company's strength was not remotely proportionate to the scale of the building activity. The increase in the number of men admitted to the freedom of the Company in the three years on either side of the Fire, up from an average of 10 to 15, represented a mere fraction of those who came to the City looking for work. Similarly, while 43 apprentices were bound in 1667, only 18 ended up becoming freemen of the Company. This actually represented a worsening wastage rate.[4]

The Company's role as a regulator of qualifications in the craft of masonry was also coming under threat. In theory at least, apprenticeship was one area where the construction companies could still flex their muscles; while the Rebuilding Act had removed the companies' power to compel masters and journeymen to become Company members, it was still the case that anyone working in London had to have completed an apprenticeship. In 1670, in support of this, the Masons' Company joined the Carpenters, Bricklayers, Joiners and Plaisterers in a petition addressed to the Lord Mayor and Aldermen, in which they sought remedy to prevent foreigners who had not completed apprenticeships from working in London. This petition appears to have had no effect.[5]

The Company was side-lined in another way also. By early October 1666, six Commissioners had been appointed to oversee the rebuilding of London, but there was no role for the construction companies in this commission, and the king did not even appoint his Master Mason, Edward Marshall, as a Commissioner. None of the City Viewers were invited to serve. The improvement in the Company's financial position was, similarly, less real than it seemed: the huge credit balance of over £358 in March 1670 was a result of the loan of £500 which Past Master George Dowswell had advanced to the Company to go towards the costs of rebuilding the Hall.[6]

With the wisdom of hindsight, therefore, we can see that the Company's ability to attract members, to regulate its craft and to sustain solvency were all under long-term threat. Yet this was not especially apparent at the time; the decision to press on quickly with the reconstruction of Masons' Hall suggests that the Court, at least, felt confidence in the Company's future. The livery showed their commitment to the Company by subscribing to the costs of rebuilding, and no doubt their optimism was bolstered by the prospect of rental income from a rebuilt Hall. But there was a growing risk that the Company might over-extend itself. In the years before the Fire, borrowed money had already been needed in order to balance the books; after the Fire, the interest charges on loans, particularly the two made by Dowswell, spiralled out of control, to absorb well over a quarter of the Company's income. It is not clear how seriously this imbalance was taken at the time; speculation was the mode of the age, and the workings of a credit system were only partially understood.[7]

As a first response, fees and fines were raised across the board. But such increases hardly made membership, now clearly a voluntary affair, a more attractive proposition. Another option open to the Court was consolidation of the debt, and in May 1676, the Company entered into an agreement to that effect with Anthony Light, a citizen and dyer of London, and his wife Anne. Light agreed to lend the Company £800 in return for 22 annual payments of £80 (a total of £1,760), secured on the 'lately new built' Company Hall. In effect, Light bought a handsome annuity. Meeting the cost of Light's annuity would cause the Company considerable trouble in the years to come.[8]

INCORPORATION

On 17 December 1677, King Charles II issued letters patent in which he 'Willed, Ordeyned, Constituted, Declared and Granted' that the Masons' Company 'shall bee one Body Incorporate and politique in Deed and in name by the name of Master, Wardens, Assistants and Comminalty of the Art or Mistery of Masons of the Cittie of London.' This was a momentous occasion in the Company's history. The newly corporate body received a large document known as an engrossment of the charter, decorated with the monarch's portrait

52 *Demise of Masons' Hall to Anthony Light on 9 May 1676.*

and heraldic devices, to the bottom of which was appended the royal seal. This original engrossment has since been lost, but two copies of the charter do survive. The first, known as the enrolled copy, is now to be found at The National Archives at Kew. The second was made by the Company in a book which is kept among the Company's records at the Guildhall Library. Another charter was issued by James II in February 1686, and subsequently nullified, with others, in the course of James's political power-manoeuvres in October 1688; the engrossed copy of this charter is also lost, although it, too, survives in an enrolled version and in a copy made by the Company, this time in the mid-19th century. Finally, in June 1702, Ephraim Beauchamp, at the end of his year as Master, negotiated a third charter from the recently enthroned Queen Anne. One of the engrossed copies either of Charles's or James's charter had by then been 'by misfortune burnt', so great care was taken to look after the copy of Anne's charter, and it survives to this day in the Company's archive.⁹

Substantial expenses were incurred by the Company in procuring these charters – more than £300 in 1677, perhaps £175 in 1686, and £20 in 1702.* A further loan was negotiated with Anthony Light in 1678, and rounds of subscriptions were taken from members. Incorporation was an expensive business, but it was evidently one that the contemporary Assistants and liverymen deemed worthwhile, for under the terms of its charter the Masons' Company became 'able and capable in law to have, take, purchase, hold, receive, possess and enjoy' properties, rents, franchises and privileges. The Company was also constituted as a body which could 'plead and bee impleaded, answer and bee answered, defend and bee defended in any Courts or places whatsoever'. The Company now had 'the immortal collective personality of a corporation'.¹⁰

The Masons' Company had existed, more or less happily, as an unincorporated association in some form or other for over three hundred years; why, then, did the Company seek incorporation when it did?

It can certainly have been no coincidence that the Master in 1677-8 was Joshua Marshall, son of Edward. Marshall was a successful mason contractor and sculptor who was responsible for the Temple Bar (one of the treasures of today's City, and recently restored with

---

* The fee of £13 6s. 8d. (20 marks) recorded on the copies of the 1677 charter was probably paid to the Chancellor rather than to the king.

help from the modern Company), the Monument to the Great Fire, six of Wren's churches and a great deal of the work at St Paul's Cathedral. He was also, from 1673 until his death in April 1678,

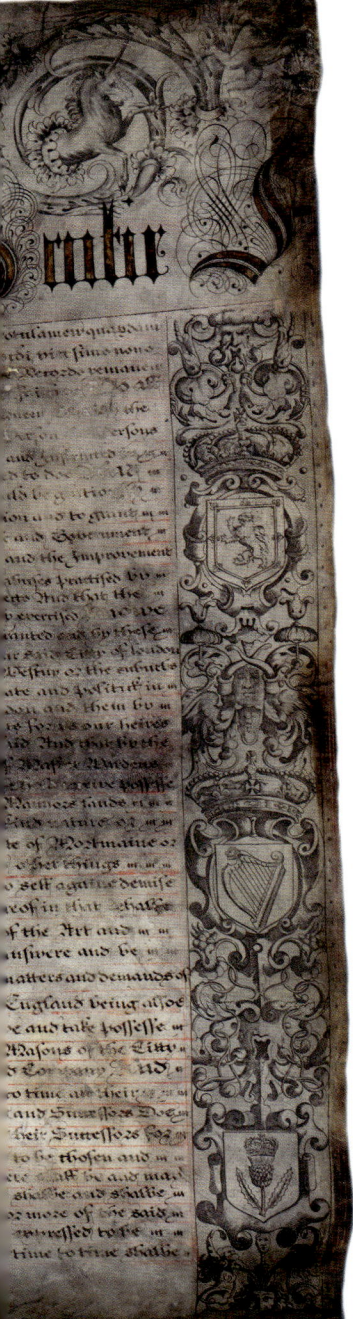

53 *Exemplification by Queen Anne of the 1677 Charter of Incorporation of the Masons' Company (5 June 1702).*

the king's Master Mason. There can have been very few livery company masters who had the access to the king that Marshall did.[11]

Marshall's privileged position, however, was not in itself sufficient cause for the move to incorporate. In fact, the Company had already begun to take steps to obtain a charter in the years preceding the Great Fire. Between 1663 and 1666, Sergeant Brome was paid £1 for providing advice about a charter, and a Mr Burke was paid £5 for his 'pains' touching the matter. If anything, rather than accelerating the process of incorporation, the Fire brought something of a halt to the preparatory work, and the Company only restarted the process in 1674-5.[12]

Incorporation may have been seen as a response to the difficulties which the Company was facing; over the course of 100 or so years, the remorseless expansion of London, coupled with economic and legal developments, had left the Company unsure of its position within the City. A royal charter might allow it to confirm and to consolidate its privileges and its jurisdiction. On the other hand, the move to incorporation may have been prompted by legal fashion, and the emergence of new and complex theories about social organisation – comparable, in their way, to the ideas that had begun to circulate about the capacities of financial credit systems.

The Company's by-laws were eventually agreed in 1678, with no little trouble, after their submission to the Mayor and Aldermen of London, as well as to the Lord Chancellor and the Chief Justices of the Courts of King's Bench and Common Pleas. The provisions in the charter and the articles in the by-laws can be divided into two broad categories. The first category dealt with the regulation of the craft of masonry in London. Under their terms, the Company's authority over the craft 'within our Cittyes of London and Westminster or the Suburbs of the same Cittyes or Seaven Miles Compasse of the same on every side thereof' was confirmed and established, with particular reference to

the necessity of qualification by apprenticeship. The Company's right to carry out the search was endorsed and the by-laws detailed how it was to be performed.[13]

In reality, however, the Company's authority over the practice of its craft was neither genuinely strengthened nor expanded in scope. The extension of the bounds of the Company's authority simply created a far larger area of jurisdiction, one that it could not hope to police effectively. Moreover, what the Crown gave with one hand, by extending the Company's jurisdiction, it took away with the other, by insisting that the Company's regulation of the craft was not 'to extend to the prejudice, obstruction or hindrance of the erecting, building and Finishing of our cathedrall church of Saint Paul within our Cittie of London, or any other Church within the same Citty which were formerly burnt downe by the late dreadfull Fyre'. This single provision hamstrung the Company's power to act on more than 50 of the largest building sites in London.

Moreover, regardless of the royal charter and the by-laws, the Company's search had already become ineffective. The Company may have hoped that its charter would augment its authority in this respect, and at the third Court meeting after the receipt of the charter, held on 22 March 1678, the Court actually invoked the charter when it agreed to send out the search, which was performed on 16, 17 and 22 April. These searches yielded 9s. 8d., along with a few small sums for arrears of quarterage. The search also failed to induce unfree masons to join the Company. On 23 April 1678, 27 foreign masons appeared before the Court and,

54 *Monument to the Great Fire of 1666, built by Joshua Marshall between 1671 and 1677.*

supposedly, asked to be 'admitted and sworne members as by the Charter is directed'.* These would seem to have been words put into their mouths by the Court Assistants, however, for not one of the 27 ever actually took up membership of the Company.[14]

The Company continued to send out the search, intermittently, until 1704, and it did from time to time yield modest amounts of money. But there is no evidence that the charter increased the effectiveness of these operations, and when, in October 1719, the Masons' Company sought the opinion of counsel on the matter, his advice was clear: those masons who worked within the bounds defined in the charter, and who were not members of the Company, were 'not subject to the View or Search of the Company unless They do voluntarily submit thereunto'. It was equally clear, long before counsel's opinion, that the Company's authority hardly prevailed even over its own members; attempts to collect arrears of quarterage met with little obvious success, and the Company's regulations regarding apprenticeship were also more honoured in the breach than the observance.[15]

* Foreign masons were those who had completed a term of seven years working in the City under the terms of the Rebuilding Acts and then joined the Company. They paid a lower fee than those joining by redemption, GL MS 5305/2, 14 Jun. 1687; By-laws, c. 31; GL MS 5304/1, 89v-90r, 94v.

55 *Company seal from 1678, shown on a 1690s document.*

The second category of provisions and articles re-established and redefined the Company's constitution. As a corporation with a legal personality, the Company gained the right to 'have a Common Seale to serve for the causes and buisnesses of the said Company'. Six weeks after the charter had passed the royal seal, the Company paid £2 15s. for two of its own seal matrices bearing the Company's coat of arms. It was to be governed by a Master and two Wardens who were to be chosen annually on 14 June and a court of 24 Assistants. The offices of Beadle and Clerk were instituted and the various oaths that all the officers and members were to take, and the manner in which they were to take them, were laid down. The fines, fees and charges associated with membership were set out, as was the detail of how and when courts were to be held.[16]

In truth, there was little here that was particularly novel. Much of this either confirmed existing practice or made minor changes to established procedure. Here and there, we do find something new. The Master, Wardens, Assistants, Clerk, Beadle, and other officers were all to swear defined oaths on taking up office, and all members had to take the oaths of allegiance and supremacy, in which each averred that the king was 'the only Supreame Governor of this Realm ... in Spirituall and Ecclesiasticall things or Causes as Temporall', and that no foreign prince or power had authority in England. Another development can be seen in article 22 of the by-laws, which required bonds of the Renter Warden.

In sum, the incorporation could hardly be described as a root-and-branch reconstruction of the Company; but it did provide a clearly-defined and well-ordered structure which supported the Company's good governance for the next 350 years.

Money Worries and the Age of Party

In April 1678, Joshua Marshall, the Master of the Company, died in office and was buried at St Dunstan-in-the-West, Fleet Street. In June 1680, Thomas Knight, who had only just finished his term as Renter Warden, died of a fever – he was buried at St Giles Cripplegate. At the time of their deaths, the Company was in debt to Marshall for £200 and to Knight for a sum probably in excess of £170. Both masons died wealthy men, and in their wills both generously remitted the sums owed to them. Knight attached no conditions to his bequest, Marshall asked that the Company 'doe yearely forever about the day of my death' pay £10 to poor widows of members of the Company.

Payments to widows of Marshall's gift began in 1679 and the names of the widows receiving money were recorded alongside those in receipt of Buckland's bequest. Forty years later, still making the payments Marshall had requested, the Company reconfirmed its recognition of his generosity.[17]

But Marshall and Knight were not the Company's only creditors. Over £321 had been borrowed to pay for the charter, and by 1680 just £28 of that had been repaid. £900 had been raised from Anthony Light, and while the first three payments of £80 were duly paid to him according to the terms of the annuity, in 1680 the Company failed to deliver. In that year, thanks to Knight's generosity, a loan dating from 1662 was finally discharged. The last debt connected with the rebuilding of the Hall, the repayment of a loan of £60 advanced by Thomas Place (Master 1675-6) in 1673, was not settled until 1693, after a suit in the Court of Chancery and much trouble.[18]

By 1680, it was clear that the Company's financial position was bad and getting worse, despite efforts to increase its revenue – in September 1679, for example, it elected 12 men to serve as Steward, at fines of £10 each, and it farmed out the profits of the search to William Hammond in return for an annual payment of £27. There is little evidence that any of these and other expedients was particularly effective, however; at least five of those elected to serve as Steward in September 1679 flatly refused to hold the office, and none of those summoned to appear and pay their quarterage in October 1681 did so. Loans had to be paid by raising further loans.[19]

In 1681, Samuel Draper, a scrivener, who had been nominated and appointed as Clerk of the Company in the charter of 1677, was dismissed under something of a cloud – perhaps related to the drawn-out process of ratifying the Company's by-laws. Subsequently, one of the bonds which the Company had given passed into the hands of someone called Lewis Newberry. Newberry claimed that he had purchased the bond for £100 from Draper, who seems never to have had the authority to sell the bond. In 1682, John Settle, the Renter Warden, stormed out of a Court meeting and one year later he was 'prosecuted for not making upp and bringing in his Account of his Renterwardenshipp.' There was evidently disquiet at Masons' Hall.[20]

These financial difficulties were greatly exacerbated by the external political tensions that arose in what is often called the 'First Age of Party', the period between 1678 and 1681, during which national politics were dominated by bitter disputes concerning religion and the succession to the throne. Radical Protestants calling for King Charles's brother, James, Duke of York, a Roman Catholic, to be disqualified on account of his religion were opposed by orthodox monarchists who believed that James's right of succession to the throne was more significant than his religious beliefs. In 1681, the 'Tory' loyalists prevailed over the 'Whig' exclusionists, and there followed a 'Tory Reaction' against political radicalism and religious dissent.

In London, a traditional breeding-ground of radical ideas, where the voting rights of the liverymen gave them significant influence in Parliament, the Crown launched proceedings against the City's charter, forcing the City to answer by what warrant it held its rights and privileges. On 12 June 1683, judgement was given against the City, and the companies now came under the spotlight. One-by-one, each was required to surrender its charters to the king. The Masons' charter was surrendered on 20 April 1684, either along with or despite a petition 'to implore his Majesties favour'. King Charles II died in February 1685, and his brother succeeded as James II, amid heightened tensions.[21]

On 9 February 1686, King James II granted the Company a revised charter. In the interim, some Company business had carried on as usual, but after the Court had voted unanimously, on 11 June 1684, to surrender the power of electing officers to the Crown, a new Master and Wardens would not be appointed until 23 March 1686. On that day, John Shorthose was sworn as Master, and John Thompson and John Young as Wardens. In terms of trade regulation, the new charter was essentially the same as its predecessor. However, in line with the Test and Corporation Acts, certain provisions concerning company personnel and administration were added to almost all charters that were reissued to the London companies. In this respect, the Masons' charter was no different. It demanded the Company and its members be loyal to the Lord Mayor and Aldermen, and it set down that all office-holders could be removed from their positions by the king. It also banned anyone who had not taken communion in the Church of England within the last six months from holding office or accepting the livery.

Furthermore, in addition to their oaths of office and the oaths of allegiance and supremacy, office-holders were now required to take the corporation oath, in which the oath-taker declared that 'it

56 James, Duke of York, subsequently King James II, painted in 1684 by Sir Godfrey Kneller.

30th martij 1686:

Wee John Shorthose John Thompson John Young Thomas Shorthose
Stephen Bumpsted Leonard Noble Abraham Story Nicholas Young John Martine
William Stanton

Doe declare that wee hold yt there lies noe Obligation upon us or
any other person from the Oath Comonly called the Solemne
League & Covent: & that the same was in itt selfe an unlawfull
Oath, & Imposed upon the Subjects of this Realme against
the knowne Lawes & liberties of the Kingdome :/

John Shorthose   John Tompson   John Young
Tho: Shorthose   The marke of   the marke of
Abr: Story   Stephen Bumpsted   Leonard L Noble
            Nicholas Young   John Martin
Wm Stanton   Chr: Kenyston   Edw mitchell
Edward Strong   Tho: Eld Will: wid John: Bennet
Tho: Stampe:l   Wm Exey   Tho: Gilbert
Gilbt Stretton

is not Lawfull upon any pretence whatsoever to take upp Armes against the King'. Finally, all office-holders and liverymen had to sign a declaration according to the terms of the Corporation Act that the Solemn League and Covenant, which had been agreed in 1643 and which called for the extirpation of popery, prelacy, superstition, heresy, schism and profanity, 'was in itt selfe an unlawfull Oath, and Imposed upon the Subjects of the Realme against the Knowne Laws and liberties of the Kingdome'.[22]

57 *Declaration against the Solemn League and Covenant, signed by the Court and Clerk in 1686.*

In March and April 1686, the Master, two Wardens, 16 Assistants and the Clerk all took the oaths and signed the declaration, a copy of which with their signatures remains in the Company's archive. However, eight Assistants refused to take all the oaths and sign the declaration. We must suppose that these were religious dissenters or political radicals – or both. In many companies, men such as these were swiftly ousted from the ranks of the assistants and from the liveries. There is no obvious evidence of such a purge in the records of the Masons' Company. For example, at the next Election Court after the regrant of the charter, held on 14 June 1687, three recusants, William Hammond, Michael Todd and Jasper Latham, were nominated, although not elected, for the office of Warden. For all the travails the Company had endured in the last 50 or so years, there is no evidence of any political or religious factionalism among the membership. In this respect, the Masons' Company appears to have been something of a broad church.[23]

With a return to some sense of constitutional stability, steps were taken to improve the Company's dire financial position. There was a drive to increase the Company's membership, and a plan was also put in place in the summer of 1686 to bring down the Company's debt. In addition, there was a clear push in the winter of 1686-7 to collect the arrears of quarterage. This had been tried before, with limited success. This time, however, it does appear to have been more focused and systematic.[24]

All this good work was thrown off course, however, by the actions of the Crown. Early in 1687, the king changed tack and moved towards a policy which supported liberty of conscience. In April, he issued a Declaration of Indulgence which removed the need to take the various oaths required by the Test Acts. This controverted his charter to the Masons, and while there is no obvious evidence that it caused disquiet among the membership, it may be significant that folio leaves from that period have been torn from the Court's minute book – two from the record of the April 1687 Court, and one from the record of the Election Court in June.

In autumn 1687, James decided to move against the 'Tories', those who had most enthusiastically supported his succession and who had gained the upper hand in the Corporation and the livery companies of London – and who, he believed, were now the most opposed to religious toleration. On 25 September, the king 'having thought fit that several members of the said several Companies shall be removed', wrote to the Londoners with orders that over 850 Masters, Wardens and Assistants be removed from office. On 10 October, the Masons' Company Court of Assistants met and James's letter was read. The Master, John Martin, and 11 Assistants were discharged of their offices. There seems to have been little rhyme or reason to the king's actions. Of the 12 dismissed men, six had taken the oaths and signed the declaration in 1686, five had not, and one had been elected as an Assistant in the interim. Two of them, Abraham Story and Thomas Shorthose, had been granted royal authority 'to give, administer and require the severall Oathes and subscriptions' to be taken by their fellow Assistants. Yet the third man named alongside them, Stephen Bumpstead, was not removed.[25]

In October, in a series of orders, the king wrote again to the Londoners, dismissing 1,795 liverymen and restoring all the liverymen and Assistants who had been in place at the time when the charters had been surrendered. As a consequence of these orders, 19 men were dismissed from the livery of the Masons' Company. This was followed in February 1688 by another city-wide purge that saw 215 Assistants and 656 liverymen removed, while 115 Assistants and 213 liverymen were restored. Within the Company, one Assistant and one liveryman were removed.[26]

Whether it was the case or not, the king must have believed that those removed were opposed to his policy of toleration – either towards Roman Catholics, or to dissenters, or perhaps both. The purges had an enormous effect on the Company in 1688. On 26 January, 'all that are left of the Assistants' were summoned to come to Court on 3 February to elect a new Master to replace John Martin. Thus, two Wardens and just six Assistants elected William Stanton, another who had taken the oaths and signed the declaration in 1686, as Master. This rather set the tone for the year. Courts were either not held or they were dismally attended. At this point even the annual cycle of accounting and auditing, maintained since 1619 throughout all the difficulties we have seen in this and previous chapters, broke down. Instead, Stanton, Mitchell, John Shorthose (he was made treasurer in December 1690) and Thomas Stampe, the Clerk, each individually kept some form of accounts for three years which were audited in October 1691.[27]

In October 1688, faced with invasion by William of Orange, James performed a series of course reversals, in which he restored the City's charter, and the charters and liveries which existed at the time of the *quo warranto*. What now was the status of all the office-holders who had been removed at various times? The Masons' Company did not wait to find out. At a Court meeting on 11 October, the Lord Mayor's letter of 7 October was read. Four days later, John Martin took up office as Master again and John Young was restored as Upper Warden. Twenty-eight Assistants and 25 liverymen were also put back in their places. Whether these restorations were strictly lawful or not is unclear, but amid the fast-moving situation of autumn 1688 men acted as they thought best, or at least safest. James's policies had destabilised the government and administration of his capital city, and it is no surprise that when William did invade, there was little support for James in London. He was deposed in December 1688, and in January 1689 the Convention Parliament offered the Crown to William and his wife Mary, James's daughter, as joint monarchs.[28]

Any hopes that Company life could quickly return to something like normal were premature. Courts did meet throughout 1689 and 1690 and some business was transacted. However, some meetings were not held, others were poorly attended, and money only dribbled in. It is hard to be sure of the exact state of the Company's finances at this time, but pensions appear to have gone unpaid and it is clear that income was not sufficient to meet expenses.[29]

It is no surprise, then, that many members were reluctant either to assume or to discharge the responsibilities of office. In June 1689, Jasper Latham was elected as Renter Warden. He refused to take up the position and by the autumn Edward Mitchell was performing the duties. In response, Stampe, the Clerk, spent money which the Company could ill afford on arresting Latham and suing him in the Lord Mayor's court. In January 1690, the Clerk was ordered to arrest John Young, too, for not bringing his warden books to Court. Young then failed, in April 1690, to attend a Court convened to audit his accounts. Two months after that, on 26 June 1690, William Hammond declined to take up the office of Master, to which he had been elected 12 days before, although he did promise to pay 'what fine ye Company shall thinke fitt' and he offered to serve in other ways.[30]

As 1690 drew to a close, the Company was weighed down with debt, its finances were in a dire position and unpaid creditors were suing the Company for redress. Attendance at meetings was scanty, and even members who had given years of service to the Company were refusing to hold office. It had just emerged from a bruising battle with a king who, despite his deposition and defeat in Ireland in 1690, was still a threat to recently-restored political stability. Could the Company ever recover from this position?

11

RESILIENCE AND RECOVERY

At the beginning of the 1690s, the Masons' Company seemed to be locked in a downward spiral of debt and decline. Its outgoings had soared as the Company rebuilt its Hall and acquired two charters, yet its long-term loss of authority over the craft of masonry had greatly reduced its income, and it was attracting nothing like the number of new recruits that it needed.

But the membership included some significant and committed figures. John Thompson, William Stanton, John Shorthose and Thomas Cartwright had been members for decades. All had been through the Master's chair, all had served the Company through thick and thin. They were joined by others equally committed to turning the Company's fortunes around: Christopher Kempster, Master in 1691 and 1700; Edward Mitchell, Master in 1692; Edward Strong senior, Master in 1696 and Treasurer from 1693 until 1716; and Ephraim Beauchamp, Master in 1701. Kempster, who had joined the Company in 1670, was 64 when he ascended the chair for the first time, and 73 when he served a second term. He, Strong and Beauchamp all hailed originally from Burford and nearby Taynton, on the borders of Oxfordshire and Gloucestershire, all had come to London in the aftermath of the Great Fire and, as we have noted, all worked together on some of the biggest building projects within and without the City of London. They had prospered mightily in London and all had advanced rapidly through to the livery and the Court after joining the Company.

The affairs of the Masons' Company, however, were in a less prosperous state than those of its leading members. To begin with, its administration was in disorder. In October 1691, for the first time

in three years, an audit was held; in June 1692, a chest was bought to hold the Company's books and, for the first time in five years, the Renter Warden's accounts began to be kept properly. At the end of that year, the Company also agreed to insure Masons' Hall to the value of £700 and policies were taken out shortly thereafter. In 1695, the Company decided to dispense with the services of Thomas Stampe, the Clerk, after mistakes and poor record-keeping on his part. A schedule of the Company's deeds and records was drawn up, and thereafter the Renter Warden's account book for the years 1704-99 is neatly and systematically laid out, with records of income on one side of the ledger and outgoings on the other.[1]

58 Edward Strong senior, Master Mason.

Still more important than good record-keeping was the need for an increase in income. Arrangements for collecting quarterage were gradually improved during the 1690s, helped by better attendance at Court meetings. The four Quarter Courts in 1693, for example, were attended by 13, 18, 14 and 16 men respectively, while 13 came to that year's Election Court. It would be too much to say that these actions 'solved' the problem of members not paying their quarterage; in 1708, 287 members owed a total of nearly £300 in quarterage; by 1714, 335 members owed over £385 – and some three dozen members owed more than £2 in both years. But the bald figures are misleading; many of these members may, in fact, have been dead – despite better record-keeping, the Company had no way of knowing how many of its members had died. In 1723, the Company hit upon the clever tactic of prioritising members who had regularly paid their quarterage or who had performed other duties when it came to electing pensioners.[2]

Even so, it is clear that the Company could not rely on quarterage receipts to improve its financial position. But the large number of debtors does draw attention to a welcome development: that is, that the number of those joining the Company had increased quite considerably. Just three men joined the Company each year in 1689 and 1690, yet in the nine years from 1691 to 1699, 118 men were admitted to the freedom of the Company, that is over 13 men a year on average – quite an improvement. Edward Strong was clearly an active recruiter; only 24 men have ever been admitted to the freedom of the Company as foreign members, but 10 joined in 1691-92, and Strong paid the admission fees for seven of them; they were presumably masons in his employ. The number of apprentices also rose, although not by quite such an impressive amount. From 1691 to 1699, 127 men were bound as apprentices, that is an average of just over 14 men each year, compared with an average of 10 in 1689 and 1690.[3]

The Company also had to reduce its debt burden. This was another problem which was tackled during the 1690s with vigour and despatch under the leadership of the briskly competent businessmen who were now running the Company. At the first Court meeting held after Kempster's election in 1691 all those who held bonds of the Company were ordered to bring them before the Court and, four months later, steps were taken to reorganise the Company's debts. The initiative met with a positive response from liverymen who clearly felt – or were persuaded to feel – loyalty to the Company. In October 1692, Abraham Story generously agreed to write off the remaining £150 he was owed. Similarly, William Stanton was 'so well affected to the Company and so desirous of its prosperity' that, in June 1695, he remitted the £195 due to him on condition that his two sons, Thomas and Edward, and his servant Richard Brown, were all admitted to the Company, clothed in the livery, and accepted as Stewards with no charge, and that his two sons were also admitted to the Court of Assistants. Several similar cases were recorded in the late 1690s.[4]

Thanks to a steadily rising income, other debts could be cleared. As Treasurer, Strong paid almost £90 to John Shorthose and £13 to Thomas Stampe, in 1693-4, in final discharge of money that had been due to them since 1691. Some belt-tightening also helped. In 1696, the Court ordered that no more expenses be run up on the Company's account and that members should pay for all their drink. In 1699, 'takeing into theire consideration the present Cercumstances of the Company and resolveing to doe what in them lies towards payment and satisfaction of theire debts', the Court agreed that no more than 40s. of the Company's money should be spent on dining on Court days.[5]

But the Company could not hope to discharge all its liabilities from measures like these. In 1693, the arrears on Lydia Light's annuity totalled £179 and she was also owed £195 on the bond her father had sealed in 1678. With the remaining five years due on the annuity, the Company's obligations to her amounted to £774. Once more, it was Edward Strong who proposed a solution. He offered Lydia Light an upfront payment of £500 to settle all the Company's obligations, a proposal that she was happy to accept. Strong and Thomas Hill each lent the Company £250, secured on Masons' Hall, at 5 per cent interest. Regular payments of both interest and principal were made to Strong and Hill until 1713, and for two years thereafter to Strong and William Knowles, son-in-law and beneficiary of Hill's estate, which settled the debt in full. The long-running issue over Lewis Newberry's debt was also resolved, and a bond for £75, owed to John Eaton since at least 1682, was settled.[6]

Despite all the improvement in the Company's financial position, however, it was still struggling to end the year in the black. When Strong's accounts as Treasurer were audited in 1694, the Company owed him just under £33; in 1695 the Company owed him over £64, in 1696 over £61 and in 1698 over £38. Many members remained unenthusiastic about holding office or coming on to the livery. In 1692, two men chose to pay a fine of £10 rather than hold the office of Renter Warden; two others did the same in 1694.[7]

Nevertheless, there can be no doubt that things had improved by 1700. The number of men joining the Company had increased. The Company's debts had been rescheduled; they were now manageable, and the Company was able, each year, to reduce the amount it owed its creditors. When, in June 1702, at the end of his year as Master, Beauchamp presented the Company with a new charter which removed all the additions which King James had made, it must have felt as if the Company was turning something of a new page in its history. Throughout this period of recovery, the names of those who were present at the Election Court in 1691 appear over and over again. John Thompson succeeded William Stanton as Master in 1690, while Christopher Kempster, Edward Mitchell, Thomas Cartwright, Edward Strong and Ephraim Beauchamp were in the chair for six of the next 11 years. The only one of the eight men present in 1691 not to serve as Master during this period was the aged John Shorthose, and he was Treasurer from 1690-93. It was truly something of a team effort, but one name does stand out above all others. Edward Strong served as Treasurer and Master, he lent considerable sums of his own money and solicited gifts to pay Light and other creditors, he collected quarterage from his teams of masons, and paid for foreign masons in his employ to join the Company. Remarkably, he did all this while simultaneously running his quarries in the Cotswolds and managing large teams of workers at St Paul's Cathedral, Morden College in Blackheath, Greenwich Hospital and several parish churches in London.

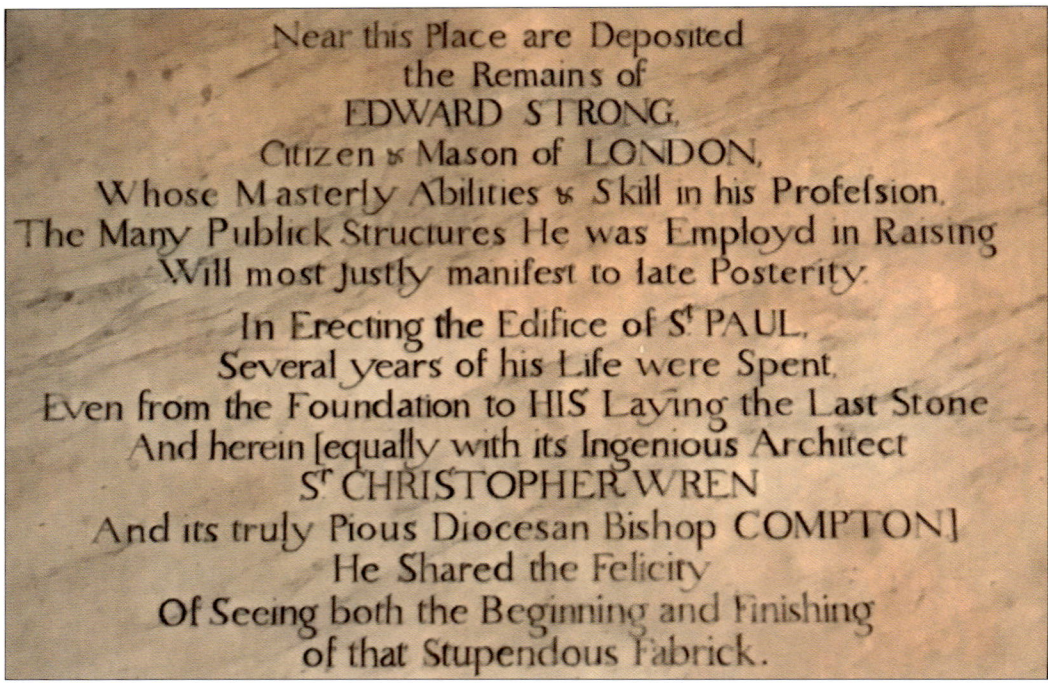

Near this Place are Deposited
the Remains of
EDWARD STRONG,
Citizen & Mason of LONDON,
Whose Masterly Abilities & Skill in his Profession,
The Many Publick Structures He was Employd in Raising
Will most Justly manifest to late Posterity.

In Erecting the Edifice of St PAUL,
Several years of his Life were Spent,
Even from the Foundation to HIS Laying the Last Stone
And herein [equally with its Ingenious Architect
St CHRISTOPHER WREN
And its truly Pious Diocesan Bishop COMPTON]
He Shared the Felicity
Of Seeing both the Beginning and Finishing
of that Stupendous Fabrick.

59 *Memorial to Edward Strong senior, d.1724, in St Peter's Church, St Albans.*

The group of powerful mason-contractors who stabilised the Company in the 1690s continued their loyal support into the opening years of the 18th century, and several of them established family dynasties which remained prominent in Company affairs for decade after decade. We have already seen how the Burford masons were tightly bound by ties of geography, family and business, but the close connections between the Company's leading families extended much further than that. Christopher Cass, who had been foreman for the Strongs at Blenheim Palace, went into business with Edward Strong junior and with Edward's former apprentice Andrews Jelfe around 1725. After Strong retired, Cass and Jelfe worked as partners in Cambridge on the Senate House and the Fellows' Building of King's College; in London, they were partners at Gibbs' St Martin-in-the-Fields, and together they worked on at least two of the new churches which were built under the terms of the Act of 1711. After Cass's death, Jelfe's most famous project was the construction of Westminster Bridge between 1738 and 1750, a task he undertook in partnership with Samuel Tufnell, master mason of Westminster Abbey. Tufnell was the son of Edward Tufnell, a man who had served his apprenticeship with Christopher Kempster, and who had been awarded the contracts to build six of the Queen Anne churches with

Edward Strong senior. It is not too much of an exaggeration to claim that the wealthiest and most successful mason-contractors formed something of an aristocracy of masons in 18th-century London.[8]

A New Membership Policy

In September 1691, the Company tried to compel masons working in London to become free of the Company. In 1694, the Court decided to go one step further and petition the Lord Mayor and Aldermen that all those working as masons in London who were members of other companies, and who bound their apprentices within those companies, should 'henceforth be presented, bound and made free of the Masons' Company'. In this petition the Company claimed that the damage wrought by indifference to the rules of livery and apprenticeship was such that they could not discharge their charitable obligations to poor members and widows, and that the Company's

60 *Westminster Bridge and the Abbey, c.1800, by Daniel Turner. The Masons' Company Charter encompasses Westminster as well as the City of London.*

membership had shrunk in comparison to former times, both of which were more or less true. The extent to which the Company was acting legally in doing this, however, is open to question.[9]

The Company had to supply more information to the Court of Aldermen before its petition was answered, in September 1694, by the passing of an Act of Common Council. This Act required all those who were working as masons in London and who had the right to be made free of other companies (e.g. by patrimony or having served an apprenticeship to a member company), to join the Masons' Company. In what was quite possibly also a breach of the Rebuilding Acts, it also required anyone who had completed an apprenticeship in London to take up the freedom on pain of a fine of £10, to be split between the Chamberlain and the Masons' Company.

Whether this was all lawful or not, the Company wasted little time in acting. Two weeks after the Act was passed, the Company sent out parties of men 'to take an account of freemen of the company, who are fit to be made free, and to collect quarterage'; two weeks after that, three men were summoned before the Chamberlain; and over the next few months, the Company had the Act of Common Council delivered to all workshops where masons worked and to 52 named companies. The first company named on the list to receive a copy of the act was the Haberdashers. All told, between 1695 and 1731, following intermittent reiterations of the Company's authority to compel membership under the terms of the Act, 36 men were forced to join the Masons' Company – of whom 10 had been apprenticed to members of the Haberdashers' Company.[10]

The Court was clearly pleased with the results of its petition. In December 1694, it paid Lawrence Purchase 10 guineas for his 'great care and paynes' in obtaining the Act and, one year later, Purchase replaced Stampe as Clerk. The Act also appears to have given the Company greater confidence to use prosecution as a tool to reinforce its authority more generally. However, as is well known, once summonses and suits are launched there are often few winners, and it must be questionable whether the time and expense which the Company spent on enforcing these requirements were worth the candle.[11]

Moreover, the Masons' Company was not the only company to have obtained an Act such as this from Common Council. In the 17th and 18th centuries many of the minor companies did so, and men were lost from the Masons' Company as a result. There is no easy way of knowing how many, but Thomas Thorpe, an innholder by trade, joined the Innholders in 1719, and two apprentices who worked with Henry Gaskin, a plasterer by trade but a member of the Masons' Company, were turned over to masters who were members of the Plaisterers' Company in 1733. The Masons' Company had attracted many gardeners and coachmakers to its ranks, too; at least eight coachmakers appeared on a list of quarterage arrears drawn up in 1686-7. In 1697, however, the Court complained that 'the Company is reduced to a very small number of Members (the Coach and Coach-harness-makers and Gardners haveing been lately drawne from them)'; nine years later, there was a similar lament that a 'greate Number of Coachmen and Gardners' had been taken from the Company's ranks 'by theire respective Charters'.[12]

In short, the traditional method of increasing membership, that is compelling people to join the Company, had again met with only limited success. The improvement in admissions that had been seen in the 1690s had run out of steam. In 1704, just seven men and one woman, Miriam Saunders, took up the freedom of the Company; in 1705, just six men were admitted and in 1706 just three. With fewer entrants coming into the Company, the burdens of office-holding also fell too quickly on those who were members, which acted as a further discouragement to those who wanted to join. For these reasons, on 2 October 1706, the Court agreed a different approach.

Resolving 'that all faire meanes be used to enlarge the Yeomandry', the Court lowered the fee for admission to the Company by redemption to 3s. 4d. Hitherto, redemptioners had paid 36s. to the Company and 46s. 8d. at the Guildhall, that is, over £4 in total; after the reduction due to the Company the new total came to just £2 10s. Moreover, the Court also ordered 'that the Clerke doe give fitting incouragement to the Ministers and officers of the Chamber that shall bring in persons to be made free accordingly'. The Masons' Company was now going to pay commissions to those working at the Guildhall for each admission they could secure for the Company.[13]

This policy had an immediate effect. In 1707, 14 men took up the freedom of the Masons' Company, five of them via redemption; in 1708, 21 were admitted, 11 of whom by redemption; and in 1709, eight of the 10 admissions that year were redemptioners. Samuel Burgis, a perfumer of gloves, was the first to be admitted by redemption, on 12 February 1707, after this policy was endorsed. In his case, it seems that no gratuity was paid to an officer at the

Guildhall, but subsequently gratuities of 2s. 6d. were regularly paid. Two months later, in order to speed up the process of admitting new members, the Court agreed that it was no longer necessary to convene a meeting of the whole Court, and that just two people, the Master or either of the Wardens, along with another Assistant, could admit new members to the Company. Thereafter, this is exactly what frequently happened; candidates were admitted at Masons' Hall, at taverns, at their houses, and at the Guildhall before just two or three Assistants. The total number of admissions, and particularly those by redemption, soared.[14]

Between 1703 and 1742, the 215 admissions by redemption accounted for almost 40 per cent of the 540 entrants to the freedom. In the 40 years prior to 1703 and the 40-year period after 1742, redemptioners accounted for less than 9 per cent of the total admissions: 42 of 495 admissions in the earlier period and just 22 of 261 in the latter. In the 10 years from 1703 to 1712, more people joined the Company by redemption than did by servitude, a phenomenon which would not be repeated until the first decade of the 19th century; while in the 10 years from 1723 to 1732, the Company admitted more members than in any other 10-year period in its history. In just one year, 1712, there were 32 admissions to the freedom of the Masons' Company, an astonishing 20 of which were by redemption.

By June 1708, however, the Court had 'Received Information That several other Companys of this City do give five shillings gratuity to the said Ministers and Officers for every Member brought by them by Redemption'. The Court thus increased both the cost of admission by redemption, to 7s. 6d., and the gratuity it would pay, to 5s. or 6s. as the Clerk 'shall think fitt'. No ledger records the gratuities paid nor the names of the recipients, but Thomas Colebatch, Clerk to the Chamberlain and a certain Mr Henshaw both appear to have received gratuities. There seems little doubt, however, that the man who was the most responsible for, and rewarded by, this policy was David Le Gros.[16]

David Le Gros was born in 1682. In June 1708 he was appointed Clerk of the Company, a position he held until February 1721; he served thereafter as an Assistant and on various committees. At the time of his appointment as Clerk, Le Gros was working in the Town Clerk's office at the Guildhall. At some point he also took up a position as an official at the Bank of England; certainly, upon his admission to the Company as a freeman in January 1721, and in

Table 10.1. Freedom admissions 1663-2012.[15]

Decade	Servitude	Redemption	Patrimony	Other	Total
1663-1672	97	10	7	0	114
1673-1682	118	26	8	0	152
1683-1692	66	2	2	24	94
1693-1702	122	4	9	0	135
1703-1712	65	67	7	1	140
1713-1722	63	48	11	0	122
1723-1732	82	71	16	1	170
1733-1742	72	29	7	0	108
1743-1752	71	10	11	0	92
1753-1762	46	5	15	0	66
1763-1772	48	5	12	0	65
1773-1782	30	2	6	0	38
1783-1792	16	5	2	0	23
1793-1802	15	10	10	0	35
1803-1812	9	17	4	0	30
1813-1822	8	10	0	0	18
1823-1832	13	13	8	0	34
1833-1842	14	3	2	0	19
1843-1852	3	9	9	0	21
1853-1862	1	7	1	0	9
1863-1872	0	20	2	1	23
1873-1882	1	11	1	0	13
1883-1892	0	18	0	1	19
1893-1902	0	20	3	0	23
1903-1912	0	16	1	2	19
1913-1922	2	10	1	4	17
1923-1932	0	17	0	0	17
1933-1942	0	13	1	0	14
1943-1952	1	45	1	1	48
1943-1953	0	1	0	0	1
1953-1962	0	39	0	0	39
1963-1972	3	32	0	2	37
1973-1982	0	40	0	4	44
1983-1992	0	42	2	2	46
1993-2002	0	47	0	1	48
2003-2012	2	81	7	5	95
GRAND TOTAL	968	805	166	49	1,988

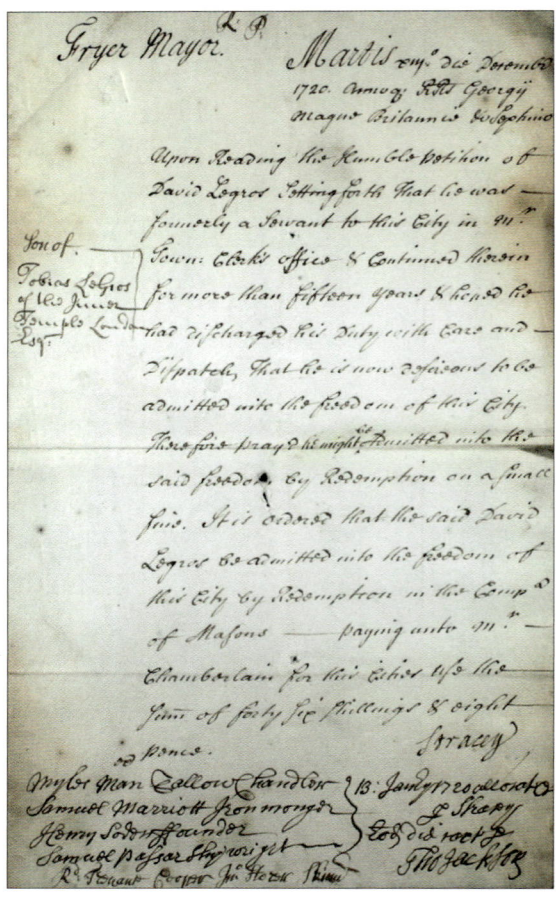

61 *David Le Gros's admission to the Freedom of the City of London in December 1720.*

subsequent quarterage records, his profession was given as a Secretary at the Bank. The Bank had been founded in 1694. He also served as secretary to a Whig political club visible in London between 1714 and 1717.[17]

Le Gros was evidently a man with a network of good contacts in the newly emergent capitalist world of the City. One month before he took office as Clerk, James Lanze and Jonathan Winthrop, two exchange brokers, were admitted to the freedom of the Company by redemption, and over the course of the next 15 years a further 17 exchange brokers joined the Masons' Company by redemption – almost one in every six redemptioners who joined in this period listed their occupation as exchange broker. The Court was under no doubt as to who should be rewarded for this development. In January 1717, it gave one of the houses adjoining the Hall to Le Gros as a reward for his 'good and faithful Services', noting 'particularly the Benefit and Advantage this Corporation doth and may receive from the many substantial Traders and others who through his means have been admitted Members thereof by Redemption' for which his salary and perquisites had not been 'proportionable'.[18]

It is striking that at least 10 of the 19 exchange brokers who joined the Company between 1708 and 1723 had names indicative of a French background. This is not surprising. Men of alien descent were very much involved in the early development of finance in London. Among the first directors of the Bank of England were Dutchmen, merchants with connections in the Portuguese wine trade, and men of Huguenot descent. In fact, seven of the first

24 directors of the Bank were Huguenots, including Sir Theodore Janssen and three brothers, John, Abraham and James Houblon – and they, as Common Councilmen, Aldermen, an MP and Lord Mayor, were men who moved easily between London's financial and administrative spheres. They were also Whigs. As indeed was Le Gros, who with his employments at the Guildhall, the Bank of England and at Masons' Hall, was equally comfortable gliding between these overlapping worlds. Who else, apart from Le Gros, was responsible for the admission by redemption of two attorneys at the Lord Mayor's Court, a clerk in the Town Clerk's office, and a clerk at South Sea House within the space of 18 months from April 1724? Who else, apart from Le Gros, could have had such extensive connections among the Huguenot brokers and traders in London?[19]

In the early 18th century, the face of the Masons' Company was changed dramatically by the huge number of admissions by redemption; brokers, traders, merchants, many of them of continental origin and several of them evidently non-conformist in their religious taste, all joined the Company. Another consequence of the new policy was that, for the first time, women who were not widows of masons joined the Company. Nine women joined the Company by redemption in these decades and most appear to have run businesses in London. Anne Baker, who joined the Company in March 1715, was a victualler in Finch Lane; Anne Sparhawke and Katherine Wight, who were admitted to the freedom together in March 1735, were milliners and business partners. There is no evidence that any of these women who joined by redemption advanced to the livery or held office in the Company, but they did play an active part in Company life. Mary Latour, who was admitted in 1712, bound two apprentices during her time as a freeman: her son, René, and Henry Rogers. Mary Paramor, who joined in July 1714 and who lived in Exchange Alley where she worked as a seamstress, was often responsible for making ribbons and cockades for the Company on Lord Mayor's Day. Women came to Company dinners, too.[20]

More dramatic, more lasting and more cumulative change, however, was occasioned by the entry into the Company of large numbers of men who worked in an enormous range of different occupations. Of the 20 admissions by redemption in 1712, three men were mercers, and John Bell appears in the Company's records as both a mercer and an exchange broker. One who seems to have changed his occupation was Richard Charlton, who is listed first as a woollen draper and

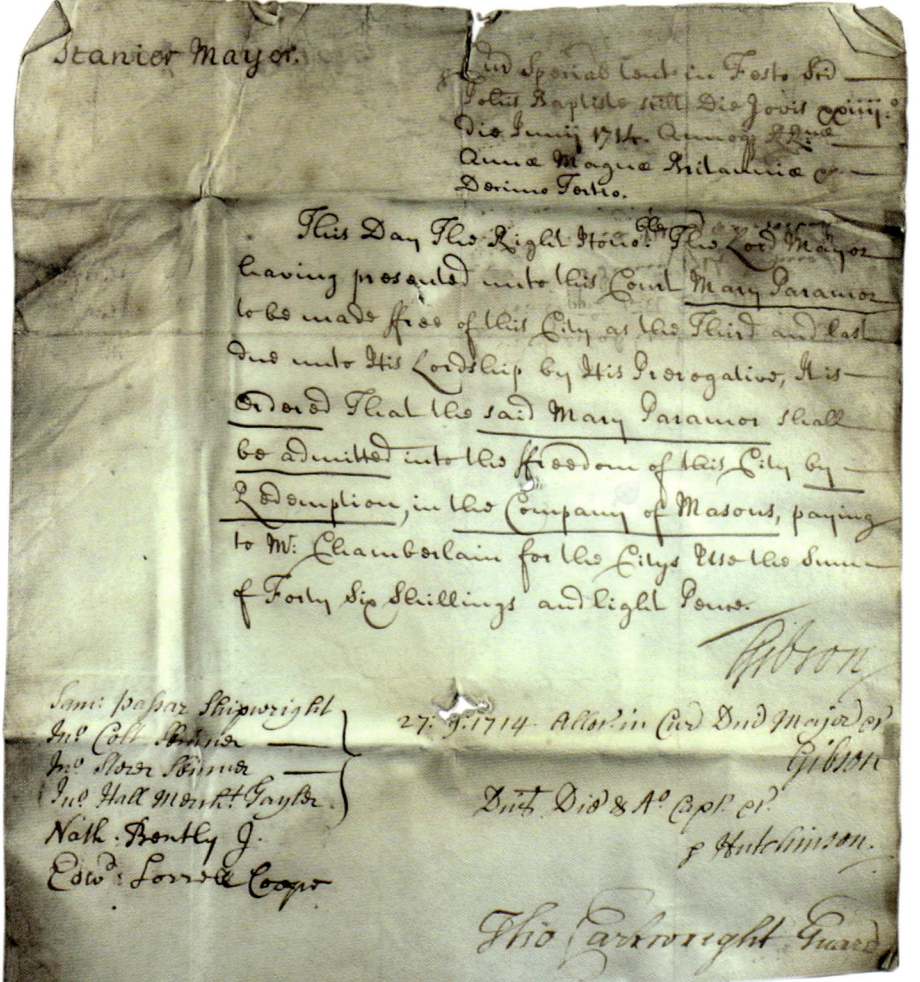

62a *Mary Paramor's admission to the Freedom of the City of London in June 1714. (Note: the handwriting is that of David Le Gros, working in his role at the Town Clerk's office at the same time as being Clerk to the Masons' Company.)*

62b *Mary Paramor's receipt for supplying ribbon in 1723.*

subsequently, presumably as the gin craze took hold of contemporary London, as a distiller. In addition there was a haberdasher of small wares, a perfumer, a tubman, a linen draper, a necklace maker, a confectioner, a victualler, a yeoman at the Poultry Compter, a hemp gang porter, a salesman, a bodice maker, a tobacconist and a warehouse keeper. Thomas Gibson's occupation is unknown, but he lodged with Bartholomew Woolfe, a mason, in East Cheap, and Thomas Robinson gave a coffee house as his address, without designating another occupation, which may suggest that he kept or worked in coffee houses – or, perhaps, earned a living with his pen.

As these new, non-mason entrants themselves bound apprentices and presented them for admission, the character of the Company was further altered. In 1724, for example, John Clark and in 1729 Robert Carr, both of whom had served apprenticeships to John Bell, sometime exchange broker and mercer, were admitted to the freedom listing their occupations as mercers. In 1741, Joshua Channing, a haberdasher of small wares, presented his former apprentice, Samuel Gainsborough, for the freedom, and in 1754 his son Howard joined the Company by patrimony. Neither worked in the craft of masonry.

In 1734, the Company submitted a list of its liverymen to the Lord Mayor. The list, presumably a complete record of the contemporary livery, contained 70 names along with their occupations and addresses. The 70 liverymen were recorded as having 24 different professions. Masonry was by far still the single largest sector in which the liverymen of the Masons' Company worked; 26 were recorded as masons, while three others, for whom no occupation was given, worked or had worked in the craft of masonry. Edward Strong junior was a wealthy mason contractor; John Gilbert, who was recorded as 'at Portland', had served an apprenticeship with Ephraim Beauchamp and was involved in the supply of stone; William Trimmer, sometime Beadle who had retired to the country, had served his apprenticeship with Bartholomew Woolfe. But masons were, all the same, only a minority of the livery: 41 of the 70 liverymen of the Masons' Company in 1734 did not work in the craft of masonry.[21]

In 1730, the Chamberlain of London began to sell freedoms by redemption to raise money. Other companies also began to pay gratuities as high as one guinea for referrals. In 1743, David le Gros died. Consequently, towards the end of the 1730s, the numbers of those joining the Company by redemption fell. By that time, however, the hard work and commitment of its members, along with

An Alphabetical List of the Company of masons of London, with the places of their abode & the time of their respective admissions returned to y Rt Honble the Lord Mayor in obedience

A

Annis John, a mason in Aldersgate Street. 1. Sep. 1727.

B

24. Feb. 1669

Bucknell William, Unknown

Beaumont Jonathan a mason at Norton falgate 29 Oct 1723.

Bonouvrier Andrew a Broker in Exchange ally. 2 Aug 1729.

Bell John an Exchd Broker in Salisbury Court. 1 aug 1729.

Bowles Richard a mason 1. Oct 1730 Shoreditch Church

Booker Richard a Distiller in Thames Street 3. Sep. 1731.

Bull Thomas a mason in Broad Street. 4 aug 1732

C

25 aug 1709

Cartwright Thomas a watchmaker under Barthlo Lane Church

Cash Christopher a mason near the horse ferry Westmr 29 Oct 1716

Channing Joshua a Habdr 7 Stars Bread Street 4. Oct 1720

Connier Francis a mason at Olivers Mount 6. Sep 1723

Cooper William a mason at London Wall 7. may 1725

Charlton Richard a Distiller just wout Aldersgate. 5 Oct 1721

Coulthurst Henry a perfumer near King's head Tavern Chelsea 4 Sep 1734

Crofts James a mercer Henrietta Street Covent Garden 14 hunting

Carter James a Threadman without Bishopsgate 2 Oct 1722

D

Dunn Thomas a mason Blackman S[tree]t Southwark 4 Oct 1709

David John a Broker in Exchd ally. 2 aug 1729

Davis Thomas Serjt at Poultry Compter. 1 Sep. 1732

Dow Ezekiel a mercer in Paternoster Row 4 Oct 1733

E

Evans Robert keeps Garways Coffeehouse. 3 may 1724

the development of an imaginative and aggressive policy to attract new members, had revitalised Company life. As the City around the Company changed, the Company had found a way to adjust to that change with benefit to its own fortunes. In 1717, the Company bought property comprising three houses and a warehouse from one of the Assistants, William Holland, for £200. In 1727, the Court bought its first stock: £200 nominal of South Sea bonds that had been issued to clear the arrears caused by the collapse of the South Sea Company in 1720. What a contrast with the 1680s and 1690s when the Company had been the issuer of bonds![22]

The improvement in the Company's financial position was obviously welcome in itself, but it was also a means to an end. It meant, for example, that the Company could make fewer demands of its members, that it could spend money on social occasions such as dinner on Lord Mayor's Day, and that it could meet its charitable obligations more generously and more regularly.

In October 1681, when William Stanton was Renter Warden, unable to find men to serve as Stewards and with no money to spare, the Company had agreed 'to have noe dinner but only a breakfast' before they went to their stands on Lord Mayor's Day. In 1739, when his grandson, also called William, was Company Beadle, the Company spent over £60 celebrating Lord Mayor's Day: among the disbursements were £2 on beer, over £4 on musicians, more than £15 on wine, and over £21 on food. In that year the Company's breakfast on Lord Mayor's Day comprised two sirloins and two rumps of beef as well as five dozen bottles of wine; whereas for dinner there were nine dishes of 'Fowles and Bacon' served, along with six ducks, six turkeys and six chines, three dishes of tongues and udders, three marrow puddings, three apple pies and 24 gallons of wine. In addition to all of which the ushers were served a boiled leg of mutton and two roasted chickens. The Company's pensioners also benefited from increased payments; in March 1740, the Company doubled the amount paid that quarter to the pensioners 'in Consideration of the Rigorousness of the late Season'. The more that can be paid to pensioners, whether old men or widows, the more attractive membership becomes, of course.[23]

In fact, throughout the 18th century, there were simply none of the financial – or, indeed, administrative and legal – stresses and strains that had beset the Company in the last four decades of the 17th century. Admittedly, the numbers of those joining the Company fell back quite significantly, but the Company never again came close to collapse into oblivion. Instead, after all the turmoil and chaos of the 1680s, the reforms and reorganisation of the 1690s, and with the increased income from its various investments, the Company's 18th-century accounts at least are reassuringly unexciting.

THE DECLINE OF ECONOMIC CONTROL

Prosperity may have abounded in 18th-century London, but uncertainty remained over the question of the livery companies' economic role. For the Masons' Company, in particular, doubt had been sharpened in two ways: first, by the legislation issued in the aftermath of the Great Fire, which left it unclear to what extent the Company had authority to control the craft of masonry in 18th-century London, and second, by the influx into the Company of so many members who were not masons by trade.

Most of the new liverymen would have joined for social reasons, and no doubt many would also have had a political motive – the voting rights of the livery were of real importance at a time when figures such as John Wilkes and William Beckford were raising the voice of London against the Crown and the aristocracy. Arguably, a greater proportion of the yeomanry were masons but, in 1761, just 37 of the Company's 73 liverymen can confidently be identified as masons: what interest did the clerks, brokers, haberdashers, coal merchants and grocers have in enforcing the Company's monopoly over a craft in which they did not work and about which they knew nothing?[24]

In their study of the London Masons' Company, Knoop and Jones argued that 'the trade functions of the Company may be regarded as of relatively little importance after the close of the seventeenth century'. The Company's authority certainly was weakened in the first two decades of the 18th century. Its searches had ceased to yield much money so the Company sent out its last search in 1704. The Company's attempts to lobby Parliament, in 1709 to prevent the import of wrought marble into Britain, and in 1712 to support the Bricklayers who were opposed to the introduction of a levy on bricks and lime, came to naught, leaving the Company only with expensive legal bills. The Company's right to ensure that all those working as masons in the City of London had completed apprenticeships was likewise undermined when it lost a case in the Court of King's Bench, in 1719-20, prosecuting Henry Taylor for working as a mason without having completed an apprenticeship.[25]

It would, however, be wrong to think that the Company gave up on its attempts to exercise its authority over its craft at the start of the 18th century. In 1719, for example, the Court redrafted its ordinances. Among the many provisions therein relating to the craft of masonry were several which reconfirmed the Company's right to levy fines on those who used and sold stones contrary to the assizes; in 1747, it appears that the Court even toyed with the idea of attempting to enforce these provisions in London.[26]

The Company's most valuable power, though, was that which it believed it had obtained from Common Council in 1694, namely the right to compel those working as masons in London to take up membership of the Company. This was a privilege which, in different ways, the Company stubbornly refused to give up. Indeed, as late as 1822, it even petitioned the Court of Common Council again for a by-law to enforce this right. That petition was unsuccessful, as were most of the Company's efforts over that century, but together they did serve to postpone for a time, in a very small manner at least, the eventual breakdown of its craft monopoly.[27]

The Act of Common Council was clear enough. Whether it was legally enforceable or not was another matter. In fact, the Company took legal advice on the validity of its ordinances and powers, at no little cost, on at least three occasions within the space of just over 80 years: in 1719 from Sir Thomas Pengelly, in 1772 from the City's Common Serjeant, and in 1802 from Sir Vicary Gibbs. In 1719, Pengelly was quite clear that he believed the Act was 'not Good in law' and that the Company could neither compel membership on any who 'Exercises the Trade of a Mason', nor could it search or view the premises or workshops of any masons without the permission of those being inspected. As a consequence, the Court redrafted the Company's ordinances to bring them into line with Pengelly's advice and only twice after 1719 did it use the Act to force masons to join the Company.[28]

However, Pengelly did advise the Court that they could prosecute unfree masons *within* the City of London under the Corporation's rules which forbade the employment of unfree labour, and the Court thus continued to summon masons for another 100 or so years. We might take just a few examples. In December 1721, it summoned 19 men to appear and take up their freedom, in December 1732 four men, and in July 1772 a further seven men – that is a total of 30 men. As late as 1812-14, the Company spent two years trying to get Richard Wilford, a stonemason working at Westminster Abbey, to take up his freedom and, as just noted, in 1822 the Court petitioned the Common Council to re-confirm its right to force masons to take up the freedom.[29]

Taking all this together, we might well conclude that the 'trade functions of the Company' hardly seem have been of 'relatively little importance after the close of the seventeenth century'. Yet we should not over-interpret the evidence to hand. First, many of the largest contractors in London were interested less in forcing their masons to join the Masons' Company and more with ensuring access to a cheap and plentiful supply of labour – free or not. If anything, journeyman masons who had taken up their freedoms had a greater interest in restricting opportunities for unfree masons than their employers did. Tensions within the craft at times like this are usually invisible in the Company's records, but in 1775 some journeyman masons did petition the Court for remedy to a problem, the nature of which the Clerk was reluctant to specify. Put another way, the contemporary craft of masonry was undergoing long-term structural changes in addition to experiencing the usual short-term, cyclical challenges of economic expansion and contraction, war and peace, and investment and retrenchment – to all of which the Company was largely incidental.[30]

Second, there is actually very little evidence to suggest that the Company's efforts to enforce its monopoly were at all effective. Just six of 30 men summoned to appear before the Court and take up their freedom on the occasions above actually became free of the Company. Wilford did join the Company in March 1814, but he promptly bound an apprentice three months later and it is quite possible that he would have taken up his freedom to do that irrespective of the Company's threats. Uncertainty about the Company's legal authority was not the only obstacle preventing the Company from enforcing its writ. When the Court summoned 19 masons to take up their freedom in 1721, four turned out to be dead and eight could not be found. The Company simply did not have the logistical or administrative capacity to impose its authority. In the end, when the Corporation swept away the final vestiges of company control in 1836 and 1856, it made little real difference to life in the Masons' Company.

In fact, the 18th-century Court clearly devoted more of its time and energy to the administration of the Company's rather modest real estate and to the social aspects of Company life than it did to its half-hearted and occasional attempts to enforce its writ. The

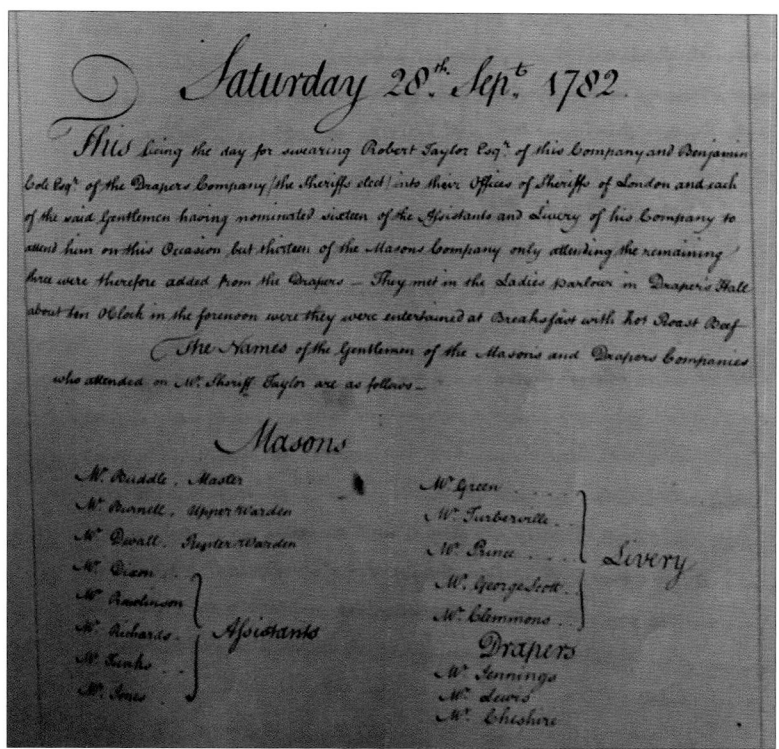

64 *Sir Robert Taylor's swearing-in as Sheriff in 1782; the opening of a five-page account in the Masons' Company Court Minute Book.*

most eye-catching entry in the Company's minutes in the late 18th and early 19th century is that which sets out detail of the splendid procession and feast which celebrated the swearing-in of Sir Robert Taylor, a liveryman of the Company, as Sheriff of London in 1782. Taylor was a celebrated civic officer and distinguished sculptor and architect who deserves his place alongside William Chambers, Robert Adam, and George Dance the younger in what was a golden age of architecture in the 30 years of peace between 1763 and 1793.[31]

For the most part, the Masons' Company in the late 18th and early 19th centuries was a Company becalmed. On 10 January 1760, 13 Assistants attended a Quarterly Court held at Masons' Hall. The minutes were read, John Shaw was admitted to the freedom, Charlotte Harris was elected a pensioner following the death of Widow Fleetwood, Sam Worrall was told to bring in his bill for erecting the stand on Lord Mayor's Day and the pensioners were paid. That was it! Over the course of the next five or six decades, Court meetings as uneventful as that are typical of Company life. In fact, many were much less dynamic even than that. In the 1770s and 1780s, and again between 1828 and 1833 in particular, Court

65 *Liveryman Sir Robert Taylor, depicted wearing the gown and chain of Sheriff of the City of London in 1782.*

meetings were often so poorly attended that it was not possible to transact important Company business. Like many other companies, the Masons had lost their traditional role. The social and fraternal side of Company life remained, albeit stripped of the religious and professional dimensions, but was that enough to justify their continued existence? The companies were about to come under the searching gaze of 19th-century reformers.[32]

12

FREEMASONRY

In 1894, Edward Conder published a volume under the self-consciously archaic title *Records of the Hole Crafte and Fellowship of Masons*, to which was added the significant subtitle *With a Chronicle of the History of the Worshipful Company of Masons of the City of London*. It is an interesting exercise in a certain sort of amateur antiquarianism, and characteristic of its period – but it is not, even in intention, a regular history of the livery company. It is, rather, a study of the connections that Conder believed to exist between 'operative masonry', his term for the practical craft of stonemasonry, and what he distinguished as 'speculative masonry', otherwise 'the modern social cult' of freemasonry. From the opening of his 'Proem', or preface, Conder asserts the identity of the Company as 'the fountain head of that vast society known as The Free and Accepted Masons', and he displays the products of his burrowings in numerous archives as 'undoubted facts' in support of his theme. On reaching the formation of the Grand Lodge of Freemasons in 1717 (or 1721?), he feels able to conclude that the butterfly of freemasonry has finally emerged from the chrysalis of the craft of stonemasonry and flown off in its own direction; so he rattles through the Company's history between 1717 and 1894 in 29 hurried and rather uninterested pages.[1]

Conder dedicated his work to 'the Court of Assistants and Freemen' of the Masons' Company; but, in reality, he wrote primarily as a member of the Quatuor Coronati Lodge (2076) of Freemasons, a lodge dedicated to studying masonic history. His primary purpose was thus not to discuss, but to assert, the identity of the Company as the origin of freemasonry.

Any discussion of the relationship between freemasonry and the Masons' Company must employ a clearly defined terminology. Hitherto, we have used the terms 'mason' and 'stonemason' to describe those who worked in the craft of 'masonry' or 'stonemasonry', and 'freemason' for those highly-skilled carvers of freestone. We shall continue to do so hereafter. To avoid confusion, we shall not employ the often-used synonym 'the craft' to describe modern freemasonry. Instead, the term 'freemasonry' (often with the qualifier 'modern' or 'Enlightenment') will be used to describe the modern initiatory and voluntary society whose members, called 'Freemasons' with a capital letter, meet in lodges which, in England and Wales at least, are today organised under the control of the United Grand Lodge of England (UGLE). There is no simple or single definition of modern freemasonry, but we might think of it as a society with secrets (many of which are actually not that secret at all), which are gradually revealed to its members, who are almost always men, by initiation and advancement through various degrees, thereby encouraging individuals to develop their own understanding of what freemasonry means to them.

THE MEDIEVAL TRADITION AND THE OLD CHARGES

There are strands of freemasonry that claim affinity with medieval antecedents. First, and undeniably, with its stress on brotherhood, commensality and charity, and with its masters, wardens and stewards, freemasonry closely resembles the medieval guilds and fraternities. More questionably, Freemasons assert that they are guardians of a body of inherited knowledge, more philosophical and esoteric than the usual expertise of a medieval craft; this knowledge, they claim, has come down by way of the lodges of medieval masons, though its origins are assigned to a far remoter antiquity. To ensure that it was only communicated to fellow masons, the medieval lodges are credited with having developed a system of degrees and passwords. The modern system of freemasonry is seen as arising in the 16th and 17th centuries, when gentlemen who were not masons began to join the lodges.

None of this proves a connection between the Masons' Company and freemasonry. The fraternal ethos and the nomenclature of the officers is one shared with the wider guild tradition and not just that of stonemasonry. Nor is freemasonry the only society to have assumed and adapted customs from the world of the medieval guilds; the Oddfellows, the Ancient Order of Foresters, the Order of Free Gardeners, the Royal Antediluvian Order of Buffaloes and many others have done so, too. What makes freemasonry unique is not that it inherited and preserved some guild practice, which it undoubtedly did, but that it survived and prospered to a quite remarkable extent. Nor is there any conclusive evidence to suggest that stonemasons generally, or the London Masons' Company in particular, preserved an ancient knowledge which was transmitted to Freemasons in the 18th century.

In not one of the sources we have considered in the previous chapters, whether institutional, such as the Company's ordinances, or individual, such as the wills of individual stonemasons, have we seen any trace of the symbols, emblems and legends which are so closely associated with modern freemasonry. We find no trace of Hiram Abif, King Solomon's temple, the five points of fellowship, the mason's word, 'true architecture', the symbolic meaning of a mason's tools, initiation into a lodge or masonic ritual. We see nothing to suggest that stonemasons in Edinburgh, London and Regensburg all believed that they formed a brotherhood of men who kept the same secrets and worked in the same tradition. No evidence has been found that members of the Masons' Company wore regalia (apart from their livery gowns) or their aprons to Court or livery meetings, or that they advanced through degrees at these same meetings. If medieval masons were preserving an ancient knowledge in secret, then they made a good job of it! Instead, the picture we have is that of a typical medieval craft and a London livery company like any other.

There is a series of texts, known by masonic scholars as the 'Old Charges', which do suggest a connection between medieval stonemasons and modern Freemasons. There are almost 130 of these documents, the vast majority of which are manuscripts now in the possession of lodges of Freemasons, and their relationship to each other has never yet been satisfactorily analysed. The oldest surviving copies of the Old Charges were drawn up in the 16th century, but they all descend, ultimately, from two Middle English texts, usually called the Regius and the Cooke manuscripts, which were both compiled early in the 15th century in the Midlands of England. Essentially, these manuscripts contain a legendary history of the craft of stonemasonry, along with ordinances and regulations for the craft of masonry and for individual masons and, in their earliest forms, they were evidently put together and copied by compilers and scribes who were close to medieval stonemasons. Regius and Cooke were probably first compiled, as Andrew Prescott has convincingly argued, at some point between 1425 and 1450 in response to government pressure on wages in post-Black Death England.[2]

The originators of these 'ur-texts' conceived a history of masonry which connected Pythagoras, Hermes, Noah's son Ham, Euclid, St Alban and King Æthelstan (whose name fortuitously means 'noble stone'), in a story designed to prove that stonemasons deserve to be fairly paid for their work. It appears that in subsequent centuries, often at times of similar wage pressure, the texts were copied, and given circulation; copies eventually found their way into various Freemasons' lodges where, known as the Old Charges, they influenced some of modern freemasonry's practice and ritual.

It must be said that this interpretation is not accepted by all. Recently, David Taillades has suggested that the Old Charges are actually records of ordinances drawn up by fraternities of medieval masons, which again passed into the hands of Freemasons in the early modern period. This seems unlikely. The Old Charges have little or nothing to say about the sort of things which typically concerned the guilds and fraternities of the Middle Ages, such as the provision of assistance for sick and aged masons, the paying of dues or the observance of feast days. It is striking, also, that the Masons' Company's iconography, regulations and ordinances seem not to have been influenced at all by the legends related in the Old Charges, something we might expect to see if the texts did indeed descend from masons' fraternities.[3]

The Old Charges are composite texts, put together over time from multiple, often contradictory or unrelated sources. Thus, we find the legend of the *Quatuor Coronati* masons and a poem on etiquette called *Urbanitatis*, alongside provisions about oaths sworn by apprentices, and sections which appear to have derived from the ordinances and regulations of the Masons' Company. There is also good evidence that their compilers appear to have misunderstood or misinterpreted some of the sources which they used. For example, some early modern compilers seem to have misconstrued the journeyman masons described as 'allowes' from the Company's 1481 ordinances, as men 'allowed' into masons' lodges even though they were not operative masons – and they are thus identified as the first Freemasons.

66 *Arms of The Masons' Company depicted in Papworth Old Charges manuscript. (Note the unusual wording of the motto.)*

Altogether, the Old Charges have to be described as a disorderly assemblage of fragmentary materials which provides us with an account of stonemasonry that is essentially dubious and in part mythical. But their value is found not in their historical veracity, but in what they tell us of conditions in the late medieval craft of masonry. They are best understood as 'origin myths' through which contemporary masons, faced with a 'problematic present', created their own 'usable past'. To put it in another way, as a response to pressure on their wages, medieval masons can be seen as having created a history of their craft, which pulled in every authority they could find, however fantastical, in order to justify their right to receive higher pay. In turn, early modern Freemasons looking to create their own usable past expanded and developed this 'history', again by turning to different sources, and it was through the transmission of these texts into the world of freemasonry that these enigmatic texts have been preserved and widely disseminated.[4]

Again, it must be said, there is little here to connect the Masons' Company and modern freemasonry. Many copies of the Old Charges bear illustrations of the Masons' Company's coat of arms, but that proves no more than that some compilers of the Old Charges wanted to use the Company's symbols to add authority to their texts. It is commonly believed that four late 17th-century copies of the Old Charges can be linked with members of the Company, but that claim does not bear closer scrutiny. The 'Antiquity MS' was supposedly copied by Robert Padgett, Clerk to the 'Society of the Free-Masons of the City of London' in 1686, but Thomas Stampe was Clerk in that year and it is odd that the Company is referred to as a 'Society' in that manuscript. The Bain MS, and the Phillipps MSS Nos. 1 and 2, may have been copied by the Masons' Company's Clerk, but he could easily have done that as a scrivener or draftsman on a private commission, and there is no evidence to support Conder's assertion that the Clerk who copied them was William Hammond – he was actually a Court Assistant. Phillipps No. 1 may have been copied for Richard Banks, another of the Company's Assistants, but that is only a tenuous link on a personal and not an institutional level. The Company does have one copy of the Old Charges, drawn up in the late 17th or early 18th century in its archive, but the Company owned several books and there is no reason to think that this one was ever anything more than a curiosity.[5]

In fact, the Old Charges seem never to have been used by the Company in a constitutional, institutional or administrative sense. Nowhere in the Company's ordinances, by-laws, charter or coat of arms is there any reference to, or representation of, any of the legends found in the Old Charges, nowhere do the Company's minutes record the reading of the Old Charges, and nowhere in the texts of the Old Charges is the Company even mentioned. If the Old Charges are a thread that joins medieval masons and modern Freemasons, then it does not appear to have been a thread that ran through the Masons' Company.

ACCEPTION

At some point between June 1630 and June 1631 the Masons' Company of London spent 6s. 6d. 'in goeing abroad and att a meeteing att the hall about the masons that were to be accepted'. This is the earliest mention of an enigmatic phenomenon known as 'acception', or the acceptance of masonry. Thereafter, the acception appears on a further seven, perhaps eight, occasions in the Company's 17th-century records. In 1645-7, the Company spent some £3 on an acception dinner and several meetings 'about the acception'. In 1649-50, four men paid £1 each, either 'uppon Acceptance of Masonry' or for 'coming on the acception', and almost £11 was spent on a dinner, presumably in their honour. It is possible that the 8s. 6d. which was 'payd upon the exception more than was received' by the Company, in 1663-4, also refers to acception. From inventories drawn up in 1665 and 1676, we learn that the Company owned a 'faire large table', or frame, which contained the names of the accepted masons, and a 'booke of the Constitutions of the Accepted Masons'. In 1677, John

Shorthose was ordered by the Court to buy a new banner with the sum of £6 0s. 5d., then in the hands of the Renter Warden, which was the 'remainder rec'd of the last accepted Masons'. Acception does not reappear in the Company's records thereafter and when an inventory of the Company's property was drawn up in January 1696, the frame containing the names of the accepted masons and the book of constitutions had both disappeared. We cannot know when the Company acquired the book and the frame mentioned in the inventories, so, from these sources at least, we must conclude that the acception was a phenomenon which flickered briefly into Company life in the middle decades of the 17th century, most obviously between 1645 and 1650.[6]

Immediately, we are struck by something of a contradiction. On the one hand, the acception appears not to have been essentially an element of the Company. There is nothing about it in the Company's constitutional records, there are no surviving records of the acception's membership or officers (if, indeed, it had any), and it appears to have had no official sanction, so it cannot have been an institutional part of Company life, nor could it have offered a route to membership in any way with which we are familiar. On the other hand, acception does seem to have been part of the Company in some sense. There are references to it in the Company's records, individuals paid money to become accepted, occasionally some of this money found its way into the Company's coffers, and the Company kept the names of accepted masons and a book of the acception's constitutions in its archive.

We learn little from these references about the actual reality of the acception. However, other contemporary references to acception or to accepted masons are not hard to find and they do throw some light on to the phenomenon. Elias Ashmole (1617-92) was a lawyer, astrologer, antiquarian and herald at the College of Arms. His wide-ranging interests, expressed in an astonishing collection of curiosities, led him in 1683 to found the museum in Oxford that now bears his name. On 16 October 1646, Ashmole famously recorded that he 'was made a Free Mason at Warrington in Lancashire', at a lodge meeting in the presence of eight other men. Thereafter, over the next 36 years, Ashmole's extensive papers and correspondence record nothing about his career as a Freemason, until on 10 March 1682 he received a summons to attend a lodge being held the next day at Masons' Hall in London where six men were 'admitted into the

67 *Elias Ashmole, 1617-92, astrologer and antiquary.*

Fellowship of Free Masons'. It has often been assumed that there was significance in the fact that Masons' Hall was the venue for this meeting, but it is a matter of prosaic reality that around this time the Company frequently let its Hall to different individuals and associations, and we know that, in the 18th century, meetings of Freemasons often took place at other livery company halls.[7]

However, it is also an indisputable fact that the lodge which met on 11 March, comprising 15 other men besides Ashmole, included at least 12 who were members – and several quite senior members – of the Masons' Company. One of those in attendance, Thomas Shorthose, had even paid £1 to the Company's Renter Warden, in 1649-50, to come on to the acception. Conder, of course, followed by others, took this as clear evidence of a connection between the Company and freemasonry. And, to add to the ambiguities of the occasion, all those present subsequently dined at the *Half Moon Tavern* in Cheapside, where they enjoyed 'a Noble Dinner prepared at the charge of the New-accepted Masons'.[8]

Evidence that by 1676, at least, the 'Company of accepted Masons' was already well-known appears in the form of a mention in *Poor Robin's Intelligence*, a satirical journal. In 1686, Dr Robert Plot (d.1696), a naturalist, antiquary and sometime Keeper of the Ashmolean Museum, explained that gentlemen were accustomed to attend lodges in Staffordshire where they learned 'certain secret signs', joined the society of Freemasons and became 'an accepted mason'. Indeed, Plot believed this to be common practice throughout England. In 1723, James Anderson opened his *Constitutions of the*

Free-Masons with reference to the 'Right Worshipful Fraternity of Accepted Free-Masons' and, in 1738, what was in effect the second edition of this book was entitled *The New Book of Constitutions of the Antient and Honourable Fraternity of Free and Accepted Masons.*[9]

What are we to make of all this? The acception appears to have been an association or fraternity through which masons and non-masons could come together, and it may well have been one of the tributaries from the confluence of which modern freemasonry flowed. Certainly, it looks more like freemasonry than anything previously seen. In London, it is sufficiently plain that it was associated in some way with the 17th-century Masons' Company. Andrew Prescott has described it as a 'social wing of the London Company of Masons' formed to 'bolster the claims and prestige of the trade' and to increase the Company's revenue at a time when the Company was in serious financial straits. That goes too far, perhaps; why would the Masons' Company, which was already quite a social fellowship anyway, need a social wing? To facilitate the admittance of new members who did not work in the craft of masonry? In that case, why did so many stonemasons who were already members of the Company also come onto the acception? That is hardly evidence of a 17th-century outreach programme. Moreover, many men who were not stonemasons had already joined the contemporary Company and, as we have seen, when the Company decided in 1706 more actively to solicit new members from other trades and professions, it did so through its existing structures and not the creation of a new one. Furthermore, if the acception was designed to bolster the prestige of the Company and increase its revenue, it failed. The Company's financial position in the 1680s was more precarious than it had been at any time in the preceding century. Indeed, many contemporary livery companies had similar financial problems, so why do we only find something like the acception in the Masons' Company? Perhaps because the acception was connected more to the craft of stonemasonry on a national level than it was to the Masons' Company? After all, men became accepted masons in Staffordshire and elsewhere in the country, and they did that through lodges rather than guilds or companies.[10]

What then, if the acception was a fraternity which many members of the 17th-century Company joined? This could explain why the 'faire large table' and book came to be kept among the Company's possessions – men who were members of both the fraternity and

Company put them there. This could also explain why we have only a few rather superficial references to the acception, which can record only a fraction of its activity, in the Company's records. Members of the acception must have dined on more than two or three occasions over five decades; one hardly needs a 'faire large table' to record the names of just a few men; and it is not possible that those few admissions could have been responsible for a credit balance of over £6 in 1677. Ashmole tells us that six men were admitted in 1682, and there is nothing about either that meeting or dinner in the Company's accounts or minutes. Perhaps, then, what we see are occasional instances when sums were diverted from acception business into the Company's accounts. These sums may have been reimbursements for expenses incurred in meetings or dinners attended by members of the acception and the Company, or voluntary donations to the Company from entrants to the acception; it is even possible that they were mistakenly, or perhaps even deliberately, recorded in the Company's ledger and not that of the acception – if indeed it had a ledger.

In the last analysis, we simply cannot know. For our purposes, we can only conclude that, in London at least, there was a connection of some sort between the acception and the Masons' Company.

THE MASONS' LODGE

Modern freemasons have adopted the term 'lodge' from the lodges of the medieval stonemasons to describe both their organisation and their meeting place. Yet even this seemingly straightforward transfer is not as simple as it first appears. Medieval masons' lodges were temporary structures occupied by itinerant craftsmen. There is no evidence, in England at least, that they were permanent or administrative institutions which could control apprenticeships, admit members or organise a craft – functions which were performed by guilds. Of course, traditions can be passed down orally and associations do not need writing to exist and thrive. All the same, no masons' lodge has left any written record of its existence and we have no evidence, from their wills or any other source, that masons 'joined' lodges.

So when Ashmole and others like him were admitted to lodges and went to lodge meetings in 17th-century England, what exactly did they join and what precisely did they do? In what tradition did they think themselves acting? Who summoned Ashmole to the

68 *Fifteenth-century manuscript with miniature depicting medieval masons' lodge.*

noble et bertueuse duchesse berthe de bourgongne

Coment berthe duchesse de bourgongne fist encomen
cher la magdalene de bezelar qui encoues est de lac
gent et grant tresor quelle p trouua par reuelation

lodge meeting at Masons' Hall? From at least 1721, freemasonry has been managed and governed through 'grand lodges', yet there is no evidence for grand lodges in the medieval craft of masonry, nor, indeed, for similar superstructures in the guild tradition. Many freemasonry lodges are special interest lodges, that is they were formed by members who have shared interests, outlooks or hobbies. There is no evidence that any stonemasons' lodge, or indeed the Masons' Company, had personalities like this. Altogether, the lodge structure and organisation of modern freemasonry in England does not obviously descend from the lodges of English medieval stonemasons.

In Scotland, however, the picture is very different, for there we find evidence, at quite an early date, that lodges did indeed operate as organisational bodies. In 1537, George Boiss was appointed mason for life by the council and kirkmaster of Dundee, according to 'the auld use and consuetude [custom] of Our Lady Luge [Lodge]'. At the end of that century, William Schaw (1549/50–1602), then Master of the King's Works, issued statutes for the reorganisation and better regulation of the craft of stonemasonry in Scotland. Among other matters, these statutes stipulated that masons ought to be organised into lodges and that these lodges should appoint secretaries and keep minutes. From these minutes, we see lodges claiming territorial jurisdiction over masons, regulating wages and production, binding apprentices, admitting freemen and providing charity and relief for their members – in short, operating in many of the ways that we would expect a guild of masons to perform.[11]

As members of the Masons' Company know, however, it is with the Incorporation of the Masons of Glasgow, and not with any lodge, that the Masons' Company is today associated. What were incorporations, then, and how are they different from lodges? Scottish incorporations were, in fact, equivalent to English guilds and there does seem to have been significant crossover in membership and officers between lodges and incorporations in Scotland. It is unclear why the two distinct yet similar bodies existed alongside each other. David Stevenson has argued that, first, incorporations were often shared between crafts, for example the masons and the carpenters, and that masons, as possessors of their own secrets, wanted their own institutions. But carpenters worked with geometry as much as, if not more than masons did, so why do we never hear about the carpenters' secrets and why would they not have wanted their own lodge-style institutions? Second, he has suggested that lodges were free from municipal or noble control and that they better met the needs of itinerant masons. To which we must then ask, why have incorporations of masons at all? Third, there is the argument that lodges offered more opportunities than the incorporations for journeyman masons to increase their social status by becoming masters. Surely, however, it would have been easier for journeymen to change the incorporations from the inside, rather than turn to an alternative structure; and did journeyman masons want the social status that may, or may not, have come with being a master mason in a lodge in the first place?[12]

The Masons' Company must have been the largest association of masons in Britain in one of Europe's largest cities, and it probably had no more than 50 members on its livery at any time in the 16th or 17th centuries – and this was certainly not because it restricted access or promotion. In fact, it was the costs of membership, and the perception that the Company was increasingly irrelevant as a craft organisation, that deterred masons from joining the Masons' Company, not the fact that it offered only limited opportunities for social advancement. It is hard to see why Scottish journeyman masons should have differed from their equivalents in London when it came to attitudes towards lodges.

Be all that as it may, lodges were organisational institutions in early modern Scotland in a way that they simply were not in England. We have evidence that by the 1630s Scottish stonemasons in their lodges possessed secrets which they called 'the Mason Word', and that men joining lodges underwent a ritual initiation. Over the course of the 17th century, gentlemen, many of whom had interests in mathematics, geometry or architecture, began to join these lodges. In May 1641, two men of very high status indeed, Robert Moray (1608/9-73), a politician and quartermaster general in the Covenanter Army occupying Newcastle, and Sir Alexander Hamilton (d.1649), general of artillery in the same army, joined a lodge of Freemasons based in Edinburgh. In 1696, the Lodge of Dunblane was founded and the majority of its members were gentlemen, making it the first lodge of its kind known to have existed in the world.[13]

As far as freemasonry was concerned, this was undoubtedly Scotland's century and it is probably no coincidence that freemasonry in this guise in England is first visible in the north. Ashmole joined a lodge in Warrington in 1646, Randle Holme (1627-1700) joined a lodge in Chester in about 1665, and Plot described the custom of gentlemen joining lodges in Staffordshire in 1686. What we have, then, is a picture of something which looks like modern freemasonry filtering down into northern England from Scotland – perhaps a consequence of the invasion of northern England, in 1640, by the Scottish Covenanter Army.[14]

RECONCILIATION?

The medieval guild traditions, with which we started this analysis, comprise just a small proportion of the ideas which have shaped the development of modern freemasonry. The influences of the Renaissance, for example, can also be easily seen in freemasonry's rituals, symbols and practices. The Renaissance was not just an artistic but an intellectual and scientific revolution; it reimagined architecture and geometry – the latter, according to Thomas Hobbes, 'the only science which it hath pleased God hitherto to bestow on mankind' – as liberal arts worthy of study by renaissance men. Today, Freemasons believe that knowledge of these disciplines, in particular, brings them closer to truth and divinity. More than anything else, though, modern freemasonry as we know it is a child of the European Enlightenment, and on a theoretical and philosophical level, freemasonry's ethos of fraternal egalitarianism, secularism, progress, perfectibility and cosmopolitanism indicates obvious legacies of the Enlightenment.[15]

It is, then, no surprise that so many of those most visibly involved in, or attracted to, freemasonry in its earliest forms are men with demonstrable interests in Renaissance and Enlightenment thought. William Schaw, who might be compared to Inigo Jones in England, was a learned, well-travelled and cultured man with an interest in hermeticism. As generals responsible for the ballistic calculations used by artillerymen, and for the design of camps, both Moray and Hamilton were well-acquainted with geometry. Ashmole was a prodigious collector of books and scientific instruments and it is easy to see how he would have been attracted to the esoteric elements of freemasonry. John Theophilus Desaguliers (1683-1744), a Huguenot who is considered one of the founding fathers of modern freemasonry, was a natural philosopher, engineer and protégé of Sir Isaac Newton. William Stukeley (1687-1765), who became a Freemason in 1721, was friends with men such as Newton, Roger Gale, Hans Sloane and Edmund Halley; a member of the Royal Society, the Royal College of Physicians and the Society of Antiquaries, he also founded a society to celebrate Britain's classical rather than Gothic architecture. The first Grand Master of Grand Lodge, John, second Duke of Montagu (1690-1749), had toured Europe in his youth and was also a member of the Royal Society and Royal College of Physicians.[16]

We should not overstate the significance of gentle, and indeed noble, participation in masonic lodges in the early days of freemasonry. Individual lodges, and Grand Lodge itself, gave prominence to non-artisan involvement in freemasonry in order to attract new members. Most Freemasons were actually drawn from what contemporaries called the 'middling sort', and operative masons were frequently keen participants. However, when the study of architecture and geometry once more became a liberal art, which was not until the late 16th and early 17th centuries in Britain, it attracted the interest of gentlemen.

Masons had no monopoly of architectural or geometrical knowledge – anyone who has stood under Hugh Herland's timber hammerbeam roof in Westminster Hall will appreciate that. But of all the crafts it was stonemasonry, with its hard practicality and subtle rationality, its soaring aspiration and stubborn durability, that most caught the imagination of the fascinated inquirer. Masonry thus became something of a noble craft, attractive to gentlemen in a way that it simply had not been hitherto, and its lodges were readily credited with a semi-legendary status as repositories of an ancient, secret and superior knowledge which had been transmitted from generation to generation.

In Scotland, men who did not work in the craft of stonemasonry began to join masons' lodges and it was this model that seems to have spread into northern England. The Masons' Company of London was a poor, small, artisan organisation which struggled to keep its head above water throughout the 17th century. It held little appeal for the quality. The mysterious acception, however, may very well have been a different thing altogether, and this fraternity may have been one forum in which masons rubbed shoulders with non-masons who had an interest in their craft. Gentlemen and others who came to lodges would have brought their own ideas, learning and embellishments with them to these meetings. It was perhaps at this time that so many of the motifs and legends we associate with modern freemasonry, which appear conspicuously absent from the medieval craft, were established as mythic elements – when the mason's tools began to be interpreted symbolically, when the idea of a 'mason's word' took hold, and when initiation rituals were developed.

This was also a time when, as Jürgen Habermas and Peter Clark have shown, a public sphere and an associational culture were taking form across the country. Between 1650 and 1800, large numbers of men – and it was primarily a masculine phenomenon – began to join voluntary associations of different hues. Clubs and societies were established in coffee houses and taverns across the land, and they soon 'permeated every nook and cranny of British social and cultural life'. It was in Britain's towns and cities that this associational culture took its firmest root and freemasonry was easily the most successful association of this time. By 1725, that is within four years of the formation of Grand Lodge, there were already 60 affiliated masonic lodges in London.[17]

This should hardly come as a surprise. Contemporary London was not just a city in the process of being almost entirely rebuilt after the Great Fire, it was spreading inexorably in every direction. As construction workers poured into the City, the livery companies had to battle to ensure their futures, but the crafts and their associated disciplines – architecture, geometry, science and design – became fashionable in a way never seen before. When before in its history had London been home to men of the stamp of Sir Christopher Wren, Nicholas Hawksmoor, Robert Hooke, James Gibbs and John James? When before had it been home to so many clubs and societies? The livery companies had been vehicles of sociability, of course, but to many contemporaries they must have appeared as relics from a bygone age. Certainly, their existence was constrained and cramped by their location in the historic City of London, by then already home to only a minority of Londoners, and it is no coincidence that we see freemasonry and other societies much more clearly in London's 'West End' and suburbs.

When all of these themes, and their supporting evidences, are brought together, it becomes possible to develop an understanding of why freemasonry emerged when and where it did. And with the benefit of that understanding, we see clearly that the Masons' Company was not a particularly important actor. The medieval guild and craft tradition which it preserved was manifestly less significant in the formation of freemasonry than Renaissance and Enlightenment philosophies were. Freemasonry's organisational structure owes more to Scottish lodges than it does to London's livery companies. Freemasonry's geographic centre was, and indeed still is, outside London's historic walls.

Uncertainties remain, but Conder's giddier speculations can surely be put to the rest for which they have long been overdue. The corruption of the Company's coat of arms and motto at the hands of early modern antiquaries does not, as he suggests, imply a connection between the Company and freemasonry: armorial bearings have for ever been subject to erroneous representation and inaccurate description. The Company did, as Conder says, begin to style itself as the Company of Masons, rather than of Freemasons, in 1653-4, but this does not provide evidence for 'the speculative element' venturing 'on a new course' outside the Company's embrace. The terms 'mason' and 'freemason' had not only been used interchangeably for centuries, they would continue to be so, even by the Company itself, well into the 19th century; if the change in name signified anything, it was that the medieval distinctions between freemasons and roughmasons, between hewers and layers, were passing into oblivion.[19]

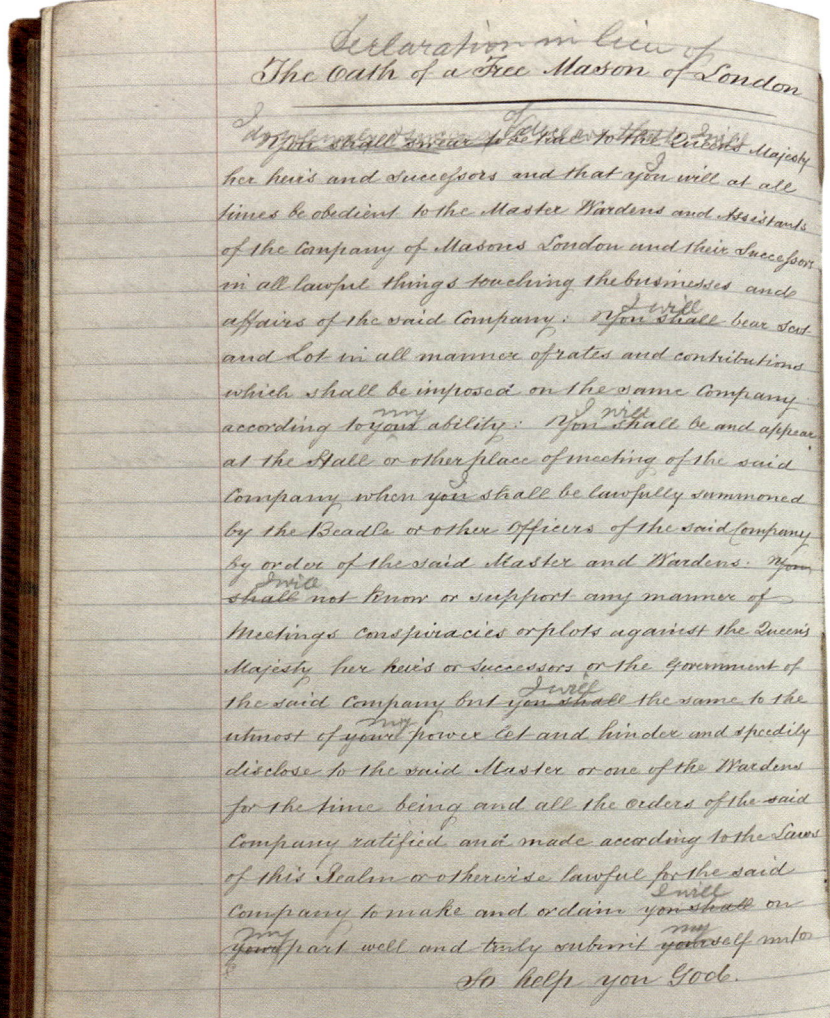

69 *The oath of a Free Mason of London, used for admission of a freeman into the 19th-century Masons' Company. The wording in the 21st century is almost unchanged.*

We should congratulate Conder for revealing the association between the 17th-century Company and the acception, but he overinterpreted the evidence which he found. We cannot possibly know if the names of Inigo Jones and Elias Ashmole were among those preserved on the frame of accepted masons. Conder goes far beyond the evidence in his assertion that, through the acception, the Masons' Company has the 'peculiar distinction, above all other gilds, of being one of the principal connecting links in that chain of evidence which proves that the modern social cult, known as the Society of Free and Accepted Masons, is lineally descended from the old Fraternity of Masons'.[18]

It is not at all 'certain', as Conder says it is, that the Company and Society of Free and Accepted Masons went hand-in-hand until 1700, at which point the 'esoteric portion' packed their bags (presumably taking their 'faire large table' and book of constitutions with them) and the two societies diverged. At the very least, one might think that if a group of members and former members of the Company had been instrumental in the establishment of a new fraternal order, which was attracting aristocrats and gentlemen to join it and which inherited and borrowed ancient knowledge that the Company had preserved for centuries, surely someone would have noted something about the fact somewhere in the Company's records! But nowhere do we find any reference to any group leaving the Masons' Company; nowhere do we even find notice of the formation of Grand Lodge. In fact, if a splinter group had left the Company early in the 18th century, it is more likely that it would have comprised operative stonemasons, unhappy at the recent influx of large numbers of non-masons into the Company.[20]

Had the Masons' Company and its members really played a significant role in the establishment of freemasonry in the 17th century, we might also expect to find continued connections, at least in terms of common membership, between the Company and the cult in the century which followed – but we do not. There are significant difficulties about identifying individuals exactly, of course – how can we know if the William Taylor who joined the Company on 2 October 1783 was the same William Taylor who appears a member of some seven or eight Freemasons' lodges in London in the 1780s and 1790s? – but at most 84 of the 654 men (12.8 per cent) who joined the Company between 1700 and 1749 may have been Freemasons; again at the very most, 56 of the 230 men (24.3 per cent) who were admitted as freemen of the Company between 1750-1799 were also Freemasons.[21]

Men who were both Freemasons and members of the Masons' Company, for example Edward Strong junior, appear to have kept Company life and freemasonry quite separate. Admittedly, some lodges do appear to have been particularly popular with members of the Masons' Company. Perhaps four of the 47 Freemasons who were members of the lodge which met at the Crown behind the Royal Exchange in 1725, and possibly seven of the 21 declared members, including both wardens of the Queen's Head Turnstile Lodge, which met in Holborn in 1723, were members of the Masons' Company. The

70 *Edward Strong junior, Master Mason 1718-19, 'A Gentleman and his Family'. Painted by Charles Phillips in 1732. Strong was a member of the Freemasons' lodge that met in the Swan Tavern in Greenwich.*

Queen's Head Turnstile was the successor to the lodge which met at the Crown tavern in Parker's Lane just off Drury Lane, that is one of the four 'time immemorial' lodges which claimed to have formed Grand Lodge, but the history of the Crown tavern lodge is very obscure and we cannot draw firm conclusions from this evidence. In short, there is nothing here at all to compare with Ashmole's account of Companymen numbering 12 of the 16 attendees at a lodge meeting in 1682.[22]

Nothing brings this into sharper relief than comparison of admissions to the Company with those of certain lodges which were wont to describe themselves as lodges of operative stonemasons. We might take samples from just three to serve as an illustration: the Masters' Lodge, subsequently known as the Royal Jubilee Lodge, which met at various locations in Soho, Marylebone and Mayfair; the Lodge of Concord, later the Operative Masons' Lodge and the Lodge of Old Concord, which met in Bloomsbury and Covent Garden; and the Domatic Lodge which met in Holborn and Clerkenwell. Between February 1768 and December 1788, 18 of the 58 new members (31 per cent) admitted to the Masters' Lodge listed their occupation as either 'mason' or 'stone carver'. Just one of these men, James Whitworth a mason from Hackney, was also a member of the Company. Between 1813 and 1836, 17 of the 210 men (8.1 per cent) and 34 of the 129 men (26.4 per cent) who joined the Lodge of Concord and the Domatic Lodge respectively listed their occupations as masons or builders. Just one, perhaps two, of these 51 masons and builders can be identified as members of the Company with anything like certainty. Indeed, if we were to draw a conclusion from this evidence it would not be that the Company and freemasonry were close, it would be that admission to a Freemasons' lodge was a more attractive proposition to stonemasons in Georgian London than was admission to the Company. After all, between 1813 and 1836, the Company admitted just 60 new members compared to the 339 who joined just two operative masons' lodges in the same period.[23]

Today, there is no institutional connection between the Worshipful Company of Masons and modern freemasonry. Freemasons are free to join the Company, of course, without let or hindrance and many have done so, but the Company also goes to great lengths to maintain its distance from freemasonry. In 1983, Standing Committee was 'firmly opposed' to the creation even of a Freemasons' lodge within the Company, primarily because it feared a blurring of lines between the two societies. In 1991, the Court was even more unyielding when it refused permission for a lodge to take the name of the Associated Companies, resolving that 'it is considered undesirable for any membership organisation, club, society or other body to be formed, the name of which implies directly or indirectly any association with or approval by the Company'. In 1996-7, a proposal that the Company change its name to the Worshipful Company of Stonemasons, to avoid confusion with freemasonry, led to a protracted and divisive debate, not just on Court and Standing Committee but also within the livery, before it was finally rejected on 7 October 1997. The re-admission of women in 2003-4 has, likewise, put more distance between the Company and modern Freemasons.[24]

There is no animosity or rivalry between the two organisations, it is just that they are entirely separate bodies; it is for the best that that distinction is unmistakable.

13

VICTORIAN SOMNOLENCE

'Local government' in the modern sense barely existed in early 19th-century England. The nation's capital was a turbulent megalopolis of some 1.5 million people which was sketchily and often chaotically administered by an anachronistic patchwork of some 90 local authorities; the 'square mile' of the City of London itself, where there was a population of perhaps 125,000, having fought to preserve its medieval privileges and institutions, was still more archaically governed. So it was unsurprising that the Whig government which came to power in 1830, having reorganised the parliamentary franchise to suit its own interests in 1832, should next consider the possibility of revising local government also. A Royal Commission of Inquiry was set up, and reported on arrangements in the country at large in 1835. Special attention was deemed necessary, however, for the ancient City and its sensibilities, and a separate inquiry headed by Sir Francis Palgrave carried out investigations between 1833 and 1835; the 'supplemental Report' of this group was eventually published in 1837.[1]

The livery companies came within the scope of Palgrave's inquiry. On paper at least, it remained the case that in the City of London only freemen could open shops or pursue a craft, while only liverymen could vote in national elections and most civic polls. Any inquiry into local government in London had, of necessity, to consider the role that the companies should and did play in the public realm. Thus, Palgrave's Commissioners asked 89 guilds and companies of the contemporary City to supply documentary evidence for their ruling bodies and constitutions, to reply to written questions about their organisation and function, and to send representatives (usually their clerks or court assistants) to answer oral questions at a public meeting at the Guildhall.

71 *Sir Francis Palgrave, lawyer and historian; etching, 1823.*

It can be fairly said that the Commissioners received a mixed response. The Corporation was for the most part helpful, but some companies simply refused to answer questions or even to appear. The Master, Wardens and Clerk of the Masons' Company were first summoned before the Commissioners at the Guildhall in December 1833. They were also expected to reply to a series of standard inquiries arranged under 16 headings which was circulated in 1834. John Aldridge, the Clerk at the time, complied more or less fully with the Commissioners' demands, supplying detailed information under nine of the headings, but not answering seven which he deemed irrelevant to the contemporary Company. His four-page handwritten replies were used to compile a summary of the Company which ran to almost five printed pages in the Commissioners' final report, and they remain in the Company's archive along with several documents in support of his replies. Aldridge's responses to the Commission's inquiries, together with other evidence contained in Palgrave's Report, supply valuable information about the activity – or lack of activity – of the livery companies at this period.[2]

By the time the report came out, in 1837, there was a new government, and the Prime Minister, Lord Melbourne, discerning no groundswell of public opinion calling for reform, was disinclined to enact change unless he absolutely had to. After all, the livery franchise gave the vote to 12,000 or so liverymen in London, or 10 per cent of the City's population, a large proportion by contemporary standards. Besides, there was the hope that the Corporation might reform itself. In 1835, it had lowered the cost of the freedom to £5 and made it possible to acquire the freedom without going through a company, while in 1856 the last restrictions on unfree labour and retailers were swept away. For the most part, however, the Corporation set its face against any proposals for reform, and the Masons' Company – or a small but committed cabal of its Assistants at least – often appeared to play its small part in opposing change. In 1852, the Court threw its weight behind the opposition to a parliamentary bill which sought further to widen the franchise to freeholders in London. In 1856 and 1863, special Courts were summoned in order to resist bills which sought electoral and administrative reform, and to amalgamate the City of London and Metropolitan police.[3]

When William Gladstone formed his second administration in 1880, therefore, the City had seen off numerous schemes for wholesale reform. The Corporation had been the subject of another Royal Commission in 1853-4, this one chaired by Henry Labouchère. On that occasion, the Commissioners did look into the Londoners' landholdings and obligations in Ulster, but the companies managed to evade closer scrutiny as the Commissioners took a very narrow view of their role and deemed them 'not constituent parts of the Corporation'. But inquiry, if not reform, was now in the air. On 1 April 1880, even before Gladstone's return to power later that month, the Court of the Masons' Company asked its Clerk, John Hunter, to search the Company's records and to prepare a report detailing how much of the Company's income came from trusts, whether any part of the Company's property was held through trusts or other third-party interests, and to pull together 10 years' worth of accounts from 1868-78.[4]

Hunter's nine-page report was ready by 12 June, and by that time Gladstone's newly elected Government had announced that another Royal Commission would be appointed, this time to inquire into the livery companies. This was to be a much more searching affair than its predecessor of the 1830s. In 1834, the Commissioners had sent the Masons' Company a single sheet with questions arranged under 16 headings; on 14 August 1880 their successors sent a 12-page questionnaire. Hunter was ordered to liaise with the clerks of other companies to find out how they would reply to the Commissioners and a committee was formed to prepare the Company's responses. After an 'exhaustive inquiry' which made 'a considerable demand upon the time of the officers' of the Company, in 1884 the Commission produced a five-volume report which ran to perhaps some three million words. The section of the printed report concerning the Masons' Company covers some 20 pages.[5]

In fact, the Commission actually produced two reports, as three conservative members issued a report which disagreed with the conclusions reached by the remaining nine Commissioners. As George Ramsey has shown, this was no simple radical/conservative political division. Rather, it was a dispute on a fundamental point of interpretation. The majority of the Commissioners concluded that the companies were public bodies with public duties and obligations. They therefore recommended that their constitutions be reformed, that steps be taken to stop them alienating estates before a large part of the income from these estates could be put to 'useful purposes', and that all trusts older than 50 years be put to public use. The minority report argued that the companies were in fact private bodies and that their right to hold private property was as inviolable as that of any private person.

The companies for their part clearly resented having to answer to a Commission which they perceived as prejudiced and hostile, and their returns were notably sullen and unaccommodating. Invited by the Commissioners to suggest ways in which the constitution or administration of the companies might be improved or altered, the Court of the Masons' Company replied that they had 'no suggestions to offer on this subject'. Many companies, including the Masons, accompanied their answers with a letter which stated that their willingness to help the Commissioners was not 'an admission on their part of any right in the Crown or any other jurisdiction to inquire into their private property, or to deal with it in disregard of their rights'. They may have felt that their cautiousness was rewarded when Gladstone's government fell in 1885 before taking any action on the Commission's report, which had reached it in the previous year.[6]

THE MASONS' COMPANY IN THE AGE OF REFORM

In many ways, Company life changed little between the 1830s and the 1880s. The Company was governed across this period, as it had been since the 1670s, by its charter and by-laws, and was managed and administered by its Court of Assistants which met seven times a year. There were four Quarterly Courts, an Election Court on 14 June, an Audit Court in August and a Court held on Lord Mayor's Day (by now 9 November). As we have already seen, the Company's retreat from its historic role as an economic regulator had been a long and drawn out affair, but it was settled by 1830. In their replies to both Commissions the Company repeated that although they still possessed some authority to superintend the craft of masonry according to their charter, 'these powers have been disused' and 'the right has not been exercised within the memory of any living member of the Company'.[7]

The 19th-century Company had only a small membership. As Aldridge himself admitted to the Commissioners, because 'they have no Notice of Deaths' the Court simply had no way of knowing how many members there were. It seems safe to say, however, that there has never been another period when the Company has had fewer members than it did between 1830 and 1880. Between 1801 and 1833, fewer than three men a year, on average, were admitted to the freedom of the Company, and in four of those years not a single admission was recorded. A list of liverymen prepared in 1822 recorded just 44 names, while 10 years later Aldridge believed there to be some 50 liverymen and 25 freemen.[8]

Under the terms of the 1832 Reform Act, the Masons were required to keep a record of the resident liverymen for the City's electoral roll, and until 1918 the Masons' Clerk was paid five guineas every year to prepare this for scrutiny by the Corporation's revising barrister. While some liverymen lived outside the City of London constituency and so were left off the list drawn up in 1833, that list recorded just 39 resident liverymen. Whatever the exact size of the membership in the 1830s, or indeed in the following decades, it seems clear that it grew smaller. In the 10 years from 1870-79 there were just 13 admissions to the freedom, and by 1880 the Court believed there to be just 41 members of the Company, all of whom were liverymen.[9]

It was not as if the Company made it particularly difficult to take up the freedom. It seems that the only bar to membership was gender. No women were admitted to the 19th-century Company and the Assistants expressed the view, both in the 1830s and 1880s, that women were not 'entitled to freedom in any case' and 'not admitted to membership of the company'. In fact, no resolution had ever been passed forbidding female admission. Nor was religious belief an obstacle to membership. Four members of the Court in the 1830s were religious dissenters, Roman Catholics were free to join and, as far as Aldridge was concerned at least, 'no feeling of religious exclusion exists in the Company'. Several Acts of Parliament were passed in the middle of the 19th century which repealed and reformed some of the more proscriptive aspects of the oaths required to hold public office and, by 1880, the question of religion was of such little import that the Commissioners did not even inquire into it. The financial implications of membership, too, were moderate. Over the course of the 19th century, the Company stopped collecting quarterage from members, and most of the fines which applicants and members paid remained unaltered throughout the period in question here. In the 1830s and 1880s, the fines for admission by servitude and patrimony were five guineas, the redemption fine seven guineas, the livery fine 15 guineas and the Court fine £5 7s. 6d.[10]

The admission process did change over the decades, for different reasons becoming slightly more formal and procedural, but it was never restrictive. In the 1830s, when apprenticeship was still a common route to membership of the Company, apprentices could be bound to a master performing any craft, and although they had to serve their full terms, it was also acknowledged 'that as to actual service the apprenticeship is often fictitious'. Even this undemanding limitation disappeared, however, as the number of bindings and admissions by servitude fell dramatically when the last vestiges of Company economic control were swept away. By 1880 apprenticeship in the Masons' Company, in its traditional sense, had passed almost completely into obsolescence.[11]

Those seeking admission by patrimony in the 1830s were not required to provide written evidence of parentage, as the members knew each other well enough. In the 1830s, applications for admission by redemption were not proposed and seconded, there was 'no precedent for such a question [admission] being determined by vote, scrutiny or ballot', and no one could remember an occasion upon which a candidate for the freedom had been refused. In 1858, the Court minutes began to record the names of those introducing or proposing entrants, and in 1863, perhaps to make the task of compiling the livery list for the City's electoral roll easier, it was resolved that all applicants had to supply their full names, occupations and addresses. Within the space of a few years, a settled and more formal rhythm of nomination by way of proposition and seconding, consideration and then approval for membership had emerged. Some of those who were proposed and approved did not go on to take up membership, but there is, again, no evidence of anyone being refused admission in these years.[12]

The fact is that the decreasing size of the Masons' Company membership was symptomatic of a wider decline, in almost every sense, of the livery in London. Between 1832 and 1855 the number of liverymen in London fell from 12,000 to 5,000 – a dozen or so companies even became extinct. To put it at its simplest, most companies had lost their sense of purpose. The Great Twelve had become, or were in the process of becoming, the prestigious and largely closed property-holding institutions that they are today. The minor companies, by contrast, had very little to offer members.[13]

The somnolence of the livery companies in the 19th century stands in some contrast to the dynamism of freemasonry, which offered its members mutual aid and financial support in times of need, as well as the chance to progress through an enriching series of degrees and side orders. The Masons' Company dispensed only small sums in charity, it offered little by way of mutual aid to its members, and it provided no opportunity for liverymen to develop as individuals. It had a longer history than Freemasons' lodges, but there is no indication that it publicised this or itself at all.

One incentive, perhaps even the biggest incentive, to join a company was the chance to become a liveryman and thereby acquire full voting rights in 19th-century London. It is no surprise, then, that in the late 1830s entrants to the Masons' Company increasingly began to take up the livery on the day of their admission; by 1880, every entrant to the Masons' Company in the previous two decades had assumed the livery upon admission. It was only in 1948 that the Company reverted to the procedure of, in some cases at least, leaving a gap between admission and promotion to the livery.[14]

A leading reason for joining the Masons' Company has always been its historic connection with the craft of masonry. In some ways, perhaps surprisingly, this was a connection which grew stronger between 1830 and 1880. In the 1830s, although the Court was of the opinion that more than two-thirds of its membership were 'practical masons', the true proportion was almost certainly much lower than that. There is little evidence that the changes we saw occurring in the 18th century had been completely unwound, and only 11 of the 31 men who joined the Company between 1820 and 1829, that is one-third of the total, can confidently be identified as masons, builders or surveyors. In 1880, by contrast, the Court informed the Commissioners that 22 of its members, that is, just over half, were employed as architects, builders, masons, engineers, surveyors, stone merchants or in other occupations connected to the craft of masonry. That seems more likely to have been true. Certainly, five of the 11 men admitted to the Company in the 1870s were employed in roles associated with the building industry.[15]

Perhaps even more surprisingly, the Company's finances were actually in quite rude health, even though less money was coming in by way of fines and legacies from the diminished membership, let alone the income it had formerly derived from its authority over the craft of masonry. In fact, between 1835 and 1880 the Company reported a financial loss in only one year, and in six of the ten years leading up to the 1880 Commission it recorded an end-of-year credit balance comfortably in excess of £100. This modest prosperity was the fruit of shrewd management of the Company's finances in the 18th century; its investments in stocks had prospered, as had its venture into real estate in Bishopsgate, and there were healthy returns on its investment in the Londonderry plantation.[16]

There had been some difficult years in the 1790s and indeed, in the 1830s, when the Company struggled to find a tenant for the Hall and the Skinners' lawsuit prevented the Company receiving its dividend from the Associated Companies venture.* At times like these, the Company would usually liquidate some of its stock; between 1833 and 1835, for example, the Company sold £200 worth of consolidated stock, reducing its holding to just £200. This was, however, a great improvement on the situation at the end of the 17th century when the Company had been forced to borrow ever greater sums at interest just to keep its head above water.[17]

The upshot of all this was that, in the 1830s, the Company could be described as well found, though not rich. In a typical year the Company's ordinary expenditure would absorb most, if not all, of its income, which averaged approximately £165 annually. It paid pensions worth £3 a year each to 12 pensioners, five men and seven women, 'being decayed members or their widows'. The Clerk was paid a salary of £25 a year, while the Beadle received £10; both men could top up their salaries with extra fees.[18]

Over the course of the next five decades, however, the Company's income rose significantly. By 1880, the Bishopsgate properties, 10 tenements standing on a site comprising some 3,300 to 3,700 sq. ft.

---

* In 1832 the Skinners filed a suit in Chancery claiming that as the companies had financed the plantation originally, the companies should receive all the income, rents and profits from the lands in County Londonderry, and that the Irish Society's lands should be distributed among the companies. The case dragged on for 13 years until judgment was finally given against the Skinners.

then known as Masons' Court in George Street and Catherine Wheel Alley, were let for £40 p.a. gross. Even allowing for inflation this was a very good return on an initial investment of £200. The dividends from the Londonderry plantations also increased. In the 1850s, the Company received an average of some £150 a year and in the 1870s more than £160 on average. Higher dividend payments enabled the Company to buy £600 worth of consols between 1838 and 1843, taking its holding up to £800 in nominal value, which produced £24 a year in coupon. This holding was liquidated to enable the Company to purchase the freehold of Masons' Hall, but once the Hall itself had been sold consols were re-purchased and, in 1880, the Company's holding was again worth £800 nominal. More generally, the sale of Masons' Hall transformed the Company's financial situation. Almost all the capital raised from the sale of the Hall was invested in property, variously at Wraysbury; 26 freehold plots in Kearsley Street and Kynaston Road, Stoke Newington; a freehold property at 48-50 Eden Street, Kingston; a mortgage on three houses in Bolton Row, Piccadilly; and freeholds in Wimbledon and Chelsea.[19]

Increasing prosperity enabled the Company to raise its profile in various ways. On 10 November 1873, that is Lord Mayor's Day, the first Master's badge, made at a cost of £27 10s., was presented to the Master, John Russell Freeman, and silver gilt Wardens' badges were bought for eight guineas in 1881. In 1871, almost £10 was spent on a

72 *Liveryman Henry Burnell's draft design of a proposed Master's insignia in 1873.*

new gown and hat for the Beadle, as it was thought his appearance had let the side down somewhat at a procession to mark the opening of the International Exhibition of Fine Arts and Industry at the Royal Albert Hall. The amount spent on dinners and entertainment went up, too, from just over £200 in 1864-5 to some £380 in 1867-8. The Clerk and Beadle both received pay rises, and the pensions were increased from £6 to £10 per head. By 1880, the Company was

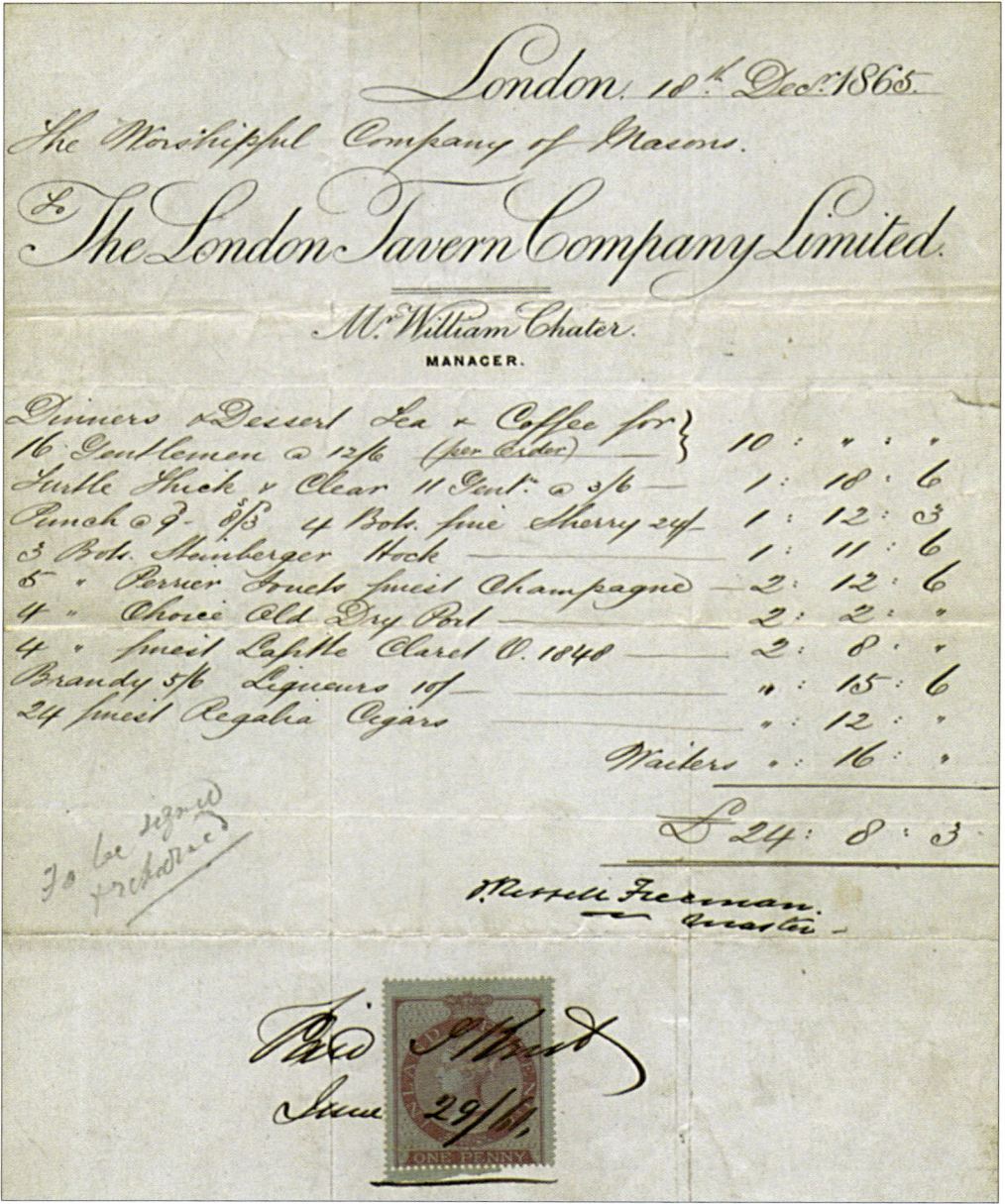

73 *The Court celebrating in style following the agreement to sell the Hall earlier that day, 18 December 1865.*

paying between £10 and £25 to nine different pensioners, totalling £125 a year.[20]

The Royal Commission of the 1880s found that other livery companies were enjoying similarly increased wealth in the period; however, there is no evidence that, where their income was ring-fenced for charitable purposes, it was being misspent. Indeed, the Commissioners noted that many companies used their corporate

74 *A page from John Hunter's handwritten summary in 1880, showing a nine-fold increase in pension payments, in contrast to Company income increasing only four-fold.*

revenues in addition to their trust income for charitable works. Although not highlighted in the published report, this was something which Hunter, the Masons' Clerk, drew attention to in his handwritten summary in 1880. The Masons' Company certainly spent more on pensions than it was bound to do by trust.[21]

However, there was no disguising the fact that by far the greater part of company income, at Masons' Hall as elsewhere, was spent for the benefit of the liverymen themselves, on entertaining, on salaries for officials, and on fees for Court Assistants. It was a picture of self-indulgence which moved the radical J.F.B. Firth to opine austerely that: 'It was difficult indeed to see, now that the companies as a whole fail to discharge any useful function in connection with the purpose of their incorporation, why they should be preserved. The best course to pursue would appear to be to dissolve them, and to vest their property in a representative London municipal authority.'[22]

Some of the companies, though not the Masons, were able to counter this criticism by pointing to the fact that they had taken steps to invest in technical education, most noticeably in the establishment, in 1878, of the City and Guilds of London Institute (CGLI). The Court of the Masons' Company, for their part, were no doubt pleased to report that 'all but one of the pensioners are connected with the trade of masons or the architects' profession'. When it came to education, however, the Masons told the Commissioners that while the question had been discussed, 'the resources of the company are so small in comparison with the magnitude of the trade, that no scheme has yet been suggested which the company has been able to carry out'. This was, to say the least, questionable. Proposals to support technical education had, in fact, been put before the Court in 1873, and rejected – and the Company had failed to join in the establishment of the CGLI. Nor was it particularly truthful to argue that the Company's resources did not allow the Company to play much of a role in technical education. Over the course of the 1870s, the Court had usually handed out a total of £115 on average each year in Court fees, and had disbursed even greater sums on entertaining itself. Seen in this light, were the resources of the Company really too small to prevent it playing a greater role in technical education?[23]

The concentration of the Commissioners, and indeed of the radicals who pressed for reform of the companies both before and after the Commissioners reported in 1884, on the question of technical education brings the failure of the 19th-century Company to engage with its craft into sharp focus. The picture which emerges, therefore, is unavoidably one of a self-interested late Victorian Court more committed to protecting its perquisites and privileges than to performing a 'useful function in connection with the purpose of their incorporation'. In June 1881, 35 guineas was paid in fees to the Assistants who came to the two Courts, and just over £50 spent on their dinners. At a Court meeting held on 5 October 1882, only two items of business were considered before the Assistants paid themselves £21 for their attendance and they retired to a dinner costing almost £17 at the Cannon Street Hotel.[24]

Of course, the expectation was that fees would encourage better attendance at Court meetings, and it was not unreasonable for Assistants to be reimbursed expenses. It was a policy which the Masons had tried for a short period between 1713 and 1728, and again, briefly, in 1844; in 1861, the Court resolved that at future meetings a sum of £5 should be divided among those attending. Typically, under this system, Assistants might get 8s. or 9s. for each meeting they attended.[25]

The policy seemed to work: once fees had been brought in, Courts were only very infrequently not quorate. That said, on occasions when fewer than eight Assistants attended, Courts were held and fees were paid regardless of the terms of the charter. The question is not so much whether fees were justified *per se*, but whether too much was finding its way into the pockets of the Assistants. In 1867, with unseemly haste after the sale of Masons' Hall, the amount set aside by the Assistants to be divided among themselves was more than doubled from £5 to £12. Still unsatisfied, however, the Assistants resolved in 1869 to double the fees again, this time to two guineas for each appearance at Court. The increase in the total paid in fees was extraordinary: in 1866 the Assistants picked up a maximum of £35, in 1868 £84, and in 1870 £131 10s. No rationale or justification for this increase was ever recorded in the minutes. That said, no rationale was ever recorded for the sale of Masons' Hall, but we can put two and two together.[26]

By 1870, the amount paid in Court fees was more or less equal to the amount paid in pensions to poor widows and members. Admittedly, the Assistants were not always so well-rewarded for their careful stewardship of the Company. In October 1874, when money was tight after a remarkable £400 had been spent on dinners and entertainment for the Court and livery in the previous year, the Court fees were lowered to one guinea. One year later, following entertaining expenses of £380, it was resolved to hold only six Courts each year to save money. Fortunately, the Assistants did not have to suffer these privations for a long time. In 1876 the Court fee was put back up to two guineas and, in 1880, the seventh Court was re-instituted.[27]

Suspicion of the motives and conduct of the 19th-century Court goes beyond the question of fees. In fact, the entire administration of the Company during this period appears both shadowy and inward-looking. In 1826, the Court resolved to stop bringing liverymen on to the Court; instead, the existing Assistants were to serve as officers in rotation. The number of Assistants subsequently declined to just a dozen or so. The Assistants justified this by claiming that as only eight were required to make a quorum, there was no need for more. In practice, this meant that significant sums of money were paid directly to a very small group of men and even more significant sums were lavished on their entertainment. The same men set the regulations under which they managed the Company, they audited their own accounts, and they elected the Master and Wardens. From 1878 to 1881 three men, William Piper, Alfred Gwilt and Henry Burnell, all served a third term as Master when many had yet to serve a single term. A quick glance at the list of Master and Wardens shows just how poor this system had become: between 1850 and 1880, 14 men served a second or third term as Master. The same small group also decided who should join them on the Court when vacancies arose and, once on the Court, Assistants served for life unless they decided to retire. As the Commissioners put it rather succinctly: 'The master, wardens, and court of Assistants of the company have the free, exclusive, and uncontrolled management of the affairs of the company.'[28]

The career of Alfred Gwilt, Surveyor to the Company from 1849 to 1884, and three-times Master, casts a clear, and possibly unflattering, light on the Masons' operations in this era of its history. His father and grandfather before him had been distinguished building surveyors and Masters of the Masons' Company, and he seems to have had no difficulty in dominating the Court's financial decisions over a long period. He collected the Company's rents, on which he charged a commission of 2.5 per cent, took his fees for attendance and claimed expenses, and made a handsome £52 10s. out of the sale of the Hall, in which he played a leading part. There is no evidence whatsoever of outright peculation on his part, and his fees do not seem to have been excessive by comparison with those subsequently charged by the external company that eventually took over his role. It is also true that the Company's property investments, made on his advice, did bring in greater revenue. On the other hand, there is, at the very least, the appearance of a conflict of interest. As a closed corporation controlled by men such as Gwilt, the Masons' Company of the later 19th century need not be condemned as absolutely corrupt; but it was undeniably exclusive, self-serving, and of little public benefit.[29]

SEE YOU IN COURT

Not all in the Masons' Company were satisfied with the immovable regime of Gwilt and his friends. In 1881, perhaps moved to action by the efforts of the Commissioners, perhaps simply frustrated at being passed over for promotion to the Court, one George Wells wrote to the Clerk asking to inspect the Company's charter and by-laws. He also demanded to know by what authority the Master had been elected and asked that the Court be increased to 24 Assistants, according to the terms of the Company's charter.[30]

Six months later, Wells launched an *ex parte* legal application to obtain a writ of mandamus designed to force the Court to elect more Assistants. Initially Wells was successful, but by March 1883 the writ of mandamus had been quashed and the case had been sent to the High Court. There followed a sequence of contested Court elections and legal challenges, in which Wells was supported by two others, Edmund Bayley and John Cox. By October the Company had incurred legal and administrative costs of £82 14s. 6d. in contesting Wells' action, and a subsequent attempt by the Court to have the case heard before a special jury was rejected on appeal by a judge who ordered the action to be heard before a judge without a jury.

The case was finally heard before Mr Justice Day at the High Court in late March or early April 1885, and he gave judgment against the Company. On 19 May, he issued a writ of mandamus chiding the Court for refusing to elect more Assistants 'to the hindrance and obstruction of the Government' of the Company and ordering them to elect 11 more Assistants, taking the number on the Court up to 24. All told, the action had cost the Company some £1,000, including Wells' costs of £600. The Assistants were no doubt relieved when Gwatkin, the Clerk, advised them that they could not be held personally liable for this amount.

Now the worst fears of the Assistants were realised. The increase in their number and the financial position of the Company dictated that the 'privileges of the Court … would have to be considerably diminished'. The number of annual Courts was reduced from seven to five, cutting the fees each Assistant might collect by four guineas a year. The next stage, inevitably, was an increasingly bitter wrangle between conservatives and reformers to capture the expanded Court. A tit-for-tat cycle of nomination even saw some entrants proposed for promotion to the Court on the day of their admission to the Company. This went on until January 1891, when a solution to the problem was finally agreed by all parties – evidence, perhaps, of a genuine rapprochement. Promotion to the Court was henceforth to be by seniority, with no liveryman eligible unless he had been in the livery for a minimum term of five years, and that he had not been declared insolvent or bankrupt.[31]

The late Victorian Assistants did take some steps to reform the Company's administration. The Court had resolved, after Gwilt died in 1884, that in future it should be the Clerk who collected the rents due on the investment freeholds. In 1888, there was an inquiry into the Company's income and expenditure, as part of which the Court agreed to dine on only three occasions a year 'in order to bring the accounts into a satisfactory state'. In the same year, a committee of seven drew up the first set of Standing Orders, which was the first substantial attempt to update the Company's regulations since the by-laws had been passed in 1678. Although only six clauses long, they set out important aspects of Court procedure. They also limited the amount of money that could be spent on Court dinners other than the Associated Companies dinner, at 12s. 6d. per head, exclusive of wine. In 1904, these regulations were updated and printed as a comprehensive, seven-page document. Provision was made for the Company to have a current account with Messrs Hoare's Bank, for the proper storage of the Company's property, and in general for the better administration of affairs. In 1907, the Court established a financial committee to decide how to invest the proceeds of the Associated Companies' venture in Londonderry. There could now be little doubt that the Company was under better management.[32]

In some other ways, however, there was little change. Some members still appear to have believed that entertainment at the Company's expense was the primary purpose of membership, and that it should be as lavish as possible. A small but characteristic illustration of this habit of mind can be seen in a proposal made in 1920 by Court Assistant Frederick Shadbolt, who 'raised the question of buying cigars for the Company'. Mr Shadbolt undoubtedly saw the Masons' Company as, quite simply, a private dining club for commercial gentlemen, and he would, of course, have been able to point to other, grander, livery companies where cigars were routinely distributed to diners at their feasts. In this instance, however, the Court, whether moved by impulses of moderation or merely by financial caution, considered Shadbolt's proposal 'inadvisable'.[33]

Before the late 1920s, there was little improvement in the Company's efforts in the field of technical education. In 1891, an application for support from the City and Guilds Institute was 'taken as read and directed to lay on the table'. In 1893, proposals that the Company pay either £100 or £30 towards the Borough Polytechnic Institute were both voted down by 13 votes to four by the Court. One year later, the Company did pay £25 to establish classes for masons and carpenters in a joint enterprise with the Carpenters' Company, but when the Carpenters wrote again in the following year to request a further £25, the Assistants supported a motion, put forward by Henry Sarson and Edward Conder, that no more money be sent as the 'Company is not in a position to repeat the donation'. In October 1919, a proposal to dedicate 20 guineas annually for prizes to apprentices and trainees in the craft of masonry was, after much discussion, 'negatived'. Such displays of parsimony stand in very obvious contrast to the liberality with which monies were disbursed in Court fees at the same meetings. In 1893, for example, when no money could be found for the Borough Polytechnic, 44 guineas was paid in attendance fees.[34]

In fact, with more Assistants on its strength, the Court may no longer have had so strongly marked an appearance as a closed shop, but the corollary of this was that ever-larger sums were paid out as fees. In January 1887, 36 guineas was paid to 18 Assistants who came to Court. The five Courts between June 1887 and June 1888 were each attended by 20 or 21 Assistants, meaning that over £212 was paid that year in Court fees. Occasional efforts to reduce or abolish the fees paid were almost always met with fierce resistance. Indeed, even the exigencies of two World Wars in the 20th century failed to stop Assistants collecting their two-guinea fees.[35]

In summary, by 1914 the Company's administration might be said to have been shaken out of its mid-Victorian coma – but the membership had hardly been stirred to any new sense of purpose. The collective conscience had yet to be stimulated sufficiently to rediscover an outward-looking and altruistically useful mission.

14

THE MODERN COMPANY

A strategic review of the Company's position was undertaken in 2004-5 under the Chairmanship of Richard Rowlandson OBE, and the exercise was repeated on a larger scale in 2012-13 during the Mastership of David Blake and under the Chairmanship of Richard Woodman-Bailey. The 9,000-word-long report of the second working party was unanimously adopted by the Court in October 2013, and brought about a significant alteration in both the direction and the level of the Company's activity, in several different respects. The reviews emerged from narrower examinations of internal Company practice, and in both instances the final objectives were broadly the same: that is, to assess 'the aims and strategy of the Company', and to consider the Company's broad 'strategic management and organisation'. The very fact that the reviews were commissioned speaks to a new ethos of professionalism and constructive thinking within the Company, quite at odds with the picture of Company life described above.[1]

In these two final chapters, we shall consider the most recent history of the Company, to which end the 2013 Strategic Review serves a useful purpose in two ways. First, because it laid out such 'a cohesive and ambitious' vision for the Company's future, it provides us with a point at which to bring our study to a close. Second, the review presented its findings under seven category headings. Five of them provide us with a useful structure through which we can examine the Company's late 20th- and early 21st-century history in this chapter. The final two headings – fundraising and charitable giving, and fostering the craft of stonemasonry – cannot be separated from each other. Indeed, more than anything else, its philanthropy

75 For hundreds of years, St Paul's Cathedral has been an iconic symbol of the City of London.

and its support for the craft define the 21st-century Company. For that reason, we shall turn to an analysis of the Company's philanthropic efforts in our final chapter.

SUPPORTING THE MAYORALTY AND THE CORPORATION

There is, and indeed always has been, a relationship of inter-dependence between the Mayoralty and Corporation of London on the one hand, and the City's livery companies on the other. Each relies on the other for support and assistance.

As one of London's smaller and poorer companies, the Masons' Company has never played an especially significant role in the City's civic life. Men from among its ranks did hold office as City Viewer or as City Mason before the offices fell into abeyance in the 17th century, and in two distinct periods of the Company's history we do find evidence for its members featuring more prominently in London's civic life. The first such period came in the second half of the 18th century, when Christopher Horsnail, Robert Easton and Charles Clavey all appear to have served as deputy, that is the senior Common Councilman in each ward, and when Sir Robert Taylor was elected as Sheriff of London in 1782. The second came in the 50 years from 1890 to 1940, when John Greenwood served as deputy, Frederick Alliston held office as Sheriff, Alderman and deputy chairman of the London County Council, and Charles Wakefield and Harry Twyford were elected as Lord Mayors of London. For their various services, Wakefield, Alliston and Twyford were knighted and Wakefield was subsequently created Viscount Wakefield of Hythe.[2]

From the late 1960s onwards the Company committed itself to supporting charities connected with the City of London, and it has honoured this pledge by providing money for purposes such as educational institutions connected with the City, the Lord Mayor's appeal, and the Sheriffs' and Recorder's Fund. Several members of the Company have been elected as Common Councilmen; in particular, John Owen-Ward served as Deputy of Bridge Ward, and he was chairman of the City's Planning Committee for many years. On the other hand, no one from the Company served on the Court of Aldermen, as Sheriff or Lord Mayor in the later 20th century, the Company seldom took part in events such as the Lord Mayor's Show, and activity with the Corporation and its officers was limited to a largely personal level.

76 *Sir Frederick Prat Alliston.*

77 *Charles Cheers Wakefield (Viscount Wakefield).*

78 *Sir Harry Twyford.*

The Company began to participate more in the City civic in the 21st century. In 2011, for example, the Company took part in the Lord Mayor's Show to support its liveryman and Lady Mayoress, Elizabeth Wootton. At about that time, Dr Christine Rigden decided to stand for election to office as London's non-Aldermanic Sheriff. With the support of the Company she was elected to office in 2015 – the Company's first female Sheriff and subsequently first female Master. This new attitude was given express sanction in the Strategic Review of 2013, which recommended that the Company embark on a policy of determined engagement with the institutions and civic activity of the City – a clear statement of fresh ambition. The report also suggested that the Company should consider moving its Clerk's office to the City of London so that the Company might have a more visible presence in the City – something effected in August 2014. It would be premature to hail recent progress on this front as a dawning of a third 'golden age' of Company participation in the civic life of the City of London, but it is a beginning.[3]

GOVERNANCE AND ORGANISATION

We have already seen how, following the turmoil of the 1880s, the Court of the Masons' Company took several steps both to reform and to codify the governance and organisation of the Company. In the interwar years, in particular, the financial committee which had

been established in 1907 expanded its remit, and as something of a standing committee it occasionally met to consider aspects of the Company's organisation and finances. However, that was for some time the high water mark of delegation and over the course of the 30 years since the outbreak of the Second World War, that standing committee convened only rarely. Well into the 1960s, the Masons' Company was managed in essentially the same way that it had been for centuries past, that is by its Court of Assistants occasionally delegating responsibility to *ad hoc* committees, but deliberating and deciding on all questions of governance, organisation and management itself.[4]

In 1966-7, the Court re-instituted a standing committee, primarily to manage the administration of John Byram's estate. Having fulfilled its original terms of reference, in November 1967 this committee was put on to a permanent footing as the Standing Committee charged with meeting four times a year, chiefly to advise the Court on which charities the Company should support, though with 'no powers other than consideration of particular meetings and reporting back to the Court'. Its remit soon grew markedly, however, and it became an integral part of a process by which the Company's management has been overhauled and professionalised. Since 1969, for instance, on the advice of the committee, the Company's Standing Orders have been subject to regular review and all alterations in Company policy have been recorded, first, in a Policy Book and then in a book

79 *Elizabeth Wootton, Lady Mayoress, with the Lord Mayor David Wootton and the Master, Derek Sayer, following presentation of a brooch from the Company in 2011.*

of Executive Rules, the latter of which is managed by the Standing Committee and which enlarges, explains or otherwise regulates 'the efficient implementation' of the Company's Standing Orders. It is no exaggeration to say that the Company's Standing Orders and Executive Rules have codified the modern Company's constitution in a way hitherto not seen.[5]

As various other committees were formed within the Company, the Standing Committee also grew into something of a 'committee of committees'. When, for example, an Investment Committee was founded in 1983, it was charged with reporting in the first instance to the Standing Committee and not the Court and, since 2013, all the Company's committees have been expected to do the same. In 1998, the Court also resolved that the chairmen of three specialist committees should sit on the Standing Committee *ex officio* and, again since 2013, all committee chairmen have been required to attend the Standing Committee, along with the Trustee chairmen, even if they do not all have voting rights.[6]

In truth, the Court had for a long time been a rather unwieldy body to govern and manage the Masons' Company. At any one time in the 20th century, its two dozen or so members comprised somewhere between a fifth and a quarter of the total membership, and perhaps even a third of the active membership. The Standing Committee, however, with no more than 12 members was much more nimble and could come to quicker decisions. Of course, there was always an overlap between the two bodies, but the demarcation between them was increasingly understood to be akin to that of a board on the one hand, and an executive committee on the other. In 2013, this distinction was set down quite clearly. The Court was to remain the Company's 'ultimate authority', and something of a legislature, whereas the Standing Committee was to have executive responsibilities and the power to take decisions delegated to it by the Court.

In the early 1980s, the Court began to establish specialist committees within the Company. These committees were to have particular terms of reference, again so as better to manage the Company's greater responsibilities and to make the most of the abilities of the Company's liverymen. We might take the example of the Technical Committee, which was established in 1982 to oversee the Company's awards and prizes. Among its first members were John Bysouth, who had spent years working as a stonemason and who owned a well-respected stonemasonry business; Peter Marsh, who was surveyor of the fabric at Canterbury Cathedral; Eric Brookes, who founded the Chichester Cathedral Works Organisation to employ stonemasons to carry out work there; Charles Harvey, who was also a stonemason and owner of a stone yard; and Alwyn Waters and Howard Lobb, both of whom were renowned architects.[7]

Since they were first formed, the specialist committees have gone through numerous iterations. The Technical Committee became the Craft Committee with an expanded remit of promoting the craft of stonemasonry; it subsequently merged, demerged, and then merged again with a more recently formed Training Committee, and today it is known as the Craft and Training Committee. In 1988, to take better account of its wider financial responsibilities, the Investment Committee was rechristened as the Finance Committee. Today there are six committees: Communications, Craft and Training, Finance, Fundraising, Membership Development, and Social. The Company administers two charitable trusts, and each trust has a group of trustees. Altogether, the committee system has not only transformed the way the Company operates, it has also provided a means through which members can become involved in Company life, offering liverymen the chance to play a role in the Company's administration at an early stage of their Company career.[8]

The traditional course of progression through the Company's ranks has also been challenged in other ways. Historically, promotion first to the Court and then to office had always been decided on seniority; this method certainly obviated competition between liverymen but it took no account either of ability or of commitment to the Company. As the livery has grown in size, from about 100 in 1974 to some 200 by 2013 – a result of policy decisions taken over those four decades – and as life expectancy has increased, the problem of progression has become more acute.

Between 1988 and 2000, a series of reports and resolutions addressed these interconnected issues. The Court's first step was the creation of the position of Honorary Court Member (subsequently Honorary Court Assistant – HCA) for those Assistants who were in no position to progress to hold office as Warden or Master. HCAs retained some of the privileges of Court membership, for example, the right to attend meetings and lunches, but they were not granted voting rights. In 1998, after the presentation of a report which showed that the average age of the 10 Masters due to serve between 1998 and 2007 would be over 67, and that five of the 10 thereafter would be over 80 when they reached the Chair, the Court resolved that Masters should not, in normal circumstances, be older than 75 years old and that new Assistants, therefore, should not normally be aged over 60. At the same time, the Court agreed to make more use of the position of HCA by informing new Assistants (who were now expected to have attended at least 60 per cent of Company events over a five-year period) that they should expect to become HCAs either at the age of 75, or five years after becoming Master, whichever was the later.[9]

These changes certainly helped to ease the problems of succession planning and an ageing Court, but it soon became clear, in the discussions which continued throughout that year, that the questions of how the Court should be comprised and how liverymen should advance through the Company's ranks had not only been unanswered, but that they were also intricately tied up with the Company's policies on membership and livery involvement.

Consequently, a Livery Involvement and Advancement Sub-Committee (LIASCOM) was set up to consider the matter in more detail. Chaired by Peter Johnson, it was an important stepping stone on the road to the two strategic reviews, and its recommendations were considered in Standing Committee and by the Court in 2000. The result was that the number of voting members on the Court was fixed at 20: seven Assistants and the two Wardens before the chair, the Master in the chair and 10 Past Masters after the chair. There was to be no limit on the number of HCAs, and each year either the longest-serving Assistant, or the one with the poorest attendance record, was to be invited to convert to honorary membership. This structure remains, although now the Court comprises the Master and seven Assistants before and after the chair.[10]

The membership of the Standing Committee was also restructured, so that it was formed of the Master and Wardens, the Deputy Master (customarily the immediate Past Master), the Renter Warden designate, three committee chairmen each serving three-year terms, and four liverymen chosen on the basis of their work and commitment on other committees each serving two-year terms. Once on the Court, advancement would still be by seniority, but new Assistants, all of whom were expected to commit to serving as Master, would ordinarily be chosen by the Court from liverymen who had served on the Standing Committee or who had chaired one of the specialist committees. Thus promotion to the Court by seniority was swept away and the Company's structure was overhauled.

These reforms have not always operated entirely as was intended, but they have certainly transformed the Company's style of business, and further change has followed in their wake.

FINANCIAL STABILITY

In 1866 and 1909, the Masons' Company received windfalls from the sale of Masons' Hall and the Associated Companies' estates in Londonderry. Although some of this money was spent unprofitably, most of it was ploughed back into investment properties and stocks. In the 20th century, the Company also increased its capital by transferring a sum 'equal to about 10 per cent of the Company's income' to its capital account. As a consequence, the Company built up a sizeable endowment which generated significant income. On the eve of the outbreak of the Second World War, the Company's stocks generated gross dividends of some £300 annually, while its remaining properties in Chelsea, Wimbledon, Stoke Newington, Kingston and Bishopsgate produced an annual income of some £400.[11]

Before the Second World War, the Court had discussed selling the properties, but the consensus was usually that they should be kept. The passing of the Town and Country Planning Act in 1947, however, seems to have alarmed some of the Assistants; certainly Claud Dennis, who owned a property business and who was the Company's surveyor *de facto* if not *de jure*, advised the Court in 1950 that they should put the Company's 'properties up for auction before they were virtually confiscated'. There was resistance to this plan, but under his advice, the Company divested itself of its Masons' Court property in Bishopsgate for £3,500 in 1949 and eight of its Stoke Newington freeholds for £2,685 between 1950 and 1952.[12]

Dennis might have planned to use the money to acquire a site in the City of London on which the Company could have rebuilt a hall, but he died in 1953 before any such plan, if indeed there was one, could be effected. Thereafter, the Stoke Newington properties were sold in dribs and drabs for hundreds of pounds each until the leases fell in during the 1970s, after which they fetched thousands each, notwithstanding their often poor condition, until the final two properties, at 16 Kersley Road and 60 Kynaston Road, were sold for £3,500 and £5,000 gross in 1980. The Company received

80 *The freehold property, Greenlaw Court in Ealing, built on land bequeathed to the Company by John Byram (d.1964).*

just over £1,300 from the sale of the freehold of 48-50 Eden Street in Kingston in 1953-4; one year later the Company sold 4 The Drive in Wimbledon for £2,250; while the two freeholds in Chelsea were sold for £1,800 in 1957-8 and £35,000 in 1980-1. The monies raised from the sales were, in almost every instance, reinvested into stocks and by 1982 the Company's investments were producing an annual income of just under £20,000.[13]

By that time the Company had benefited, and would continue to benefit, from the Dray and Byram bequests, which we shall shortly analyse in greater detail. Most bequests that have subsequently come in have usually been destined for one or both of the Company's charitable trusts. From 1984 to 1993, the Company had a policy of transferring stock into its charitable trusts in order to meet its charitable commitments; since then, it has allocated 'either in cash or suitable investments 10 per cent (say) of its annual net revenue' to its charitable trust in order to strengthen the trust's capital base.[14]

The value of the funds in the Company's account and trusts changes daily and it is, of course, difficult to value the Company's property interests at Greenlaw Court, but two trends are very clear over the last 40 or so years. First, with several generous bequests and judicious financial management, the Company's capital has grown a great deal; and second, thanks to the legacies and stock transfers, the capital value of the two charitable trusts has increased by more than that of the Company fund. By 1987, the investments held in the Company account were worth just over £600,000 with a further £35,000 in the two charitable trusts. That is to say, the trusts accounted for just over 5 per cent of the Company's total endowment. By 1993, the Company's stocks were valued at around £1m, of which 10 per cent was held in the trusts, and by 1998 the trusts held just over 12 per cent of a portfolio valued at almost £2m. By 2013, however, the Company's investment portfolio was worth some £3.35m, of which just over £1m, that is about 30 per cent of the Company's capital, was held in the trusts. In that year, the income from this endowment was worth over £135,000.[15]

Before 1983, the Court had decided on the Company's investment strategy and portfolio with the advice of the Company's brokers; after 1983, responsibility was delegated to the Company's Finance (originally Investment) Committee. By the end of the 1990s, there were some Assistants who believed that the growth in the value of the Company's portfolio over the last two decades had vindicated the Finance Committee's decision-making. Others, however, were beginning to have doubts about the wisdom of entrusting the management of a £2m portfolio to Company members, however knowledgeable and experienced they were. For some Assistants, it would have been preferable for the Company's brokers, J.M. Finn, to manage the Company's portfolio on a discretionary rather than advisory basis and, between 1999 and 2003, there were many discussions about whether the Finance Committee should be relieved of its 'stock-picking' responsibilities. A small discretionary fund set up in 1999, which aimed at capital rather than income growth under Finn's management, achieved better returns than the funds under the Company's direction which, indeed, seem to have underperformed the market. This, coupled with the realisation that it was no longer considered best practice for a finance committee to manage investments in this way, led to a Court resolution in 2003 that removed the Finance Committee's responsibility to pick stocks. Instead, the committee was tasked with overseeing asset allocation and keeping an eye on the investment manager's performance. One year later, the Company decided that all its investments were henceforth to be managed on a discretionary basis.[16]

Over the long course of its history, the Company has experienced some perilous financial episodes. The investment portfolio brought unprecedented strength in depth during the 20th century, but still the Company could never be called rich; indeed, there were times in the second half of the 20th century when the Company's expenditure again exceeded its revenue. In 1949, after the Company had spent beyond its means, John Byram put up a loan of £200 to save the Company the trouble of borrowing from Hoare's. Against the backdrop of high inflation in the late 1970s, the Company often found itself spending more on day-to-day Company business than it received in income: £881 in 1976-7, £760 one year later, and £1,667 in 1981-2. At this time, the argument would often be advanced that high spending was justified because the Company had a reputation in the City to maintain, but others grew quite exercised by what they perceived as profligacy or reckless generosity.[17]

In theory, it should not be difficult for the Company to ensure that its ordinary revenue is sufficient to cover its expenditure. However, as we have seen many times in the Company's history, the reality is different and it has proved no less a challenge in recent decades. Increases in membership numbers have brought both benefits and challenges, and different views of the Company's identity and function have come into contention under financial pressures. In particular, two questions which have a very long and troubled tradition in the Company, namely whether Assistants should be paid for attending Court, and whether members should pay quarterage, have required decision in recent times, and need attention here.

In the first half of the 20th century, there were occasional efforts to reduce or abolish the fees paid to Assistants. After income tax was increased to finance the national effort in the Great War, and the Company's cash balance reduced as a consequence, a proposal that the two-guinea attendance fee be halved to one guinea was defeated on a vote. In June 1940, just after the fall of France and as the nation readied itself for a Nazi invasion, a proposal that the Court fees be reduced was not even put to the vote after at least three Assistants spoke out against it. Three years later, another attempt to lower the Court fees miscarried as the correct procedure in bringing forward the motion had not been followed. When the Company was flush with cash, or at least the prospect of cash following Byram's bequest, in January 1965, it was suggested that as the fees had not been reviewed since 1910 – which was not actually true, they had just not been increased – the Assistants' fees should be 'brought into line with those of other companies'. In the end, this proposal came to nothing, but only after the Assistants had realised that surtax would be payable on any increase. Instead, therefore, they cancelled the 10s. fee that each Assistant paid for his lunch. In January 1968, however, fears of surtax were set aside and the Court fees were more than doubled to £5 each. This significantly increased the Company's expenditure. In 1966-7, the Assistants paid themselves fees totalling £176, two years later, the total was £530, and they continued to comprise a substantial portion of the Company's outgoings for the next 20 years.[18]

In the mid-1980s, however, within the context of wide-ranging discussions about the Company's finances and commitments, the question of fees again came to the fore and, following a Standing Committee review, the Court finally abolished them on 8 June 1987. There was little fanfare or controversy; the minutes tersely record the resolution in just 19 words and only three of the 24 Assistants voted to keep them. Four years later, the Standing Committee did discuss their reinstatement, but there was little appetite to bring them back. Indeed, the committee resolved that 'bearing in mind other free lunches and the Byram Dinner enjoyed by Court members it was felt to be inappropriate and unnecessary to re-instate the Court expenses for members.' A new ethos was thus established: that service on the Court was a privilege, and that payment for service was at odds with the Company's modern philosophy.[19]

If one vexed question was brought to a conclusion in 1987, however, another one opened. As part of the discussions around the Company's financial position that saw fees abolished, the idea of quarterage was raised in Standing Committee. There was nothing 'new' about asking members to pay quarterage: according to the Company's ordinances and by-laws, all members have always been liable to pay it, and the Court has never rescinded these provisions. What happened is that, at some point in the middle of the 19th century, the Company simply gave up trying to collect it. Instead, over the last 150 or so years the Court regularly raised the entry, and indeed other, fines paid by members until they reached quite a high level. In 1994, for example, a candidate would pay £1,100 upon his admission to the freedom and the livery.[20]

In 1987, the Standing Committee 'were unanimous in the view that quarterage should not be levied'. However, the question never went away, and at times when the Company found itself with the problem of falling income and/or rising expenditure, a revival of quarterage was inevitably suggested as a solution. Debate rumbled on until September 2005, when the Court was asked to vote on four financial policy proposals. Should the Company increase the subsidy it paid towards the two formal events? Should Assistants pay £100 annually towards Court lunches (which at that time cost some £7,300 per year) and should HCAs pay £25 for each lunch they attended? Should entry fines be lowered to £100 for the freedom of the Company and £500 for taking the livery? And finally, although existing members would be exempt as they had paid higher entry fines, should the Company levy quarterage on all new liverymen at £150 and new freemen at £50 annually? The proposals sought to strike a careful balance: on the one hand maintaining, if not boosting, the number of members while increasing the income the Company derived from those members; on the other hand, keeping the cost of attending Company events at as low a cost as possible. After much discussion, all four proposals passed by comfortable margins.[21]

The re-introduction of quarterage was symbolically important, but in the first few years it brought in very little money indeed. Certainly, when the credit crunch of 2008 precipitated a recession that had a severe effect on the Company's finances and its charities, the amount collected in quarterage was not enough to obviate cost-saving measures. For example, in 2009, the Court invited guests to only two of its lunches to save money and it was necessary to cut the amount available in student support grants from £32,500 to £27,500. In this context, it was inevitable that focus would turn once more to improving the Company's ordinary revenue, and expanding the scope of quarterage was an obvious way of achieving that. The Court resolved, therefore, that quarterage was to be levied on all members who were under the age of 75 from 1 July 2009. Four years later, the age limit was raised to 80. Of course, the rates at which quarterage is levied have also increased over the years. Today, liverymen pay £440, freemen £110, and yeoman masons (of whom more in the next chapter) £10.[22]

With its large portfolio of investments and the Charitable Trust's property at Greenlaw Court, the Masons' Company is now a well-capitalised organisation. It also has a regular stream of income from a growing membership. It does not exist, however, to produce profits for their own sake.

The Worshipful Company of Masons

DINNER

HELD AT

GROCERS' HALL

ON

Tuesday, 23rd February, 1954

Master :
WILLIAM DUCHATEL WOELLWARTH, Esq., M.C.

NURTURING THE FELLOWSHIP

Fellowship has always been central to Company life. In the 21st century each candidate for admission will almost certainly have come to a Company event before applying for membership, when there would have been the opportunity to see the importance of camaraderie within the Company's ranks. At interview by members of the Company's Membership Development Committee, the candidate would have heard talk of the Company's fellowship and, on the very first page of the members' information booklet, the new member is told that commitment to the Company 'brings with it a belief in the fellowship that is common to all Livery Companies in the City'.

There has never been a time in the Company's history when the ideal of fellowship was not compromised, or even broken, by internal disputes. In the mid-20th century, there was a minor

81 *William Duchatel Woellwarth, a Roman Catholic who felt unable to make the Declaration required of officers. This was subsequently resolved. (Note the original Master's Badge, worn at a Masons' Company Dinner with the Lord Mayor, Sir Noel Bowater.)*

disagreement concerning the declaration in lieu of the oath taken by Roman Catholics elected as officers of the Company.

More seriously, around 1970 there was a bitter falling-out between Sidney Loweth and his fellow Assistants over alleged mismanagement of the Company's affairs. The trouble appears to have arisen from personal animosities rather than any material ill-doing, but it was still an unhappy affair.[23]

Perhaps the most substantial matter to divide the membership in the last two decades of the 20th century was the admission of women to the livery. The passage of the Sex Discrimination Act in 1975 prompted a discussion, in January 1976, among the Assistants about whether its provisions opened up membership of the Company to women. During this debate, Spencer Rodgers noted that 'there was nothing in Standing Orders to preclude a woman joining the Livery and one could only await events'. He was right, of course. Women had joined the Company previously and there was nothing in the Company's charter, ordinances, by-laws or Standing Orders that prohibited women from joining. In fact, there had been at least one 20th-century attempt to introduce a woman member: in 1920, Frederick Dray, who was something of a reformer on the Court, gave notice of his intention to propose his daughter, Evelyn Muriel Dray MBE, for admission to the Company. The Company's minutes are silent on what happened next, but Dray would go on to hold office as Master for a fourth time in 1925-6, in which year, unhappily, Evelyn died. He was, of course, a very generous benefactor to the Company, so it seems unlikely that he would have fallen out with his fellow Assistants over this issue. Instead, it seems that the matter was quietly set aside.[24]

The later 20th-century discussion over female membership was more prolonged. In October 1984, Spencer Rodgers informed the Court that he would like to propose his daughter, Elizabeth Rodgers, for membership. At that time, Dame Mary Donaldson was just coming to the end of her year as the first female Lord Mayor of London and Elizabeth, a liveryman of another company, a Common Councilman, and the daughter of a Past Master of the Masons' Company, was in all other respects an excellent candidate for membership. Three months later, the Court in a secret ballot voted nine to eight in favour of admitting women, but the consensus was that an issue as significant as this could not be decided by so slender a margin, so the ban on women members remained.[25]

In 1993, again in a secret ballot, there was another majority in favour of re-admitting women, but once more it was felt that the 15-9 vote did not constitute a super-majority. In that year, the Company had chosen Philippa Thomerson as the first student to be supported at the Building Crafts Training School. She came to the livery dinner and, as the Company was eager to increase the number of its members who worked in the craft of stonemasonry, there was even some discussion about offering her the freedom of the Company. In the end, this was deemed 'not practical' under existing Standing Orders, but the Company did support another female student, Stephanie Bierkandt, at the same college shortly thereafter. At that time, then, the Company was in the unfortunate position of refusing to allow women with whom it had close relationship and who worked in the craft of stonemasonry into the Company, while welcoming men with no connection to the industry whatsoever.[26]

In 1999, liveryman David Beattie asked what the Company's legal position was in the matter of female membership; he was told by the chairman of LIASCOM that women could easily join through patrimony. By 2002, some 80 per cent of London's companies admitted women, and when the Mercers voted to allow them in that year, the Masons' established a sub-committee chaired by Beattie to look into the matter again. On 1 April 2003, the matter again came before the Court when the Master, Peter Johnson, put a resolution which opened by stating that 'the balance of advantage lies in accepting the principle that women should be admitted'. This time, although not all members of the Court were happy with the decision, all those with a vote cast theirs in favour of the motion and just over one year later, after a period of some 250 years, the Masons' Company again admitted its first three women: Elaine Marson, Caroline Copland and Lady Fairhaven.[27]

Over the course of the 1990s, the Court also instituted a system for removing an 'inactive' liveryman from the Company's roll if he could not 'show in some physical or material way, an interest in the activities of the Company'; it took steps to lower the cost of attending Company events, to make them more attractive to liverymen; and it re-instituted the office of Steward, allocating to it the responsibility of encouraging the livery to be involved in the Company, maintaining contact with liverymen, acting as intermediary between the livery and the Court, and recommending liverymen for certain roles within the Company. It was this spirit of reform that gave birth to LIASCOM in 1998.[28]

The decision to re-admit women also led directly to a wider reconsideration of the Company's membership protocols. In March 2004, the Court resolved that it would henceforth vote on admitting candidates by a show of hands (a secret ballot could only be called by the Master) and that it would take three negatives for a candidate not to be admitted. These provisions were designed to prevent one or two Assistants clandestinely blackballing any female candidate.[29]

The Court also voted to relax its nationality requirements so that citizens of foreign countries could join the Company as long as they were prepared to swear the City of London's declaration of a freeman. (There is no evidence that aliens were prevented from joining the Company before 1916, when anti-German feeling saw the Company limit its freedom to British subjects, 'independently of all considerations of race and colour as against all other inhabitants of the Globe'.) Finally, the Court also instituted a Membership Committee 'to consider the applications of candidates for membership' (in practice to interview each candidate and to draw up a brief report on each applicant's suitability) and to 'advise the Court on longer-term membership policy'.[30]

The role of the Company's Membership Committee has expanded considerably since it was set up in 2004. For example, following the 2005 Strategic Review, it was tasked with overseeing an increase in the size of the Company's livery to 175, and in 2011 its remit expanded further, to encouraging existing members to be more prominent in Company life and to nurture the talent within the Company's ranks. For this reason, it is now known as the Membership Development Committee (MDC). The MDC's responsibilities are closely aligned with those of the Social (originally Fellowship) Committee, which is itself in control of the incoming Master's social calendar. In a typical year, the Social Committee might arrange lectures, outings, or drinks receptions, but it usually does not play a role in organising the Company's regular cycle of major annual events (e.g. the Master's Banquet or the Livery Dinner with the Associated Companies), although it is expected to encourage good attendance at these events, too. Together, the Social Committee and the MDC aim to create the conditions under which the Company is an interesting, vibrant, friendly and warm-hearted organisation for its members.[31]

ENGAGEMENT AND PUBLIC RELATIONS

It took a long time, and much effort on the part of a minority of the livery, to reverse the inward-looking mentality of the early 20th-century Company. Willingness to adopt a public stance gradually developed, however, as the Company increased its commitment to a policy of fostering and supporting its ancient craft of stonemasonry, from the 1980s onwards.

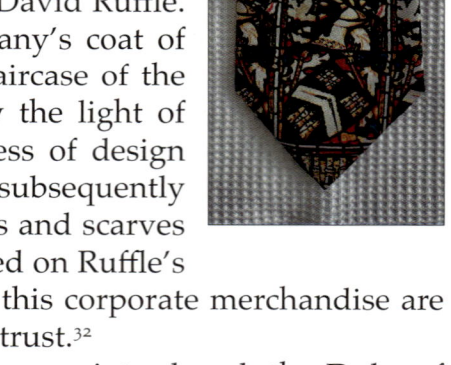

82 *The original Company tie and its 1996 replacement – now one of the most noticed in the livery movement.*

A minor, but symbolic, move was the decision taken in 1986 to commission a Company tie. The first tie, supplied by Melland Brothers, bore the Company's arms depicted in black on either a grey or red background – a sober, restrained, and not especially memorable affair. The current tie, a riot of colour and almost certainly the most distinctive tie among the City of London's livery companies, was designed by David Ruffle. Based on a depiction of the Company's coat of arms in the 1874 window of the staircase of the Guildhall old library, it finally saw the light of day in 1996 after a four-year process of design and redesign; the Company has subsequently added cufflinks, lapel pins, brooches and scarves to its collection, all of which are based on Ruffle's design. The profits from the sale of this corporate merchandise are paid into the Company's charitable trust.[32]

In the same year that the first tie was introduced, the Duke of Gloucester presented the prizes at the inaugural Natural Stone Craft Awards ceremony (NSCA). The awards, run with the London Association of Master Stonemasons (LAMS – an organisation that subsequently combined with others to form the Stone Federation of Great Britain – SFGB), were to be presented, originally, every four years in two categories: best new building and best repair project.

However, they went from strength to strength and as a result soon expanded. In 1990 there were 26 entries, in 1998 there were 32, and in 2007, by which time prizes were awarded in four different fields, over 300 people attended a glorious prize-giving ceremony at Mansion House. Thanks to the excellent efforts of David Blake (a corporate communications director), Gerry Everett and Richard Rowlandson

83 *The Duke of Gloucester presenting the Natural Stone Craft Awards, 5 November 1986. Seated (left to right) David Bishop (Clerk), Alwyn Waters (Chairman of Judges), Robert Woodward (Upper Warden), Rex Wisby (Master), Sir Michael Harrison (Master Mercer), Richard Rowlandson (Renter Warden) and Ron Hebb (Beadle).*

in attracting sponsorship, the two award ceremonies in 2003 and 2007 even managed to raise £50,000 for the Company's craft fund. In this way, thanks to imaginative thinking, the Company's charitable trusts have benefited and continue to benefit from the Company's engagement with the world around it.[33]

The Masons' Company has also raised its profile by associating itself, more or less formally, with external organisations. Many of these, such as the Weald and Downland Museum or the Building Crafts College (BCC), are charities or educational institutions which the Company supports through its charitable giving. Others, however, such as the Incorporation of Masons of Glasgow, are linked through the Company itself. In 1986, the Deacon of the Incorporation attended the Company's Ladies Banquet and, four years later, the Master in return visited the Incorporation. Over the course of the 1990s, these visits became an annual convention and the two organisations agreed more formal connections; more recently, Bob Morrow became the first Master Mason to be admitted to the Incorporation.[34]

In 1990, the Company also signed articles of association with the Corps of Royal Engineers, based in Chatham. Although the Company has a long tradition of contributing to military charities or subscribing money for war loans and defence bonds, this was its first formal association with a specific military organisation. This support to the armed forces has evolved in recent years, with affiliations also being signed with HMS Portland, the Royal Regiment of Scotland and 14 Squadron Royal Air Force in addition to the relationship with the Royal Engineers being re-focused specifically on 36 Engineer Regiment. As part of these relationships, the Company's Charitable Trust funds 'The Masons' Company Prize' to each unit, with recipients and their Commanding Officers being invited to one of the Company's annual formal events where the prizes are presented – social events that are reciprocated each year with visits by the Master and Clerk. Reinforcing these links by supporting the wider military family, the Charitable Trust also makes regular donations to both the Royal British Legion and the Royal Engineers' Corps Museum, and funds prizes for the Best Detachment and Best Instructor in 15 Company South West London Army Cadet Force.[35]

In 1984, as part of a discussion about charity and governance, Colin Jeffries, then Upper Warden, asked his fellow Assistants what chance there was of getting the livery to contribute to the Company's charities if members 'knew comparatively little of Company affairs'. Consequently, the Company created its first newsletter, and between 1984 and 1999 the Company produced a plain but informative sheet for its members. In the latter year, the newsletter was rechristened *Tablets*, and it was printed in full colour, often adorned with many photographs. In 2008, not long after David Blake had taken over as editor, it went even further, becoming something of a glossy magazine, the production of which, at £1,282 for 500 copies (including design and setting), was far from cheap. At that time, there was a real desire to develop the content of *Tablets* as a vehicle for expounding the Company's structure and promoting its activities. That project was reined back in 2014, however, and with frequent e-bulletins there was no longer any need for *Tablets* to be printed twice a year. Now the Clerk produces the less frequent but very well regarded *Journal of the*

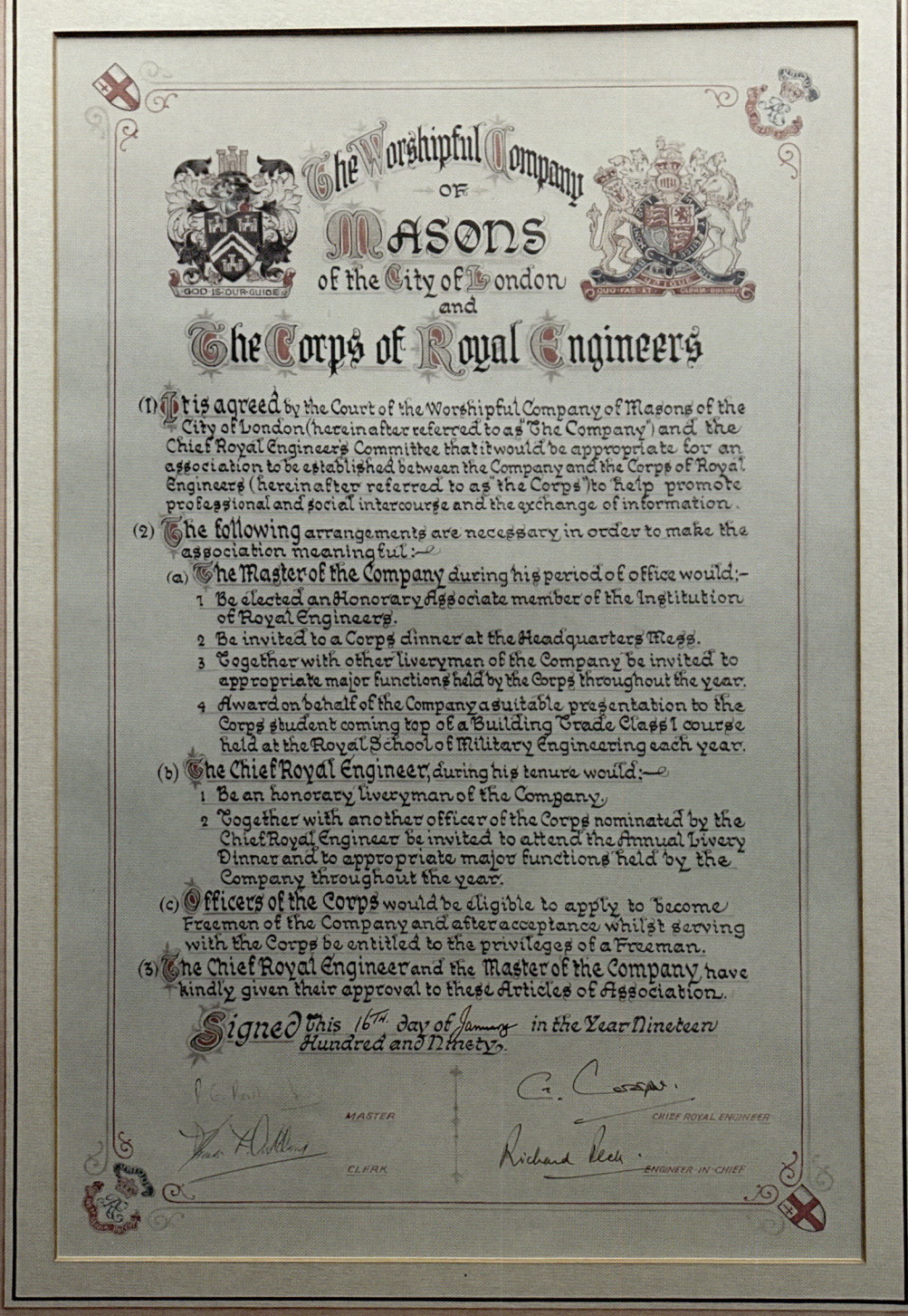

84 *The Articles of Association between the Worshipful Company of Masons and the Corps of Royal Engineers.*

Worshipful Company of Masons annually, and this has as much an external audience as an internal one.[36]

Today, the Company remains in more frequent contact with its members through email updates and its website. In 1999 the newly-formed Publicity Committee (soon renamed the Public Relations and Communications Committee) developed the Company's first website and brought it online the following year. Initially, it was little more than a shop window for the Company – a role that of course it still fulfils today. Two subsequent iterations in 2007 and 2013, however, have made greater use of technology so that the website saves the Clerk valuable administrative time, increases transparency and the Company's profile, and facilitates communication both horizontally between members and vertically between members and the Company.[37]

When we look back over the 20th century, there have undoubtedly been times when the Company has reformed or reorganised itself with greater energy and resolve than at others. One period stands out a little more than the rest. The 1980s really were a time of profound and long-lasting change within the Masons' Company. It was in this decade that the Company formed its first specialist committees, that the long process by which women would be admitted to the Company began, that the Company established the NSCA and overhauled the prizes it presented to apprentice masons, that it got its first tie, that it issued the first Company newsletter, and that it took its first steps to developing formal associations with external bodies. More than that, it was then that the Company began to get all these different pieces on the chessboard to work together, for example by raising money for its charitable efforts from its Awards, by better communication with its members, and by the sale of its merchandise. It was also in that decade that it instituted its Craft Fund, an event that transformed the Company's philanthropic objectives.

15

PHILANTHROPY

The late 20th and early 21st centuries have seen a great revolution in the activity, and even the nature, of the Masons' Company. Prompted from without by the zeitgeist of the times, and from within by the strong enthusiasm of a group of talented and dynamic individuals, the Company has become a consciously philanthropic organisation focused, without benefit to itself, on supporting an ancient and artistically valuable form of craftsmanship, and the people who practise it. This truly charitable re-invention of the Company's purpose and identity may be said to have grown out of an age-old concern for charity in its traditional sense of care for the disadvantaged and enfeebled; but the modern Company has transformed that marginal benevolence into a matter of existential importance.

HISTORIC CHARITY
Charitable activity was an invariable characteristic of the guilds of medieval London, and as the guilds developed into livery companies and acquired corporate status in the 15th century, they accumulated endowments for charitable purposes which matched, and after the Reformation came to exceed, those administered by the Church.

We have only occasional and limited glimpses of the Masons' Company's earliest charitable efforts. We know that the Company paid 26s. 8d. towards the re-foundation of St Bartholomew's Hospital in 1548, and £5 towards the re-establishment of Christ's Hospital three years later. We know, too, from surviving property deeds that from the 1560s onwards, if not before, the Company leased rooms at Masons' Hall to widows at what appear to have been below-market rates. Unfortunately, we do not know how these widows were chosen for support, nor if the Company provided for them in other ways.[1]

The better survival of the Company's records from the 17th century onwards allows the fog to clear somewhat. The reports of the Royal Commissions of 1833-5 and 1884-5, together with the records of the Clerks' preparatory investigations, do throw useful light on what the Company at those times believed its charitable history to be (although modern analysis can tell a somewhat different story). In the first half of the 20th century, the Company began to issue and update standing orders in which, among other things, clear guidance was laid down as to how the Company should administer charity. In the second half of that century, the Company took steps which gave overall structure and purpose to its charitable provision; the Masons' Company's Charitable Trust and Craft Fund were established, and each year since then, trustees have reported on the funds' activities and performance. Together, all these sources provide us with a rich picture of the Company's charity.

From 1600 to 1900 the Masons' Company's provision for its poor and pensioners formed a substantial part of the Company's financial business. In the second half of the 19th century, however, the Company's membership became more middle-class and, following the introduction of state-funded old-age pensions in 1908 and the subsequent development of a welfare state, there was plainly less need for the Company to support its own poor – at least financially. In the 20th century, the focus of the Company's charitable efforts changed, and the establishment of the Charitable Trust in 1968 gives us a good understanding of the evolution of the Company's charitable ethos.

The Trust as then established had four objectives: the relief of poverty, the advancement of education, the advancement of religion, and such other charitable purposes as the trustees should think fit. The first three objectives were clear enough, and they were deeply rooted in the Company's history. The fourth objective was open to greater interpretation. In the five or six decades before the creation of the Trust, there had been a developing awareness among the Company's members that support for the craft of stonemasonry should properly be an important feature of the Company's charitable ambitions. So in the years following the foundation of the Trust, the fourth objective came to be understood as meaning that the Company should support the craft of stonemasonry. This objective gradually came to assume such importance that in 1985 the Company created a second, separate charitable trust, entitled the Craft Fund, more of which later.

THE COMPANY'S POOR

In 1623-4, the Company paid a total of 7s. 6d. to two widows of its members, and in 1632-3, the sum of 6d. to Isaac Gardener, a 'poor brother'. Although the Company had almost certainly been supporting its own poor from the time of its foundation, these are two of the earliest documented examples of such activity. The Company's donations covered a range of needs: a loan in 1638-9 of 5s. to Leonard Perkin, a young mason who had just been made free of the Company, may have been made in order to help him acquire tools, pay for his admission or otherwise to set him up in business; in January 1729, as the unfortunate Michael Fleetwood languished in Ludgate Gaol – he was probably a debtor – he must have been very grateful for the four sacks of coal that the Company sent him; in October 1758 the Assistants authorised the payment of five guineas to William Morris, the Beadle, 'on Account of his long Illness and Misfortunes.' There was always sympathy and support for wives and widows of members. Two typical examples might be the cases of Sarah Stephens who, in June 1764, was given a guinea by the Court after she had been left destitute when her husband had deserted her; and widow Lee who, in 1859, was given £10 so that she might emigrate to Australia. The Company was usually also willing to help pay funeral costs. In 1683-4, it gave £2 to widow Bowser so that she might bury her husband, in 1845-6 it provided money for the funerals of three widows, and in 1880 found £5 to go towards the cost of widow Malcott's burial.[2]

Of course, there were occasions on which charity was denied. Many, perhaps even most, of these instances are probably invisible to us, as applicants deemed undeserving would almost certainly have been discouraged or disallowed from appearing before the Court. When we do see charity denied, it is usually impossible to know why. We might take the example of Edward Stanton. Edward descended from a very successful dynasty of mason contractors, at least 10 of whom were prominent members of the Company over four or five generations, but who seem to have fallen on hard times in the middle decades of the 18th century. In 1755 and 1756, Stanton put in a series of applications for charity to the Court. Twice he asked for the return of his £5 livery fine, 'on account of his great Misfortunes', and once for £4 'on account of his indigent Circumstances', all of which requests the Court refused without explanation.[3]

PENSIONERS

From 1625 to 1632, widow Thomas was paid sums ranging from 1s. to 3s. on eight occasions. These payments are not regular or consistent enough to suggest that they were a pension; rather, they appear to have been *ad hoc* disbursements made upon receipt of petitions. Thanks to the munificence of two benefactors, the Company began to pay regular pensions in the 1670s. The first benefactor was Robert Buckland, who had lent the Company £120 with the proviso that only the interest due on the loan, and not the capital, should be paid for as long as the Company gave 10 'of the most auntient and poore ffreemen of this Companie or the widdowes of ffreemen' an annual pension of 10s. after he and his wife had died. Buckland died in 1653 and his widow Margaret died in 1672. In that year, the Company bought a book to record the names of those who were to receive money of Buckland's gift. Shortly thereafter, in March 1678, Joshua Marshall, the king's Master Mason (1673-8) and current Master of the Company, died. Perhaps inspired by Buckland's generosity, in his will Marshall remitted a debt of £200 owed to him by the Company, as noted in chapter 10, on condition that the Company pay pensions totalling £10 to as many poor widows of members 'as they should think fitt'. The first pensions of his gift were paid in 1679 and they were disbursed until 1990.[4]

The Company soon developed procedures both for choosing its pensioners and paying their pensions. Pensioners were expected to appear at Masons' Hall in person, not on the anniversary of Marshall's death but at the quarterly Court meetings to collect their pensions, where a special room was set aside for what was probably something of a ritualised ceremony. After the sale of the Hall in 1866, the Company saved the pensioners the bother of following the itinerant Court by allowing them to collect three of their quarterly payments – they still had to appear before the Court in January – from the offices of Hunters in Lincoln's Inn. Whenever there was a vacancy for a pensioner, candidates would submit petitions to, and sometimes be interviewed by, the Assistants.[5]

Once elected, a pensioner would ordinarily receive their pension for life, but this was not invariably the case; in 1768, for example, widow Huddleston lost her pension after she was admitted to a workhouse. There were almost always more female than male pensioners, but women, whether daughters or widows of members, could only continue as pensioners so long as they remained single.[6]

There were other ways, apart from cash subsidies, of disbursing benefits to the Company's worthy dependents. By a convention which was in widespread use throughout the 18th and early 19th centuries, nominal or sinecure employment might be used as a disguised form of pension, and the Company frequently made use of this device in the appointment of its Beadles. When a vacancy occurred in the office, it was customary for the Company's Court to select a successor from among petitioners in the ranks of its aged members or existing male pensioners. In the years 1772 and 1783, for example, John Strong and George Lee, both of whom were already pensioners of the Company, were elected Beadle. The duties of this office were light, but it was not a mere sinecure, and some Beadles proved more satisfactory than others.[7]

In fact, some of these 18th-century Beadles appear to have been rather a rascally lot. In June 1717 Beadle John Miller was imprisoned for reasons unknown, whereupon John Shield and William Trimmer both submitted 'humble petitions' to the Court in advance of the election of a successor, emphasising both their neediness and their readiness to defer to the Court's authority. Trimmer, who was the chosen candidate, particularly stressed his Whig credentials, which might suggest that Miller, a Tory, had landed himself in hot water following the failed 1715 uprising. Whether that was the case or not, shortly thereafter Trimmer was himself suspended, after he had behaved 'himself very insolently and spoke several slighting and reproachful words to the Court'. His replacement was John Shield. William Stanton succeeded Shield in 1738. At the time of his election, Stanton claimed that he was 'under some Difficultys in regard to his Circumstances' and he was given further financial assistance on top of his Beadle's salary. However, he was soon 'displac'd' from his office after he was accused of pocketing quarterage payments that should have been paid to the Company. This was perhaps a misunderstanding; certainly he was reinstated shortly afterwards, although with the caveat that his appointment was only 'during his good behaviour'. He served a further 13 years as Beadle, seemingly without trouble, until his death in 1753, at which point it was discovered that he had pawned his gown![8]

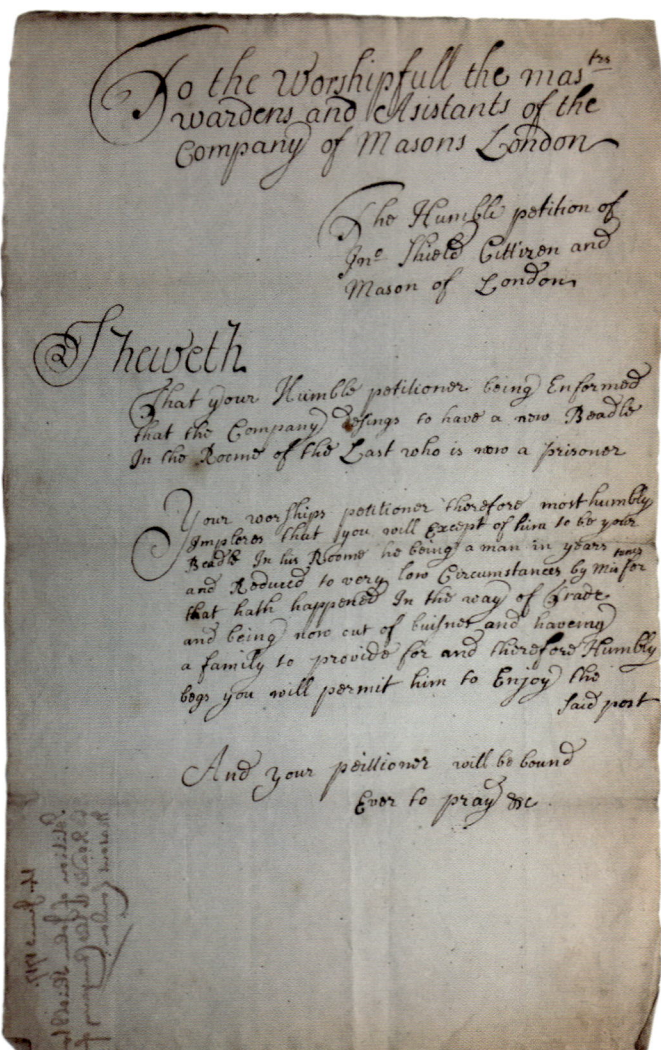

85 *'The Humble petition of John Shield, Cittizen and Mason of London' to be appointed 'Beadle in the Roome of the Last who is now a prisoner'.*

Quasi-pensioner Beadles apart, over the course of the next two centuries the number of pensioners varied. At times there might perhaps be as many as 12 or 13 on the Company's books, at other times as few as five. The general trend, however, was for the Company, as its finances recovered, to support more pensioners at higher rates. A bequest by a widow of a member, Elizabeth Commines (d.1745), enabled the Company to double the amount paid to women pensioners, from £1 to £2, bringing their pensions into line with the sums paid to the men. Higher dividends from the Associated Companies' venture in Ulster between 1825 and 1842 helped the pensions to double again from £3 to £6 and, after the Company had sold Masons' Hall in 1866, the pensions were all raised to £10, with an additional Christmas box worth £1.[9]

The Company was proud of the support it offered its pensioners. After the turmoil of the late 17th century, it always paid its pensions promptly and fully. Indeed, throughout the 18th and 19th centuries, the provision for its pensioners is one of the most prominent features of the Company's activities. In 1780-1, for example, when the Company's turnover was a little over £112, it paid pensions worth £25. When the Clerk, John Hunter, appeared before the royal commissioners in the 1880s, he pointed out that, while in the preceding 200 years the Company's income had grown four-fold, the amount paid in pensions had increased by a factor of nine. In 1910, the Company was still paying a total of £96 annually to its six pensioners. Thereafter, however, vacancies were simply not filled, and in 1990-91 the Company brought more than four centuries of pension provision to a formal end, when it transferred £200 worth of gilt-edged stock, that is a sum equivalent to Marshall's original bequest, from the Company's funds to the Company's Charitable Trust to establish within it a separate Joshua Marshall bequest fund. Ten years later, this special fund was finally rolled into the Charitable Trust's general funds.[10]

MODERN BENEFACTORS

The Company's charitable activity, in the traditional sense of the words, has continued to expand in modern times thanks to the generosity of many benefactors. Henry Grover commemorated his year as Master (1924-5) by donating £100 in stock, while his successor, Frederick Dray, left the Company an annuity worth £500 gross after his death in 1941. Upon his death in 1964, John Byram left the Company land in Ealing, comprising some three-quarters of an acre, worth about £66,000 freehold, which the Company leased to the City of London Housing Society; the Society then built 34 flats and garages on the site, paying the Company a consideration of £50,000 and an initial ground rent of £1,000 per annum. Today, the ground rent on Greenlaw Court, as the building is known, produces £30,000 per annum, and over the course of the last 50 years the Company has received a sum comfortably in excess of £700,000 in premiums from leaseholders who have extended their leases. In 1980, Max Weldon left the Company £500, 10 years later Gordon Coates left the Company £1,000, and five years after that Sydney Mason gave £20,000 while he was still alive. Since then Colin Jeffries has bequeathed £5,000, Eric Brookes £90,000, Rupert Wood just over £100,000, and Richard and Jill Burrows some £400,000. In 2013-14, Peter Clark asked that half of his salary be given to the Company's charities and his successor in the role, Giles Clapp, raised £2,500 for the Company's charities when he walked the length of Hadrian's Wall in 2018. Collections made at banquets, services and other occasions swell the coffers with quiet regularity.[11]

COMMEMORATION

The Company has not always given its benefactors the recognition that they have deserved. For a long time, in fact, Joshua Marshall was the only one whose memory seems to have been thought worthy of preservation – perhaps because he was king's Master Mason, one of the most famous masons of his age, and the Company's first Master under its charter. When he appeared before the royal commissioners in the 1880s, John Hunter stated that 'the only charity under the management of the company is one under the will of Mr Joshua Marshall'. When Conder wrote his history of the Company he likewise referred only to Marshall's will, and the habit of treating Marshall's name almost as a representative symbol of the Company's charitable activity has persisted into recent times – a phenomenon which can be found to have parallels in the histories of many other institutions, and is the result of the laziness of collective memory.[12]

86 *The Dray family grave in Highgate Cemetery.*

In the 20th century, the Company began to recognise the importance of commemorating all its benefactors. Under the terms of Dray's will, for the Company to receive the annuity, the Master, Wardens and Clerk of the Company must visit his family's grave in Highgate Cemetery each year on or close to 21 July, in order to lay a wreath and then to submit a report on the condition of the grave to the trustees of his estate. In 1947, the Court bought three loving cups in Dray's memory, and his anniversary has been kept ever since. Following Byram's bequest, the Court decided to hold an annual dinner for the Assistants in his honour and to purchase some silver in his memory. Today, this dinner is known as the Benefactors' Dinner and, since the year 2000, it has begun with the reading of the Byram Grace, commissioned by Basil Rushton, which recalls, 'with thanksgiving, those benefactors who across the centuries have dedicated their lives to this Company and to the service of others'.[13]

A CHANGE OF DIRECTION: EDUCATION AND TRAINING

The evolution of the Company's charitable activity in the later 20th century might appear to have followed a simple course. John Byram left a substantial endowment to the Company and, consequently, the Company established its Charitable Trust in 1968. As a result of the reforming zeal of the 1980s, the Craft Fund was created in 1985, and today these two well-endowed trusts, between them, provide tens of thousands of pounds annually in support of the Company's charitable objectives. In reality, however, the story is somewhat more complex.

The Court actually gave consideration at various times in the first half of the 20th century to the subject of utilising to best effect the tax advantages afforded to charities, and the idea of creating a charitable trust had been raised in 1950, 18 years before it was actually established. Nor was the Trust immediately endowed with the proceeds of Byram's bequest. In fact, its initial endowment was just £100 and it was only from 1974 that the Company began to use the Trust to meet its charitable commitments. It would be another 10 years before the Company would begin to endow its Trust properly by transfers of stock, the income of which was used to support the Company's charitable aims; and only in 1993 did it start allocating some of its profits, usually 10 per cent but sometimes more, into the Trust. The freehold of Greenlaw Court, by far its most valuable asset, was not transferred to the Charitable Trust until 2006. In short, the endowment of the Masons' Company Charitable Trust has been a process, not an event.[14]

As we have noted, providing for the craft of stonemasonry was not one of the objectives listed in the deed which instituted the Charitable Trust. But the Company could still fulfil the objectives of the Trust while supporting its craft, albeit vicariously, and the City of London. For example, the relief of poverty was readily accepted as a duty if it came with particular connections to the building industry. Thus, the Company had supported the Builders' Benevolent Institution (BBI), a charity which provides support for builders or their dependents who find themselves in need, with ad hoc payments in 1885, 1900 and 1903. Since 1970, with some brief interruptions, the Company has contributed annually to this charity's work.[15]

Since the Trust was founded, the advancement of religion has usually come to mean support for the restoration of church buildings, normally in London, and much of the Company's educational provision has been connected with the City of London. In 1969, for instance, the Company covenanted £150 to assist City University. In the last 30 years the Company has regularly given money in aid of the Treloar Trust, a charitable organisation founded by the Lord Mayor of London in 1907, which runs a nursery, school and college for children and adolescents with physical disabilities. It has also contributed money each year to support pupils, through bursaries and prizes, at King Edward's Witley, another school which can trace its history back to a foundation in 16th-century London (Bridewell Hospital); and the City of London Freemen's School which was established by the Corporation of London in 1854. Each year the Company also assists the Livery Schools Link, a voluntary body which brings together livery companies and schools in Greater London.[16]

The Masons' Company was not one of the 16 City companies which supported the founding of the City and Guilds of London Institute (CGLI) in 1878, even if some in the Company came to believe that it was. Nor was it in any other way committed to formal or structured technical education at that time, despite gallant and persistent efforts on the part of George Wales, Master in 1873. Wales, who was a surveyor by profession, had been involved in discussions on technical education at Mansion House and at the end of his year he presented the Court with a detailed proposal for how the Company might involve itself with 'some distinct practical Benevolent work connected with our Craft'. He had studied the Company's income and expenditure in some detail, as well as inquiring into the 'honourable example' set by other companies. His constructive, costed recommendations for the support of 'Technical Education bearing on Masonry and the Masons' Craft' concluded with the suggestion that while 'the ancient charter rights of our Company have become obsolete ... it should be the object of our day to throw out new energies and find new fields for usefulness in connection with Masonry and not allow ourselves to become an effete body.'[17]

The Court's response to Wales' proposal was tepid; Wales was thanked for his 'great services rendered' and, one year later, the Court appointed a sub-committee to explore how best to 'promote higher Technical knowledge among the Operative Masons of London'. But thereafter little was done, and when the Royal Commissioners of the 1880s asked the Court for a 'statement as to whether the company does anything to subsidize or encourage education, whether general or technical', the Company replied that it did not have the resources. In reality, Wales' proposal was rather modest in scope; certainly it would have cost about half the £115 which the Assistants paid themselves, on average, each year for attending Court meetings. It is hard to explain this lack of interest on the Company's part. In the 1880s, some 22 members of the Company, that is over one half of the livery, were 'connected with the building trade, being either architects, engineers, surveyors, builders, masons or stone merchants', and the Company also had a well-established charitable ethos. It seems simply to have been the case that Wales's fellow Assistants had different ideas of what the Company's purpose should be.[18]

Over the course of the next 50 years, some Assistants pressed the Company to do more to support training in its craft, but with only very limited success. In 1894, the Court did authorise the payment of £25 to establish classes in masonry and carpentry in partnership with the Carpenters' Company at the newly-founded Carpenters' Company Trades Training School, subsequently the Building Craft Training School and then the Building Crafts College (BCC). But the donation was not repeated, and subsequent suggestions to the Court about support for technical scholarships and apprenticeships usually fell on deaf ears.[19]

Towards the end of the 1920s, however, thanks to the efforts of energetic and imaginative members who worked in the construction industry, things began to change. In June 1927, Henry Grover, a quantity surveyor and senior member of the Company, volunteered to respond to an invitation sent to the Company to adjudicate on the masonry competition at the Eisteddfod of Wales, entirely at his own cost; shortly afterwards, perhaps shamed by Grover's example, and very much through the good offices of Sidney Young, a surveyor, and John Greenwood, a builder, the Company instituted three prizes for technical study. The first of these was for students at the Northern Polytechnic Institute in Holloway and the famous LCC School of Building in Brixton; the second was given to the student who performed best in the theoretical and practical examinations held by LAMS; the third was awarded for the best individual piece of finished masonry exhibited by any one of the schools at the annual Building Trades Exhibition held at Kensington Olympia.[20]

The Second World War interrupted the Company's efforts, but after the war there was an urgent demand for building craftsmen, which appears to have focused minds on the Court. By the end of the 1940s, the Company was providing £30 each year to LAMS for prizes and, in 1953, the Court contributed money so that LAMS apprentices could travel to Canterbury and Rochester for lectures on the cathedrals there. Discussions took place with construction companies as well as training institutions, and with representatives of the Ministry of Works, in the light of which the Company agreed in 1950 to subscribe £21 to the CGLI for prizes, thereby beginning a relationship with an institution that had existed in London for over 70 years. Shortly thereafter, the CGLI formed a committee for education in stonemasonry, on which Mark Lemon was the Company's first representative.[21]

By the mid-1960s the Company was giving over £133 a year to CGLI and LAMS for prizes, that is over six times the amount it had provided some 30 years earlier. John Byram's generosity allowed the Company to make quantitative and qualitative changes in its provision for craft training. In 1969, the Masons' Company began its long association with what is now the BCC, covenanting to support them with an annual donation of £100. Within the space of a few years the Company had agreed new covenants worth a total of £225 with the City and Guilds of London Art School (CGLAS); the Orton Trust, a charity based in Northamptonshire dedicated to 'the advancing of public education in the arts of stone masonry'; and the CGLI. It had also appointed representatives to work with the latter two institutions and the Committee for Natural Stone.[22]

In recent years, the Company has also celebrated its support for education and training by paying the £2000 cost of the Portland stone used at the entrance of the BCC's new premises in Stratford, east London, and by commissioning two new stone public benches in London, one on the corner of Cheapside and Foster Lane and the other at Grant's Quay adjacent to Old Billingsgate. Both benches were made by trainee masons from institutions which the Company supports to designs of students that had won competitions which the Company had backed. It also generously supported the European Stone Carving competition which was held at Lincoln Cathedral in 2013. This event brought more than 110 masons together for a three-day event, at which the Master, John Burton, presented the prizes.[23]

HERITAGE

After the Second World War, there was a pressing need to restore churches and cathedrals across the country and, between 1947 and 1962, the Company supported the Bishop of London's church appeal, as well as restoration projects at St Paul's and Canterbury Cathedrals and Westminster Abbey. In 1962, a sub-committee met to formulate a policy on how the Company should respond to appeals for donations. It suggested that the Company give £300 annually to appeals and that giving should be 'restricted to structural efforts in the City of London and in particular those of an Ecclesiastical nature', which was unanimously approved by the Court in the following year. A decade later, the Court re-affirmed its commitment to supporting the 'the preservation and restoration of Cathedrals and historic buildings primarily in London but also in other parts of England'.[24]

As a consequence of these resolutions, significant sums of money were paid to churches and cathedrals within and without London and the Company established a model for charitable giving which remains to this day. In fact, more than one-third of the money disbursed by the Company's Charitable Trust in recent years has gone to stone conservation, restoration and improvement projects, mostly at religious buildings, in grants of various sizes.

It was perhaps in 1972-3, as part of the celebrations surrounding the quincentenary of the Company obtaining its coat of arms, that the Company really began to think about how it might celebrate its connections with the country's built environment in imaginative and lasting ways. The first example of this approach came in October 1972, when a plaque was unveiled in the crypt of St Paul's Cathedral to commemorate Thomas and Edward Strong, and all the other

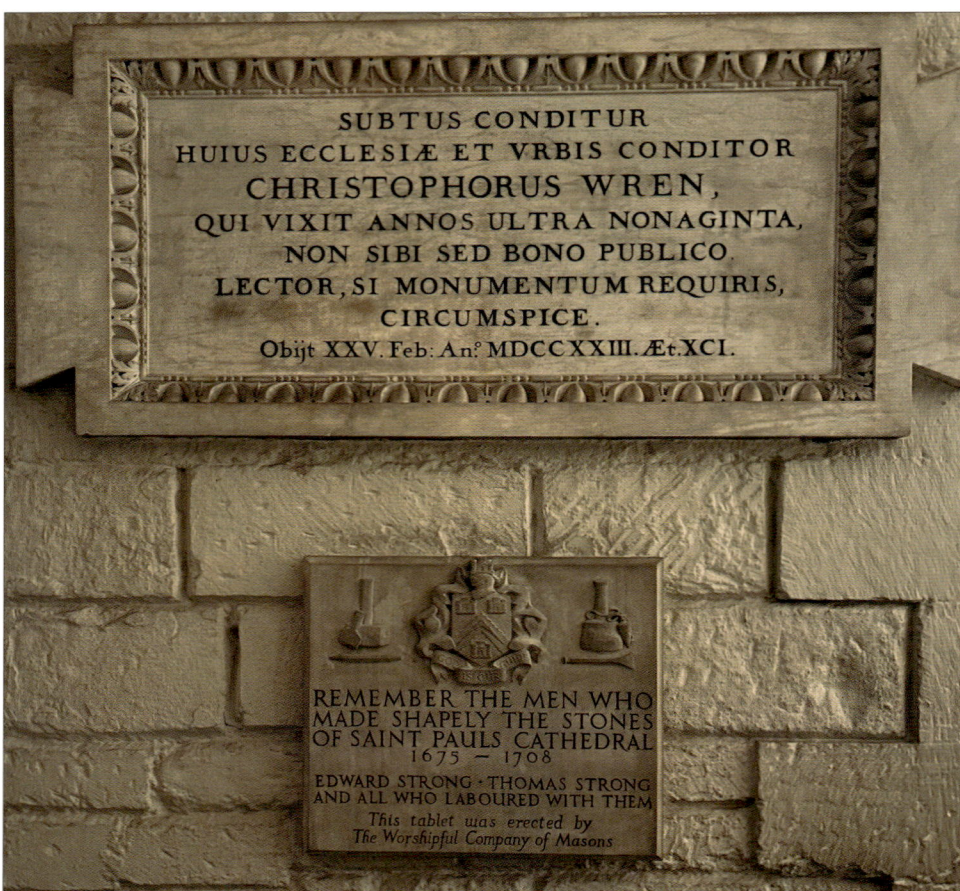

SUBTUS CONDITUR
HUIUS ECCLESIÆ ET VRBIS CONDITOR
CHRISTOPHORUS WREN,
QUI VIXIT ANNOS ULTRA NONAGINTA,
NON SIBI SED BONO PUBLICO.
LECTOR, SI MONUMENTUM REQUIRIS,
CIRCUMSPICE.
Obijt XXV. Feb: Anᵒ MDCCXXIII. Æt.XCI.

REMEMBER THE MEN WHO
MADE SHAPELY THE STONES
OF SAINT PAULS CATHEDRAL
1675 — 1708
EDWARD STRONG · THOMAS STRONG
AND ALL WHO LABOURED WITH THEM
This tablet was erected by
The Worshipful Company of Masons

87 Plaque unveiled by the Master Mason in 1972 adjacent to the tomb of Sir Christopher Wren, commemorating Edward and Thomas Strong along with others who built St Paul's Cathedral.

stonemasons who had worked on the cathedral; it had been paid for by the Company and had been carved by liveryman Sir Charles Wheeler KCVO CBE, the first sculptor to hold the presidency of the Royal Academy. It does not appear that the Company had ever previously remembered any of its anniversaries, the achievements of its members, or its support for masonry work in buildings in this way.[25]

Six months after the event at St Paul's, Cyril Thatcher, then Master, presented the Dean of York with a solid silver bowl which commemorated the joint quincentenaries of the completion of York Minster and the Company's grant of arms. The Company's connections with York Minster were not as deep as those it enjoyed with St Paul's Cathedral, but the depiction of medieval and modern craftsmen on the bowl's handle was a fitting representation not just of a shared anniversary but also of a common theme in the Company's and the Minster's history.[26]

This stone bearing the mark of SIR CHRISTOPHER WREN was found near the site of an ancient wharf at Portland from whence stone was transported by sea and the River Thames for the building of the Cathedral. It was shipped to London in 1972 aboard the Sailing Barge MAY with other Portland Stone for restoration work and was received at the wharf by the Dean, and by the Master and Wardens of the Worshipful Company of Masons who were exercising their ancient right of inspection.

88 *Portland stone (right) placed above Wren's tomb in St Paul's Cathedral. On 17 August 1972 it was ceremonially inspected by the Master and Wardens when it was brought from Portland to a quay on the River Thames close to the Cathedral.*

Since then, there have been many examples of the Company celebrating the use of natural stone in London's built environment. In 1989, the Company's Charitable Trust paid some £1,000 for a stone bench, made at John Bysouth's works, which was unveiled at the Guildhall as part of the commemorations to mark the 800th anniversary of the mayoralty of London.

The Company also provided £1,000 for restoration work on the Albert Memorial in Kensington Gardens, this time by using money from Rupert Wood's bequest as he had long had connections with the Royal Albert Hall, by sponsoring the restoration of the stone sculpture of Francis Bird on the Memorial's Frieze of Parnassus. Bird (1667-1731) was a famous sculptor best known for his carving work at St Paul's

89 *Illuminated vellum recording the presentation of a silver bowl to York Minster in celebration of joint quincentenaries.*

Cathedral, and Neil Barnes, then Master, attended the ceremony to celebrate the reopening of the Memorial on 21 October 1998. In November 2000, the first plaque in St Paul's Cathedral was joined by another, this one the Company's Millennium Gift to the cathedral, which was installed just outside the OBE chapel in the crypt. It was carved by Richard Kindersley, stone carver to the cathedral and subsequently a liveryman of the Masons' Company, and it remembers the surveyors to the cathedral's fabric, among whom were Robert Potter OBE and Martin Stancliffe, two distinguished liverymen of the Company; it will be updated by the Company in the centuries to come.[27]

90 Inscription on the bench situated in Guildhall Yard.

An important project with which the Company was already involved was the re-siting of Temple Bar. From medieval times, the Bar marked the extent of the City of London's jurisdiction to the west and, therefore, the boundary between the historic cities of London and Westminster. In 1670-72, a new gateway was built of Portland stone on the site, perhaps to designs by Wren. It was certainly carved

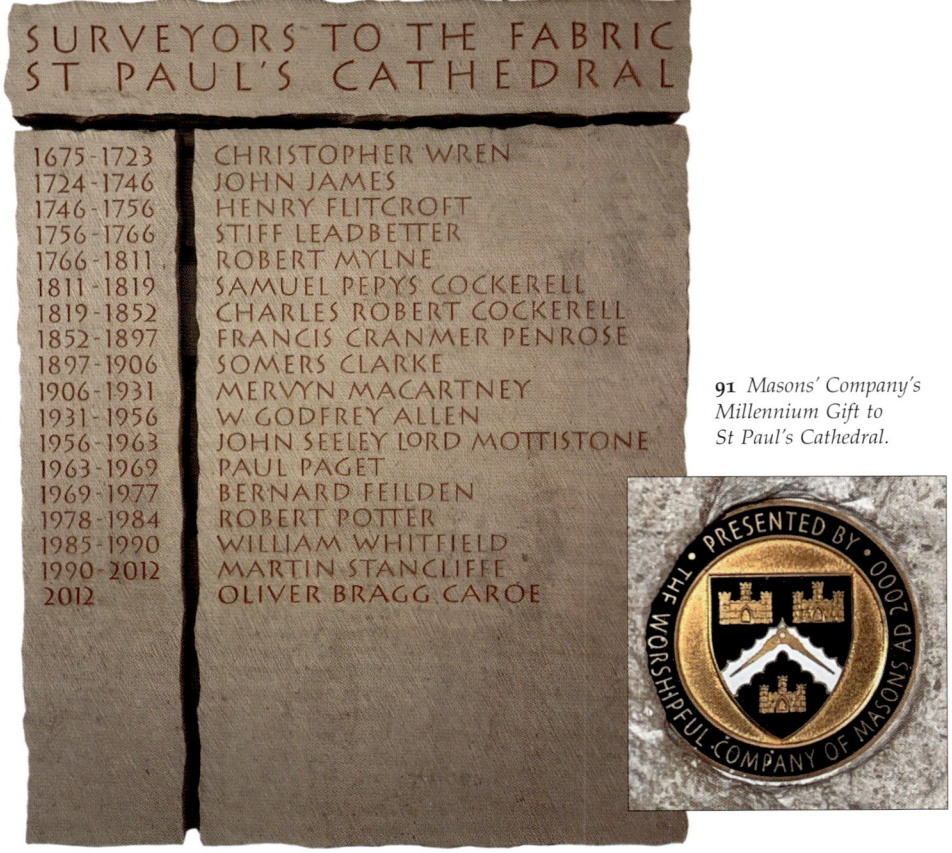

SURVEYORS TO THE FABRIC
ST PAUL'S CATHEDRAL

1675-1723	CHRISTOPHER WREN
1724-1746	JOHN JAMES
1746-1756	HENRY FLITCROFT
1756-1766	STIFF LEADBETTER
1766-1811	ROBERT MYLNE
1811-1819	SAMUEL PEPYS COCKERELL
1819-1852	CHARLES ROBERT COCKERELL
1852-1897	FRANCIS CRANMER PENROSE
1897-1906	SOMERS CLARKE
1906-1931	MERVYN MACARTNEY
1931-1956	W GODFREY ALLEN
1956-1963	JOHN SEELEY LORD MOTTISTONE
1963-1969	PAUL PAGET
1969-1977	BERNARD FEILDEN
1978-1984	ROBERT POTTER
1985-1990	WILLIAM WHITFIELD
1990-2012	MARTIN STANCLIFFE
2012	OLIVER BRAGG CAROE

91 *Masons' Company's Millennium Gift to St Paul's Cathedral.*

by Thomas Knight, City Mason, and Joshua Marshall, one of the most famous members of the 17th-century Company, and possibly also by his father, Edward. It stood at the junction of Fleet Street and the Strand for some 200 years until, having become regarded as an obstruction to traffic, it was removed in 1878 and bought by Sir Henry Bruce Meux, a scion of the brewing dynasty, to be reconstructed at his family's estate in Theobalds Park in Hertfordshire.[28]

It seems that the Masons' Company first became aware of a campaign to return the Temple Bar to London, perhaps even to a public park, in 1973, in which year Sir Hugh Wontner, the first chairman of the Temple Bar Trust, became Lord Mayor of London. For a decade or so little happened, but in 1984 the Trust bought the gateway from the Meux Trust for £1 and in the following year the Company donated £200 to the Trust's appeal. Again, things moved slowly, but in July 2001 Sir Alexander Graham, a Mercer and a trustee of the Temple Bar Trust, came to a Court lunch to discuss a

new appeal which would, it was hoped, raise £5m to relocate the gateway in the new Paternoster Square development adjacent to St Paul's Cathedral. A few months later, the Corporation of London decided to back the project, which made it much more likely to succeed, and in September 2002, the Masons' Company, keen once more to celebrate the achievements of one its most famous sons, pledged as much as £15,000 in support.

92 *Engraving of Temple Bar sited on the junctions of Fleet Street and Strand.*

With funding from other livery companies, too, matters now moved reasonably quickly. The Lord Mayor laid the foundation stone on 16 October 2003 and the gateway was officially opened on 10 November 2004, during all of which time Court Assistant David Beattie steadfastly held a watching brief on the project. Many representatives of the Company attended the ceremony, at which they were given a private tour of the gateway by liveryman Bernard Burns of the Cathedral Works Organisation, who had led the rebuilding project. At the rebuilt Temple Bar itself, the representatives would also have seen two bronze plaques, inscribed with the arms of the Company and the Corporation of London, which commemorate both the Marshalls and the Company.

Another significant project concerned a small piece of Clipsham limestone known as London Stone, which was sited in what is now Cannon Street. John Stow famously noted that he knew not what the stone actually was, nor how or why it had come to reside in Cannon Street, but that it had 'long continued there' as something of a landmark since at least the time of the Conquest. Our knowledge of its history is little better than Stow's, but

93 *Temple Bar, re-sited in Paternoster Square in 2004. Commemorative plaques were set in the adjacent paving.*

94 *London Stone, shown in its latest setting opposite the entrance to Cannon Street Station.*

we do know that London Stone had been re-positioned on several occasions throughout the centuries until, in 1961-2, it was housed, rather unloved and unnoticed, in an uninspiring office block built on the site of Wren's bomb-damaged St Swithin's church, which housed the Oversea-China Banking Corporation (OCBC). The Company had been in contact with the OCBC since 1995 with a view to increasing the visibility of the Stone and doing more to preserve and celebrate its enigmatic history. Over the course of a decade, however, despite numerous plans, meetings and discussions, very little progress was made.[29]

In 2006, Minerva plc, a development company, acquired the site and they were much more favourably inclined to the suggestion that the Company should have a role in the improved presentation of the Stone. Sandy Copland, with support from John Burton and Derek Sayer, spent the next five years representing the Company in discussions with Minerva, but proposals to relocate the Stone some 50 yards to the west in the frontage of their new Walbrook building were opposed by English Heritage and other preservation societies and, in the end, they were rejected by the Corporation of London. The site was eventually redeveloped by Adrian Fu, a Hong Kong businessman, and with the help of London and Oriental's project manager and the Museum of London, plans were finally agreed. In October 2018, the Lord Mayor unveiled the Stone, now re-sited in a Portland stone casing, at a ceremony again attended by many members of the Company. Through its efforts to improve the position and visibility of the Stone, the Company has acquired something of a role – completely self-designated, wholly unofficial, but one that will itself perhaps be 'long continued' – as guardians of London Stone.

Fostering the Craft of Stonemasonry

Grants that were made in the late 1960s represented something new. Previously, most of the money the Company had given to educational institutions had been used to support prizes, but now it was giving money for actual training. Still more important, the Company was beginning to focus its support, quite deliberately, on the teaching of skills involved in working not just with building materials generally, but with natural stone. Over the course of the 1970s, the Company gave grants to enable apprentice stonemasons to pay for tools and books, and it also began to sponsor apprentices, albeit modestly, engaged at cathedrals across the country. In 1982 the Company founded its first specialist committee, the Technical (subsequently 'Craft') Committee, to promote the craft of stonemasonry. All these developments came to a head on 9 May 1985, when the Company constituted its Craft Fund by deed, with the objectives of encouraging the exercise and maintaining the standards of the craft of stonemasonry, preserving and improving the craft, and promoting public interest in stonemasonry.[30]

There was a great deal of enthusiastic support among the livery for the new Craft Fund. Not only was it quick to be established, within just six months of being proposed by Colin Jeffries, but, in the first year of its existence, the livery paid or promised cash or covenants to the fund worth over £23,000 – more than twice the amount initially sought. Indeed, the Craft Fund very quickly became worth more than the Company's Charitable Trust, an imbalance which prompted a review of the Charitable Trust's aims, with the result that in 1991 the Court resolved that the trustees of the Charitable Trust should 'give precedence at all times to Charitable objectives connected with stonemasonry but not to the complete

95 *Stonemasonry workshop at the Building Crafts College (BCC).*

exclusion of other, more general projects within the provisions of the Trust Deed'. This refocusing has succeeded, to an extent at least, in equalising the sums given in the form of annual donations by liverymen as individuals. But the Craft Fund has attracted the most spectacular legacies, with gifts altogether worth in excess of half a million pounds.[31]

The remit, as well as the size of the Craft Fund, has developed since it was established. The initial expectation was that the Craft Fund would support the Company's awards, prizes and certificates, and make occasional grants to 'deserving causes connected with our craft'. This began to change in 1993. At that time, the economic recession and changes in the way that the government allocated funding for courses were having a negative impact on courses offered at the BCC. As a consequence, the Carpenters' Company asked the Court of the Masons' Company if it would consider sponsoring one or more students taking a newly-established one-year diploma in stonemasonry, approved by the CGLI and which would count towards a National Vocational Qualification (NVQ). The Company was already supporting the BCC to the tune of some £750 annually, which was three-quarters of the Company's total training budget. The cost of the course, however, was £3,800 – a significant increase. Consideration was given to the proposal in the context of wide-ranging discussions about training, involving construction companies and the City authorities, the end result of which was an agreement to sponsor a student.[32]

To meet its commitments, the Court established a special training fund within the Craft Fund, initially with £10,000 from the Associated Companies' Joint Venture Scheme, but with the aim of increasing its balance to £50,000 with donations from the livery and elsewhere. This time the response from the livery was less enthusiastic, but with further monies from the Joint Venture Scheme (the receipts from which have for the most part always been used to support training), donations from members, internal transfers and investment returns, the training fund did grow steadily over the course of 10 years. By May 1999 it was worth some £70,000, yielding over £3,000 a year for training, and by the end of 2004 it had grown to some £97,000, providing over £5,000 a year. By then, though, the Company had decided to merge the training fund back into the main Craft Fund to reduce administration, on condition that half of the total income from the Fund be used for the training of stonemasons, and the other half more generally, for example in grants to training institutions and prizes. This, combined with some very generous legacies from members, has had the effect of making even more money available for grants to students.[33]

The decision to provide direct grants to students in this way represented more than a mere increase of expenditure: it marked a significant change in practice. Although the ring-fenced training fund only existed for little more than a decade, for the first time ever in its history the Company had set up a charitable fund to be used solely to support training. Furthermore, rather than giving money to institutions, the Company was now supplying subsidies to people. This new form of commitment clearly required management by way of regular policies and procedures. So, in October 1993, the Court approved the establishment of a Training Committee 'to review the training available for prospective stonemasons' and 'to improve the Company's participation in the area of training'.[34]

In agreeing to give direct support to students as individuals, the Company could expect to have more personal relationships with its chosen students. The first Masons-sponsored student was Philippa Thomerson, who provided a working demonstration of masonry on the Company's stand at the livery exhibition at the Guildhall in 1994. Before long, the Company was presenting its students with a précis of its history, while representatives of the Company would

96 *Diamond Jubilee. Left to right: Kevin Calpin; Lucy Winn; Brad Steele; Heather Newton; Derek Sayer (Master); Sebastian Brooke; Pourang Tajally; Adrian Munns; Catherine Ladd; Richard Woodman-Bailey (Deputy Master).*

make annual visits to both the BCC and CGLAS, where they would meet sponsored students and inspect some of their work. Although Philippa Thomerson never joined the Company, other former students have done so. Tom Brown and Tom Nicholls, for example, both demonstrated their skills as volunteers at the Company's exhibition at the Weald and Downland Museum in Sussex and both were admitted as yeoman masons of the Company. Brown went on to take up the freedom of the Company. Close relationships with students (and indeed staff) at the various colleges have been forged in other ways, too. Thanks to the generosity of the Master, Derek Sayer, when the Company hosted a table at HM The Queen's Diamond Jubilee Luncheon at Westminster Hall on 5 June 2012, the Court invited Catherine Ladd, one of its sponsored students at the CGLAS, in addition to four working stonemasons with whom the Company had a relationship, and three others working at stone industry organisations with which the Company was associated.[35]

Since it was established in 1993, the Training Committee has overseen a great increase in both the number of students the Company sponsors and the institutions through which it offers support. After Sydney Mason had given £20,000 to establish the 'Sydney Mason Fund for the Furtherance of Stonemasonry' in 1995, the Company began assisting students taking courses in stone carving at the CGLAS. In 2000, the Company agreed to find £10,000 over three years to fund a student taking a diploma in Building Craft and Restoration run jointly by the BCC and Canterbury Cathedral. By that time, the Company was supporting seven other students at the BCC, one at Weymouth College and one at the CGLAS.[36]

On 9 October 2006, David Beattie, then Master, and Dr Dick Reid and John Burton, chairmen of the Training and Craft Committees, were present at the launch of the Cathedral Workshop Fellowship (CWF) at Gloucester Cathedral. The CWF brought together masons' workshops at eight Anglican cathedrals and Westminster Abbey to improve training in stonemasonry, especially with regard to conservation and preservation, and the Company was soon working with the CWF to support its apprentices. In 2006-7, the Company

97 *Zoë Wilson, a recipient of grant money from the Craft Fund, working on her graduation project at CGLAS.*

provided grants worth some £30,000 to 18 students: seven at the BCC, six at the CGLAS, three at Weymouth College, and an apprentice at each of York Minster and Salisbury Cathedral. The growth in the value of the Company's Craft Fund since that time has enabled the Company to make even more money available for student grants. Today, the Craft Fund might pay grants worth some £50,000 to students at the various institutions with which it is associated.[37]

FREEMEN AND YEOMAN MASONS

The membership of the Masons' Company has never been completely divorced from the craft to which it is attached, but one of the most noticeable trends of the Company's recent history has been a steady growth in the number of its members connected, more or less directly, with the stone industry. On the one hand, this is hardly remarkable. The Court needed only to resolve that it should admit more members associated with the craft of masonry, then tweak its admission policies and try to attract suitable candidates. This is exactly what happened in 2005, when the Company set itself a target that 25 per cent of its livery would have 'a working knowledge of the [stone] trade' within five years. Of course, there are different ways of defining what a working knowledge of the stone industry actually is, but the Company appears to have made good progress in achieving this goal. By July 2007, more than half of the 33 candidates elected, admitted or progressing to the livery of the Company were connected to the construction industry, and nine of them were 'closely involved' with stone.[38]

On the other hand, it was evidently not quite as simple as setting a target or changing a policy. Those who work in the craft have to feel that there is an incentive to join and that they can afford the costs of membership. It had long been understood that many in the stone industry, especially young masons, found the cost of becoming a liveryman too high. One answer to this problem was to expand the freeman category of membership, which had an entry fine of just £100, by recruiting more stonemasons as freemen. Attempts were therefore made to render the status of freeman more attractive. From 1991, new freemen could join by servitude upon completion of a 'contract of training', and they were granted certain privileges, such as the right to attend some Company events and to receive Company publications.[39]

In June 2001, the freedom was opened up to those who had completed 'appropriate training' or to 'persons who have been sponsored by the Company and have successfully completed an approved course of training in stonemasonry and who are invited by the Court to apply.' This led to initial success. Five of the six people invited to become free under these new arrangements did so and there can be little doubt that this group of five strengthened the Company's connections with the craft of stonemasonry. John Taylor MBE was Director of the BCC, while John Helps was a senior instructor at the same place; Jeremy Thompson and Michael Moody were two students associated with the Company; and Allan Daire was a senior instructor at the Royal School of Military Engineering.[40]

On 19 May 2007, the Company instituted another innovation when, with the special permission of the Chamberlain of London and the Dean of Salisbury Cathedral, it broke with a 700-year tradition and carried out its first admission ceremony outside the City of London, admitting Lee Andrews, an indentured apprentice at the cathedral, as a freeman of the Company by servitude. Even so, altogether these changes were less successful than might have been hoped. By February 2008, there were only 11 freemen on the Roll.[41]

The Company wanted to attract and retain working stonemasons, especially winners of prizes it had instituted and students whom it had sponsored, but it was clear that the freedom of the Company was not an especially attractive offer. Many of its former students were not based in London and they were unlikely to put on a suit and tie to travel to the City simply to attend a Company event. What did the freedom of the Company realistically have to offer them? Peter Clark had earlier suggested that the Company create an entirely new category of membership, and in 2003 a similar proposal, this time that the Company admit 'working members of the stone industry' as 'yeoman masons' for an annual subscription of a modest £20, was again mooted in Standing Committee. Five years later, after much discussion, the Court approved the creation of this new tier of membership, with the designation 'Yeoman Mason', for a trial period of five years, during which time entrants would pay no membership costs. The benefit for the Company was that it would 'gain in influence and reputation if persons working in the craft of stonemasonry' were connected with the Company in some way, while applicants would benefit from an association with the Masons' Company, through which they would have opportunities to network and to come to social and educational events, some of which could be held outside London, perhaps in various cathedral cities. In May 2010, at a reception held at the BCC, the first seven yeoman masons were admitted to the Company and presented with their membership certificates and, three years later, yeoman masons were made a permanent category of Company membership.[42]

STRATEGY

Questions about strategy have, inevitably, risen in importance as the scale of the Company's philanthropy has increased. Is it best that the Company supports dozens of students with smaller grants, or fewer with larger sums? Would the Company's bounty be better spent if it were directed to working stonemasons looking to improve their skills, rather than on new entrants who may never go on to work in the industry? How should the Company choose the students it wishes to assist? Should a London livery company focus its attention on training within London, or should it support the craft nationally? With these questions and others in mind, in 2009 Adrian Sarson, then Master, asked liveryman Janet Nelms, an educational consultant, to review the Company's training strategy. This was a considerable task. It brought together both the Craft and Training Committees, the trustees of the two charitable trusts, and it involved an analysis of national provision for vocational training. It took four years for the recommendations of the Nelms review to be finalised and then adopted.[43]

Following the recommendations of the review, the Court established two separate training programmes: the Masons' Company Training Scheme, to support students studying to NVQ level three or higher at educational institutions with which the Company has a relationship; and the Masons' Company Apprentice Graduate Scheme, which would work with the CWF and the Livery Companies Apprenticeship Scheme (LCAS), to support apprentices to the tune of some £5,000 a year in employment at a cathedral or other appropriate national institution throughout their formal training period. Furthermore, although it was not a consideration or a recommendation of the Nelms review, it was clear at this time that there was a significant overlap in the work of the Craft and Training committees and that there was a good case for bringing them together. As a consequence, on 1 September 2011 a newly-formed Craft and Training Committee met under the chairmanship of Martin Low, with Dick Reid, an architectural carver of stone and wood appointed an OBE for his services to heritage and famous for his restoration work at Windsor Castle, Westminster Abbey, Hampton Court Palace and York Minster in particular, as its deputy chairman and training co-ordinator.[44]

The 2013 strategic review set out that 'it is the Craft and Training Committee that is core to our raison d'être, as it centres on the prime objective of Fostering Our Craft'. Its responsibilities are various, and they speak to the Company's comprehensive engagement with the craft of stonemasonry. The committee acts as a judging panel for the Duke of Gloucester Awards and it considers applications for membership of the Company as yeoman masons. It manages the Company's participation in the Construction Liveries Group's (CLG) Master Certificate Scheme, engaging with the CLG and other bodies associated with it, such as the Livery Companies Skills Council and the CGLI, as well as with the several colleges with which the Company is connected. More recently, also overseen by Martin Low, supported by Adam Stone, the Craft and Training Committee initiated a Journeyman Mason's Certificate for eligible masons with 10 years' post-qualification experience, and since then certificate awards have been created for apprentices – again the committee's work. Separately, prize-winning students benefit from vouchers enabling them to buy tools of their choice.[45]

The activity of the Craft Fund has been increasingly complemented by that of the Charitable Trust, and in fact the Company has taken steps from time to time to rationalise its provision for the craft by switching payments from one fund to another. For example, in 1999-2000 the Court resolved to make its payment to the Associated Companies' Joint Venture Scheme from its Charitable Trust, and its donations to the BCC and CGLAS from the Craft Fund. Similarly, the Charitable Trust has also taken on responsibility for funding the Company's commitments to the museums at Ironbridge Gorge in Shropshire and Portland in Dorset, the Weald and Downland Museum in Sussex, and the RSME in Chatham, Kent. It is the Charitable Trust which makes grants to the Orton Trust, to the Lettering and Commemorative Arts Trust, and to the cathedrals at Canterbury and Salisbury for school outreach days on which older children are given the opportunity to come to the cathedrals and learn about careers in the craft of masonry. The Company's charter gave the Company authority over the craft of stonemasonry 'within our Cittyes of London and Westminster' and in recent years the Company has demonstrated its support for stone projects in both cities through its trust. It gave a significant grant to Westminster Abbey to assist in the creation of HM The Queen's Diamond Jubilee Galleries in the triforium, and the trust's single largest payment in 2019-20 was £10,000 to St Paul's Cathedral for its equal access project, the most significant external change to the Cathedral in the last 300 years, through which two ramps have been built to allow access for those who cannot manage the steps to enter the church through the door of the north transept.[46]

Not all of the Company's initiatives to support the craft have been equally successful. The Company has sometimes had difficulties in its relationships with outside organisations and it had to discontinue its NSCA as they were just too similar to ones awarded by the SFGB. Support in the form of voluntary contributions from the livery has varied over time, too. Surveys taken between 2010 and 2013 found that fewer than half of the Company's liverymen donated money to the Company's charitable trusts – this despite it having been an established part of the agenda for discussion at interview for membership. More than half of the money that the Company disburses each year, then, comes from investments as opposed to its donations from its members. There are, of course, other ways in which members can support charities, such as by giving their time or by finding sponsors for Company events. Thus, in 2013, following a recommendation in the Strategic Review, the Court established a Fundraising Committee to 'coordinate all Company fundraising activities.'[47]

THE DUKE OF GLOUCESTER AWARDS

The Company has been awarding prizes at colleges, training institutions, exhibitions and to apprentices for some 100 years. Its Duke of Gloucester Awards, however, are something different. The Award Scheme has gone through several iterations since its inception in 2007, but it has always recognised early- or mid-career stonemasons, as opposed to students, for excellence in their craft. Following the establishment of the Duke of Gloucester Awards, the Court formed a Craft Awards Committee to 'develop, manage and promote any awards organised by the Company, other than those aimed at students and apprentices'. Chaired first by David Blake, and then for some nine years by Major-General John Milne CB, this committee has since transferred its responsibilities to the Craft and

Training Committee, and it is this latter body that ensures, through its Duke of Gloucester Awards, that the Company raises its profile in the stone industry while celebrating the use of natural stone in the built environment.

Additionally, the most prestigious accolade has been created. The Duke of Gloucester Gold Medal for Outstanding Achievement in Stonemasonry

98 *Craft Awards, 2007. Left to right: Sir David Brewer (Lord Mayor), the Duke of Gloucester, Gary Collier (medallist) and Gerry Everett (Master).*

is something of a lifetime achievement award given to an individual whose professional excellence and contribution to the stone industry

99 *Dr Dick Reid receiving the Gold Medal for Outstanding Achievement from the Duke of Gloucester.*

is acknowledged by his peers. The medal is co-sponsored by the Company and the SFGB. It was conceived in 2008 and first presented to John Bysouth in 2010. It has since been awarded triennially to Richard Kindersley, Dick Reid and Peter Harrison.[48]

CONCLUSION

At the start of the 20th century, the Masons' Company had little interest in doing much, if anything, to support its craft. Over a period of 100 years, that has changed entirely. More than anything else, it is now the promotion, celebration and encouragement of its craft which defines the Company's role in the modern world.

A similar transformation in philosophy can be seen across the livery movement. The establishment of new livery companies in the 20th century, closely tied to their respective professions, forced the older companies to rethink their missions. However, much credit must also go to the energetic and imaginative Masters, Assistants and liverymen who have brought their dynamism and experience to the service of the Company. They have both stimulated and utilised an impressive flow of benefactions.

The Company has set itself a vision for the 21st century: to support the mayoralty and the City of London, to play a leading role in the livery movement, to promote its charitable objectives to the wider public and, above all, to be highly respected for supporting the craft of stonemasonry. Conder concluded his history with a variant of the usual Masons' Company toast: 'prosperity to the Masons' Company, root and branch, and may it flourish forever.' The Company has indeed flourished and prospered since, and well might we wish the Company future success in its ambitions.

SUPPORTERS

Sandy Copland, Master 1997-8, arranged a Millennium Gift from the Company to St. Paul's Cathedral, being a stone plaque installed in the Crypt that lists the Surveyors to the Fabric.

Neil Barnes, Master 1998-9, joined the livery in 1975, and was Chairman of the Finance Committee, Governance Group, and the Charitable Trust, during which time he instigated the schools outreach programme.

Master in 2002-3, Chartered Civil Engineer Peter Johnson was elected to livery in 1977 and Court in 1990. He was Finance Committee Chairman and founder Chairman of the Governance Group.

Fr. Derek Mottershead became a liveryman in 1986 and Master in 2008-9. He was valued serving as Chaplain to some 15 Masters, and as a trustee of the Charitable Trust.

David Blake JP was admitted in 1991, and elected Master in 2012-3. He chaired Membership Development, Communications and Craft Awards Committees, was Craft & Training Deputy Chairman and edited the *Tablets* newsletter.

Richard Hurley, a Chartered Surveyor and a liveryman since 1991, had a career in property and heritage, but upon retirement moved to Devon with his family and purchased an Inn.   *In memoriam.*

Charles Gilbert became a liveryman in 1993 and, with over 40 years' experience in the restoration of heritage buildings, has been a great supporter of the Company's aims and objectives.

Past Master Nicholas Payne has long been fascinated by the heritage of the livery, and trusts that its traditional nurturing of the craft continues to increase through the modern age.

Roger May was admitted to the livery in 2002 under the auspices of Past Master Ernest Harry Turner, and happily served on the Craft Awards Committee from 2007 through to 2019.

Court Assistant John Peat has regularly enjoyed the social events for some 20 years, as well as putting his professional expertise to good effect whilst serving on the Finance Committee.

Dr Michael St John Parker joined the livery in 2006. He is a Fellow of the Society of Antiquaries, honorary archivist of the Masons' Company, and editor of this volume.

Alistair Wood, LVO MBE, Master 2022-3, liaised with the Company when he was Private Secretary to TRH The Duke and Duchess of Gloucester, and became a liveryman in 2008.

Adam Woodman-Bailey is an intensive care doctor. His grandfather was Aubrey Bailey MBE, who for many years was the historic buildings' architect responsible for Stonehenge and the country's other Ancient Monuments.

Peter Blincow, Renter Warden in 2022-3, has spent his working life in property as a Chartered Surveyor. An enthusiastic liveryman, he has chaired both the Social and the Fundraising Committees.

Liveryman Graham Holland was elected in 2015, the first family member to join a livery company. Mayor of Bexley in 1990-1, he worked at the Foreign and Commonwealth Office.

Liveryman Alan Kraven, a Chartered Civil Engineer, was elected in 2015. Promoting the use of natural stone on public realm schemes within London, he is a member of the Fundraising Committee.

Michelle Turner was elected to the Court in 2019, and her passion for the training and development of stonemasons has enabled her to lead the Company's Craft and Training Committee.

Liveryman Craig Bryce is keenly involved in Company activities including as Chair of the Charitable Trust, and is also Collector of the Incorporation of Masons of Glasgow. He is a London-based payments specialist.

Carol Heidschuster became the first female UK Cathedral Works Manager (Lincoln) in 2003. She was elected a Freeman in 2016 in recognition of her development and promotion of stonemasonry training.

Commodore Adrian Munns OBE was the Cathedrals' Workshop Fellowship's Administrator. He became Craft and Training Committee Chairman 2018-21, Court Assistant in 2020, and then Chairman of the Craft Fund charity.

Liveryman George Niblett, a Past Master of the Guild of Mercers Scholars, enjoyed a distinguished career as a City stockbroker, but he pays tribute to his ancestors who were stonemasons.

Liveryman Mark Macdonald, a Chartered Certified Accountant, joined in 2017 and considers membership a privilege. He has become a Trustee of the Charitable Trust, and now acts as its Treasurer.

Bernard Grundy has spent his working life in the City as a stockbroker and an investment banker. He has an interest in the livery movement, particularly in heritage and stonemasonry.

Tony Woellwarth	Anthony Johnson
Adrian Sarson	John Burton
John Wilson	Roger Adcock
David Beattie	Bernard Briggs
Michael Jepson	William Gloyn
Benjamin Woodward	Ward Parshall
Nicholas Woellwarth	John Milne
Andrew Smith	Emily Aldrich

Nicholas Fennemore
James Edgedale
John Crook
John Taylor
George Laverick
Stephen Green
Simon Bish
John Woodman
Neil Budd
Graeme Knowles
Matthew Burton
Elizabeth Hirst
Morris Lockwood
Alexandra Haynes

Tony Phillips
Jonathan Baker
Richard Nichols
Graham Wilks
Philip Hynard
David Collier
Jeremy Pett
Rachel Beszant
Mark Peachey
Geoffrey Cheshire
Robert Merry
Edward Garty
Richard Noviss
Anonymous

OFFICERS

The Company has a long tradition of electing its officers. Men titled as 'masters' and 'wardens' of the craft of masonry are visible in the City's records from as early as 1386, although we know nothing of how they were chosen nor of their responsibilities. From 1481 until 1607 'persones enfraunchesed' of the Company met every two years to elect 'twoo honest and discrete persones' to serve two-year terms as Wardens of the Company. From 1607, the liverymen elected a Master and two Wardens annually. Since 1677, the Company has chosen its officers according to the terms of its royal charter.[1]

Although the Company's records only provide us with a complete list of officers from 1619 onwards, we can discover the names of some incumbents before that year from documents produced at the Guildhall or from deeds or leases in the Company's archive. In these sources, scribes sometimes used the terms Master and Warden interchangeably; in the list which follows, the term Master is only used after 1607 when the office was officially instituted. We must also note that these sources only tell us the name of an officer on the date that the record was created; they tell us nothing of when the incumbent had been elected or how long he had served.

The Company's charter gave the Master, Wardens and Assistants of the Company the power to 'nominate, elect, chuse and constitute a Clerke, Beadle and other officers to serve for the affaires of the said Company'. Both offices existed long before that, however. Edmund Roberts served as Clerk from at least 1625 to 1638 and we can trace a more or less continuous line of succession ever since. The Company's first Clerks were almost certainly scriveners or draftsmen by trade who worked part-time, very much like secretaries, to keep a record of the Court's meetings. In the 18th century, as the duties of the role

expanded, the Company began to appoint attorneys as clerks, and from 1741 to 1987 the Company's Clerks were all men who worked for the firm now known as Hunters Law LLP. The Clerk's workload and responsibilities are greater now than they have ever been – we should probably imagine the role as not less than a chief operating officer. For this reason, the Clerk is employed on a full-time basis to run the day-to-day affairs of the Company and the Company has, since 1996, employed an Assistant Clerk or Administrator.[2]

The Beadle was first mentioned in the Company's ordinances of 1481, and the earliest known incumbent was John Taylor, who was succeeded in 1628 by William Withers. Before the 20th century, Beadles were usually aged members of the Company. Today, the Beadle officiates at Court meetings and Common Hall, and he acts as toastmaster and master of ceremonies at ceremonial functions. When fulfilling these roles, he will usually carry his staff, which reminds us of his historic duties as the enforcer who summoned

100 *Ladies Banquet, Mansion House, 27 February 1984 (From left to right) Howard Greenacre, Tony Woellwarth, Gordon Coates, Howard Lobb, Gordon Tait (Master), Frank Maddison (Beadle), Thomas Hollister, Spencer Rodgers, Aubrey Christlieb and Clifford Culpin.*

members to attend meetings, feasts and funerals; who acted as caretaker at Masons' Hall; and who accompanied the Assistants when they searched the premises of masons of London. To maintain independence and impartiality in the professionalised and modernised 21st-century Company, no member should be employed as Clerk or Beadle, but since Frederick Gwatkin took up the freedom of the Company in 1868, every Clerk bar one has become a member of the Company, usually upon or close to their retirement.[3]

WARDENS

1386   John Clifford, Thomas Malling, Simon at Hook, John Westcote, Henry Wylot
1416   William West, John Croxton
1417   Henry Boston, William Massam
1418   Richard Grove, William Finch
1419   Edmund Werlowe, John Croxton
1428   Edmund Symond, John Wymmyg
1441   John Hardy, William Goodburgh
1481   Thomas Hill, Richard Rede
1573   John Tanner, Martin Harberd, Robert Purkle
1585   William Kerwin and Thomas Kettle

MASTERS AND WARDENS

Year	Master	Upper Warden	Renter Warden
	Reign of James I		
1619-20	James Gilder	William Warde	John Abraham
1620-21	John Dowse	Richard Middleton	Richard Moreton
1621-22	Henry Parkins	William Warde	Edward Kinsman
1622-23	William Warde	Thomas Turpin	Benjamin Richardson I
1623-24	Richard Middleton	William Wilson	Gilbert Arnold
1624-25	Thomas Turpin	Thomas Jordan I	Henry Walton
	Reign of Charles I		
1625-26	William Wilson	John Hince	Richard Chilton
1626-27	Thomas Jordan I	Gilbert Arnold	Nicholas Stone
1627-28	John Hince	Henry Walton	Thomas Priestman
1628-29	Gilbert Arnold	Richard Chilton	James French
1629-30	Richard Middleton (2nd time)	Nicholas Stone	Timothy Townsend
1630-31	Richard Middleton (3rd time)	Richard Hide	William Smith
1631-32	Richard Chilton	Thomas Priestman	John Shuttleworth I
1632-33	Nicholas Stone	James French	Daniel Challoner
1633-34	Nicholas Stone (2nd time)	Edmund Kinsman	Richard Llewelyn
1634-35	Edmund Kinsman	Hugh Jones	Thomas Moore
1635-36	Thomas Priestman	John Gardner	William Dorbar
1636-37	James French	William Smith	Thomas Stanley
1637-38	Hugh Jones	John Shuttleworth I	Richard Banks
1638-39	John Gardner	Richard Llewelyn	Guy Glendoning
1639-40	William Smith	Thomas Moore	James Holmes
1640-41	John Shuttleworth I	William Dorbar	William Mills
1641-42	Richard Llewelyn	Thomas Stanley	Henry Wilson I
1642-43	Thomas Moore	John Young I	Edward Marshall
1643-44	William Dorbar	Richard Banks	Thomas Richardson
1644-45	Thomas Stanley	John Collis	Humphrey Mayer
1645-46	John Young I	Henry Wilson I	John fitz Williams
1646-47	Richard Banks	Edward Marshall	Robert Lewis
1647-48	John Collis	Thomas Richardson	Thomas Florrey
1648-49	Henry Wilson I	Humphrey Mayer	Thomas Jordan II
	Interregnum		
1649-50	Edward Marshall	Roger Lewis	Andrew Mervin
1650-51	Thomas Richardson	Richard Mildmay	Abel Palmer
1651-52	Richard Mildmay	Thomas Florrey	John Young I
1652-53	Humphrey Mayer	Thomas Jordan II	Benjamin Richardson II
1653-54	Roger Lewis	Abel Palmer	Richard Herunden
1654-55	Henry Wilson I (2nd time)	John Young I (2nd time)	Clement Cole
1655-56	Thomas Jordan II	Benjamin Richardson II	Thomas Shorthose
1656-57	John Young I (2nd time)	John Parker	John Lewis

Year	Master	Upper Warden	Renter Warden
1657-58	Benjamin Richardson II	Thomas Stanton	William Drew
1658-59	John Parker	Thomas Moore	Francis Hayley
1659-60	Thomas Stanton	Richard Herunden	Stephen Switzer
	Reign of Charles II		
1660-61	Thomas Moore (2nd time)	Clement Cole	George Dowswell
1661-62	Richard Herunden	Thomas Shorthose	John Young I (2nd time)
1662-63	Clement Cole	William Drew	Richard Smith
1663-64	Thomas Shorthose	Stephen Switzer	Thomas Shadbolt
1664-65	Thomas Shorthose (2nd time)	George Dowswell	Henry Banks
1665-66	Stephen Switzer	John Shuttleworth II	Joshua Marshall
1666-67	George Dowswell	Thomas Shadbolt	James Masters
1667-68	John Shuttleworth II	Henry Banks	Richard Crook
1668-69	Thomas Shadbolt	Joshua Marshall	Thomas Burman
1669-70	Henry Banks	James Bryan	Thomas Place
1670-71	Joshua Marshall	James Masters	William London
1671-72	James Bryan	Thomas Cartwright I	Thomas Berrow
1672-73	James Masters	Richard Crook	Leonard Noble
1673-74	Thomas Cartwright I	Thomas Burman	Abraham Story
1674-75	Richard Crook	Thomas Place	Nicholas Young
1675-76	Thomas Place	Thomas Berrow	Henry Wilson II
1676-77	Thomas Berrow	Stephen Bumpstead	John Shorthose
1677-78	Joshua Marshall (2nd time), d. & repl. Thomas Cartwright I	Leonard Noble	John Parsons
1678-79	Stephen Bumpstead	Abraham Story	John Martin
1679-80	Leonard Noble	Nicholas Young	Thomas Knight
1680-81	Abraham Story	Henry Wilson II	William Hammond
1681-82	Thomas Wise	John Shorthose	William Stanton
1682-83	Nicholas Young	John Martin	John Settle
1683-86*	Henry Wilson II, died in office†	William Stanton	John Thompson
	Reign of James II		
1686-87	John Shorthose	John Thompson	John Young II
1687-88	John Martin, removed by order of King James II, repl. William Stanton	John Young II	Christopher Kempster
1688-89	John Martin (2nd time)	John Young	Edward Mitchell
	Reign of William III and Mary II		
1689-90	William Stanton	Christopher Kempster	Edward Mitchell
1690-91	John Thompson	Edward Mitchell	Michael Todd
1691-92	Christopher Kempster	Michael Todd	William Standborough
1692-93	William Mitchell	William Standborough	Edward Strong I

* No elections in 1684 and 1685 owing to suspension of the Company's Charter under the *quo warranto* proceedings.
† No replacement but Richard Crook, Abraham Story, Nicholas Young, Thomas Wise, Stephen Bumpstead, and Leonard Noble all stood in for Wilson.

Year	Master	Upper Warden	Renter Warden
1693-94	William Standborough	Edward Strong I	John Clarke
1694-95	Thomas Cartwright I (2nd time)	Thomas Wise	John Crook

Reign of William III

Year	Master	Upper Warden	Renter Warden
1695-96	John Young II, d. & repl. John Thompson	Thomas Hill	William Wise
1696-97	Edward Strong I	William Wise	Giles Stretton
1697-98	John Clarke	John Crook	Ephraim Beauchamp
1698-99	Thomas Wise	Ephraim Beauchamp	Robert Smith
1699-1700	Thomas Hill	Robert Smith, d. & repl. Thomas Craven	William Collins
1700-01	Christopher Kempster (2nd time)	William Collins	William Kempster

Reign of Anne

Year	Master	Upper Warden	Renter Warden
1701-02	Ephraim Beauchamp	William Kempster	John Walker
1702-03	Thomas Craven	John Walker	William Woodman
1703-04	William Wise	William Woodman	Thomas Stainer
1704-05	William Collins	John Walker	Thomas Cartwright II
1705-06	William Kempster	Thomas Cartwright II	James Hardy
1706-07	John Walker	Thomas Stainer	Richard Garbutt
1707-08	William Collins (2nd time)	James Hardy	Richard Crutcher
1708-09	William Woodman	Richard Garbutt	Thomas Sleamaker
1709-10	Thomas Stainer	Thomas Cartwright II	James Paget
1710-11	Thomas Cartwright II	Richard Crutcher	Edward Buckingham
1711-12	James Hardy	Thomas Sleamaker	William Holland
1712-13	Richard Garbutt	James Paget	Edward Strong II
1713-14	Richard Crutcher	Edward Buckingham	Edward Stanton

Reign of George I

Year	Master	Upper Warden	Renter Warden
1714-15	Thomas Sleamaker	William Holland	Bartholomew Woolfe
1715-16	James Paget	Edward Strong II	Thomas Cartwright II (2nd time)
1716-17	Edward Buckingham	Edward Stanton	Charles Gardiner
1717-18	William Holland	Bartholomew Woolfe	Thomas Watts
1718-19	Edward Strong II	Thomas Cartwright II (2nd time)	John Cooper
1719-20	Edward Stanton	Charles Gardiner	Christopher Casse
1720-21	Bartholomew Woolfe, d. & repl. Edward Stanton	Thomas Watts	Samuel Saunders
1721-22	Thomas Cartwright II (2nd time)	John Cooper	Joshua Fletcher I
1722-23	Charles Gardiner	Christopher Casse	Thomas Dunn
1723-24	John Gilbert	Samuel Saunders	Robert Kidwell
1724-25	John Cooper	Joshua Fletcher I	Richard Lissiman
1725-26	Christopher Casse	Thomas Dunn	Humphrey Highgate, d. & repl. Joshua Channing
1726-27	Samuel Saunders	Robert Kidwell	Joshua Channing

Year	Master	Upper Warden	Renter Warden
	Reign of George II		
1727-28	Thomas Dunn	Richard Lissiman	John Stanley
1728-29	Robert Kidwell	Joshua Channing	James Watts
1729-30	Richard Lissiman	John Stanley	Robert Taylor
1730-31	Joshua Channing	James Watts	Christopher Horsnail
1731-32	John Stanley	Robert Taylor	Thomas Iden
1732-33	James Watts	Christopher Horsnail	Martin Wardell
1733-34	Robert Taylor	Thomas Iden	Oliver Kidwell
1734-35	Christopher Horsnail	Martin Wardell	Francis Commines, d. & repl. George Greaves
1735-36	Thomas Iden	Oliver Kidwell	Edward Townsend
1736-37	Martin Wardell	George Graves	Samuel Worrall
1737-38	Oliver Kidwell	Edward Townsend	Richard Charlton
1738-39	Edward Townsend	Samuel Worrall	Walter Lee
1739-40	Samuel Worrall	Richard Charlton	Andrews Jelfe
1740-41	Richard Charlton	Walter Lee	John Annis, d. & repl. David Shrimpton
1741-42	Walter Lee	Andrews Jelfe	James Crofts
1742-43	Andrews Jelfe	David Shrimpton	Thomas Scott
1743-44	David Shrimpton	James Crofts	John Gresham
1744-45	James Crofts	Thomas Scott	Thomas Bull
1745-46	Thomas Scott	Thomas Bull	Richard Bowles
1746-47	Thomas Bull	Richard Bowles	Joshua Fletcher II
1747-48	Richard Bowles	Joshua Fletcher II	Edward Anderson
1748-49	Joshua Fletcher II	Edward Anderson	James Wardell I
1749-50	Edward Anderson	James Wardell I	John Bell
1750-51	James Wardell I	John Bell	Benjamin Hunt
1751-52	John Bell	Benjamin Hunt	Clement Hart, d. & repl. William Bull
1752-53	Benjamin Hunt	William Bull	Charles Easton
1753-54	Walter Lee (2nd time)	Charles Easton	Alexander Rouchead
1754-55	Charles Easton	Alexander Rouchead	Charles Clavey
1755-56	Alexander Rouchead	Charles Clavey	John David
1756-57	Charles Clavey	John David	William Walker
1757-58	John David, d. & repl. Christopher Horsnail	William Walker	William Deller
1758-59	William Walker	William Deller	John Deval I
1759-60	William Deller	John Deval I	Samuel Gainsborough

By this time, it had been established that officers served as Wardens and Master in successive years, therefore, only the names of Masters are given hereafter.

Reign of George III

1760-61	John Deval I
1761-62	Samuel Gainsborough
1762-63	Joseph Kenleside
1763-64	George Mercer
1764-65	William Richards
1765-66	Samuel Steemson
1766-67	James Annis
1767-68	Moses Waite
1768-69	John Dueffell I
1769-70	Ralph Hotchkin
1770-71	Henry Gregory I
1771-72	Thomas Stephens
1772-73	James Wardell II
1773-74	Thomas Gayfere
1774-74	John Scott
1775-76	Joseph Dixon
1776-77	John Rawlinson
1777-78	William Gates
1778-79	John Richards I
1779-80	Richard Tunks
1780-81	John Wynne
1781-82	Thomas Beard
1782-83	Richard Buddle
1783-84	Thomas Burnell I
1784-85	John Deval II
1785-86	Richard Jones
1786-87	William Bailey
1787-88	Churchill Harper
1788-89	John Walter
1789-90	Thomas Green
1790-91	George Gwilt I
1791-92	John Hinchcliffe
1792-93	Thomas Waller
1793-94	George Prince
1794-95	George Prince (2nd time)
1795-96	George Scott
1796-97	Henry Scrimshaw
1797-98	John Richards I (2nd time)
1798-99	John Prince
1799-1800	Henry Gregory II
1800-01	James Perry
1801-02	John Dueffell II
1802-03	Thomas Swithin
1803-04	George Whitlock
1804-05	Thomas Burnell II
1805-06	Samuel Ireland
1806-07	Thomas Wood
1807-08	John Green

1808-09	John Peter Holloway
1809-10	Benjamin Marshall
1810-11	John Cadogan
1811-12	John Richards III
1812-13	John Malcott
1813-14	Thomas Piper II
1814-15	Joseph Meymott
1815-16	Henry Burnell
1816-17	William Cadogan
1817-18	Thomas Grundy
1818-19	William Henshall
1819-20	William Archer Dixon

Reign of George IV

1820-21	Martin Stutely
1821-22	John Moginie
1822-23	Robert Shout
1823-24	George Parminster
1824-25	Richard Heale
1825-26	John Rowden
1826-27	William Clayton Storey
1827-28	John Paulin
1828-29	John Harkness
1829-30	William Freeman I

Reign of William IV

1830-31	Thomas Burnell II (2nd time)
1831-32	John Richards III (2nd time)
1832-33	John Malcott (2nd time)
1833-34	Thomas Piper II (2nd time)
1834-35	Henry Burnell (2nd time)
1835-36	George Gwilt II
1836-37	William Cadogan (2nd time)

Reign of Victoria

1837-38	John Moginie (2nd time)
1838-39	John Rowden (2nd time)
1839-40	William Clayton Storey (2nd time)
1840-41	James Richards
1841-42	Thomas Piper III
1842-43	Martin Stutely (2nd time)
1843-44	Philip Flood Page
1844-45	John Meriscoe Pearce
1845-46	Thomas Burnell III
1846-47	George Gwilt II (2nd time)
1847-48	John Richards III (3rd time)
1848-49	Henry Nicholson
1849-50	William Piper
1850-51	Alfred Gwilt

1851-52	William Freeman I (2nd time)	1900-01	Herbert John Moore
1852-53	Thomas Piper III (2nd time)		
1853-54	Henry Burnell (3rd time)		**Reign of Edward VII**
1854-55	George Gwilt II (3rd time)	1901-02	Henry Wells Dewhurst Theobald
1855-56	Charles Henry Storey	1902-03	George Pocock
1856-57	Henry Nicholson (2nd time)	1903-04	William Clarke
1857-58	John Meriscoe Pearce (2nd time)	1904-05	Percy Peet
1858-59	Philip Flood Page (2nd time)	1905-06	Alfred Somerville Dodson
1859-60	Henry Hockey Burnell	1906-07	Arthur William Donne
1860-61	Wilson Thomas Piper, repl. Henry Hockey Burnell	1907-08	Frederick George Dray
		1908-09	William Henry Rylands
1861-62	Joseph Freeman	1909-10	Sir Frederick Prat Alliston OBE[†]
1862-63	Edward Bull		
1863-64	George Richard Wales		**Reign of George V**
1864-65	George Rowden Burnell	1910-11	Alfred Lister Blow
1865-66	John Russell Freeman	1911-12	Frederick Toulmin Shadbolt (2nd time)
1866-67	Henry Robertson		
1867-68	Wilson Thomas Piper (2nd time)	1912-13	George Pocock (2nd time)
1868-69	William Piper (2nd time)	1913-14	Alfred Somerville Dodson (2nd time)
1869-70	Alfred Gwilt (2nd time)	1914-15	Arthur William Donne (2nd time)
1870-71	Henry Hockey Burnell (2nd time)	1915-16	Arthur William Donne (3rd time)
1871-72	Edward Bull (2nd time)	1916-17	George Henry Judd
1872-73	George Richard Wales (2nd time)	1917-18	Frederick George Dray (2nd time)
1873-74	John Russell Freeman (2nd time)	1918-19	Frederick George Dray (3rd time)
1874-75	Henry Robertson (2nd time)	1919-20	Robert Lewin Hunter
1875-76	Sir John Hawkshaw	1920-21	Sydney Michael Young
1876-77	John Greenwood I	1921-22	John Francis Greenwood
1877-78	Edward Conder I	1922-23	Robert Lewin Hunter (2nd time)
1878-79	William Piper (3rd time)	1923-24	Thomas Howard Deighton
1879-80	Alfred Gwilt (3rd time)	1924-25	Henry Archibald Grover
1880-81	Henry Hockey Burnell (3rd time)	1925-26	Frederick George Dray (4th time)
1881-82	Arthur John Baker	1926-27	Alfred Page
1882-83	Hon. Gerald Talbot*	1927-28	William Richard Pumfrey
1883-84	John Hunter	1928-29	George Emmerson
1884-85	Henry Sarson	1929-30	Alfred Lewis Whealler
1885-86	Russell Selby Freeman	1930-31	John George Kipling
1886-87	John Greenwood II	1931-32	George Emmerson (2nd time)
1887-88	Edward Hudson Bayley	1932-33	HH Willoughby Bullock
1888-89	Edward Cozens Smith	1933-34	Edward Percival Richardson
1889-90	John Cox	1934-35	William Thomas Osborne
1890-91	Henry Benson James	1935-36	Alfred Page (2nd time)
1891-92	Thomas Wigglesworth		
1892-93	Edward Spencer Stidolph		**Reign of Edward VIII**
1893-94	Leonard James Williams	1936-37	Sir Harry Edward Twyford[‡]
1894-95	Edward Conder II		
1895-96	Henry Logsdail Sarson		**Reign of George VI**
1896-97	Frederick Toulmin Shadbolt	1937-38	Sir Herbert Edward Morgan
1897-98	Dr Edwin Freshfield	1938-39	George William Reynolds, d. & repl.
1898-99	Frederick John Cox		Sir Herbert Edward Morgan
1899-1900	Thomas Skinner Peet	1939-40	John Meadows Theobald

* Never sworn. Arthur John Baker served the year as Acting Master.

[†] Alderman.
[‡] Alderman. Sheriff 1934-5, Lord Mayor 1937-8.

1940-41	William Anthony Rayner, d. & repl.	1981-82	Thomas William Hollister
	John Meadows Theobald	1982-83	Alwyn Brunow Waters CBE GM
1941-42	Richard George Percival Wyatt	1983-84	Gordon Tait
1942-43	Charles Aaron Pearcey	1984-85	Colin Jocelyn Jeffries MBE
1943-44	John Byram	1985-86	Ernest Harry Turner
1944-45	Henry Smalley Sarson	1986-87	Rex Alastair Wisby
1945-46	Alfred Strachan Bennion	1987-88	Colin Jocelyn Jeffries MBE (2nd time)
1946-47	George Frederick Ridley	1988-89	Dr Robert John Woodward
1947-48	Stanley Arthur Phillips	1989-90	Richard Graham St John Rowlandson OBE
1948-49	Charles George Surtees Shill		
1949-50	Maj. Henry Richard Watling OBE JP	1990-91	Charles Edward Woodward
1950-51	Claud William Dennis JP	1991-92	Graham Barry Leslie Gale
1951-52	Evan Rees JP	1992-93	John Bysouth
		1993-94	Robert Arthur Waters

Reign of Elizabeth II

		1994-95	Sydney Mason CBE, d. & repl. Robert Waters
1952-53	Charles Ernest Miles Emmerson		
1953-54	William Duchatel Woellwarth MC	1995-96	Ralph John French OBE
1954-55	Hugh Murchison Clowes	1996-97	Barry Murray Woodman
1955-56	Henry Soady Bell	1997-98	Patrick Alexander Copland
1956-57	Andrew Money Woodman	1998-99	Neil Richard Barnes
1957-58	Vincent Boys Richardson	1999-2000	Basil James Rushton
1958-59	William James Parsons	2000-01	David Ruffle
1959-60	Hubert Walter Dennis MC	2001-02	Thomas Francis Ackland
1960-61	Frederick William Friday	2002-03	Peter Jacques Johnson
1961-62	Henry Denniss Hubble	2003-04	Gavin Nicholas Tait
1962-63	Audrey Frederick Christlieb	2004-05	Michael John Peachey
1963-64	Gordon Lionel Coates	2005-06	John Wilfred Wilson
1964-65	Sir Stanley Graham Rowlandson MBE JP	2006-07	David Beattie CMG
		2007-08	Gerald Francis John Everett
1965-66	Sidney Harold Loweth	2008-09	Fr Derek Mottershead
1966-67	Eric Leslie Gale	2009-10	Adrian Mark Henry Sarson
1967-68	Spencer Carlton Rodgers	2010-11	Richard Woodman-Bailey
1968-69	Sir John Rodgers Bt.	2011-12	Derek Roger Sayer JP
1969-70	Frank Martin Webster	2012-13	David Blake JP
1970-71	Robert Freeman Mansell	2013-14	John Michael Burton MBE
1971-72	Alan Francis Phillpotts	2014-15	Robert Anthony Henry Morrow
1972-73	Cyril Francis Thatcher	2015-16	William Joshua Gloyn
1973-74	Clifford Ewart Culpin OBE	2016-17	Nicholas John Denis Payne TD
1974-75	Howard Leslie Vicars Lobb CBE	2017-18	Peter Francis Clark
1975-76	Rupert More Wood MVO	2018-19	Andrew Bowles
1976-77	John Grahame Bentley	2019-20	Christopher David Radmore
1977-78	Richard James Bernard McCarthy	2020-21	Dr Christine Holliday Rigden*
1978-79	Howard John Henry Greenacre	2021-22	Martin Paul Joseph Low
1979-80	Howard Anthony Woellwarth	2022-23	Alistair Angus Wood LVO MBE
1980-81	Robert Nott TD DL		

CLERKS

-1625	Thomas Paskins
1625-38	Edmund Roberts
1638-39	Edmund Hamlet
1638-60	John Pickering
1660-71	William Brome I
1671-77	William Brome II
1678-81	Samuel Draper
1681-95	Thomas Stampe
1695-1708	Lawrence Purchase
1708-21	David Le Gros
1721-38	Miles Mann
1738-41	Edward Gross
1741-70	Richard Newton
1770-96	Joseph Newton
1796-1839	John Aldridge
1839-1872	Frederick Gwatkin
1872-81	John Hunter
1881-86	Arthur John Campbell Gwatkin
1886-1913	Robert Lewin Hunter
1913-20	Robert Cecil Hunter
1920-47	Hugh Murchison Clowes
1947-69	Alan Francis Phillpotts
1969-86	Henry John Maddocks
1986-87	Thomas David Bishop
1987-99	Thomas Francis Ackland
1999-2009	Peter Francis Clark
2009-13	Heather Margaret Rowell
2013-14	Peter Francis Clark
2014-date	Giles Benedict Clapp

BEADLES

-1628	John Taylor
1628-	William Withers
1677-?	Josiah Tully
?	John Miller
1691-97	Thomas Shadbolt
1697-1714	Robert Wright
1714-17	John Miller
1717-21	William Trimmer
1722-38	John Shield
1738-53	William Stanton
1753-61	William Morris
1761-71	John Nicholson
1771-72	Richard Stevens
1772-77	John Strong
1777-83	Thomas Barker
1783-90	George Lee
1791-97	John Hockley
1797-1800	William Taylor
1800-06	William Sluin
1806-16	Richard Peters
1816-31	David Moffatt
1832-33	James Davies
1833-49	William Davies I
1849-98	William Davies II
1898?-1910	William John Richards
1910-27	E.H. Powney
1927-50	Charles Gogarty
1950-57	Leslie Charles Birch
1957-84	Frank Leslie Bernard Maddison
1984-95	Ronald Albert Hebb
1996-2006	Peter Sidney Hards
2006-2014	Richard Birtchnell
2015-date	Edward William Prior

CHAPLAINS

There is little recorded about this role. For the period 1928 to 1937, the Guild Vicar at St Margaret Pattens, Rev. St Barbe Sladen, was Honorary Chaplain to the Company, and at some point later in the century the Master began appointing a chaplain of his choosing at the beginning of his year of office. For many years from 1988, Fr. Derek Mottershead served 15 Masters in that role, and in 2007 he proposed the creation of a Company Chaplain. This was agreed by the Court, and subsequently in 2010 the Rev. Canon Nicholas Fennemore was appointed to the position, which he continues to fulfil. The Master still appoints his own chaplain, which can be the Company Chaplain if wished.

BADGES

In modern times, badges are ubiquitous at any formal livery event. Although the Company's medieval ordinances and the 17th-century oaths of the Master and Wardens all charged the Company's officers to look after and account for the 'Goods, Plate, Jewells or Money' that came into their possession, there is no evidence to suggest that the Company's officers wore badges before the late 19th century. Badges never appear in the inventories of the Company's property that various Clerks drew up over the centuries, and there is nothing to suggest that a newly elected Master or Warden was invested with a badge when he took his oath of office.

In 1870, the Company had recently rediscovered the original grant of its armorial bearings and there was, therefore, renewed interest in the Company's historic symbols and motifs. Still reasonably cash rich from the money received from the sale of Masons' Hall, there was evidently a sense among those contemporary Assistants that the Masons' Company should use some of this money to improve its corporate image, as referred to in chapter 13.

The first badge was that presented to the Master, John Russell Freeman, on Lord Mayor's Day, 10 November 1873. Eight years later, the two sterling silver gilt Wardens' badges were bought. They were made by Henry Thomas Lamb, a jeweller in Clerkenwell noted for making masonic insignia. At first sight, they might look identical, but closer inspection reveals a very slight variation: the windows and doors on the three castles are depicted in white on one and black on the other. This allowed for differentiation between the Upper Warden's badge and that used by the Renter Warden, although this practice has not been followed of late.

101 *Master's Badge, 1873.*   **102** *A Warden's Badge, 1881.*

All three badges had the Company's coat of arms enamelled at their centres, around which was engraved 'In the Lord is all our Trust', the motto then in use, and the year '1472', in which year the Company had been granted its armorial bearings. Each provides, then, more evidence for how many in the Company had come to associate the grant of arms in 1472 with the Company's foundation.

For some 100 years, these three badges adorned the necks of the Company's Masters and Wardens. In May 1972, there was something of a scare when Clifford Culpin lost his Renter Warden's badge, but he found it before the Company progressed too far down the road of replacing it. Unfortunately, worse news was to follow in December of that year, when the Master's badge was stolen in a burglary at the home of Cyril Thatcher, then Master. The Company had wisely insured all its insignia and the insurers paid out £1250 for the stolen badge, almost all of which the Company promptly spent on a new badge made by Hicklenton and Phillips – a very well-regarded jewellery firm whose director, Stanley Phillips, was Master of the Masons' Company in 1947-8. The new badge comprised a gold oval

103 *Master's Badge, 1973.*

set within a border of 9ct gold loops. On the oval, in silver and gold, as well as black, white, blue, pink and green enamel, is the Company's arms as depicted in the exemplification prepared for the 500th anniversary of the grant of arms in 1972, complete with a shield, helm and crest. By then, however, the Company was using 'God is our Guide' as its motto and it is this which is engraved at the base of the oval.

The badges worn by the Past Masters are by far the most numerous badges on show at a Masons' Company event. They are, too, the most varied. The first eleven badges were presented to Past Masters in October 1892; Edward Stidolph had generously agreed to bear the costs of ten of them, as well as the production of the die, to celebrate his year as Master. Formed of a six-pointed gold star, they were engraved with the now disused version of the Company's motto, upon which was set an enamel representation of the Company's arms, all of which was hung on a ribbon in the Company's colours. For decades afterwards, the Company would pay for a new badge to be struck annually which would be presented to an outgoing Master, at costs rising from £3 to £6.

104 *Past Master's Badge, 1892.*

105 *Past Master's Badge, 1946.*

106 *Past Master's Badge, 1964.*

After the Second World War, a gold ring was added to surround the star, but the design remained essentially the same. By 1959, however, many Assistants had concluded that the Past Master's 'jewel was not sufficiently dignified', and there followed extensive discussions about what might be better. Eventually, in 1964, the Court resolved to have 18 badges made, at a cost of about £100 each, which would be the property of the Company and returnable upon the death of a Past Master. These gold and enamel oval badges were much more impressive than those previously given to Past Masters – although, unfortunately, two were lost within three years. In any case, due to the rise in life expectancy in recent decades, the Company has made a further 12, so there are now 28 badges in circulation.

107 *The Clerk's Badge with ribbon, 1982.*

The other badges are all more recent. Between 1977 and 1983, three men presented badges to the Company to commemorate their years in office as Master. In 1977, John Bentley gave a miniature pendant of the Company's arms which can be worn by the Mistress Mason; Thomas Hollister, 1981-2, bestowed a silver gilt badge for the Clerk to wear; and, in 1983, Alwyn Waters presented a 9ct gold and enamel brooch on a 9ct gold chain, also to be worn by the Mistress Mason, alternatively known as the Master's Consort.

In 2010 it was decided to use another badge of unknown provenance as the Company Chaplain's badge, and in 2014 badges were commissioned for use of the consorts of Past Masters. Finally, in 2017 the Masons' Company Medal was introduced to recognise special service to the Company.

108 *Mistress Mason Pendant, 1977.*

109 *Mistress Mason Brooch, 1983.*

Company Possessions

Prior to 1866, the Masons' Company's records and chattels were all kept at Masons' Hall in a series of iron chests and safes. The officers were usually responsible for their safekeeping. After the sale of the Hall, the Company's books, records and possessions were entrusted to the care of the Clerk, Frederick Gwatkin, at the offices of his company, Hunters, at Lincoln's Inn, while the flags, 'armorial escutcheons', and many of the deeds and leases were committed to the care of the Surveyor, Alfred Gwilt. In January 1904, the Company opened a bank account with Messrs Charles Hoare & Co. and the Company's records, other than those in use by the Clerk, were stored there in five deed boxes until they were transferred to the Guildhall Library in 1949. Here they are maintained in good repair by the archivists and librarians, and they can be freely consulted by readers and researchers. This was not always the case. Previously, the records could only be viewed with the permission of the Court (subsequently the Master only) and permission was occasionally refused.[1]

Over the course of the 20th century, the Company's possessions were stored variously in the vaults of Messrs Gilliam & Co., Messrs Garrard & Co., Messrs Hicklenton and Phillips, and then with the National Safe Deposit Company. Since 1977, they have been kept in the vault at Mercers' Hall. It is the Clerk's responsibility, via an annual inspection and audit, to ensure that they are 'maintained in a good state of repair' and 'kept fully insured against fire, burglary, theft, and all other appropriate risks'. Some items, for example the badges worn by the Officers and Past Masters, are the responsibility of those to whom they are entrusted, and together the Clerk and the Officers verify their existence each year.[2]

There is no evidence that any of the Company's records were destroyed in the Great Fire of London. However, inventories drawn up in 1665, 1673, 1675, 1676, 1696, 1722, 1859 and 1873 do furnish us with a sobering account of the care and attention devoted to the Company's documents and possessions. The original grant of arms, made to the Company in 1472, vanished from view for more than 150 years until it turned up in the possession of Ebenezer West in 1870. Wooden carvings of the arms of the Company and Corporation of London went missing for some 45 years after the sale of Masons' Hall. In 1918, the Clerk found 'certain Elizabethan and other old deeds' at his office. It is not clear if Conder had sight of these documents at the time he compiled his history of the Company. As late as 1991, the Company was still finding some 'old archive records' and delivering them to the Guildhall Library. Unfortunately, the rummer engraved with the Company's arms, a fragile item, broke in the vault at Mercers' Hall.[3]

At least the rummer's fate is known, and the grant of arms, the carvings and deeds were found – eventually (albeit the carvings seem again to have gone missing, quite possibly at the Museum of London following their apparent transfer from Guildhall in the latter part of the 20th century). Many more items have been lost. Andrew Eliot's 'grete maser', the earliest known gift of silver or plate made to the Company, the original lease for Masons' Hall from Holy Trinity Priory, and the Company's first charter have all disappeared. We know that the Company sold silver from time to time, but that does not account for the loss of some items. John Tanner and Philip Paskin's mazers, and a ribbed silver cup, the gift of Joshua Marshall with two handles and the arms of the Company engraved on the bottom, were last listed among the Company's possessions in 1722. No silver was sold after that date. In 1643, William Lloyd presented the Company with a Latin translation of books I-V of Sebastiano Serlio's *Tutte l'opere d'architettura* and his *Extraordinary Book of Doors*, which was printed in Venice in 1569 by Francesco de' Franchesci and Johann Kruger. It was still in the Company's possession as late as 1905 but it subsequently disappeared. In 1852, for no obvious reason, William Freeman was presented with two books at the end of his year as Master: a 'large folio Bible bound in Russia Leather with Brass Clasps printed at London by Robert Barber' in 1613, and 'a small folio Common Prayer Book bound in Russia Leather with Brass Clasps printed at London by Bonham Norton and John Bell' in 1625. In 1918, the Company engaged Miss Shilton at the Guildhall Library to examine and report on the newly found deeds, but her report and abstracts have unhappily since disappeared.[4]

Mazers were probably used in the late Middle Ages in the same way that loving cups are now. Eliot's bequest to the Company of his mazer with the symbol of the Trinity, indicating that he wanted his devotion to the Trinity to be remembered in the fraternal surroundings of Masons' Hall – perhaps even at the recreation held there after members had been to their annual mass at the Priory. He evidently felt great fondness towards the Company, and in subsequent centuries members have followed his example by presenting items as tokens of their affection. After the Reformation, religious symbols appear less frequently on gifts. Tanner and Paskin inscribed their marks on their mazers, while the two oldest items in the Company's possession, drinking vessels presented by Edward Gerard and Edward Marshall in the 1640s, were both engraved with their names – Marshall also had his own arms and those of the Company etched onto his gift. Thereafter, whenever members have presented items to the Company, almost without fail they have ensured that their individual identity and the Company's identity as a body, often through a representation of its arms, are visible on the gift. In this way, they serve a two-fold purpose of remembrance. Most often, these gifts have been made of silver, and it has become commonplace to refer to these items as 'the Company's silver' or 'the Company's plate'. However, members have presented many pieces which are primarily neither silver nor plate: books, bowls, a ballot box, a cigar box, place mats, and even two lapel microphones to ensure that no member has ever to sit through an inaudible speech again! So more generically they are simply the 'Company's Possessions', the detailed listing of which starts with the newest, is followed by the three oldest items, and the remainder are grouped together as shown.[5]

110 THE STONEMASON

Commissioned in celebration of the 550th anniversary of the grant of arms by King Edward IV in 1472.

Presented by Mr Martin Low and Mrs Susan Low, Master & Mistress Mason 2021-2022.

(Featuring Yeoman Mason Tom Nicholls at work.)

Mappin & Webb, 2022.

Height 10" on a 3" plinth.

111 THE GERARD GOBLET

The Gift of Edward Gerard to the Worthy Companie of Masons 1647.

Maker: unknown, 1639.

Height 7"

112 THE MARSHALL TANKARD

The Guift [*sic*] of Edward Marshall, Master 1649.

(Engraved with family arms on the tankard's cover.)

R.E., 1649.

Height: 6"

113 THE BEADLE'S EBONY STAFF HEAD

The Gift of George Mercer Esq, Father of the Worshipful Company of Masons, on 29th September 1791.

Phipps & Robinson, 1791.

Height 17″

114 THE BENNION CUP

The Gift of Arthur Strachan Bennion, Master, Victory Year 1945-46.

William Fennell, 1800.

Height 15″

115 THE DENNIS CUP

The Gift of Claud William Dennis, JP, CC. Master 1950-51.

William Hall, 1800.

Height 19″

116 THE DRAY COMMEMORATION CUPS

Three cups.

In memory of Fred G Dray, a Benefactor of this Company – Died 1941. Master 1907-08, 1917-18, 1918-19, 1925-26.

Peter & William Bateman, 1807, 1809 & 1816.

Presented by Charles George Surtees Shill 1948.

Height 13"

117 THE FRIDAY CUP

The Gift of Fred W Friday Master 1960.

B & J Smith, 1810.

Height 13"

118 THE CASTLE CUPS

One presented by the Master and Wardens 1873 (each named).

One presented by the Court of Assistants 1875 (each named).

William Hattersley, 1872-1874.

Height 11"

119 THE WOODMAN-BAILEY CUP

To commemorate his year as Master Mason, Richard Woodman-Bailey 2010-2011.

And in memory of Honorary Court Member Thomas Aubrey Bailey 1912-2001 (engraved with family arms on reverse side).

Mappin & Webb, 1924.

Height 14"

120 THE EMMERSON STEEPLE CUP

Reproduction of cup by Benvenuto Cellini, presented by George Emmerson, Master 1928-29.

James Garrard, 1890.

Height 20"

121 THE MERCERS CUP

Reproduction of the Trinity Cup presented by the Masons to the Mercers, February 1616.

Gifted by the Mercers' Company, 1910, as a memento of nearly 300 years of association.

Carrington, 1909.

Height 9"

122 THE CULPIN OFFICERS' GOBLETS

One original and two copies, each engraved The Gift of Clifford Ewart Culpin OBE, Master 1973-4.

The original is engraved with the Company's arms and inscribed Master's Goblet, the others have the inscription Upper Warden's Goblet, and Renter Warden's Goblet.

B.D., 1974

Height 6"

123 THE GREENACRE GUESTS' GOBLETS

Two silver gilt goblets.

The Gift of Howard John Henry Greenacre, Master 1978-79.

Christopher Lawrence, 1977.

Height 6"

124 THE McCARTHY CLERK'S GOBLET

Presented to the Masons' Company by Richard James Bernard McCarthy, Master 1977-78, for the use of their Clerk.

(A Charles & Diana Wedding goblet, gifted in 1982.)

Aurum Designs, 1981.

Height 7"

125 THE WOODWARD DEPUTY MASTER'S GOBLET

Presented to the Masons' Company by Past Master Robert John Woodward in 2000.

A Westminster Abbey Jubilee cup made by order of the Dean and Chapter of Westminster to Commemorate the Silver Jubilee of Her Majesty Queen Elizabeth II.

Aurum Designs, 1977.

Height 7"

126 THE WOODWARD EPPING FOREST FLAGON

Presented to the Masons' Company by Past Master Robert John Woodward in 2000.

Aurum Designs, 1977

Height 13"

127 THE WOODWARD CANDELABRAS

Presented to the Masons' Company by Past Master Robert John Woodward in 2000.

Aurum Designs, 1977.

Height 11"

128 THE JUDD VICTORY BOWL

The Victory Bowl. Presented by P.M. George Henry Judd.

(Engraved with family arms.)

The wood base (not pictured) states: Presented to the Worshipful Company of Masons in commemoration of the victorious conclusion of the Great War, 1914-1918, by George Henry Judd Esq. JP, Order of Mercy, Master of the Company, 1916-17.

W.C., 1895.

Diameter 12"

129 THE HUNTER BOWL

Presented to the Worshipful Company of Masons by Robert Lewin Hunter, in memory of Robert Cecil Hunter, Clerk from 1913 to 1920, died 6th November 1921.

H.E., 1902.

Diameter 16"

130 THE DENNIS TRAY

Silver tray presented in October 1971: The Gift of Past Master Captain Hubert W Dennis MC.

The Worshipful Company of Masons 1472-1972.

Walker & Hall, 1906.

Length 26"

131 THE DRAY SALVER

The Gift of Fred G Dray, Master, 1907-08, 1917-18, 1918-19, 1925-26.

Walker & Hall, 1905.

Diameter 15"

132 THE LEMON ROSEWATER BOWL

The Gift of Mark Lemon, MM, 24th November 1960.

Features the Greek legend of the Calydonian Boar.

Omar Ramsden, 1934.

Diameter 16"

133 THE TWYFORD SALVER

Presented to the Right Honourable The Lord Mayor, Sir Harry Twyford KBE, by the Mayors of the Metropolitan Boroughs 1937-38.

Added to the Masons' Company plate by Sir Harry Twyford KBE, Master 1936, as a mark of appreciation of the services to the Company of Evan Rees, OBE (Master 1951).

Hicklenton & Phillips, 1937.

Diameter 18"

134 THE WHEALLER SALT

An ornate silver gilt salt with Corinthian columns and a canopied top with a raised cupola.

The Gift of Alfred Lewis Whealler, Master 1929.

P G Dodd, 1929.

Height 11"

135 THE SURTEES SHILL SALT

Reproduction of the Summer Salt AD 1679 in the possession of the Mercers' Company.

Presented in 1951 to the Masons' Company by Major C G Surtees Shill, Master 1948-49.

Maker: unclear, 1911.

Diameter 7"

136 THE WATERS' QUEEN ELIZABETH II BOWL

A silver bowl with decorative lid produced to mark the 60th birthday of Her Majesty The Queen in 1986.

Inscribed: The Gift of Alwyn Brunow Waters CBE, GM. Master 1982-83.

Hector Miller, 1986.

Diameter 7"

137 THE PHILLIPS MERCERS' BOWL

Presented by the Mercers' Company to Stanley A Phillips under a Resolution of the Court of Assistants 13th November 1942.

Added to The Masons Company's Plate by permission of the Court of Assistants 26th June 1947.

Cornassau, 1722.

Diameter 7"

138 THE YORK MINSTER QUINCENTENARY BOWL

The Gift of Charles Adolph Hemming Stenholm to commemorate the joint quincentenaries of the completion of York Minster and the grant of arms of the Company, 1972.

Number 500 of a limited edition made by order of the Dean and Chapter of York.

Bowl number 1 was presented to the Dean & Chapter; see chapter 15.

Aurum Designs, 1972.

Diameter 7"

139 THE WESTMINSTER ABBEY JUBILEE BOWLS

Presented to the Masons' Company by Past Master Robert John Woodward in 2000.

A pair of Westminster Abbey Jubilee bowls made by order of the Dean and Chapter of Westminster to Commemorate the Silver Jubilee of Her Majesty Queen Elizabeth II.

Aurum Designs, 1977.

Diameter 7"

140 THE SARSON SNUFF BOX

The Worshipful Company of Masons.
Presented by Henry Sarson, Master 1885.

George Unite, 1884.

Size 5" x 4"

141 THE HUBBLE CIGAR BOX

A thuya wood cigar humidor with the Company's arms on the lid.

Silver plate inscribed: Presented by Henry Denniss Hubble, Master 1961-62.

London 1965
Size: 13" x 8"

142 THE BYRAM CIGARETTE BOXES

Four silver cigarette boxes engraved with the Company's arms, inscribed:

In memory of John Byram, a benefactor of this Company. Died 1964. Master 1943-44.

Purchased by the Company.

Goldsmiths & Silversmiths, 1967-8.

Size 6" x 4"

143 THE MASTER'S GAVEL

Silver mounted ebony gavel with the Company's arms, presented by and engraved Sidney Michael Young, Master 1920-21.

Maker: unclear, 1920.

Length 7"

Also silver mounted gavel block presented by Stanley Phillips in 1960 (not pictured).

Hicklenton & Phillips, 1960.

Diameter 5"

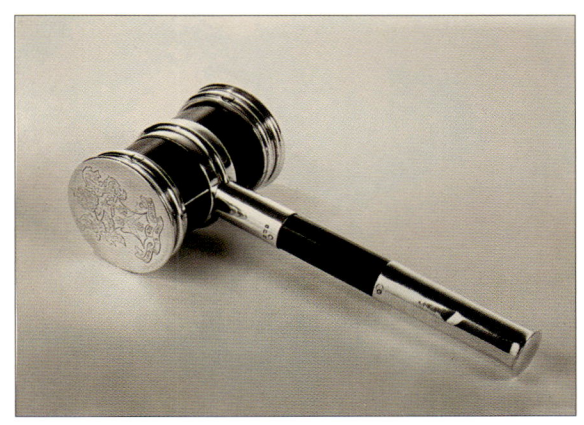

144 THE CLARK STONE SAMPLERS

Presented to the Masons' Company by Peter Clark to mark his retirement as Clerk.

Four wooden boxes made by students at the Building Crafts College, containing four different types of stone carved by three freemen of the Company employed at the BCC.

145 THE ADCOCK PLACE MATS

The Gift of liveryman Roger Adcock in 2003, and subsequently.

Twenty personalised ancient oak place mats made by apprentice joiners at the donor's firm, Killby and Gayford, using computer programmed high-pressure machines. Four were presented to the Company's Officers and Clerk, and a further 16 were personalised to individual liverymen.

Size 12" x 10"

146 THE RIGDEN PLACE CARDS

Presented by Sheriff Dr Christine Rigden, 2015. (Master 2020-21)

Three silver place cards, each with the Company's arms and inscribed with an Officer's title.

Grant Macdonald 2015.

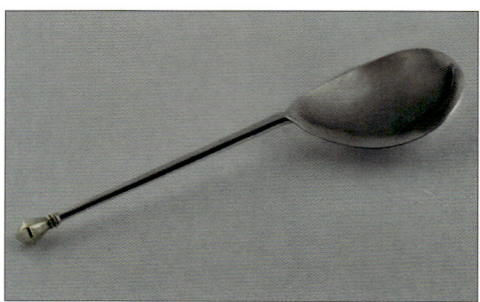

147 THE MERCERS' SEXCENTENARY WHITTINGTON SPOON

The Whittington Spoon.

Presented by the Mercers' Company on 8th June 1994.

Marking the 600th Anniversary of their Charter.

F.L., 1993.

Length 7"

148 THE HOARE & CO. BONBON DISH

A bonbon dish presented to the Worshipful Company of Masons in 1972 to mark the tercentenary of C. Hoare & Co., who were the Masons' Company bankers.

It is engraved 1672 – 1972, and the bank's eagle emblem features in the centre.

C. H & Co. 1972.

Diameter 4"

149 THE BERN STONEMASONS GUILD MEDALLION

The Gift of Zunftgesellschaft zum Affen at Bern in 1994, courtesy of David Beattie, HM Ambassador to Switzerland.

Obverse: The Guild of the Ape.

Reverse: The Craft of the Stonemasons in Bern.

Founded in 1321, the guild has many similarities to the Masons' Company.

150 CHAPLAIN'S STOLE

The Chaplain's Stole was presented in 2002 by Peter Johnson, then Master. There are now two. (Pictured courtesy of the Rev. Canon Nicholas Fennemore, also wearing the Company Chaplain's Badge.)

151 A WARDEN'S GOWN

There are seven gowns, including two black ones for the Clerk and the Beadle. The badge on the arm of each Officer gowns were the gift of Peter Johnson in 2003. (Pictured courtesy of Alistair Wood, 2021.)

152 MASONS' BANNER, POSSIBLY 19TH CENTURY

Very little is known about the origin of this painted silk banner, except that it seems to have been languishing for many years in a basement storeroom at Mercers' Hall until it was rediscovered in 1999. Whilst its age has not been determined, some indication may be derived from the style, and use of the earlier motto.

153 20TH-CENTURY MASONS' COMPANY BANNER

This banner was presented to the Company in 1975 by Rupert More Wood as a mark of appreciation for being installed as Master.

154 21st-CENTURY MASONS' TABARDS & BANNER

Awaiting the 2011 Lord Mayor's Show procession to commence, pictured are liverymen wearing the six new tabards, and new banner, acquired by the Company a short time previously.

The tabards are worn by freemen at their swearing-in during Court meetings.

ITEMS NOT ILLUSTRATED INCLUDE:

THE BALLOT BOX

A mahogany ballot box with a silver plaque featuring the Company's arms and inscribed: The Gift of Stanley Arthur Phillips, Master 1947-8. Also a leather carrying case.

THE MASTER'S CHAIN

Three-strand 9ct gold chain for formal use with badge and gown presented by Hubert Walter Dennis in 1960.

TUDOR STYLE BONNETS

Three traditional velvet bonnets for use of the Master and Wardens, presented by Howard Anthony Woellwarth in 1989.

WOODEN BOWLS

Two turned wood bowls, 20th century.

COMPANY SEAL

A Company seal embossing press, for use by the Clerk on documents when authorised by the Court of Assistants.

MICROPHONES

A pair of lapel microphones, gifted by Adrian Sarson, Master 2009-10.

SUGAR SIFTER

A 1902 ornate silver sugar sifter, gifted by Robert Morrow, Master 2014-15.

MASONS' HALL WOODEN CARVINGS

The Company-owned decorative arms of the City and the Company, likely to be 17th-century armorial escutcheons from Masons' Hall, placed for safekeeping at the Guildhall Museum in 1911 (see page 123).

REGULATIONS, ORDINANCES AND CHARTER

Full transcriptions, and where necessary translations, of all the regulations and ordinances set out below are available on the Masons' Company website.

On 1 February 1356, the Mayor and Aldermen of London ratified a set of regulations 'touching the craft of the masons'. These regulations, in Latin and French, were entered into London's *Letter Book G*. Henry Riley prepared an almost full translation of the text which has been printed twice. In medieval London, when the Mayor and Aldermen ratified corporate ordinances, they established a set of rules which usually applied both to the administration of the company in question and to the craft or trade to which that company was connected. As we have already noted, it is not clear whether a mistery of masons existed at that point in time or not. For that reason, we should understand these provisions as a set of regulations for the craft of masonry rather than as corporate ordinances.[1]

The Company ratified its first set of ordinances on 15 October 1481. They were drafted in English and copied into London's *Letter Book L*. They set out clear rules for the better administration of the Company and several ways in which the Company might regulate the craft of masonry in London.[2]

On three occasions in the 16th century, the Company's representatives appeared before the Mayor and Aldermen of London to ratify additional sets of ordinances. In all these instances, the Company is described variously as a craft, mistery, or company, either of masons or freemasons.[3] The provisions in these ordinances were always more focused than those of 1481; they aimed to resolve specific difficulties in the contemporary craft of masonry, rather than to provide a comprehensive framework in which the Company might work. In 1510 and 1580, the Company's primary concern was the quality of stone in use in London – on the later occasion particularly Purbeck stone – and the Company's right to search for stone in the City and thereby uphold the provisions in its ordinances. In 1521, at a time when wages in the building industry were low, the 'good men of the craft or mistery of masons of the City of London' sought powers to restrict employment opportunities for unfree workers and apprentices. These are the only ordinances which gave the Company any authority to regulate wages.

In 1607, the Company successfully amended its ordinances, establishing the office of Master and moving to a system of annual election to office. This was the final occasion on which the Mayor and the Aldermen of London ratified or altered the Company's ordinances. In 1677, it obtained its royal charter, the text of which is below:[4]

Charles the second by the grace of God of England, Scotland, France and Ireland King, Defender of the Faith etc. To all to whom these presents shall come, greeting. Whereas in and by a Statute made in the fifth yeare of the Reigne of Queene Elizabeth the Art or occupation of a Mason is reckoned as a distinct Art or occupation of itt selfe, and by the same Act all and every person or persons useing or exerciseing the said Art or occupation is and are enabled, and may be compelled, to take Apprentices to bee taught and instructed in that occupation in manner and forme as other Artificers and handicrafts men in the same Act particularly are inabled or may bee compelled to doe. And Whereas the Masters, Wardens and Assistants of the Company of Masons London by their humble petition to us have prayed that Wee would be gratiously pleased by our letters Pattents under our great Seale of England to Incorporate them into a Body Politique To have perpetuall Succession and to grant them such Liberties, powers and priviledges as to us in our Princely wisdom shall seeme requisite and necessary for the better Order, rule and Governement of the said Company and the Members thereof. And Wee willing and intending the support and Continuance of the said Company and the Improvement of the said Art or Mistery of Masons by all just and Lawfull meanes, and to the end they may bee impowred to Suppresse and reforme all abuses practized by persons who take upon them without *sufficient Skill and knowledge to worke att the Masons Trade to the greate Damage of our Subjects, and that the said Art and Mistery of Masons within the said Citty and places herein after mentioned may from henceforth be artificially and truely exercised, Know Yee, therefore, that Wee of our especiall grace, certaine knowledge and meere motion Have Willed, Ordeyned, Constituted, Declared and granted, and by these presents for us, our Heires and Successors doe Will, Ordeyn, Constitute, declare and Grant that all and singular Masons Freemen of our said City of London, and all other our Subjects That now doe or hereafter shall use the same Trade, art or Mistery within our Cittyes of London and Westminster or the Suburbs of the same Cittyes or Seaven Miles Compasse of the same on every side thereof by Vertue of these presents shall bee one Body Incorporate and politique in Deed and in name by the name of Master, Wardens, Assistants and Comminalty of the Art or Mistery of Masons of the Cittie of London; and them by the name of Master, Wardens Assistants and Comminalty of the Company of Masons of the Cittye of London Wee doe by these Presents for us, our heires and Successors Really and fully make [m. 14], ordeyne, create, erect,* Constitute and declare one body Corporate and Politique by the name aforesaid. And that by the same name they and their Successors shall and may have perpetuall Succession and that they and their Successors by the same name of Master, Wardens, assistants and comminalty of the Company of Masons shalbe for ever hereafter Persons able and capable in Law to have, take, purchase, hold, receive, possesse and enjoy to them and their Successors, as well of us, our heires and Successors as of any other person or persons whatsoever, aswell any Mannors, Lands, Tenements, Liberties, Jurisdictions, Franchises, Rents, Revertions, priviledges and other hereditaments to them and their Successors of what kind, nature and quality soever they bee, in fee or perpetuity or for terme of life or lives or yeares or otherwise in what manner or sorte soever, the Statute of Mortmaine or any other Statute, Law, Usage or Custome to the Contrary in any wise Notwithstanding, As also all and singuler Goods, Chattells and other things whatsoever, and the same Lands, Tenements, Rents, Revertions, Goods and Chattells and other the premisses and every parcell thereof to sell againe, demise and grant, and to make, Seale and accomplish*

---

* Inserted above the line.

all Deeds, Evidences and Writeings of, for or concerneing the same and every parte thereof in that behalfe needful, necessary or convenient to bee had or made. And that by the same name of Master, Wardens, Assistants and Comminalty of the art and Mistery of Masons of the Citty of London they shall and may bee persons able and capable in Law to plead and bee impleaded, answer and bee answered, defend and be defended in any our Courts or places whatsoever, in all and all manner of Complaints, Pleas, Causes, Matters and demands of whatsoever kind or nature they bee in the same manner and forme as other our Leige People and Subjects of this our Realme of England being also persons able and capable in Law may plead and bee impleaded, answer and bee answered, defend and bee defended, have, purchase, receive and take, possesse, give grant, let, sett assigne or dispose of. And that they, the said Master, Wardens, Assistants and Comminalty of the Company of Masons of the Citty of London, and their Successors for ever hereafter shall and may have a Common Seale to serve for the Causes and Buisnesses of the said Company, and that it shall and may bee lawfull to and for them and their Successors to breake, change, alter and make new the said Seale from time to time att their pleasures as they and their Successors shall thinke fit. And further Wee will and ordeyne, and by these presents for us, our Heires and Successors doe give and grant unto the said Master, Wardens, Assistants and Cominaltye of the Company of Masons of the Citty of London, and to their Successors for ever, That for ever hereafter there shall bee some one of the said Company in manner and forme hereunder in these presents mentioned to bee Chosen and named who shall bee and shalbe called the Master of the said Company of Masons of the said Citty of London. And likewise that there shall bee and may bee Two of the said Company and Corporation in manner and forme hereafter in these presents mentioned to bee Chosen and named who shall bee and shall bee called the Wardens of the Company of Masons of the Citty of London. And also that there shall or may bee Foure and Twenty or more of the said Company, according to the discretion of the Master and Wardens for the time being in manner and forme hereafter in these presents expressed to bee named and chosen which shall bee and shall bee called the Assistants of the said Company of Masons of the Citty of London, and from time to time shall bee Assisting and Aydeing to the said Master and Wardens of the said Company. And that the said Master, Wardens, Assistants and Comminalty of the said Company of Masons of the Citty of London for the time being or any Eight or more of them, whereof the Master and one of the Wardens for the time being to bee allwaies Two, shall and may have full power and authority by vertue of these presents To make, constitute, ordeyne and sett downe from time to time, and also from time to time to alter, change, amend or make new such reasonable Laws, acts, orders, Ordinances and Constitutions in writing which to them or any eight or more of them as aforesaid (Whereof the Master and one of the Wardens for the time being to bee two) shall seeme good, necessary and expedient and according to their best discretions for, touching and concerneing the Improvement of the said Trade, art or Mistery of Masons and the good order, rule and Governement of the said Company and Corporation and every Member thereof; and for punishment and Reformation of such abuses, deceipts, falsityes and other wrongfull practices and misdemeanors from time to time to be comitted, used or practised in their Trade or in anything apperteineing or in any wise belonging to the art or Mistery of Masons whereby our loveing Subjects may bee wronged, dampnified or abused or any other wrong, cousenage or deceipt or abuse Offered or used in the said Trade att any time whatsoever within the said Cittyes of London and Westtminster and the liberties thereof or within any other place or places within the Lymitts aforesaid. And also for defraying and beareing the publicke and necessary Charge of the said Company and Corporation, and for declaration after what manner and forme the said Master, Wardens, Assistants and Comminalty of the said Company, and their Successors and all and every other person and persons that now doe or hereafter shall lawfully use or exercise the said Trade, art or Mistery of Masons within our said Cittyes of London and Westminster and the Liberties thereof, or within Seaven Miles Compase of the same, shall behave, demeane and carry themselves, either in or concerneing their said Trade, for the publicke good and common profitt of all our Loveing Subjects by whome the said Artists shall bee employed, and all other matters and things touching the Improvement of the said Trade, Art or Mistery. And that the said Master, Wardens and Assistants for the time being, or any eight or more of them (whereof the Master and one of the Wardens for the time being to bee allwaies two), shall have power and

*authority to make, sett, ordeine, impose and lymitt such reasonable
penalties by mulcts and Amerciaments, or by any other Lawfull wayes
or meanes [m. 15] whatsoever, upon all Offenders or breakers of any such
Lawes, ordinances, orders and Constitutions by them soe made and
established as aforesaid as to them or any eight or more of them as
aforesaid shall seeme necessary, reasonable, fitt and convenient to bee
made, sett, imposed, limitted and provided for the keepeing of the same
Lawes, Ordinances, Orders and Constitutions; and that the same Master,
Wardens, Assistants and Comminalty of the said Company of Masons
of the Citty of London and their Successors shall and may from time to
time by vertue of these presents have, take and Recover the same Penalties,
Mulcts and Amerciaments to their owne onely use by distresse, Action
of Debt or any other wayes or meanes according to Law without the lett
or hindrance of Us, our Heires or Successors and without giveing or
rendring any account or thing to Us, our Heires or Successors for the
same or any parte thereof. All which Lawes, acts, Orders, Ordinances
and Constitutions soe to be made, altered or new made, as is aforesaid,
Wee doe by these presents for us, our Heires and Successors confirme,
ratifie and establish, and also will and Comand to bee from time to time
observed and kept, under the paines and penalties to bee therein contained,
so always as the same Lawes, Statutes, Ordinances and Constitutions,
Penalties, Mulcts and Amerciaments (as is aforesaid) bee reasonable and
not repugnant or contrary but as neare as may bee Agreable to the Lawes
and Statutes of this our Realme of England, and not derogatory to our
Prerogative Royall nor to the Priviledges, Customes or Usages of our
Citty of London and bee first Confirmed according to the Statute in that
behalfe and also presented to and allowed of by the Court of Lord Mayor
and Aldermen of our said Citty and Inrolled amongst the Records of the
said Citty. And for the better executeing of this our Grant in that behalf,
Wee have assigned, named, Constituted and made, and by these presents
for us, our heires and Successors doe assigne, name, constitute and make,
our wellbeloved Subject Joshua Marshall Esquire, our Master Mason, to
be the first and present Master of the said Company of Masons of the
Citty of London, to continue in the said office untill the Foureteenth day
of June which shalbe in the yeare of Our Lord One thousand six Hundred
Seaventy eight (if hee shall soe long live), and from and thence untill one*

other of the said Company shalbe Chosen and named unto the office of Master of the said Company and Corporation in due manner according to the Ordinances and Provisions hereafter in these presents expressed and mentioned Unlesse hee shall in the meane time upon just Cause bee removed from the said Office of Master. And also wee have assigned, named, Constituted and made, and by these presents for us, our heires and Successors doe assigne, name, constitute and make our welbeloved Subjects Leonard Noble and John Parsons to bee the first and present Wardens of the said Company and Corporation to continue in the said office of Wardens untill the said Foureteenth day of June which shalbe in the said yeare of our Lord One Thousand six hundred Seaventy and eight (if they, the said Leonard Noble and John Parsons, shall soe long live) and shall not for some just cause in the meane time bee lawfully removed from their Offices, and from thence untill Two other of the said Company and Corporation bee chosen unto the said office of Wardens of the said Company and Corporation according to the Ordinances and Provisions in these presents expressed and declared. And wee have assigned, named, constituted and made, and by these presents for us, our heires and Successors doe assigne, name, constitute and appoint our welbeloved Subjects John Young senior, Thomas Shorthose, Thomas Shadbolt, James Bryon, James Masters, James Bussey, Thomas Cartwright, Richard Crooke, Thomas Barrow, Stephen Bumpsted, Abraham Story, Nicholas Young, Henry Wilson, John Shorthose, Thomas Knight, William Hammond, John Grove, William Stanton, John Settle, John Tompson, Thomas Strong, John Young junior, Michaell Todd and Richard Banks to bee the first and present Assistants of the said Company and Corporation to continue in the said Office of Assistants dureing their naturall lives respectively, unlesse they or any of them shall misbehave him or themselves in their said offices or for some other lawfull or reasonable cause shalbe removed. And also that the said Joshuah Marshall, Leonard Noble and John Parsons from and after such time as they or any of them shall leave and have discharged their said severall offices shall dureing their respective lives bee Assistants of the said Company and Corporation unlesse they or any of them shall misbehave him or themselves in the said office of Assistants or for some other reasonable or lawfull cause shalbe removed from the same. And our will and pleasure is and wee doe hereby authorize, appoint and require that the said first and present Master and Wardens by us nominated, as aforesaid, shall every of them respectively take their Corporall Oathes before the Lord Mayor of the Citty of London for the time being well and truely to execute their said severall and respective offices of Master and Wardens according to the true meaneing of these presents before hee or they take upon them the exercise or execution of their said offices or places; To which said Lord Mayor Wee doe by these presents give power and authority to administer the said Oathes accordingly. And that the said Master and Wardens, soe being sworne, the said Master or one or more of the said Wardens shall have power and authority by vertue of these presents to give unto all and every the persons aforesaid named to bee the First Assistants of the said Company and Corporation an Oath, well and truely to execute their said Offices according to the true meaneing of these presents before they, the said Assistants, take upon them the exercise or execution of their said places of Assistants. And further wee will and by these presents for us, our heires and Successors doe grant unto the said Master, Wardens, Assistants and Comminalty of the Company of Masons of the Citty of London, and to their Successors, that they or the greater number of them, whereof the Master and one of the Wardens [m. 16] for the time being to be alwaies two, from time to time for ever hereafter shall have full power and authority by vertue of these presents to assemble and meete together once in every yeare, in their common hall or other convenient place upon the Foureteenth day of June (if it bee not Sunday), and if it bee Sunday then upon the next day after, to elect and nominate either the last preceding Master or one of the Wardens or Assistants of the said Company and Corporation of Masons of the Citty of London to bee Master of the said Company and Corporation for one whole yeare from thence next ensueing, and from thence untill one other of the Wardens or Assistants of the same Company or Corporation bee chosen into the said Office of Master of the said Company and Corporation, according to the Ordinances and Provisions in these presents expressed and declared. And that hee which shalbee soe chosen and named into the said office of Master, before hee bee admitted to enter into the Execution of the said Office of Master of the said Company and Corporation, shall take his oath before the last Master of the said Company and Corporation, his predecessor and one or both of the last Wardens of the said Company and Corporation for the time being well and truely to Execute the said Office of Master of the said Art or Mistery of Masons in all things concerneing the said Office. To which said last Master and one or more of the Wardens of the said Company for the time being, wee doe for us, our heires and Successors give full power and authority to administer the said Oath to the said master accordingly, and that after the said Oath soe to be taken, as aforesaid, hee shall have and exercise the said office of Master for one whole yeare, and from thence for soe long time and untill one of the said Wardens or assistants bee Chosen and sworne into the said Office of Master as aforesaid (if hee shall soe long live), and shall not in the meane time for just cause bee removed from his office of Master. And likewise that they shall or may elect, nominate and chuse two other out of the said then remaineing Wardens and Assistants to be Wardens of the said Company and Corporation for one whole yeare from thence next ensueing for soe long time and untill two other of the said then remaineing Wardens and Assistants bee chosen into the said office of Wardens of the same Company and Corporation according to the Ordinances and Provisions in these presents mentioned, expressed and declared. And they which shall bee soe Chosen and named unto the offices of Wardens of the said company and Corporation, before they bee admitted to enter into the said office shall take their Corporall Oathes before the preceeding Master and Wardens of the same Corporation, or any two of them, well and truely to execute the said Offices of Wardens in all things touching and concerneing the same office. To which said Master and last Wardens or any two of them Wee doe give full power and authority to Administer the said oath to the said Wardens accordingly, and after the oath and oathes soe as aforesaid taken, they shall and may exercise the said offices of Wardens for one whole yeare then next ensueing and from thence untill Two others of the said Wardens and Assistants bee chosen and sworne unto the said offices of Wardens of ye same Company and Corporation in manner and forme before in these presents expressed and declared. And further wee will and by these presents for us, our heires and Successors doe grant unto the said Master, Wardens, Assistants and Comminalty of the Company of Masons of the Citty of London, and to their Successors, for ever that if it shall happen the said Master and

Wardens of the said Company & Corporation for the time being, or any of them att any time within one yeare after that they or any of them bee chosen unto his or their office or offices, to Decease or bee removed from his or their office or offices, Which said Master and Wardens or any of them Wee will shalbe removeable and removed by the greater Number of the said Master, Wardens and Assistants of the said Company and Corporation for the time being, whereof the Master and one of the Wardens for the time being to bee allwayes two, for evill Governement or Misbehaviour or any other lawfull and reasonable cause, That then and soe often it shall and may bee lawfull to and for such and soe many of the Master, Wardens and Assistants which shall be living and remaineing, or the greater number of them as is aforesaid, att their pleasures to choose and sweare other or others of the said Wardens or Assistants to bee Master or Wardens of the same Company and C'orporation according to the Ordinances and Provisions before in these presents expressed and declared, to execute and exercise the said offices of Master and Wardens of the said Corporation respectively untill the Foureteenth day of June then next following, and from thence untill some others bee chosen in his or their stead, or they bee removed or dye as aforesaid, the said Master and Warden or Wardens soe to bee elected and chosen takeing his and their Corporall oath and oathes in manner and forme as is aforesaid and soe often as the case shall require. And moreover wee will and by these presents for us our heires, and Successors doe give and grant unto the said Master, Wardens, Assistants and Comminalty of ye Company of Masons of the Citty of London, and to their Successors, that when ever it shall happen any one of the Assistants of the said Company and Corporation to dye or bee removed from his or their office or offices, all which Assistants and every or any of them wee will shalbe removeable and bee removed by the greater part of the said Master, Wardens and Assistants of the said Company and Corporation for the time being, whereof the Master and one of the Wardens for the time being to bee allwayes Two, for evill governement and misbehaviour or for any other lawfull or reasonable cause, That then and soe often it shall and may bee lawfull to and for the Master, Wardens and the remaineing part of the Assistants which shall then survive or remaine [m. 17], or any eight of them whereof the Master and one of the Wardens for the time being to bee allwayes two, att their wills and pleasures from time to time to choose and name [one] or more other or others of the said Company or Corporation to be Assistant or Assistants of the same Company or Corporation in his or their place or stead which shall soe happen to dye or be removed as is aforesaid; and that hee or they, after they bee soe chosen and named to bee Assistant or Assistants of the said company or Corporation, shall take their Corporall Oathes before the Master and Wardens of the same Company and Corporation or any [one] or more of them for the time being, well and truely to execute the said office or offices of Assistant or Assistants. To which said Master and Wardens or one or more of them, Wee doe by these presents give full power and Authority to Administer the said Oath accordingly. And for the better rule and governement of all and singuler persons which now doe or hereafter shall lawfully use the Trade, art or Mistery of Mason, or any part thereof within the said Society and Corporation, Wee doe by these presents for us, our heires and Successors give and grant unto the Master, Wardens, Assistants and Comminalty of the said Company of Masons, That the said Master, Wardens and Assistants for the time being, or any Five or more of them, whereof the Master and one of the Wardens for the time being to bee allwayes Two, shall have full power and authority in Lawfull manner att all covenient times in the day time, as well by Land as by water, in any place or places within the Citties of London and Westminster and the Liberties thereof, or within Seaven Miles of the said Citty of London, where any Stones to be used in the Art or Trade of Masonry shall bee brought or laid to Search and see whether the same bee of due goodnesse, measure, length and thicknes, and whether the same bee well and sufficiently Wrought; and if any such Stones, of what nature or quality soever, att any time upon and after such view and Search shall bee duely and Legally found and adjudged to bee ill wrought, and not amended at the charges of the Owner before the same bee put to Sale, or that any of them are soe faulty that they cannot be amended and made good in Assize, thicknes and goodnesse, that then the same shalbe disposed of according to Law. And Wee doe also further grant to the said Master, Wardens, Assistants and Comminalty of the said Company that the said master Wardens and Assistants of the said company for the time being, or any eight or more of them, shall have full power and liberty under the Common

Seale of the said company from time to time to constitute and depute such and soe many fitt persons as they in their discretions shall approve of and chuse to bee their Deputyes or Agents, to make and execute all veiws and Searches and to act and doe all matters and things thereunto relateing as fully as the said Master, Wardens and Assistants or any of them [as] are by these presents impowred to make, execute, doe and performe. And Wee doe by these presents for us, our Heires and Successors give full power and authority to the said Master and one or both of the Wardens for the time being to Administer all and every such fitt oath and oathes to all and every Member and Members of the said Society, as shall according to Law bee approved and allowed of, in Order to the good Governement of the said Corporation and the Improvement of the said Trade without further or other Warrant or Warrants in that behalfe for us our heires or Successors to bee procured or obteined. And further wee will and by these presents for us, our Heires and Successors doe grant unto the said Master, Wardens, Assistants and Comminalty of the Company of Masons of the Citty of London, and to their Successors, that the Master, Wardens and Assistants for the time being, or any eight of them, shall and may from time to time nominate, elect, chuse and constitute a Clerke, Beadle and other officers to serve for the affaires of the said Company, and to bee serviceable to and attendant on the said Master, Wardens and Assistants of the said Company in all matters touching the same; and to allow the said Clerke, Beadle and other officers respectively such Sallaries, Fees and Rewards as they shall think fitt; and them, or any or either of them respectively, for reasonable and just Cause to displace and remove and other persons in their place to chuse and elect, which said Clerke, Beadle and officers soe elected and constituted, before they bee admitted to the Execution of their said offices, before the Master, Wardens and Assistants of the said company for the time being, or two or more of them shall take their Corporall Oathes well faithfully and honestly to demeane & behave themselves in the execution of their offices respectively. To which said Master, Wardens and Assistants, or any two or more of them, Wee doe hereby give power and authority to administer such like oathes as well to the said Clerke, Beadle and other officers, as to all other person or persons which shall from time to time bee admitted into the said company. And wee doe hereby nominate, appoint and

*confirme our Trusty and Welbeloved Subject Samuell Draper of London,
Scrivener, to bee first and present Clerke of the said company, To hold
and enjoy the said office of Clerke dureing such time and soe long as hee,
the said Samuell Draper, shall well demeane himselfe therein, and to bee
exercised by himselfe or his sufficient Deputy in that behalfe, and to bee
sworne according to the power and authority in that behalfe herein before
expressed. And forasmuch as wee are informed that many and great
deceipts, frauds and abuses are dayly used & practised, chiefely by Sundry
persons who never duely served as Apprentices to the said Art or Mistery
of [m. 18] a Mason, and haveing noe Judgement or skill therein, Wee
therefore intending the speedy reformation of the said abuses doe ordeyne
and firmely charge and comand that noe person or persons whatsoever
from henceforth doe use, exercise or practise the Art or Misterv of a
Mason, either as Master or Journeyman, unlesse hee or they shall first
have served as an Apprentice or Apprentices for the space of Seaven
yeares att the least unto a Freeman of the said Company or to some other
person Lawfully useing or exerciseing the Art or Mistery of a Mason
upon paine of being proceeded against according to the Lawes and
Statutes of this our Realme. And considering that the good order and
honest practise of the Art and Mistery aforesaid will conduce much to
the good and benefitt of the Artists of the said Society, being for the most
part under the governement of the said Citty of London, the Offenders
in the said Trade are like to bee more effectually punished and those that
doe use or exercise the same as they ought to doe the better encouraged,
Wee doe hereby declare our will and pleasure to be That the Lord Mayor
and Aldermen of the Citty of London for the time being doe cause and
allowe these our Letters Patents to bee Inrolled within the Common
chamber of the said Citty amongst the records thereof, to the intent that
those that are and shalbe Freemen of London and Members of the said
Company of Masons may bee subject to the Governement of the said
Citty and may enjoy the benefitt thereof. And further wee will and by
these presents for us, our heires and Successors doe firmely charge and
comand all and singuler Justices of the Peace, Mayors, Sheriffes, Bailiffes,
Constables and other Officers and Ministers of us, our Heires and
Successors to whome it shall apperteine, That they bee and shalbe aydeinge
and assisting to the aforesaid Master, Wardens and Assistants for the*

time being, and the Deputy and Deputyes of the said Master and Wardens for the time being, respectively in all things touching the powers and authorityes hereby granted according to our pleasure herein before declared. And moreover wee will and by these presents for us, our heires and Successors doe grant unto the aforesaid Master, Wardens, Assistants and Comminalty, and their Successors, that these presents or the Inrollment of the same and all and singuler other matters and things therein contained from time to time shalbe good, firme and effectuall in the Law in and by all things according to the intent and meaneing thereof, and shalbe expounded and construed beneficially and largely for the benefitt and advantage of the aforesaid Master, Wardens and Assistants and Comminalty and their Successors. Provided alwaies and our Royall will and pleasure is That nothing in these our Letters Patents conteined shall extend or be construed to extend to the prejudice, obstruction or hindrance of the erecting, building and Finishing of our cathedrall church of Saint Paul within our Cittie of London, or any other Church within the same Citty which were formerly burnt downe by the late dreadfull Fyre which happened in London. Provided further and our will and pleasure is that the Master, Wardens and Assistants of the said company for the time being, and all other person and persons to bee from time to time admitted into or ymployed by the said Society, before they bee admitted to enter uppon the execution of their respective offices and places or become Members of the said Society by admittance thereunto, shall severally take the Oathes of Allegiance and Supremacy before the Master and Wardens for the time being, or two of them whereof the Master to bee one, save onely in the case of [the?] Master who shall take the said Oathes before the Wardens for the time being, to whome wee doe hereby give full power and authority to administer the same oaths accordingly. In Witnesse etc. Witnese our selfe att Westminster the Seaventeenth day of December.

By Writt of Privy Seale.

ILLUSTRATION ACKNOWLEDGEMENTS

These individuals have created the following photographic images, and have kindly allowed them to be used in this publication; with further acknowledgement in brackets if appropriate.

Angelo Hornak
Images: front endpapers, *frontispiece*, 75, 93, 111, 112, 114, 115, 116, 117, 118, 119, 120, 121, 122, 123, 124, 125, 126, 127, 128, 129, 130, 131, 132, 133, 134, 135, 136, 137, 138, 139, 140, 141, 142, 143, 144, 147, 148, back endpapers

Richard Woodman-Bailey
Images: 3, 8, 18 (Guildhall), 29, 41 (Catherine Martin, carver), 47, 72, 82, 84, 86, 87, 88, 90, 91, 94, 102, 103, 110, 113, 145, 146, 149, 150, 151, 153, 154, back cover

Ian Stone
Images: XII, 10, 11 (The National Archives), 19, 23 (The National Archives), 25, 28, 32, 33, 34, 36, 38, 43, 55, 57, 62b, 63, 64, 69, 74, 85

Jolanta Glas
Images: 104, 105, 106

Martin Low
Images: 108,109

Giles Clapp
Image: 107

Paul Ostwind
Image: 42

SDS Heritage
Images: 35, 73

Marble carving on the cover of Richard Nichols' special presentation binding, courtesy of Catherine and Richard Martin of Heritage Stone Access.

These organisations/individuals have a copyright in the following photographic images, which is acknowledged:

© London Metropolitan Archives (City of London)
Images: 1, 5, 13, 21, 24, 31, 53, 61

BIBLIOGRAPHY

1: MANUSCRIPT SOURCES
THE RECORDS OF THE MASONS' COMPANY

Records stored at Guildhall Library (GL MSS)

Constitutional records

5332	Exemplification by Queen Anne (5 June 1702) of the charter granted to the Company by Charles II, 17 September 1677.
5333	Contemporary copy of the charter of 17 September 1677; extracts from the repertories; formulae of oaths of allegiance to the king and realm, 30 March 1686.
5334	Ordinance and oath book.
5335	Copies of the charter and ordinances of 1677, mid-18th century.
5336	Copies of the charter granted to the Company by James II, 9 February 1686, and of the exemplification by Anne, 5 June 1702
5986	Draft of ordinances 1719
5992	Miscellaneous papers 1677-1841

Court records

5304/01-10	Minutes of the Court of Assistants 1677-1955
Uncatalogued	Minutes of the Court of Assistants 1955-2019 [CM]
5305/01-11	Rough Court minute books 1677-1784
5979/01-15	Rough minutes and accounts 1715-34
5306/01-4	Clerk's agenda and rough Court minute books 1888-1948
24502	Standing orders passed at the quarterly Court of Assistants 1904-17
Uncatalogued	Standing Orders 1967-2018 [SO]
21031	Standing Committee minute book 1919-35
Uncatalogued	Standing Committee Minutes 1967-2019 [SC]
Uncatalogued	Policy Book 41 1971-2002
Uncatalogued	Strategic Review 2013 [SR]

Membership records

5307	Register of freedom admissions 1694-1780
5308	Alphabetical list of freemen 1677-1795
5309	Alphabetical list of apprentices 1694-1795
5310	Register of apprentices 1772-96
5311	'An account of severall persons that served their apprenticeships to some of the members of the company of Masons and have not taken up their freedoms', with names of Masters
5312	Register of apprentice bindings with an account of orphans' duty paid into the Chamber of London 1694-1856
5313	'Quarteredge booke'; inventories; general accounts; quarterage, admissions; apprentice binding registers; other memoranda, 1663-1701
5314/01-3	Quarterage books 1686-1697
5981	List of Masters and Wardens 1675-1708
5982	Livery lists 1685-1734
5983	Lists of Court of Assistants, livery and yeomanry 1708
5984	List of apprentices 1694-1719
9470	Court, livery and members' list c.1731-50
9471/01-3	Livery list, giving trades and addresses 1809-32
9471A	A list of admissions 1787-1836
5987/01-3	Quarterage books 1708-14

Financial records

5303/01-3	Renter warden's account books 1620-1888
5317	'The book of assessment for Corne' 15 November 1630
5322	Miscellaneous accounts, bills and receipts 1669-1841
5323	Ship money assessment 26 July 1636
5985	Bonds of renter wardens 1700-19
5991/01-2	Miscellaneous vouchers and papers 1723-4
21032	Cash book 1910-51
Uncatalogued	Cash books 1951-86

Trade records

5320	Order by the commissioners for building in the City of London 22 November 1637
5329	Record of the quantity of stone searched 1691
19629	Note of two Acts of Parliament, 2 & 3 Edward VI c.16 and 3 & 4 Edward VI c.20
19633	Warrant for the arrest of Masons who are 'refractory and refuse to obey the orders and ordinances of the company' 1664

Clerk's records

5319	Writs commanding the Master to restore Thomas Stamp to the office of Clerk 1695-6
5330	Miscellaneous administrative papers 1685-1917
5331	Collection of bills, menus, invitations etc 1797-1914
5337	Formulae of oaths used by the Company 1677-mid-19th century
5980	Miscellaneous papers 1702-19
5990	Precepts from the Mayor and Sheriffs to the Company 1697-1720
9472	Copy of Clerk's answers to the Municipal Corporations Commissioners 1833
19631	Copy order of Lord Mayor and Court of Aldermen relating to procedure for election of Master and Wardens 1607
19632	Heralds' visitation 1634
24500	Copy out-letter book 1928-34
24501	Register of seals 1917

Charity and estate

5315/01-2	Irish estates: account books 1832-1909
5316	Inventories of company goods, plates and records etc. and a copy of *The City Press* containing an article on Masons' Company plate 2 June 1897, 1675-1897
5318	List of widows in receipt of benefit 1672-91
5321	Rental of estates and account of stock 1820-4
5324	Deeds and documents relating to Masons' Hall 1562-1707
5325	Irish estates: abstracts for the Court of Assistants 1609-1737
5326	Irish estates: mortgage, dated 30 June 1696, between the Company and John Martin
5327	Irish estates: copy of Mercers' Company accounts and dividends paid to the Masons' Company 1626 & 1628
5328	Irish estates: mayoral precepts to the Company and receipts for moneys paid into the Chamber of London by the Company, 1609-15
5328A	Irish estates: accounts and reports 1831-42
5338	Clerk's report on trust relating to charity 12 June 1880
5988	Copy of a lease by the Company to Thomas Morton 3 September 1707
5989	Counterpart lease by the Company to Caleb Smith 1 May 1710
10741	Brief on the suit between the Skinners' Company and the Irish Society 1838-45
19630	Bond for observance of covenants contained in a lease 1559
20961	Schedules of documents in 'boxes 1,2 and 3' *c*.1880

	Miscellaneous
Uncatalogued	62 issues of the Company's news-sheet/magazine (*Tablets/Journal of the Worshipful Company of Masons*) 1985-2018
Uncatalogued	Statement made by the House Warden of the Mercers' Company, the Cooks', Broderers' and Masons' Companies winding-up the Irish Estate 1908.
Uncatalogued	Assorted photographs

Stored at the British Library
Add. Ch. 19135   Grant of arms by William Hawkeslowe, Clarenceux King of Arms 1472-3

Stored at the Clerk's office
Standing orders (current)
Executive rules (current)
Members' information booklet

OTHER MANUSCRIPT SOURCES
British Library, London [BL]
Add. Ch. 7589
Maps Crace Port 2.55
MS Tiberius D X
MS Harley 839
MS Harley 472
MS Harley 1049
MS Harley 1098
MS Harley 1464
MS Harley 2167
MS Harley 2198
MS Harley 2220
MS Harley 6363
MS Harley 6860

College of Arms, London [CA]
1st H. 7
2nd C. 24
G 10
Vincent 199

Guildhall Library, London [GL]
GL Bside 11:45

Library and Museum of Freemasonry [LAMF]
GBR 1991 OC   Old Charges
Uncatalogued   Membership Registers 1751-1921

London Metropolitan Archives, London [LMA]
COL/AD/01/001-044   Letter Books A to TT
COL/CA/01   Repertories of the Court of Aldermen
COL/CC/01   Journals of the Common Council
COL/CHD/FR   Freedom admissions
DL/C/0355   Register of Wills, Westminster
DW/PA/5/1563/88   Register of Wills, Surrey
DL/AL/C/002/MS09051 Register of Wills, Archdeaconry Court of
                     London
DL/C/B/004/MS09171   Register of Wills, Commissary Court of
                     London
P69/BOT2/A/016/MS09232 Register of Burials, St Botolph Aldgate
P69/GIS/A/002/MS06419 Registers General, St Giles Cripplegate,
                     London

Sir John Soane's Museum, London
Uncatalogued The Letter Book of Edward Strong junior [Memorandums]

The National Archives, London [TNA]
C 8/513/3   Court of Chancery, Garbutt vs Masons' Company
C47 41/154   Return of the Lincoln Guild of Masons, 1388-9
C66/3197   Patent Roll, 29 Chas. II.
C66/3279   Patent Roll, 2 Jas. II.
SC12/3/12   Rental of tenements late of Christ Church, London
SC12/11/16   Christ Church Priory, rent roll
PROB/11   Wills proved and enrolled in the Prerogative Court of
               Canterbury

2: WORKS OF REFERENCE
A Biographical Dictionary of British Architects 1600-1840, ed. H.M. Colvin
    (1978)
A Biographical Register of the University of Oxford to A.D. 1500, 3 vols., ed.
    A.B. Emden (1957-59)
Dictionarium Britannicum; or a more compleat universal etymological English
    Dictionary than any extant, ed. N. Bailey, 2nd ed. (1736)
English Mediæval Architects. A Biographical Dictionary down to 1550, ed. J.
    Harvey, rev. edn. (1984)
Index to Testamentary Records in the Commissary Court of London (London
    Division): now preserved in the Guildhall Library, London, vols. I-IV, ed.
    M. Fitch (1969-1998)

Index to Testamentary Records in the Archdeaconry Court of London, now preserved in the Guildhall Library, London vols. I-II, ed. M. Fitch (1979-85)

Ninth Report of the Royal Commission on Historical Manuscripts, Part 2 (London, 1884)

Masonic Records, orig. ed. J. Lane and updated by LAMF

Pevsner Architectural Guides: The Buildings of England. London I: The City of London by Bradley S. and Pevsner, N. (2002); and *London 2: South* by Cherry, B. and Pevsner, N. (1983)

The Book of Common Prayer. The texts of 1549, 1559, and 1662, ed. B. Cummings (2011)

The History of the King's Works, eds. H.M. Colvin et al, 6 vols (1963-73)

The Oxford Dictionary of National Biography

The Oxford Dictionary of Saints, ed. D.H. Farmer (1978)

The Statutes of the Realm

3: PRINTED PRIMARY SOURCES

Accounts of the Churchwardens of the Parish of St Michael, Cornhill, 1456-1608, ed. W.H. Overall (1871)

Calendar of Early Mayor's Court Rolls preserved among the archives of the Corporation of City of London, 1298-1307, ed. A.H. Thomas (1924)

Calendar of Letter-Books preserved among the archives of the Corporation of the City of London, 1275-1498, Books A-L, ed., R.R. Sharpe, 11 vols. (1899-1912) [CLBA-L]

Calendar of Plea and Memoranda Rolls preserved among the archives of the Corporation of the City of London, eds. A. H. Thomas & P. E. Jones, 6 vols. (1926-1956)

Calendar of the Close Rolls. Preserved in the Public Records Office: [CCR]

Elias Ashmole (1617-1692). His Autobiographical and Historical Notes, his Correspondence, and Other Contemporary Sources Relating to his Life and Work, ed. C.H. Josten, 5 vols. (1967)

J. Howes' MS., 1582, Being a Brief Note of the Order and Manner of the Proceedings in the first erection of the three Royal Hospitals of Christ, Bridewell & St Thomas the Apostle, introduction and notes by W. Lempriere (1904)

Letters and Papers, Foreign and Domestic, of the Reign of Henry VIII: preserved in the Public Record Office, the British Museum, and elsewhere in England (1862-1932) [L&P]

London and Middlesex Chantry Certificate 1548, ed. C.J. Kitching (1980)

London Assize of Nuisance 1301-1431, eds. H.M. Chew and W. Kellaway (1973)

London Bridge: Selected Accounts and Rentals, eds. V. Harding and L. Wright (1995)

London politics 1713-1717; Minutes of a Whig Club 1714-1717; London Pollbooks 1713, eds. H. Horwitz, W.A. Speck, W.A. Gray (1981)

London Viewers and their Certificates, 1508-1558: Certificates of the Sworn Viewers of the City of London, ed. J.S. Loengard (1989)

Memorials of London and London Life in the XIIIth, XIVth and XVth Centuries, ed. H.T. Riley (1868)

Munimenta Gildhallæ Londoniensis; Liber Albus, Liber Custumarum et Liber Horn, ed. H.T. Riley, 4 vols. (1859-62)

Parish Fraternity Register: Fraternity of the Holy Trinity and SS. Fabian and Sebastian in the Parish of St. Botolph without Aldersgate, ed. P. Basing (1982)

Report of the Royal Commissioners appointed to inquire into the Livery Companies of the City of London, 5 vols. (1884)

Second Report of the Commissioners Appointed to Inquire into the Municipal Corporations in England and Wales. London and Southwark and London Companies (1837)

Stow, J., *A Survey of London*, ed. C.L. Kingsford, 2 vols. (1908)

Stow, J., *The Survey of London … now finished by … A[nthony] M[unday] H[umphrey] D[yson] and Others* (1633)

Strype, J., *A Survey of the Cities of London and Westminster*, 2 vols. (1720)

Two Tudor Subsidy Assessment Rolls for the City of London: 1541 and 1582, ed. R.G. Lang (1993)

The Bede Roll of the Fraternity of St Nicholas, eds. N.W. and V.A. James (2004)

The Cartulary of Holy Trinity Aldgate, (ed.) G.A. Hodgett (1971)

The Church Records of St. Andrew Hubbard Eastcheap c.1450-c.1570, ed. C. Burgess (1999)

The Minutes of the Grand Lodge of Freemasons of England 1723-1739, ed. W.J. Songhurst (1913)

The Note-Book and Account Book of Nicholas Stone, Master Mason to James I and Charles I, ed. W.L. Spiers (1919)

The Religious Houses of London and Middlesex, eds. C.M. Barron and M. Davies (2007)

4: SECONDARY WORKS

Anderson, J., *The Constitutions of Free-Masons, Containing the History, Charges, Regulations & c.* (1723), p. 1

Anderson, J., *The New Book of Constitutions of the Antient and Honourable Fraternity of Free and Accepted Masons* (1738)

Archer, I.W., 'The charity of early modern Londoners', *Transactions of the Royal Historical Society* [*TRHS*], vol.12 (2002)

Archer, I.W., 'The livery companies and charity in the sixteenth and seventeenth centuries', in I.A. Gadd and P. Wallis (eds.), *Guilds, Society & Economy in London, 1450-1800* (2002)

Archer, I.W., *The Pursuit of Stability: Social Relations in Elizabethan London* (1991)

Ashton, R., *The City and the Court 1603-43* (1979)

Barron, C.M., *London in the Later Middle Ages: Government and People* (2004)

Barron, C.M., *The Medieval Guildhall of London* (1974)

Barron, C.M., 'The parish fraternities of medieval London' in C. Harper-Bill & C.M. Barron (eds.), *The Church in Pre-Reformation Society: Essays in Honour of F.R.H. Du Boulay* (1985)

Berlin, M., '"Broken all in pieces": artisans and the regulation of workmanship in early modern London', in G. Crossick (ed.), *The Artisan and the European Town, 1500-1900* (1987)

Blair, J., 'English monumental brasses before 1350: types, patterns and workshops', in Coales, *The Earliest English Brasses*

Brigden, S., *London and the Reformation* (1989)

Brigden, S., 'Religion and social obligation in early sixteenth-century London', *Past & Present [P&P]*, No.103 (1984)

Brigden, S., 'Youth and the English Reformation', *P&P*, No.95 (1982)

Bromley, J. and Child, J., *The Armorial Bearings of the Guilds of London* (1960)

Campbell, J.W.P., *Building St Paul's* (2007)

Clark, P., *British Clubs and Societies 1580-1800: the Origins of an Associational World* (2000)

Coldstream, N., *Medieval Architecture* (2002)

Coldstream, N., *Medieval Craftsmen: Masons and Sculptors* (1991)

Conder, E., *Records of the Hole Crafte and Fellowship of Masons with a chronicle of the history of the Worshipful Company of Masons of the City of London* (1894)

Cooney, E.W., 'The origins of the Victorian master builders', *EcHR*, vol.8, No.2 (1955)

Curl, J.S., *The Honourable the Irish Society and the Plantation of Ulster, 1608-2000* (2000)

Curl, J.S., *The Londonderry Plantation, 1609-1914: the History, Architecture, and Planning of the Estates of the City of London and its Livery Companies in Ulster* (1986)

Day, J.F.R., 'Primers of honor: heraldry, heraldry Books, and English Renaissance literature', *The Sixteenth Century Journal*, vol.21, No.1 (1990)

Doolittle, I.G., *The City of London and its Livery Companies* (1982)

Doolittle, I.G., *The Mercers' Company 1579-1959* (1994)

Dussek, I., *Children of Stones: A History of the Worshipful Company of Paviors of the City of London* (1999)

Epstein, S.R., 'Craft guilds, apprenticeship and technological change in preindustrial Europe', *Journal of Economic History*, vol.58 (1998)

Esdaile, A., 'The Stantons of Holborn', *The Archaeological Journal*, vol.85 (1928)

Forey, A.J., 'The military order of St Thomas of Acre', *The English Historical Review [EHR]*, vol.92, No.364 (1977)

Gadd, I.A., 'Early modern printed histories of the London livery companies' in I.A. Gadd and P. Wallis, *Guilds Society & Economy in London*

Gadd, I.A. and Wallis, P., 'Reaching beyond the city wall: London guilds and national regulation, 1500-1700', in S.R. Epstein and M. Prak, eds., *Guilds, Innovation and the European Economy*, 1400-1800 (2008)

Grannum K. and Taylor, N., *Wills and Probate Records: A Guide for Family Historians*, 2nd edn. (2009)

Günther, H.,'Vincenzo Scamozzi comments on the architectural treatise of Sebastiano Serlio', *Annali di architettura: rivista del Centro Internazionale di Studi di Architettura Andrea Palladio* 27. 2015 (2016)

Habermas, J., *The Structural Transformation of the Public Sphere: An Inquiry into a Category of Bourgeois Society*, trans. T. Burger and F. Lawrence (1991)

Harding, V., 'The population of London, 1550-1700: a review of the published evidence', *The London Journal*, vol.15 (1990)

Heal, F. and Holmes, C., *The Gentry in England and Wales,* 1500-1700 (1994)

Hill, P.R. and David, J.C.E., *Practical Stone Masonry* (1995)

Hislop, M., *Medieval Masons* (2014)

Jeffries Davis, E., 'The beginnings of the Dissolution: Christchurch, Aldgate, 1532', *TRHS*, vol.8 (1925)

Jeffries Davis, E., 'The transformation of London' in R.W. Seton-Watson (ed.), *Tudor Studies* (1924)

Jordan, W.K., *The Charities of London 1480-1660: The Aspirations and Achievements of Urban Society* (1960)

Kahl, W.F., *The Development of London Livery Companies: An Historical Essay and Select Bibliography* (1960)

Keene, D., 'From Conquest to Capital: St Paul's, c.1100-1300' in *St Paul's: The Cathedral Church of London* 604-2004, eds. D. Keene, A. Burns and A. Saint (2004)

Kellett, J.R., 'The breakdown of gild and corporation control over the handicraft and retail trade in London', *EcHR*, New Series, vol.10, No.3 (1958)

Knights, M., 'A City Revolution: The remodelling of the London livery companies in the 1680s', *EHR*, vol.112, No. 449 (1997)

Knoop, D. and Jones, G.P., [K&J] 'London Bridge and its builders. A study of the municipal employment of masons mainly in the fifteenth century', *Ars Quatuor Coronatorum [AQC]*, vol.47 (1934)

Knoop, D. and Jones, G.P., *The Genesis of Freemasonry. An account of the Rise and Development of Freemasonry in its Operative, Accepted and Early Speculative Phases* (1947)

Knoop, D. and Jones, G.P., 'The impressment of masons in the middle ages', *EcHR*, vol.8, No.1 (1937)

Knoop, D. and Jones, G.P., 'The London mason in the seventeenth century', *AQC*, vol.48 (1935)

Knoop, D. and Jones, G.P., *The London Masons' Company*, repr. from *Economic History* (1939)

Knoop, D. and Jones, G.P., *The Mediæval Mason*, 3rd ed. (1967)

Kynaston, D., *Till Time's Last Sand: A History of the Bank of England 1694-2013* (2017)

Lang, J., *City and Guilds of London Institute Centenary 1878-1978* (1978)

Leunig, T., Minns, C. and Wallis, P., 'Networks in the premodern economy: the market for London apprenticeships, 1600-1749', *The Journal of Economic History*, vol.71, No.2 (2011)

Liddy, C.D., *Contesting the City: The Politics of Citizenship in English Towns, 1250-1530* (2017)

Maclagan, M., 'Genealogy and heraldry in the sixteenth and seventeenth centuries', in L. Fox (ed.), *English Historical Scholarship in the Sixteenth and Seventeenth Centuries* (1956)

Maitland, W., *History of London from its foundation to the present time* (1739)

Masters, B. R., *The Chamberlain of the City of London, 1237-1987* (1988)

McKellar, E., *The Birth of Modern London: the Development and Design of the City, 1660-1720* (1999)

Minns, C. and Wallis, P., 'Rules and reality: quantifying the practice of apprenticeship in early modern England', *EcHR*, vol.65, No.2 (2012)

Minns, C. and Wallis, P., 'The price of human capital in a pre-industrial economy: premiums and apprenticeship contracts in 18th century England', *Explorations in Economic History*, vol.50 (2013)

Noorthouck, J., *A New History of London including Westminster and Southwark* (1773)

Önnerfors, A., *Freemasonry: A Very Short Introduction* (2017)

Paye, A., *Stone: The Decay and Repair of Historic Façades* (2014)

Pearl, V., *London and the Outbreak of the Puritan Revolution: City Government and National Politics, 1625-43* (1961)

Pevsner, N., 'The term "architect" in the Middle Ages', *Speculum*, vol.17, no.4 (1942)

Plot, R., *Natural History of Staffordshire* (1686)

Prescott, A., 'A history of British freemasonry 1425-2000', *Centre for Research into Freemasonry and Fraternalism at the University of Sheffield*, Working Paper Series No. 1

Prescott, A., 'The old charges' in H. Bogdan and J.A.M. Snoek (eds.), *Handbook of Freemasonry* (2014)

Prescott, A. and Sommers, S.M., '1717 and All That', circulation paper for debate organised by Quatuor Coronati Lodge No.2076, 15 February 2018.

Ramsey, G.D., 'Victorian historiography and the guilds of London: the report of the Royal Commission on the Livery Companies of London, 1884', *The London Journal*, vol.10, No. 2 (1984)

Rappaport, S., *Worlds within Worlds: the Structures of Life in Sixteenth-Century London* (1989)

Rawlins, S.W., *Visitation of London 1568 with Additional Pedigrees 1569-90, the Arms of the City Companies and a London Subsidy Roll, 1589* (1963)

Reddaway, T.F., *The Rebuilding of London after the Great Fire*, repr. (1951)

Reynolds, S., *An Introduction to the History of English Medieval Towns* (1997)

Rosenfield, M.C., 'Holy Trinity, Aldgate, on the eve of the Dissolution', *The Guildhall Miscellany*, vol.3, No. 3 (1970)

Rosser, G., *The Art of Solidarity in the Middle Ages: Guilds in England 1250-1550* (2015)

Salisbury, E., 'List of the liverymen and freemen of the city companies, 1538', *Middlesex and Hertfordshire Notes and Queries*, iii and iv (1897 and 1898)

Salzman, L.F., *Building in England down to 1540: a documentary history* (1952)

Salzman, L.F., *English Industries of the Middle Ages*, 2nd. edn. (1923)

Sampson, G.V., *Statistical Survey of the County of Londonderry, with Observations on the Means of Improvement, Drawn up for the Consideration, and under the Direction of the Dublin Society* (1802)

Scanlan, M.D.J., 'The origins of freemasonry: England' in Bogdan and Snoek, *Handbook*

Schalk, R., Wallis, P., Crowston, C. and Lemercier, C., 'Failure or flexibility? Apprenticeship training in premodern Europe', *Journal of Interdisciplinary History*, vol.48, No. 2 (2017)

Schofield, J,, *The Building of London: from the Conquest to the Great Fire* (1999)

Sharpe, R.R., *London and the Kingdom*, 3 vols. (1894-5)

Smith, A., *Wealth of Nations* (1776)

Spiegel, G.M., *Romancing the Past: The Rise of Vernacular Prose Historiography in Thirteenth-Century France* (1993)

St John Hope, W.H., *Windsor Castle. An Architectural History*, 3 vols. (1913)

Stalley, R., *Early Medieval Architecture* (1999)

Stephenson, J.Z., *Contracts and Pay: Work in London's Construction 1660-1785* (2017)

Stevenson, D., 'Four hundred years of freemasonry in Scotland', *The Scottish Historical Review*, vol.90, No. 230, Pt. 2 (2011)

Stevenson, D., 'The origins of freemasonry: Scotland', in Bogdan and Snoek, *Handbook*

Stevenson, D., *The Origins of Freemasonry. Scotland's Century, 1590-1710* (1988)

Stone, I., 'Huguenots, Whigs, and the Remodelling of the London Masons' Company, 1680-1740', *Huguenot Society Journal*, 35 (2022)

Summerson, J., *Georgian London*, new edn. (2003)

Swanson, H., 'The illusion of economic structure: craft guilds in late medieval English towns', *P&P*, vol.121 (1988)

Taillades, D., 'A new approach of the Old Charges', *AQC*, vol.133 (2020)

Taylor, H.M. and Taylor, J., *Anglo-Saxon Architecture*, 3 vols. (1965)

Unwin, G., *The Gilds and Companies of London*, 3rd ed. (1938)

Veale, E.M., 'Craftsmen and the economy of London in the fourteenth century', in R. Holt and G. Rosser (eds.), *The Medieval Town: A Reader in English Urban History* (1990)

Veale, E.M., '"The Great Twelve": mistery and fraternity in thirteenth-century London', *Historical Research*, vol.64 (1991)

Wagner, A.R., *Heralds and Heraldry in the Middle Ages: An Inquiry into the Growth of the Armorial Functions of Heralds*, 2nd. edn. (1956)

Waller, F., *Arms of the City Companies* (1852/1863)

Wallis, P., 'Apprenticeship in England' in P. Maarten and P. Wallis (eds.), *Apprenticeship in Early Modern Europe* (2020)

Wallis, P., 'Apprenticeship and training in premodern England', *The Journal of Economic History*, vol.68, No.3 (2008)

Wallis, P., 'Controlling commodities: search and reconciliation in the early modern livery companies', in Gadd and Wallis, *Guilds, Society & Economy*

Wallis, P., 'Labor, law, and training in early modern London: apprenticeship and the city's institutions', *Journal of British Studies*, vol.51, No.4, (2012)

Walters, H.B., *London Churches at the Reformation with an account of their contents* (1939)

Welch, C., *Coat Armour of the London Livery Companies* (1914)

Welch, C., *The Worshipful Company of Paviors of the City of London* (1909)

Whitaker, J., *An Almanack for the Year of Our Lord* 1894 (London, 1893)

Williams, W.J., 'Archbishop Becket and the Masons' Company of London', *AQC*, vol.41 (1929)

Williams, W.J., 'Masons of the City of London. Gleanings from the letter books and other records A.D. 1293 to A.D. 1654', *AQC*, vol.45 (1932)

Williams, W.J., 'The gild of masons at Lincoln', *AQC*, vol.54 (1941)

Wright, B., *The armes of all the cheife corporatons of England W^t the Companies of London described by letters for their severall collores* (1596)

5: UNPUBLISHED RESOURCES

Diamond, M.C., 'The Irish Estates of the Mercers' Company, 1609-1906', Unpublished M.Phil thesis (New University of Ulster, 1974)

Doolittle, I.G., 'The Government of the City of London, 1694-1767', Unpublished PhD thesis (Oxford University, 1979)

Hovland, S.R., 'Apprenticeship in Later Medieval London (*c.*1300-*c.*1530)', Unpublished PhD thesis (Royal Holloway, University of London, 2006)

Mobus, M.A.C., 'The Burford Masons and the Changing World of Building Practice in England, 1630-1730', Unpublished PhD thesis (Open University, 2011)

Stephenson, J.Z., 'The Organisation of Work and Wages in the London Building Trades in the Long Eighteenth Century', Unpublished PhD thesis (London School of Economics, 2015)

Notes

INTRODUCTION

1. Stow, *Survey*, i, 285; GL MS 5304/8A, 140; Conder, *Records*, iii-v.
2. Conder, *Records*, 280.
3. GL MS 5304/10, 160, 165-6; CM, 27 Jun. 1957, 27 Mar. 1958, 13 Jan. 1959, 9 Feb. 1960; SC, 7 May and 3 Sep. 2009, 16 May 2012, 20 Nov. 2013.

CHAPTER 1   BEGINNINGS

1. Chew and Kellaway, *Nuisance*, ix-xxi; *Lib. Cust.*, i, 86-8.
2. Barron, *London*, 207; K&J, 'Masons' Company', 158-9.
3. Liddy, *Contesting*, 142-53.
4. Salzman, *Building*, 68-72; K&J, *Mediæval Mason*, 99-100, 210-14; Harvey, *Architects*, 268; Hope, *Windsor*, 132; Riley, *Memorials*, 253-8; *Statutes*, i, 311-13.
5. K&J, *Mediæval Mason*, 100, 112, 211; *CPMR*, 1323-64, xxx-xxxi; *CLBG*, 115-18; *CCR*, 1360-4, 262-3; *Statutes*, i, 366-7; *King's Works*, i, 184-5; K&J, 'London Bridge', 27-9.
6. *CLBG*, 116-17.

CHAPTER 2   THE MASON

1. Salzman, *Building*, 69-72; GL MS 5304/4, 27 Mar. 1777; GL MS 5304/6, 15 Jun. 1807.
2. GL MS 5313, 1696-7; GL MS 5304/3, 42r, 110v, 178v.
3. Salzman, *Building*, 30-34, 63-4; *King's Works*, i, 427-8; K&J, *Mediæval Mason*, 73-7; Blair, 'English monumental brasses', 140, 166-67.
4. K&J, *Mediæval Mason*, 78.
5. Blair, 'English monumental brasses', 168-9; *CLBE*, 55-6.
6. *ODNB*; Salzman, *Industries*, 103-4.
7. Pevsner, 'The term "architect"', 549-62.
8. L.R. Shelby, 'The geometrical knowledge of mediaeval master masons', *Speculum*, vol. 47, no. 3 (Jul., 1972), 395-421; Coldstream, *Medieval Architecture*, 65-71.
9. K&J, 'London mason', 21.
10. GL MS 5317; GL MS 5323; GL MS 5303/1, 85v-86r, 328r-30r; GL MS 5304/1, 92-92v; K&J, 'London mason', 60.
11. Stephenson, *Contracts*, 50-2, 65; Stephenson, 'Organisation', 89-95; Colvin, *Dictionary*, 21; Campbell, *St Paul's*, 72-3.
12. McKellar, *Modern London*, 86.
13. Stephenson, 'Organisation', 60-61; Campbell, *St Paul's*, 60; *King's Works*, v, 40-1.
14. *King's Works*, v, 39-46; K&J, ''London mason', 31-32, 38-39, 46, 48-49; 'Memorandums', 2-3.

15. 'Memorandums', 7; K&J, 'London Mason', 38-39, 42; Stephenson, 'Organisation', 66.
16. Stephenson, *Contracts*, 68-9.
17. Cooney, 'Origins', 167-76; McKellar, *Modern London*, 93-113.
18. *King's Works*, vi, 607-8; Cooney, 'Origins', 173; *ODNB*.
19. Salzman, *Building*, 50, 127-8; K&J, 'Masons' Company', 163-5; Hislop, *Medieval Masons*, 50; Riley, *Memorials*, 238, 361, 569-70, 626.
20. CM, 22 Sep. 2009; SC, 5 Nov. 2009, 12 May 2010, 18 May 2011.

CHAPTER 3   THE MEDIEVAL COMPANY
1. TNA PROB 11/2B/220; Williams, 'Archbishop Becket', 137-8; Harvey, *Architects*, 313-14.
2. Veale, 'Craftsmen and the economy', 125; Reynolds, *English Medieval Towns*, 83-4,165-6; Rosser, *Solidarity*, 152-3.
3. Barron, *London*, 209, 214-15.
4. Reynolds, *English Medieval Towns*, 83-4; Barron, *London*, 206-8, 233; Swanson, 'The illusion', 33-39; *Statutes*, i, 379.
5. Officers and Badges; Barron, *London*, 230.
6. K&J, *Mediæval Mason*, 135-8; Salzman, *Industries*, 114; Regulations, Ordinances and Charters; Veale, 'Craftsmen and the economy', 128-29; Veale, '"The Great Twelve"', 237.
7. Rosser, *Solidarity*, 3-4, 50; Unwin, *Gilds*, 51-5, 93-126; Barron, 'The parish fraternities', 13, 23-5, 28-31.
8. LMA MS 9171 1, 177; TNA C47 41/154; Williams, 'Gild of masons at Lincoln', 108-110; Unwin, *Gilds*, 103-4; Veale, 'Craftsmen and the economy', 125-26; Barron, 'Parish Fraternities', 14-17; Barron, *London*, 206-7.
9. Harvey, *Architects*, 194, 364; Rosser, *Solidarity*, 48-9.
10. Forey, 'The military order of St Thomas of Acre', 500-03.
11. Veale, 'Craftsmen and the economy', 125-6; Rosser, *Solidarity*, 4.
12. GL MS 05440, 11v; *CPMR*, 1437-57, 7-8, 58; Barron, *London*, 218-19; Officers and Badges; Regulations, Ordinances and Charters.
13. Barron, *London*, 209-210.
14. Salzman, *Industries*, 114-15; Salzman, *Building*, 33-41; K&J, *Mediæval Mason*, 55, 135, 142-3, 154; Coldstream, *Masons*, 11-12; Coldstream, *Medieval Architecture*, 98-100.
15. Regulations, Ordinances and Charters.
16. *CLBL*, 246; Barron, *London*, 209-11; Unwin, *Gilds*, 160-72.
17. LMA COL/AD/01/011, 150v-51v, 219r-220r; *CLBL*, 170, 233-4; Welch, *The Worshipful Company of Paviors*, 7-12; Dussek, *Children of Stones*, 16-24; LMA COL/CC/01/08, 169v-170r.
18. *Albus*, 527-28.
19. K&J, *Mediæval Mason*, 140-1; Liddy, *Contesting*, 133-36, at 134.
20. Unwin, *Gilds*, 217-21; Barron, *London*, 226-7.
21. Unwin, *Gilds*, 223-231; Barron, *London*, 211-14.
22. Schofield, *Building of London*, 117-18; *CLBK*, 290; *CLBL*, 67, 73, 132.
23. Harvey, *Architects*, 78, 165; LMA MS 9051 1 179.
24. Farmer, *Saints*, 155-56; Stow, *Survey*, i, xxxiii.
25. LMA COL/CC/01/10, 373v.
26. Regulations, Ordinances and Charters.

CHAPTER 4   THE COMPANY'S ARMS
1. Bromley and Child, *Armorial Bearings*, v-viii, xviii-xix, 73.
2. Bromley and Child, *Armorial Bearings*, vii-viii, 162-4; BL, Add. Ch, 19135; Conder, *Records*, 89.

3. BL Add. Ch., 19135; CA MS, 1st H. 7, 60v; CA MS G. 10, 123v; GL MS 19632; CA MS, 2nd C. 24, 7; Rawlins, *Visitation*, ix, 131; Heal and Holmes, *Gentry*, 28.

4. Maclagan, 'Genealogy and heraldry' 31; Heal and Holmes, *Gentry*, 20-47; Day, 'Primers of honor', 93.

5. BL MSS: Tiberius D x, 62r; Harley 839, 51r; Harley 6363, 18r; Harley 2220, 10r; Harley 472, 16v; Harley 6860, 76r; Harley 1464, 91r; Harley 2198, 183r; Harley 2167, 183r; Harley 1049, 1r-7r; Harley 2167, 188v, 249v54r; LAMF MSS: GBR OC 1/15; GBR OC 1/16; Papworth MS Old Charges; GBR OC 1/22; GBR OC 1/36; GBR OC 1/9; GBR OC 1/33; GBR OC 1/40; Wright, *The armes of all the cheife corporatons*; Stow, *Survey… now finished…AM HD*, 630; Gadd, 'Early modern printed histories', 38-40, 43-5.

6. GL MS 5304/3, 1v; GL MS 5304/8, 6 Oct., 9 Nov. 1870, 30 Mar., 14 Jun. 1871; GL MS 5330.

7. GL MS 5304/7, 1 Apr. 1841; GL MS 5304/8, 9 Nov. 1872; CM, 1972-4, *passim*.

8. CM, 1 Oct. 1968, 1 Apr. 1969; *Tablets*, 50, 12-13.

9. BL MS Harley 472, 16v; Welch, *Coat Armour*, 42-43.

10. Bromley and Child, *Armorial Bearings*, 128, 151, 154, 213; GL MS 5304/8A, 155, 159, 163-4, 173; GL MS 5330.

CHAPTER 5   REFORMATION

1. Jeffries Davis, 'The beginnings of the Dissolution', 127-29; Rosenfield, 'Holy Trinity, Aldgate', 170-73.

2. E. Jeffries Davis, 'Transformation', 289-90, 304-10; Stow, *Survey*, i, 142.

3. Bromley and Child, *Armorial Bearings*, viii-ix; Brigden, *London and the Reformation*, 428-9; Kitching, *Chantry Certificate*, xxxiii.

4. TNA PROB 11/6/428; LMA COL/CC/01/04, 55v; Grannum and Taylor, *Wills*, 33-36; Fitch, *Commissary Court of London*; Fitch, *Archdeaconry Court of London*; Sharpe, *Calendar of Wills*.

5. Robert Vertue, d.1506, TNA PROB 11/15/340; Robert Janyns, d.1506, TNA PROB 11/15/251; Walter Martyn, d.1513, TNA 11/17/397; Thomas Bristall, d.1516, LMA MS 01971/9, 5r; Nicholas Merche, d.1517, LMA MS 09171 9, 43r; John Warner, d.1519, LMA MS 09171/9, 112r-v; Mark Lincke, d.1525, LMA MS 09171/10, 63v-64r; Thomas Wells, d.1526, LMA MS 09171/10, 82r-83r; William Vertue, d.1527, TNA PROB 11/22/103; William Hill, d.1527, LMA MS 09171/10, 99v; Thomas Raynton, d.1527, LMA MS 09171/10, 92v-93r; Thomas Herunden, d.1534, TNA PROB /11/25/213; Thomas Pope, d.1533, LMA MS 09171/10 202v-203r; Nicholas Searle, d.1533, LMA MS 09171/10, 213r; Richard Aylmer, d.1533, LMA MS 09171/10, 215r; Thomas Redman, d.1536, LMA MS 09171/10, 276r; John Painter, d.1536, TNA PROB 11/25/152; George Simpson senior, d.1536, TNA PROB 11/25/532.

6. Robert Hawte, d.1540, LMA MS 09171/11, 40v-41r; Francesco Benall', d.1544, LMA MS 09171/11, 136v; John Orgar, d.1546, TNA PROB 11/31/367; William Holmes, d.1546, LMA MS 09171/11 178v; John Molton, d.1547, LMA DL/C/0355, 101v-102r; John Aylmer, d.1548, TNA PROB 11/32/184; Gilbert Burpham, d.1550, LMA MS 09171/12, 118v-119r; William Chamberlain, d.1550, LMA MS 09171/12, 39v; Thomas Fant, d.1550, LMA MS 09171/12, 58r; Geoffrey Orgar, d. 1551, LMA MS 09051/2 30r-v; George Simpson junior, d.1556, TNA PROB 11/38/139; John Paskin, d. 1557, LMA MS 09171/13, 138r-v; Thomas Harris, d. 1563, LMA DW/PA/5/1563/88; Thomas West, d. 1564/5, LMA MS 09171/15 195v; Gabriel Caldham, d.1570, LMA MS 09171/16 5v; Thomas Beacher, d.1571, LMA MS 09171/16 53r; Peter Maye, d.1574, LMA MS 09171/16 173v; Thomas Watson, d.1578, LMA MS 09171/16, 368r-v.

7. Brigden, *London and the Reformation*, 30.

8. LMA MS 09171/6, 296v-297r; LMA MS 09171/5, 116v; TNA CP 40/829, rot.521, 538; TNA C1/533/23; Salisbury, 'List of liverymen', iii, 39-43, iv, 19-20; GL MS 30737/d;

Lang, *Two Tudor Subsidy Rolls*, 254; LMA MS 09171/14, 73r; BL MS Harley 1464, 91v; James and James, *Bede Roll*, pt. I, 3, 119, 120, 135.

9. LMA MS 09171/6, 371v; LMA MS 09171/13, 63r-v; Burgess, *St. Andrew Hubbard*, 159.
10. Brigden, *London and the Reformation*, 34.
11. Brigden, *London and the Reformation*, 37.
12. Basing, *Register*, xii, 5-7, 9, 25-26, 43-44, 50-51; LMA MS 09171/5 1, 90r.
13. Barron, 'Parish fraternities', 24-5; Unwin, *Gilds*, 53-4, 122-3; Brigden, *London and the Reformation*, 35-6.
14. James and James, *Bede Roll*, I, xxviii, 110, 120.
15. Brigden, *London and the Reformation*, 28; Brigden, 'Religion and social obligation'; 67-86; Prov., 19:17.
16. Archer, *Stability*, 175.
17. John Clerk (d. 1459) and William Rolls (d. 1480), LMA MS 09171/5, 268r.
18. Brigden, *London and the Reformation*, 381-2, 606-12; Walters, *London Churches*, 186.
19. Salisbury, 'List of liverymen', iii, 39-43, iv, 19-20; Rappaport, *Worlds*, 322-6; Loengard, *Viewers*, lxvi.
20. Brigden, *London and the Reformation*, 304-5, 383-9.
21. Jordan, *Charities*; Archer, 'Charity', 223-30, 232-44; Archer, *Stability*, 163-5, 167-9, 175-82; Brigden, *London and the Reformation*, 481-2.
22. TNA PROB: 11/101/566, 11/169/152, 11/457/142; GL MS 5303/1, 160v; GL MS 5304/1, 57r.

CHAPTER 6   THE EARLY MODERN COMPANY

1. K&J, 'Masons' Company', 160-61; *Mediæval Mason*, 199.
2. Unwin, *Gilds*, 244-5, 329-51; Kahl, *Livery Companies*, 1-2, 25-29; Gadd and Wallis, *Guilds*, 1-3; Kellett, 'Breakdown', 381-2; Rappaport, *Worlds*, 213-14; Ashton, *City and the Court*, 165-7.
3. Unwin, *Gilds*, 346-7; Berlin, '"Broken', 77; Spiers, *Note-Book* 1-19; *King's Works*, iii, 408; *ODNB*; GL MS 5303/1, 43r, 71r, 92r, 99r.
4. Regulations, Ordinances and Charters.
5. Kellett, 'Breakdown', 383-4; Berlin, '"Broken', 78; Ashton, *City and the Court*, 51-70.
6. GL MS 5303/1, 147v, 152r, 204r, *passim*.
7. *Statutes*, iv, pt. 1, 58-9, 120; GL MS 19629; K&J, *Mediaeval Mason*, 100-1; Rappaport, *Worlds*, 401-7.
8. GL MS 5303/1, 6r, 19r, 25r, 28v, 51r-52r, 58v, 148r; K&J, *Mediæval Mason*, 203-4; *King's Works*, iii, 147.
9. Ashton, *City and the Court*, 60-61; GL MS 5303/1, 86v, 115r, 118v, 122r. But Cf. 144r.
10. GL MS 5303/1, 10v, 17r, 27r, 48r-v, 86r-v, 93v-94r, 134v, *passim*.
11. GL MS 5303/1, 32v, 34r, 65v, 73r, 75v, 112r, 188v, 203v; Berlin, '"Broken', 79-81; Epstein, 'Craft guilds', 693-4.
12. Rappaport, *Worlds*, 192; Archer, *Stability*, 32-9; Unwin, *Gilds*, 240-41.
13. LMA: COL/AD/01/015, 217r, COL/CC/01//01/20, 560r; COL/CC/01/01/21, 19r, 426r-v; COL/CC/01/01/22, 37v; COL/CC/01/01/18, 31r; GL MS 5303/1, 114r-15v, *passim*.
14. GL MS 5303/1, 147v-50v, 160v-1v; Reddaway, *Rebuilding*, 250-56.
15. LMA/COL/CA/01/20, 560r; GL MS 5303/1, 56v, 147v-9v, 156r-9v, 161r, 167r-68v, 217v; GL MS 5324.
16. 1620-21, 1641-45, 1648-49, 1654-55, 1660-61, 1663-64.
17. LMA COL/AD/01/024, 57v; Williams, *Masons*, 151-2.
18. GL MS 5303/1, 74r-6v.
19. GL MS 5303/1, 12v, 33v, 74r; GL MS 5303/2, 60; GL MS 5304/3, 141v.
20. GL MS 5303/1, 49r, 51r, 74r-76v, 96v, 97r, 156r.

21. GL MS 5303/1, 89r.
22. *King's Works*, iii, 140-7.
23. Chew and Kellaway, *Assize of Nuisance*, xix-xx; Loengard, *Viewers*, xi-xxi, xxx-xxxvi, xlv- xlviiii.
24. Lang, *Two Tudor Subsidy Rolls*, 132, 133, 152, 172, 196, 254, 277, 289.
25. Loengard, *Viewers*, xiii-xv, lix-lx; Reddaway, *Rebuilding*, 55-9.
26. *Statutes*, iv, pt. 1, 419; Minns and Wallis, 'Rules and reality' 556; Kellett, 'Breakdown', 393-4.
27. Rappaport, *Worlds*, 24, 232, 294, 311-12; Minns and Wallis, 'Rules and reality', 559; Wallis, 'Apprenticeship and training', 836.
28. K&J, *Mediæval Mason*, 72, 149-50; Salzman, *Building*, 587-8; *ODNB*.
29. K&J, *Mediæval Mason*, 62-5, 144; Hovland, 'Apprenticeship', 45, 267-71; *Lib. Cust.*, i, 86; Coldstream, *Craftsmen*, 13; Harvey, *Architects*, 305.
30. K&J, *Mediæval Mason*, 143-50; K&J, 'London Bridge', 33; LMA MS 9171 1, 154v; LMA MS 9051 1, 179r; TNA PROB 11/2B/192, Harvey, *Architects*, 187-9; LMA MS 9171 3, 323v; TNA PROB 11/2B/220; TNA PROB 11/15/340; TNA PROB 11/17/397; LMA DL/C/0355, 101v-102r; TNA PROB 11/32/184; LMA MS 9171/12, 51v; TNA PROB 11/38/139.
31. Barron, *London*, 205-6; Wallis, 'Labor, law and training', 794; Rappaport, *Worlds*, 186-8, 294-5.
32. Smith, *Wealth*, i, ch. 10, Pt. 2; Rappaport, *Worlds*, 104-10, 324-6; Wallis, 'Apprenticeship and training', 852.
33. GL MS 5304/2, 15v, 131v, 177v.
34. GL MS 5304/4, 10 Jan. 1765.
35. Rappaport, *Worlds*, 311-15; Wallis, 'Labor, law and training', 795-7; Minns and Wallis, 'Rules and reality', 570; GL MS 5304/3 and GL MS 5304/4, *passim*; Swanson, 'Illusion', 46.
36. GL MSS 5307, 5308, 5312, 5313, 9471A.
37. GL MS 5303/1, 36v-38r.

CHAPTER 7   HENRY WILSON – A 17TH-CENTURY LIVERYMAN

1. GL MS 5303/1, 2v, 26r, 36r, 47v; Rappaport, *Worlds*, 24-5, 48, 294-5, 322-4; *Statutes*, iv, pt. 1, 419; *Albus*, 272.
2. Rappaport, *Worlds*, 48-53; Gadd and Wallis, *Guilds*, 5; GL MS 5303/1, 65v, 117v.
3. Rappaport, *Worlds*, 188-9, 216-17; Archer, *Stability*, 83, 219-20.
4. GL MS 5303/1, 79r-80v, 187v.
5. Williams, *Masons*, 154-5; GL MS 5303/1, 203v; GL MS 5304/2, 89r-97v; GL MS 5304/3, 57v, 67r-v, 69r, 76v; GL MS 5304/6, 9 Nov. 1808, 12 Jan. 1809.
6. GL MS 5317; GL MS 5303/1, 85v-86r; GL MS 5323.
7. Archer, *Stability*, 101-2, 114.
8. Rappaport, *Worlds*, 345, 349-51, 357-9; Archer, *Stability*, 19-20.
9. GL MS 5303/1, 192v.
10. GL MS 5303/1, 5r, 96r-7r, 152v.
11. 1631-32, 1633-35, 1639-44, 1645-46, 1647-49, 1650-51, 1652-53, 1659-60 and 1664-65.
12. GL MS 5303/1, 154v, 158r, 161v, 165v, 222r-3r.
13. GL MS 5334, 10r-11v; GL MS 5985; GL MS 5303/1, 199v.
14. GL MS 5303/1, 169r, 176v, 180r, 203r.
15. GL MS 5303/1, 48r-v, 73v, 86v, 89r, 100v-1r; 112v, 119v-120r, 134v-5r, 147v, 185r, 189r, 193r, 196v, 200r, 204r, 207v, 211v, 215v, 218r.
16. TNA PROB 11/303/154; Archer, *Stability*, 28-32, 58-63; Rappaport, *Worlds*, 29, 215.

CHAPTER 8   MASONS' HALL

1. Stow, *Survey*, i, p. 285; Strype, *Survey*, iii, 68; Noorthouck, *New History*, ii, 550.
2. GL MS 5324.
3. Barron, *London*, 216-17.
4. GL MS 5313; GL MS 5316; GL MS 5304/3, 1r-4r; Schofield, *Building*, 115-17.
5. TNA SC12/3/12; TNA SC12/11/16, 4v; Rosenfeld, 'Holy Trinity, Aldgate', 161, 171-72; *L&P*, vol. 20 pt. 1, 219-20; GL MS 5324; *ODNB*.
6. GL MS 5324; GL MS 5303/1, unfoliated fly leaf.
7. Salisbury, 'List of liverymen', iii, 39-43, iv, 19-20; Lang, *Two Tudor Subsidy Rolls*, 141; GL MS 5324; LMA 9051/5, 174v; Williams, *Masons*, 150-1.
8. GL MS 5324.
9. GL MS 5324; GL MS 5303/1, 6r.
10. GL MS 5303/1, 121r; GL MS 5324.
11. GL MS 5324; GL MS 5303/1, 3v, 78v, 134r, 146r-211r, 166v.
12. GL MS 5303/1, *passim*.
13. GL MS 5303/1, 272v-75v; GL MS 5324; GL MS 5303/2, 1-6; GL MS 5304/1, 150r, 155r; GL MS 5304/2, 103v, 104v, 118v, 191v, 196v, 198r, 207r; GL MS 5304/3, 103r; GL MS 5989; GL MS 5303/3, 1840-41.
14. GL MS 5303/1, 236r, 237v, 241v, 276v-79r; GL MS 5322; GL MS 5324.
15. GL MS 5304/3, 14r; GL MS 5304/4, 14 Jun., 29 Jun. and 4 Aug. 1769, 9 Jan. 1777; GL MS 5303/2, 121, 177.
16. GL MS 5303/3, 1829-35; GL MS 5304/6, 4 Aug. and 24 Aug. 1826, 1831-5 *passim*.
17. GL MS 5304/2, 107r; GL MS 5980; GL MS 5304/3, 212r; GL MS 5304/4, 14 Jun., 27 Jun. and 1 Aug. 1782.
18. GL MS 5303/1, 216r-19v, 227r; GL MS 5324.
19. GL MS 5322; GL MS 5303/1, 249r-71v; GL MS 5304/2, 54v.
20. Reddaway, *Rebuilding*, 252-3; GL MS 5303/1, 246r-56r, 261r-7r, 272v-79r; GL MS 5304/2, 202r; GL MS 5304/3, 3v, 52v, 55v; GL MS 5324.
21. GL MS 5304/7, 15 Oct. 1857; GL MS 5324; GL MS 5303/1, 252r-56r, 265r-67v.
22. GL MS 5324; GL MS 5989.
23. GL MS 5304/4, 4 Aug. and 1 Oct. 1767, 1 Jul. 1773; GL MS 5324.
24. GL MS 5303/1, 265r-67v, 272v-75v; GL MS 5303/2, 1-6, 113, 133, 153; GL MS 5304/2, 191v; GL MS 5304/3, 14r, 71v, 92r, 124r; GL MS 5988.
25. GL MS 5304/2, 81r; GL MS 5991/01; GL MS 5304/3, 141r; GL MS 5304/4, 31 Mar. 1791.
26. Reddaway, *Rebuilding*, 80; GL MS 5304/6, 25 Jun. 1807, 7 Feb. 1811, 24 Aug. 1826; GL MS 5304/7, 7 Aug. 1840, 15 Oct. 1857.
27. GL MS 5304/3, 55v; GL MS 5303/2, 104, 106, 219; GL MS 5304/4, 1 Mar. and 28 Mar. 1751, 1767-8 *passim*, 14 Jun. 1770; GL MS 5304/6, 1826 *passim*, 29 Mar. 1827, 10 Nov. 1834, 8 Jan. 1835.
28. GL MS 5304/2, 191v; GL MS 5304/4, 11 and 16 May 1789, 10 Feb. 1790.
29. GL MS 5304/9, 92-3, 102-3, 124; GL MS 5304/7, 11 Jan. 1866; Conder, *Records*, 275, n.1; Museum of London, ID nos. 10351, 10352.
30. BL MS Harley 1464, 91v; GL MS 5304/3, 162r, 164v-65r; GL MS 5313.
31. Schofield, *Building*, 117-18; GL MS 5304/4, 11 and 16 May 1789; GL MS 5304/6, 14 Jun. 1831.
32. GL MS 5304/2, 81r; GL MS 5991/01; GL MS 5304/4, 9 Jan. and 2 May 1755, 31 Mar. 1791; GL MS 5303/2, 242.
33. GL MS 5304/6, 7 Jan. and 31 Mar. 1836; GL MS 5303/3, 1841-4, 1853-5; GL MS 5304/7, 7 Aug. 1840, 30 Jun. 1842, 12 Jan. and 30 Mar. 1843, 7 Dec. 1853, 1855-7 *passim*; GL MS 5330.
34. CH Minutes, 474, 482-3; GL MS 5304/7, 1858-60 *passim*; GL MS 5330.

35. GL MS 5304/7, 1860-2 *passim*, 14 Jun. and 30 Jun. 1864; 1861 Census.
36. GL MS 5304/7, 1865-6 *passim*; GL MS 5330.
37. GL MS 5304/7, 10 Jan. 1867.
38. GL MS 5330; GL MS 5304/7, 28 Mar. 1861, 28 Mar. 1867; GL MS 5304/8, 6 Aug. 1869.
39. GL MS 5303/3, 1869-70, 1880-1, 1887-8; GL MS 5304/10, 87-90, 120-21, 152-54.
40. GL MS 5304/8, 1868-70 *passim*, 14 Jun. 1882.
41. GL MS 5304/10, 324-8; CM, 29 Mar. 1956, 2 Jul. 1985, 1979 *passim*, 8 Jan. and 25 Mar. 1980, 17 Mar. and 9 Jun. 1992, 16 Mar. and 15 Jun. 1993, 17 Jul. 2012; *Tablets*, 57, 3.

CHAPTER 9   THE IRISH VENTURE AND THE ASSOCIATED COMPANIES

1. Livery Dinner Menu Card.
2. For the narrative outline in this section, see Curl, *Irish Society*, 28-138; Curl, *Londonderry*, 22-90; Diamond, 'Irish Estates', 14-52.
3. Doolittle, *Mercers'*, 57.
4. Curl, *Londonderry*, 34.
5. GL MS 5328.
6. Curl, *Londonderry*, 122-9; Doolittle, *Mercers'*, 58-9.
7. Curl, *Irish Society*, 138; Diamond, 'Irish Estates', 31.
8. Sharpe, *London*, ii, 44; GL MS 5327; GL MS 5303/1, 73r, 80v, 87r, 101r, 107r.
9. Pearl, *Puritan Revolution*, 81-8; For the narrative outline in this section, Curl, *Irish Society*, 139-154; Curl, *Londonderry*, 90-5; Diamond, 'Irish Estates', 74-91; GL MS 5303/1, 137r-39r.
10. GL MS 5325, 9, 11; Sharpe, *London*, ii, 143-50, 167-8.
11. For the narrative outline in this section, Curl, *Irish Society*, 154-230; Curl, *Londonderry*, 96-121; Diamond, 'Irish Estates', 92-142.
12. GL MS 5303/1, 233v, 359v-85r, *passim*; GL MS 5325, 13; GL MS 5304/1, 65r-6r, 116r-v, *passim*; GL MS 5304/2, 11v, 14v-15r, 35v-36r, 47v, 50r, 57r; GL MS 5326; GL MS 5322.
13. GL MS 5304/2, 117v; GL MS 5304/4, 13 Oct. 1751.
14. GL MS 5303/2, *passim*; GL MS 5303/3, *passim*; GL MS 5304/4, 5 Oct. 1752, 2 Oct. 1766.
15. GL MS 5304/6, 9 Jan. and 10 Mar. 1812.
16. Doolittle, *Mercers'*, 140. For the narrative outline in this section, Curl, *Irish Society*, 231-60; Curl, *Londonderry*, 133-52; Diamond, 'Irish Estates, 157-81.
17. GL MS 5315/01-02; GL MS 5304/8, 9 Nov. 1872 and all the entries for the election courts 1875-9.
18. GL MS 5304/8, 9 Nov. 1883; GL MS 5304/9, 60, 80, 87-8, 106; Mercers' Company, 1/54/2/9, 1, 14.
19. GL MS 5325; GL MS 5304/3, 247r, 248v, 270v; GL MS 5304/6, 13 Jan. and 30 Mar. 1815, 1831 *passim*; GL MS 5304/8A, 110, 332; GL MS 5404/9, 15; Doolittle, *Mercers'*, 140; Diamond, 'Irish Estates', 127-8.
20. GL MS 5304/10, 367, 373; Cash Book 1951-73, 1951-52.
21. GL MS 5304/10, 377-8, 390; CM, 1956-8 *passim*, 11 Jan. and 12 Jul. 1994; SC, 1994 *passim*.
22. GL MS 5304/10, 222-4, 241-2; CM, 16 and 26 Jun. 1958, 16 Jan. 1962, 29 Mar. 1977, 2 Jul. 1985, 17 Mar. 1992; 26 Mar. and 1 Oct. 2002, 31 Mar. and 21 Jul. 2009; SC, 9 Nov. 2000, 17 May 2001. Cf. CM, 5 Oct. 1999.
23. CM, 16 Jan. 1962, 13 Jan. 1981, 30 Mar. 1982, 1985-7 *passim*, 21 Mar. 1989; SC, 1983-6 *passim*.
24. GL MS 5304/10, 289, 340; CM, 29 Mar. 1956.
25. CM, 13 Jun. 1988, 8 Jan. 2002; SC, 26 Nov. 1987, 24 May 1988, 5 Sep. and 8 Nov. 2001, 6 Sep. 2007.
26. CM, 21 Jul. 2009, 15 Jun. and 28 Sep. 2010, 11 Jan. 2013; SC, 2009 *passim*, 23 Feb. and 18 May 2011; *Tablets*, 53, 14.

CHAPTER 10   TURBULENCE

1. Reddaway, *Rebuilding*, 22-25; GL MS 5303/1, 247r.
2. Reddaway, *Rebuilding*, 32, 68-111, 121-6, 181-9, 255-8, 284-300; *Statutes*, v, 603-12, 665-82; GL MS 5313.
3. GL MS 5303/1, 233r-241v, 246r-256r; GL MS 5313, 1663-73.
4. For the Company's admissions and bindings, see GL MSS: 5307, 3308, 5309, 5310, 5313, *passim*.
5. Reddaway, *Rebuilding*, 116-17.
6. Reddaway, *Rebuilding*, 55-9; GL MS 5303/1, 257r-59v.
7. GL MS 5303/1, 218r-28v, 236r-50v, 265r-75v; LMA P69/GIS/A/002/06419/007; GL MS 5313, 1673-4.
8. GL MS 5303/1, 265r-67v, 276v-79r; GL MS 5322; GL MS 5324.
9. TNA C66/3197, 29 CII, Pt. 10, m. 13-18; TNA C66/3279 JII, m. 1-10; GL MS 5333, 1r-20v; GL MS 5336, 1-23, 26-54; GL MS 5304/2, 56r; GL MS 5304/3, 2r; GL MS 5332.
10. GL MS 5330; GL MS 5304/1, 10v, 84r; GL MS 5324; GL MS 5303/1, 301r-06r, 322r-24v; GL MS 5304/2, 56r, Unwin, *Gilds*, 158.
11. Colvin, *Dictionary*, 539; *ODNB*.
12. GL MS 5303/1, 234r-37r, 272v-75v; Unwin, *Gilds*, 164-6; Gadd and Wallis, *Guilds*, 6.
13. GL MS 5304/1, 3r, 10r, 26v, 31r, 32r; GL MS 5334, unfol. leaf, 1r-2r; GL MS 5333; GL MS 5992.
14. GL MS 5304/1, 10v-14v, 16v; GL MS 5303/1, 294r-99r; K&J, 'London mason' 10-17.
15. K&J, 'London mason', 20-1; GL MS 5330; GL MS 5304/2, 179v-82v; GL MS 5304/1, 57v-8r; GL MS 5308, *passim*; GL MS 5313, *passim*.
16. GL MS 5303/1, 287r-91v; GL MS 5304/1, 10r; GL MS 5334, 10r-11v, 22v.
17. LMA P69/GIS/A/002/06419/10; GL MS 5304/1, 31r-v, 45v-46r; GL MS 5303/1, 252r-56r, 301r-306r; TNA PROB 11/356/428, PROB 11/363/243; GL MS 5318; *ODNB*.
18. GL MS 5303/1, 301r-06r, 348v; LMA P69/BOT2/A/016/09232/001; GL MS 5304/1, 30r-v; GL MS 5313, 1673-4.
19. GL MS 5303/1, 307r-20v; GL MS 5304/1, 33r-35r, 57r-8r, 66r, 70r.
20. GL MS 5304/1, 26v, 40r-v, 46v, 51r-52v, 59v, 65v-68v, 70r, 168r; GL MS 5333, 17r.
21. For what follows, Masters, *Chamberlain*, 48-9; Doolittle, *London*, 16-19; Knights, 'Remodelling', 1141-1178; GL MS 5304/1, 73v, 74r, 86v.
22. GL MS 5336, 14-21; GL MS 5333, 21r-22v; GL MS 5337.
23. GL MS 5304/1, 87r-88v, 99v-101v; GL MS 5333, 22v; GL MS 5304/1, 87r-v.
24. GL MS 5304/1, 88v-102v; GL MS 5308, 28 and *passim*; GL MS 5330; GL MS 5983, *passim*; GL MS 5987, *passim*; GL MS 5303/1, 312r-16r, 328r-30r; GL MS 5314/1; GL MS 5336, 4.
25. *HMC Lords*, 1689, 293-4; Knights, 'Remodelling', 1158; GL MS 5304/1, 94r, 104r; GL MS 5336, 15.
26. Knights, 'Remodelling', 1159-62; *HMC, Lords*, 1689, 294-7.
27. GL MS 5304/1, 106r-110r, 127v, 135r-36v; GL MS 5313, 1688-90; GL MS 5303/1, 331v-40v.
28. GL MS 5304/1, 110v-14v; GL MS 5330.
29. GL MS 5304/1, 114r-20r, 127r-28r, 135r-37r; TNA PROB 11/383/414; GL MS 5303/1, 330v-340v; GL MS 5318; TNA C 8/513/3.
30. GL MS 5304/1, 116r-18v, 121r-25r, 147r; GL MS 5303/1, 339r-40v; K&J, 'London mason', 23, esp. fn.4.

CHAPTER 11   RESILIENCE AND RECOVERY

1. GL MS 5303/1, 331v-340v, 346v-50r; GL MS 5304/1, 135r-36v, 140v-43v, 157r; GL MS 5304/2, 2v-5r, 8r, 9v-11r; GL MS 5324; GL MS 5319.
2. GL MS 5304/1, 138r-v, 145v-153r; GL MS 5313, 1673-4; GL MS 5304/2, 25r-27r, 50v;

GL MS 5887, 29, 37; GL MS 5304/3, 11r.

3. GL MS 5303/1, 347r; GL MS 5304/1, 142v-43r, 144r; table 11.1 and fig. 11.1 below.

4. GL MS 5304/1, 59r, 92v, 122v, 130r-33v, 137r-38r; 143v-44r; GL MS 5304/2, 2r-v, 9r, 18r-v, 29v, 45v, 47r-v; GL MS 5303/1, 346v-48v, 360v, 362v, 374r; TNA PROB 11/457/142.

5. GL MS 5303/1, 355r-57v; GL MS 5304/1, 149v-50r; GL MS 5304/2, 15r, 36v.

6. GL MS 5304/1, 58r, 146r-48r; GL MS 5324; GL MS 5303/1, 349v, 359v-85r; GL MS 5303/2, 1-14; GL MS 5322; GL MS 5326; GL MS 5304/2, 11v-12r, 15r, 22v, 28v, 36v, 57r.

7. GL MS 5304/1, 140v-142r, 147v-48r, 156r-57v.

8. Colvin, *Dictionary*, 456-7; GL MS 5304/1, 141r; GL MS 5304/2, 71r; GL MS 5308, 32; *ODNB*.

9. GL MS 5304/1, 154v-56r; GL MS 5304/2, 181r-82r; K&J, 'London mason', 15-18, 83-4.

10. GL MS 5304/1, 12v-14v, 160r-69v; K&J, 'London mason', 18, 36-7, 76-83; GL MS 5308, *passim*; GL MS 5304/2, 20r-v, 24r, 131v.

11. GL MS 5304/1, 167r; GL MS 5303/1, 357v; GL MS 5304/2, 15v, 24r, 25v, 38r, 41r-42r, 67r, 83r, 131v, 177v, 220v.

12. GL MS 5304/2, 24r, 47v, 79r, 161r, 175v; GL MS 5314/1; GL MS 5304/3, 120r-v.

13. GL MS 5304/2, 79r; K&J, 'London mason', 16.

14. GL MS 5304/2, 80v-81v, 82v, 85v, 86r, 139v; GL MS 5308, 5; GL MS 5983.

15. The data in this table is compiled from GL MS 5313; GL MS 5308; GL MS 5307, various livery lists and Court Minutes.

16. GL MS 5304/2, 87r-88r, 90r, 125v; GL MS 5304/3, 8v.

17. GL MS 5304/2, 88r, 203r-4r; GL MS 5982; GL MS 5322; LMA COL/CHD/FR/02/0397; Horwitz et al., *London Politics*, i-x; TNA PROB 11/728/410.

18. GL MS 5304/2, 87r, 153v-54r and *passim*; GL MS 5304/3, *passim*.

19. Kynaston, *Till Time's Last Sand*, 22; Stone, 'Huguenots, Whigs'; GL MS 5304/3, 27r-v, 31r, 47r.

20. Mary Pricto, Miriam Saunders, Anne Baker, Anne Knight, Margaret Wise, Anne Sparhawke, Katherine Wright, GL MS 5308, *passim*; GL MS 5304/2, 137r, 149r, 185r, 199v, 213v; GL MS 5304/3, 9r, 21r, 233v, 242r, 261r.

21. Not including William Bucknall of 'unknown' occupation, GL MS 5982. Cf. GL MS 5304/3, 134v-35r.

22. Masters, *Chamberlain*, 57; Doolittle, 'Government', 160; GL MS 5304/2, 155r, 160r, 191v-92r; GL MS 5303/2, 112-13.

23. GL MS 5304/1, 57r; GL MS 5303/2, 168-70; GL MS 5304/3, 176r-v, 180r.

24. GL MS 5304/4, 9 Nov. 1761.

25. K&J, 'Masons' Company', 163; GL MS 5304/2, 10v-11r, 13r-14r, 53r-v, 54r, 70v, 94v-99r, 118v, 177v, 179r-82v, 184r-85r, 186v, 192v, 200v-201v.

26. GL MS 5986, 15-17; GL MS 5304/3, 242r.

27. GL MS 5304/6, 4 Oct. 1821 to 9 Nov. 1822; Kellett, 'Breakdown', 393.

28. GL MS 5304/2, 177v-82v; GL MS 5304/4, 7 Aug. 1772; GL MS 5304/5, 9 Nov. 1801 and 1 Apr. 1802; GL MS 5304/6, 29 Apr. 1819; GL MS 5986; GL MS 5330.

29. GL MS 5304/2, 212r, 215r, 216r-17r, 220v; GL MS 5304/3, 118v; GL MS 5304/4, 16 Jul. and 1 Oct. 1772; GL MS 5304/6, 26 Mar. 1812, 1814 *passim*.

30. Kellett, 'Breakdown', 388; GL MS 5304/4, 12 Jan. and 30 Mar. 1775.

31. GL MS 5304/4, 28 and 30 Sep. 1782; Summerson, *Georgian London*, 100, 105-7, 111-34; *ODNB*.

32. GL MS 5304/4, 10 Jan. 1760, 9 Nov. 1776; Kellett, 'Breakdown', 393-4.

CHAPTER 12   FREEMASONRY

1. Conder, *Records*, iii-v, 1-14, 252, and *passim*; Prescott and Sommers, '1717'.

2. Prescott, 'Old charges', *passim*.

3. Taillades, 'A new approach', *passim*.
4. Spiegel, *Romancing*, 1-5.
5. LAMF GBR 1991 OC MSS: 1/6, 1/10, 1/12, 1/15; Conder, *Records*, 208, 256-7; Prescott, 'Old Charges', 33-6, 49; GL MS 5992. Perhaps Conder misread the minutes for April 1678? GL MS 5304/1, 11v.
6. GL MS 5303/1, 82v, 171v, 175r, 184v, 186v, 235r, 281r-85v; GL MS 5313, 1672-73.and inventory 8 Apr. 1673; GL MS 5304/1, 2v, 10r; Scanlan, 'Origins', 63-81. Probably not the 'account of the Antiquity, Rise and Progress of the Art and Mistery of Masonry', GL MS 5304/3, 1v; Conder, *Records*, 256-8.
7. *ODNB*; Josten, *Elias Ashmole*, ii, 395-6, iv, 1699-1701; Songhurst, *Minutes*, 47-9.
8. Thomas and William Wise, Thomas and John Shorthose, Thomas Shadbolt, Nicholas Young, William Hammond, John Thompson, William Stanton, William Woodman, William Grey, Samuel Taylor. Should we identify Ashmole's Mr Waindsford esq. with Rowland Raynsford? GL MS 5303/1, 184v.
9. *Poor Robins Intelligence*, 17 Oct. 1676, 3; Plot, *Natural History*, 316-18; Scanlan, 'Origins', 74-5; Anderson, *Constitutions*, 1; Anderson, *New Book*.
10. Prescott, 'Old Charges', 45; Prescott, 'British freemasonry', 11-12.
11. For much of what follows, see Stevenson, *Origins*; Stevenson, 'Four hundred years'; Stevenson, 'Origins'.
12. Stevenson, 'Origins', 52-4; Stevenson, 'Four hundred years', 282.
13. Stevenson, 'Origins', 57-8; Stevenson, 'Four hundred years', 282-3.
14. Scanlan, 'Origins', 74; Prescott, 'British freemasonry', 10-11; *ODNB*.
15. Hobbes, *Leviathan*, 1:4; Önnerfors, *Freemasonry*, 46.
16. Stevenson, 'Origins', 54-6; *ODNB*.
17. Habermas, *Public Sphere*, 58-67; Clark, *British Clubs and Societies*, 4, 309-12, *passim*.
18. Conder, *Records*, 11-13, 90-6, 173, 208; GL MS 5303/1, 199r; 'declaration in lieu of the oath of a free mason of London', GL MS 5304/8.
19. Conder, *Records*, 1, 7-10.
20. Conder, *Records*, 13-14, 246.
21. GL MS 5308, 68v; LAMF, Membership Registers, London, vol. 1, 280, 411 and *passim*. I cross-referenced the names of every entrant to the Company with Songhurst's *Minutes* and the membership records of the Antients (from 1751), the Moderns (from 1768), and UGLE (from 1813-1921).
22. Crown: Thomas Davis, John Deane, William Lesow, Robert Taylor. Queens: Samuel Broomehall, Richard Burchard (warden), William Hale, Thomas Hill junior, Nicholas Mitchell (warden), William Perkins, Matthew Worral, GL MS 5308, 4-6, 7, 12, 13, 28-29, 40, 44, 57, 68, 72v; GL MS 5982; Songhurst, *Minutes*, 4, 12, 29-30.
23. GL MS 5308, 74; Thomas Grundy and James Davis.
24. CM, 9 Jul. and 1 Oct. 1991, 1996-7 *passim*, 7 Jan. 2003; SC, 23 Sep. 1991, 5 Aug. 1983, 1996-7 *passim*.

CHAPTER 13   VICTORIAN SOMNOLENCE
1. *Second Report*. 1; Doolittle, *London*, 21-36.
2. *Second Report*, 1-4, 55, 152-6, 178, 226; Doolittle, *London*, 25; GL MS 9472; GL MS 5304/6, 1834 *passim*.
3. Kellett, 'Breakdown', 394; Doolittle, *London*, 28-30, GL MS 5304/7, 1852 *passim*, 14 Jun. 1856, 28 Apr. 1863; GL MS 5303/3, 1851-2, 1854-5.
4. *Report of the Royal Commission on the Corporation of the City of London* (Parliamentary Papers (Cmd. 1772), 1854, XXVI), x; GL MS 5304/8, 1 Apr 1880.
5. GL MS 5338, 1-12; Ramsey, 'Victorian historiography', 156-7; Doolittle, *London*, 89-102; GL MS 5304/8, 9 Nov. 1880, 21 and 31 Mar. 1881; 1884 *Report*, iii, 573-92.
6. 1884 *Report*, iii, 451, 573, 580; GL MS 5308/8, 14 Jun. 1881.

7. *Second Report,* 152-6; 1884 *Report,* iii, 574-5; GL MS 9472.

8. GL MS 9472; GL MS 5304/6, 6 Jul. 1822, 12 Jan. 1832; GL MS 9471/3.

9. GL MS 5304/7, 1 Oct. 1840; GL MS 5303/3, 1844-5; GL MS 5304/9, 276; GL MS 9472, 3; 1884 *Report,* iii, 576.

10. *Second Report,* 153-6; 1884 *Report,* iii, 575-6; GL MS 5304/7, 9 Nov. 1854, 3 Aug. 1866; GL MS 5304/8, 1 Jul. 1869; GL MS 5330.

11. *Second Report,* 153.

12. *Second Report,* 153; GL MS 5304/7, 14 Jun. 1858, 26 Mar. 1863; GL MS 5304/8, 1868-72 *passim.*

13. Doolittle, *London,* 89-90.

14. GL MS 5304/10, 311.

15. *Second Report,* 154; 1884 *Report,* iii, 576.

16. GL MS 5303/3, 1835-80, the loss occurred in 1874-5; 1884 *Report,* iii, 578.

17. GL MS 5303/2, 345-54; GL MS 5303/3, 1829-35.

18. *Second Report,* 155-6.

19. 1884 *Report,* 578; GL MS 5303/3, 1838-43, 1878-9, 1881-4; GL MS 5304/8, 1878 *passim,* 27 Mar. 1879, 1881-3 *passim;* GL MS 5304/10, 2-3, 216-17; GL MS 5304/8A, 296, 299; GL MS 5304/9, 74-6.

20. GL MS 5304/8, 14 Jun. and 5 Oct. 1871, 9 Nov. 1872, 1873 *passim,* 6 Oct. and 9 Nov. 1881; GL MS 5330; GL MS 5303/3, 1864-5, 1867-8, 1881-2; GL MS 5304/8A, 340; 1884 *Report,* iii, 574; Officers and Badges.

21. Ramsey, 'Victorian historiography', 156; Doolittle, *London,* 98-9; GL MS 5338; GL MS 5303/1, 301r-6r.

22. Doolittle, *London,* 92-3, 98; J.F.B. Frith, *Reform of London and of City Guilds* (1888), 116.

23. 1884 *Report,* 577, 579. GL MS 5304/8, 14 Jun. 1873, 14 Jun. 1874.

24. GL MS 5304/8, 5 Oct. 1882; GL MS 5303/3, 1880-3.

25. GL MS 5304/2, 129v; GL MS 5304/3, 71v; GL MS 5304/7, 17 Oct. 1844, 2 Oct. 1845, 7 Aug. 1846, 9 Jan. and 27 Mar. 1861; GL MS 5303/3, 1845-6.

26. GL MS 5304/8, 6 Aug. 1869; 1884 *Report,* iii, p. 577.

27. GL MS 5303/3, 1873-5; GL MS 5304/8, 1 Oct. 1874, 14 Jun. 1875, 5 Oct. 1876, 14 Jun. 1880.

28. GL Ms 5304/6, 14 Jun. 1826; 1884 *Report,* iii, 575, 577; Officers and Badges.

29. GL MS 5304/7, 14 Jun. 1849, 28 Mar. 1850; GL MS 5303/3, 1853-8, 1869-70, 1879-80, 1883-44; GL MS 5304/8, 7 Jan. 1879; Colvin, *Dictionary,* 369-72; *ODNB*; GL MS 5304/9, 277.

30. For this case, GL MS 5304/8, 6 Oct. and 9 Nov. 1881, 1882-5 *passim;* GL MS 5304/8A, 3; GL MS 5303/3, 1884-5.

31. GL MS 5304/8A, 8, 12-14, 22-4, 28-9, 32-3, 36, 39-41, 43-5, 50, 101, 104-7; Cf. GL MS 5304/8, 2 Oct. 1873.

32. GL MS 5304/8, 10 Jan. 1884; GL MS 5304/9, 35, 276-7; GL MS 5304/8A, 56-57, 61, 63, 68, 71-4, 330-1, pastedown; GL MS 24502; SO 29 Mar. 1917.

33. GL MS 5304/9, 309.

34. GL MS 5304/8A, 126.145, 151, 166, 171, 173, 176, 182, 187, 191; GL MS 5304/9, 299.

35. GL MS 5304/8A, 37; GL MS 5303/3, 1887-8.

CHAPTER 14   THE MODERN COMPANY

1. CM, 30 Mar. and 20 Jul. 2004, 14 Jan. 2005, 17 Jul. 2012, 16 Jul. and 1 Oct. 2013; SC, 13 May and 4 Nov. 2004, 15 May 2013; *Tablets,* 42, p. 1; *Tablets,* 58, 14-15; SR.

2. GL MS 5304/4, 12 Jan. 1758, 28 Oct. 1767, 14 Jun. and 28 Sep. 1782; GL MS 5304/9, 2, 15, 51, 205, 215; 5304/10, 114, 146, 166, 176, 196, 308; *ODNB*.

3. CM, 12 Jul. 2011, 10 Jan. 2012; *Tablets,* 55, 4-5.

4. GL MS 5304/9, 35, 39, 56, 74-6, 227-8, 232-8, 270, 276-7, 280, 286-93, 310-13; SO 29

Mar. 1917, 3; GL MS 21031; GL MS 5304/10, 78, 158, 169-71, 288, 309.

5. CM, 10 Jan. 1967, 14 Jun. 1968; SC, 9 Mar. and 21 Nov. 1967, 29 Jul. 1969; Policy Book; ER.

6. CM, 6 Oct. 1983, 16 Jun. 1998; SR, 12-13.

7. CM, 30 Mar. 1982, 3 Oct. 1984; SC, 18 Feb. 1982. Cf. SC, 20 Nov. 1980.

8. CM, 28 Mar. 1984, 12 Jan. 1988, 16 Oct. 1995, 14 Jan. 2005; SC, 16 Feb. 1984, 7 May 2009.

9. CM, 1 Oct. 1974, 12 Jan. 1982, 17 Jun. 1985, 12 Jan. and 22 Mar. 1988, 1998 *passim*, 30 Mar. 2004; SC, 9 May 1985, 1987-8 *passim*, 17 Feb. 1999, 11 Feb. 2004.

10. CM, 11 Jan. and 21 Mar. 2000; SC, 16 Feb. 2000.

11. GL MS 5304/9, 74-6; GL MS 5304/10, 216-17.

12. GL MS 5304/10, 58-9, 197, 217-18, 314-19, 322-30, 345, 349; GL MS 21032, 187-97.

13. GL MS 5304/10, 343, 354-55, 402; CM, 3 Oct. 1957, 9 Jan. 1958, 27 Mar. and 26 Jun. 1973, 17 Jun. 1975, 6 Jan. and 16 Mar. 1976, 10 Jan. 1978, 27 Mar. 1979, 1980-1 *passim*; SC, 21 Nov. 1974, 30 Apr. 1975, 23 Nov. 1978, 22 Nov. 1979; Cash Book 1951-73, *passim*; Cash Book 1974-87, *passim*.

14. CM, 16 Mar. 1993.

15. CM, 1 Jul. 1987, 12 Jan. 1993, 26 Mar. 2013; SC, 13 May 1998; SR, 17.

16. SC, 9 Sep. 1999, 17 May and 5 Sep. 2001, 6 Nov. 2003, 11 Feb. and 13 May 2004; CM, 5 Oct. 1999, 9 Jan. 2001, 7 Oct. 2003, 22 Jun. 2004.

17. GL MS 5304/10, 318-19; GL MS 21032, 183-8; Cash Book 1974-87, 1976-7, 1977-8, 1981-2; CM, 9 Jan. and 27 Mar. 1979; SC, 15 Feb. 1979.

18. GL MS 5304/9, 270, 277; GL MS 5304/10, 226, 257-8; CM, 12 Jan. and 30 Mar. 1965, 9 Jan. 1968; Cash Book 1951-75, 1966-7, 1968-9.

19. CM, 2 Oct. 1985, 8 Jun. 1987; SC, 3 Sep. 1991.

20. SC, 25 Feb. 1987, 23 Feb. 1994; GL MS 5303/3, 1809-10; *Second Report*, 153.

21. CM, 15 Mar. and 4 Oct. 1994, 11 Mar. 2000, 2003-5 *passim*; SC, 11 May 1993, 23 Feb. 1994, 2003-4 *passim*.

22. CM, 31 Mar. 2009; SC, 18 Feb and 3 Sep. 2009; SR, 17-19.

23. GL MS 5304/10, 373-7, 385; CM, 1970-1 *passim*, 9 Jan. 1973; SC, 29 Jul. 1969, 26 Feb. 1970.

24. CM, 6 Jan. 1976; GL MS 5304/9, 316.

25. CM, 3 Oct. 1984, 8 Jan. 1985; SC, 23 Aug. and 15 Nov. 1984.

26. CM, 12 Jan. and 5 Oct. 1993, 4 Oct. 1994, 10 Jan. 1995; SC, 22 Nov. 1994, 22 Feb. 1995, 11 Sep. 1996.

27. CM, 1 Oct. 2002, 1 Apr. 2003, 22 Jun. 2004. SC, 9 Sep. 1999, 16 May and 4 Sep. 2002, 13 Feb. and 6 Nov. 2003.

28. CM, 12 Jun. 1990, 19 Mar. and 11 Jun. 1991, 6 Oct. 1992, 1993 *passim*, 14 Mar. and 13 Jun. 1995, 18 Jun. 1996, 13 Mar. 1997, 1998 *passim*, 13 Jul. 1999; SC, 15 May 1991, 23 Feb. 1993, 11 May 1994, 10 May 1995, 22 Feb. and 11 Sep. 1996, 18 Feb. 1997, 8 Sep. 1998, 12 May 1999, 16 May 2002.

29. SC, 11 Feb. 2004; CM, 30 Mar. 2004.

30. GL MS 5304/9, 221, 227-8, 232; CM, 30 Mar. 2004.

31. CM, 14 Jan. 2005; SC, 12 May 2005; SR, 8-11.

32. CM, 1986 *passim*, 13 Jan. 1987, 6 Oct. 1992, 16 Mar. and 13 Jul. 1993, 14 Mar. and 16 Oct. 1995, 9 Jan. and 1 Oct. 1996, 13 Jul. 1999; SC, 1985-6 *passim*, 22 Feb. 1996, 9 Nov. 2000, 13 Feb. and 16 May 2002.

33. CM, 1984-5 *passim*; 10 Jul. 1990, 12 Jul. 1994, 7 Oct. 1997, 14 Jul. and 6 Oct. 1998, 2003 *passim*, 6 Jan. and 30 Mar. 2004, 19 Jul. 2005, 29 Mar. and 25 Jul. 2006, 9 Jan. 2007, 8 Jan. 2008; SC, 23 Aug. 1984, 18 Feb. 1998, 5 Nov. 2002, 11 Feb. 2004, 3 Nov. 2005, 11 May and 9 Nov. 2006, 8 Nov. 2007; *Tablets*, 45, 1, *Tablets*, 46, 8-9.

34. CM, 7 Jan. 1986, 2 Oct. 1990, 1998 *passim*; SC, 18 Feb. 1998, 13 Sep. 2000; *Journal*, 2015-16, 28-9.

35. CM, 12 Jan, and 13 Jun. 1988, 16 Jan. 1990, 1 Oct. 1991, 13 Mar. and 7 Oct. 1997, 9 Jan. and 27 Mar. 2001, 29 Mar. 2011; SC, 10 Sep. 1997, 24 May 1988, 29 Nov. 1989, 14 Feb. 2001.

36. CM, 3 Oct. 1984; SC, 1984 *passim*, 9 May 1985, 6 Feb. and 6 Nov. 2008; *Tablets*, 59, 2; *Journal*, 2014-15, 24-25; *Journal*, 2018-19, 23.

37. CM, 6 Oct. 1998, 23 Mar. 1999, 8 Jan. 2008, 11 Jan. and 11 Jul. 2000, 18 Jun. 2013; SC, 17 Nov. 1999, 10 May and 13 Sep. 2000, 9 Nov. 2006, 6 Sep. 2007, 12 Sep. 2012; SR, 11.

CHAPTER 15   PHILANTHROPY

1. LMA COL/CA/01/15, 399r-v; Lempriere, *J. Howes' MS.*, 58-9; Chapter eight.

2. GL MS 5303/1, 29r, 95v, 135r-v, 322r-24v; GL MS 5304/3, 80v; GL MS 5304/4, 5 Oct. 1758, 28 Jun. 1764; GL MS 5303/2, 246; GL MS 5304/7, 2 Oct. 1845, 8 Jan. 1846, 31 Mar. 1859; GL MS 5303/3, 1845-6; GL MS 5304/8, 1 Jul. 1880. Rappaport, *Worlds*, 337-8, 372-6.

3. Esdaile, 'The Stantons', 24; GL MS 5304/4, 4 Oct. 1753, 9 Jan. 1755, 1756 *passim*.

4. GL MS 5303/01, 40v, 51v, 74r-75v, 87v, 89r, 95v, 167r-68v, 261r-64v, 265r-67v; LMA P92/SAV/3003, 339; GL MS 5318; GL MS 5304/1, 31r-v; TNA PROB 11/356/428; CM 2 Oct. 1990, 1 Oct. 1991; SC, 4 Sep. and 28 Nov. 1990.

5. GL MS 5304/8A, 331, 339; GL MS 24502; GL MS 5304/2, 74r, 118r, 132v.

6. GL MS 5304/4, 26 Jun. 1766, 31 Mar. 1768; GL MS 5304/6, 1 Apr. 1819.

7. GL MS 5304/4, 25 Jun. 1772, 14 Jun. and 2 Oct. 1783. Cf. GL MS 5304/8A, 237, 334.

8. GL MS 5980; GL MS 5304/2, 157v, 207v-8r, 211r, 213v, 216v; GL MS 5304/3, 162r, 174v, 179r-81r, 182v, 197v; GL MS 5304/4, 1753 *passim*, 10 Jan. 1754.

9. GL MS 5303/2, 201-2; GL MS 5304/3, 233r, 238v-39r, 250v, 253v; TNA PROB 11/743/361; GL MS 5303/3, 1825-6; GL MS 5304/6, 5 Aug. 1825; GL MS 5304/7, 9 Jan. 1840, 31 Mar. 1842, 28 Mar. 1867.

10. GL MS 5303/3, 1877-8, 1887-8; GL MS 5303/2, 321-2; GL MS 5338; GL MS 21032, 1-6; CM, 1 Oct. 1996, 10 Jul. 2001.

11. GL MS 5304/10, 51, 239, 242, 262-3, 279-82; GL MS 21032, *passim*; SC, 24 May 1988, 18 Nov. 1997, 13 May 1998, 17 Feb. 1999, 13 Feb. 2003, 9 Sep. 1999, 5 Sep. 2001, 22 Feb. and 12 Sep. 2012, 20 Nov. 2013; CM, 1964-70 *passim*, 4 Oct. 1982, 13 Jun. 1988, 12 Jun. 1990, 19 Mar. 1991, 4 Oct. 1994, 1995 *passim*, 9 Jan. 1996, 14 Jul. 1998, 15 Jun. 1999, 27 Mar. and 10 Jul. 2001, 8 Jan. 2002, 1993 *passim*, 7 Jan. 2003, 6 Jan. 2004, 21 Jun. 2011; Cash Book, 1957-73, *passim*; Cash Book 1974-87, 1979-80.

12. GL MS 5338; GL MS 5304/6, 9 Nov. 1820, 11 Jan. 1821, 12 Jan. 1837; Conder, *Records*, 269; *Journal*, 2014-15, 20.

13. GL MS 5304/10, 249, 262-3, 268; *Tablets*, 51, 12; *Tablets*, 56, 11; CM, 14 Jun. 1966, 26 Mar. 1968, 13 Jul. 1999; SC, 10 May 2000.

14. Deed of Trust, 26 Mar. 1968, Charity no. 263137; GL MS 5304/9, 290-1; GL MS 5304/10, 333; Cash Book 1951-73, 1967-8; SC, 20 May 1969, 22 Nov. 1973, 21 Feb. and 21 Nov. 1974, 16 Feb. 1984, 23 Feb. 1993, 18 Feb. 1998, 9 Nov. 2000, 4 Sep. 2002, 10 Sep. 2003, 7 Sep. 2005, 8 Feb. 2006; CM, 2 Oct. 1973, 1974 *passim*, 1984 *passim*, 16 Mar. and 5 Oct. 1993, 16 Oct. 1995, 27 Sep. 2005, 10 Jan. and 29 Mar 2006.

15. GL MS 5304/8, 26 Mar. 1885; GL MS 5304/8A, 282, 319; The Builders' Clerks' Benevolent Society was dissolved in 1999 and its assets taken over by the BBI; CM, 6 Oct. 1970, 27 Mar. 1973, 11 Jan. 1994, 9 Jan. 2001; SC, 15 Feb. 1973, 18 Feb. 1998, 14 Feb. 2001.

16. CM, 17 Jun. 1969, 17 Mar. and 7 Jul. 1992, 15 Jul. and 7 Oct. 1997, 6 Jan. 1998; SC, 10 Sep. and 18 Nov. 1997.

17. GL MS 5304/8, 4 Nov. 1869, 27 Jun. and 2 Aug. 1872, 14 Jun. 1873; Lang, *City and Guilds*, 11-18; CM, 11 Jan. 1977.

18. GL MS 5304/8, 26 Jun. 1873, 14 Jun. 1874; 1884 *Report*, 577-9.

19. GL MS 5304/8A, 142, 145, 151, 166, 171, 173, 176, 182, 187, 191, 244; GL MS 5304/9, 96, 103, 260-1, 263, 268, 270, 276-7, 279, 299; SC, 27 Aug. 1986.

20. GL MS 5304/10, 84, 88, 101, 103, 105-6, 110-11, 115, 122-6, 135-8, 154-5, 164-5, 177-80, 186, 196-9, 201, 211.

21. GL MS 21032, 142-67, 183-91; GL MS 5304/10, 282, 287, 324, 327, 330-3, 388-9, 399; CM, 6 Oct. 1955.

22. CM, 28 Mar. 1963, 1 Apr. and 7 Oct. 1969, 12 Jan. and 30 Mar. 1971; GL MS 21032, 133-41; Cash Book 1951-73, 1967-8; Charity no. 304232.

23. SC, 10 May 2000, 17 May and 5 Sep. 2001, 20 Nov. 2012; CM, 10 Jul. 2001; *Tablets*, 51, 7; *Tablets*, 56, 7.

24. GL MS 5304/10, 289-94, 297, 383, 386, 362, 402; CM, 8 Jan. 1963, 29 Mar. 1966, 14 Jun. 1972, 8 Jan. and 7 Apr. 1974; SC, 17 Feb. 1972.

25. CM, 15 Jun. and 5 Oct. 1971, 22 Mar. and 14 Jun. 1972.

26. CM, 27 Jun. and 3 Oct. 1972, 1973 *passim*; SC, 24 Aug. 1972, 3 May 1973.

27. CM, 5 Jul. 1988, 1989 *passim*, 1998 *passim*, 15 Jun. 1999, 2000 *passim*, 10 Jul. 2001; SC, 15 Aug. and 23 Nov. 1988, 13 May and 17 Nov. 1998, 16 Feb. and 13 Sep. 2000, 5 Sep. 2001.

28. For what follows, CM, 27 Mar. 1973, 10 Jan. and 22 Mar. 1978, 28 Mar. 1985, 10 Jul. 2001, 17 Jul. 2003, 30 Mar. and 22 Jun. 2004, 14 Jan. and 15 Mar. 2005; SC, 15 Feb. 1973, 21 Feb. 1974, 5 Sep. 2001, 4 Sep. 2002, 13 Feb. 2003, 2004 *passim*; *Tablets*, 42, 2.

29. For what follows, CM, 11 Jul. 1995, 6 Jan. and 24 Mar. 1998, 10 Jul. 2001, 27 Mar. 2001, 21 Jul. 2009; SC, 18 Feb. and 10 Sep. 1997, 18 Feb. and 8 Sep. 1998, 17 Feb. 1999, 13 Feb. 2002, 7 Feb. 2007; Stow, *Survey*, i, 223-5; *Tablets*, 56, 3; Private correspondence with Sandy Copland.

30. CM, 9 Jan. and 27 Mar. 1973, 16 Mar. 1976, 17 Jun. and 3 Jul. 1980, 12 Jan. 1982, 1985 *passim*; SC, 15 Feb. 1973, 17 May 1976, 15 Nov. 1984, 14 Feb. and 9 May 1985; Cash Book 1974-87, 1980-1; Deed of Trust 9 May 1985, Charity no. 292070.

31. CM, 2 Jul. and 2 Oct. 1985, 16 Jun. 1986, 10 Jan. and 11 Jul. 1989, 19 Mar. 1991; Policy Book, no. 20; SC, 3 Nov. 2005.

32. SC, 15 Nov. 1984; CM, 1993 *passim*, 15 Mar. and 14 Jun, 1994; SC, 11 May 1993, 23 Feb. and 11 May 1994; Carpenters' Company Education Committee Minutes, 26 Nov. 1992, 19 Jan. 1993.

33. SC, 12 May 1999, 8 Sep. 2004; CM, 14 Jan. 2005.

34. CM, 5 Oct. 1993.

35. CM, 4 Oct. 1994, 10 Jan. 1995, 6 Jan. and 24 Mar. 1998, 22 Jul. 2008, 27 Mar. 2012; SC, 22 Nov. 1994, 23 Feb.1994, 22 Feb. 1995, 10 Sep. 1997, 7 May 2009, 22 Feb. 2012; *Tablets*, 56, 6.

36. CM, 10 Jan. 1995, 15 Jul. and 7 Oct. 1997, 2000 *passim*; SC, 13 May and 10 Sep. 1997, 13 Sep. 2000.

37. SC, 2006 *passim*, 7 Feb. 2007; *Tablets*, 45, 5-6, 12; *Tablets*, 46, 4; Craft fund trustees' report 2019-20, 7.

38. CM, 14 Jan. 2005, 24 Jul. 2007.

39. CM, 5 Jul. 1988, 19 Mar. and 13 Jun. 1991; SC, 7 Feb. 1991.

40. CM, 10 Jul. and 2 Oct. 2001; SC, 17 May and 8 Nov. 2001.

41. CM, 20 Mar, 2007; SC, 6 Feb. 2008; *Tablets*, 46, 14.

42. SC, 6 Nov. 2003, 10 May and 8 Nov. 2007, 8 May and 6 Nov. 2008, 12 May 2010; CM, 24 Jul. 2007, 22 Jul. 2008, 5 Jan. 2010; *Tablets*, 48, 11, *Tablets*, 52, 10; SR, 6-7.

43. SC, 3 Sep. 2009, 18 May 2011, 12 Sep. 2012; CM, 22 Sep. 2009, 8 Jan. and 16 Jul. 2013; SR, 5.

44. SC, 7 May 2009; *The Telegraph*, 29 Jan. 2021; *The Times*, 29 Jan. 2021.

45. SR. 5; ER, no. 49; *Tablets*, 59, 4.

46. SC, 17 Nov. 1999; CM, 4 Oct. 1988, 10 Jan. and 3 Oct. 1989, 12 Jun. 1990, 11 Jun. 1991, 11 Jan. 2000; Charitable fund trustees' report, 2019-20, 11-12.

47. SC, 17 Nov. 1999; 13 Sep. and 9 Nov. 2000, 14 Feb. 2001, 6 Sep. 2006, 22 Feb. 2012; CM, 3 Oct. 2000, 27 Mar. 2001, 26 Sep. 2006; 22 Sep. 2009, 28 Sep. 2010; *Tablets*, 44, 15; *Tablets*, 47, 13; *Tablets*, 58, 12, 16; SR, 2-4; ER, no. 50, at 50.2.3.

48. SR, 5; SC, 3 Nov. 2005, 9 Nov. 2006, 6 Sep. 2007, 8 May and 6 Nov. 2008, 12 Sep. 2012, 20 Nov. 2013; CM, 27 Sep. 2005, 10 Jan. and 29 Mar. 2006, 25 Sep. 2007, 8 Jan. and 22 Jul. 2008, 21 Jul. 2009, 5 Jan. 2010; *Tablets*, 45, 1; *Tablets*, 46, 1, 10-11; *Tablets*, 50, 4; *Tablets*, 51, 9; *Tablets*, 53, 4; *Tablets*, 57, 10; *Tablets*, 58, 10.

OFFICERS

1. CLBH, 274; LMA COL/AD/01/011, 165r; LMA COL/AD/01/28, 235r.
2. GL MS 5334, 20v-21r; SC, 12 May 2005.
3. GL MS 5303/1, 12r, 66v; Company Standing Orders, no. 15.

COMPANY POSSESSIONS

1. GL MS 5304/7, 11 Jan. 1866; GL MS 5304/8A, 344; GL MS 5304/9, 10; GL MS 5304/10, 300, 315, 319; CM, 19 Jun. 1974; GL MS 24502; A List of the Livery of the Worshipful Company of Masons, privately published 2 January 1905, p.11. Hereafter, 1905 Livery List.

2. GL MS 5304/9, 130, 137, 140; GL MS 5304/10, 304; CM, 13 Jan. 1970, 29 Mar. 1977; Company Standing Orders, no. 39; *Tablets*, 57, 5; Black Book, 1st ed., 23.

3. GL MS 5313; GL MS 5316; GL MS 5304/2, 10v; GL MS 5304/3, 1v-4r; GL MS 5304/7, 9 Nov. 1859; GL MS 5304/8, 27 Mar. 1873; GL MS 5304/9, 260, 263-4, 266, 276, 288, 326; SC, 9 Sep. 1999; CM, 5 Oct. 1999.

4. GL MS 5304/3, 1v; GL MS 5304/7, 14 Jun. and 1 Jul. 1852; GL MS 5304/9, 276, 288, 362; CM, 19 Mar. 1991; GL MS 20961; H. Günther, 'Vincenzo Scamozzi comments on the architectural treatise of Sebastiano Serlio', *Annali di architettura: rivista del Centro Internazionale di Studi di Architettura Andrea Palladio* 27. 2015 (2016), 47-60, at 47-48. With gratitude to Vaughan Hart, Professor of Architecture at Bath University, for his help in tracing the editions of Serlio's books; 1905 Livery List, p.10.

5. GL MS 5304/3, 1v-2r; for Tanner and Paskin's marks, see 23, 72; *Tablets*, 53, 3.

REGULATIONS, ORDINANCES AND CHARTER

1. LMA COL/AD/01/007, 41r; CLBG, 51; Riley, *Memorials*, 280-2; K&J, *Mediæval Mason*, 224-6.

2. LMA COL/AD/01/011, 165r-67r; K&J, *Mediæval Mason*, 226-31.

3. LMA/COL/AD/01/012, 168; LMA COL/AD/01/013, 175v-77r; LMA COL/AD/01/023, 57v-58r; Williams, *Masons*, 142-9; K&J, *Mediæval Mason*, 231-3.

4. LMA COL/AD/01/028, 235r-v; Williams, *Masons*, 152-3; TNA C66/3197, 29 CII, Pt. 10, m. 1.

Index

Page numbers in **bold** indicate illustrations. The letter n following a page number denotes that the reference will be found in a note, the letter t in a table, e.g. 187t. All buildings and streets are in London unless specified otherwise.